Advance Praise for *Mark Twain's Literary Resources*

"Alan Gribben is a scholar's scholar, and *Mark Twain's Literary Resources* is his masterwork. It will retain its fertile usefulness so long as Twain studies exist. Volume One isn't just a bounteous treasure of information and an important corrective to the most common misperception of Twain. It's also an engaging record of Gribben's tireless, lifelong adventure in literary sleuthing."
—**FREDERICK CREWS**, Professor of English Emeritus, University of California, Berkeley

"*Mark Twain's Literary Resources* lets readers cozy up to Mark Twain and peep over his shoulder as he reads: a rare and rewarding vantage point." —**KEVIN J. HAYES**, author of *Mark Twain: A Brief Critical Biography* and *George Washington: A Life in Books*

"Mark Twain knew that you can't write if you don't read, and his reading was as wide and deep as his beloved Mississippi River, flowing through his life and writings from beginning to end. It is in large measure thanks to Alan Gribben's *Mark Twain's Literary Resources* that we understand how Twain's extensive reading nourished his authorial genius. Gribben's achievement is no mere library catalog, but rather a voyage of discovery that expertly navigates the complex channels of Twain's literary sources. They are all charted here, awaiting further exploration, beckoning both the avid reader and serious scholar, and often as entertaining as Twain's own published writings. Here is a masterpiece of research and presentation that will serve as a model for all future inquiries into the wellsprings of the creative process." —**KEVIN MAC DONNELL**, Mark Twain scholar, foremost Mark Twain collector

"One of the foundational sources of Mark Twain studies for nearly forty years, Alan Gribben's *Mark Twain's Library: A Reconstruction* has long been a scholarly treasure. Gribben's revised and much expanded compendium, *Mark Twain's Literary Resources: A Reconstruction of His Library and Reading*, will prove to be the standard reference guide on the topic for the next many decades. These volumes belong in all research libraries and on the shelves of all nineteenth-century Americanists." —**GARY SCHARNHORST**, Distinguished Professor Emeritus of English, University of New Mexico

"*Mark Twain's Literary Resources* is the definitive guide to Mark Twain's intellectual universe. Alan Gribben discusses everything from the elaborately bound parlor-table gift books known by titles such as *Friendship's Offerings* to the literary, historical, and religious works that directly influenced America's greatest writer. This book, the most useful reference book on Twain ever written, is a classic. And despite what Twain said about classics, this one will be read again and again." —**JOE B. FULTON**, Professor of English at Baylor University; author of five books on Mark Twain, including *Mark Twain Under Fire: Reception and Reputation, Criticism and Controversy 1851–2015*

"Dr. Alan Gribben's *Mark Twain's Literary Resources* offers a fascinating peek into the mind of an American literary genius. The book's mind-boggling wealth of information could only have been gathered using extraordinary research skills and dogged determination. The work is an invaluable tool for Mark Twain scholars and sets a new standard for generations of scholars to come." —LAURA SKANDERA TROMBLEY, President, University of Bridgeport

"Alan Gribben's critical masterpiece, *Mark Twain's Literary Resources: A Reconstruction of His Library and Reading*, asserts itself as one of a handful of truly invaluable resources in Mark Twain studies. A heroic compendium of analytical essays, annotated catalogs, critical bibliographies, and index guides, this work is the definitive study of the literary, philosophical, historical, and scientific texts that shaped Mark Twain's mind and art." —JOSEPH CSICSILA, Professor, Eastern Michigan University, and coauthor of *Heretical Fictions: Religion in the Literature of Mark Twain*

"From the day I discovered Alan Gribben's *Mark Twain's Library: A Reconstruction*, it became one of only two reference works that I have kept within arm's reach of my desk. Gribben's research served as an inspiration and guidepost enabling me to make my own discoveries. His new updated and expanded Mark Twain's Literary Resources has been one of my most eagerly anticipated publications throughout the years. With hundreds of new entries, it is the most extensive mapping of Mark Twain's intellectual development that will ever be undertaken. It is an essential reference work for any Mark Twain researcher or biographer."—BARBARA SCHMIDT, publisher, www.twainquotes.com; Mark Twain scholar

"Alan Gribben has devoted decades to cataloging and studying this legendary author's lifetime of reading. His *Mark Twain's Literary Resources* is the magnificent result. It complements Twain's autobiography and biographies of Twain, and will enhance any reference library."— MAXINE HONG KINGSTON, author of *The Woman Warrior* and other novels

"Alan Gribben's *Mark Twain's Literary Resources: A Reconstruction of His Library and Reading* brings together in three volumes a series of interconnected essays, many revisions of his earlier published works, and a significant update of annotated titles in Twain's personal library. This new edition replaces the invaluable *Mark Twain's Library: A Reconstruction*—long out of print and nearly impossible to obtain. The introductory essays in the first volume render in toto a penetrating critique of the reader behind the writer who, as Ernest Hemingway once said, reinvented American literature." —JEROME LOVING, author of *Mark Twain: The Adventures of Samuel L. Clemens*

MARK TWAIN'S
LITERARY RESOURCES

VOLUME ONE

Mark Twain's Literary Resources

A Reconstruction of His Library and Reading

VOLUME ONE

ALAN GRIBBEN

FOREWORD BY R. KENT RASMUSSEN

NewSouth Books

Montgomery

NewSouth Books
105 S. Court Street
Montgomery, AL 36104

LIBRARY OF CONGRESS CATALOGING-IN-PUBLICATION DATA

Names: Gribben, Alan, author.
Title: Mark Twain's literary resources : a reconstruction of his library and reading / Alan Gribben.
Other titles: Mark Twain's library
Description: Montgomery : NewSouth Books, [2019] | Includes bibliographical references and index.
Identifiers: LCCN 2018040870 (print) | LCCN 2019000462 (ebook) | ISBN 9781603064538
(Ebook) | ISBN 9781588383433 | ISBN 9781588383433(hardcover)
Subjects: LCSH: Twain, Mark, 1835–1910—Library—Catalogs. | Twain, Mark,
1835–1910—Books and reading. | Private libraries—United States—Catalogs.
Classification: LCC PS1342.B6 (ebook) | LCC PS1342.B6 G7 2018 (print) | DDC
818/.409—dc23
LC record available at https://lccn.loc.gov/2018040870

Design by Randall Williams

Printed in the United States of America by the Maple Press

On the front of the dust jacket:
Portrait of Mark Twain, 1907 (from the collection of Caroline Harnsberger,
who donated it to the *Mark Twain Journal* in 1988)

On the front of the hardcover case:
The library of the house in Hartford where the Clemenses lived from 1874 to 1891 was a center of
family life. (Courtesy of the Mark Twain House and Museum, www.marktwainhouse.org)

For Irene Wong,
who married a scholar and his book

Contents

Foreword

R. KENT RASMUSSEN

Whenever a truly innovative work about Mark Twain appears, I often wonder what Twain himself would have thought of it. In the case of this greatly expanded new edition of Alan Gribben's *Mark Twain's Library: A Reconstruction* (1980), I find it easy to imagine Twain sitting up all night reading it and muttering sounds of astonished incredulity at what it reveals about him. Considering how many other books have tried to understand Mark Twain, it may seem strange to suggest that something as mundane as a scholarly reference work might evoke that kind of reaction, but Alan's book is different. Perhaps more than any other published study of Mark Twain, *Mark Twain's Literary Resources: A Reconstruction of His Library and Reading* probes deeply into his mind and life experiences, providing information essential to what he knew and how he knew it, where he got his ideas, and how his mind worked. Alan has done all this by attempting something not only that no one else has ever done for Mark Twain but also something never done in the same depth for *any* author. Not only does he try to account

for every publication Mark Twain ever owned or read, he also attempts to show how each of them influenced Mark Twain's life and work. When it comes to inventive reference tools, *Mark Twain's Literary Resources* stands alone. Moreover, considering that the books, magazines, newspapers, and other publications Alan discusses within these pages number in the thousands, to call his reference work "monumental" is almost an understatement.

As one who has himself written reference books—including several on Mark Twain—and who also spent many years working as a full-time reference-book editor, I have naturally developed some strong ideas about what constitute the standards of a good reference work. I can thus confidently attest that Alan's work exceeds all those standards. The first thing that users want from a reference book are answers to the questions they bring to it. For example, readers desiring to know how the writings of Charles Dickens influenced Mark Twain will quickly find answers here in richly detailed and fascinating mini-essays on each Dickens novel Mark

Twain read. These entries reveal what Mark Twain thought of Dickens's works and where their influence can be found in his own writings. Meticulously sourced, the entries are authoritative and trustworthy. Readers don't have to guess where their information comes from, as Alan provides chapter and verse for everything. *Mark Twain's Literary Resources* is also clearly and logically organized. Readers looking for any author's titles can merely turn to the alphabetically arranged entries. These volumes are also strongly supported by cross-references and a variety of indexes. Volume One collects all of Alan's research on Mark Twain' reading, while the forthcoming Volumes Two and Three will contain the Annotated Catalog.

Though it seems difficult to believe, I have been intimately acquainted with Alan's earlier version, *Mark Twain's Library*, for almost a quarter of a century, during which time I have also had the pleasure of periodically communicating with him about the progress of his revisions and making occasional contributions and suggestions myself. Even now, all these years later, I can vividly remember the first time I pulled the volumes of *Mark Twain's Library* from a low shelf in the stacks of UCLA's Research Library. I was then beginning work on my own reference book, *Mark Twain A to Z* (1995). As a newcomer to the field of Mark Twain studies, I eagerly examined every book on Mark Twain I encountered and usually had about fifty library books checked out at any given time. Alan's book, however, initially confounded me: "Two whole volumes doing nothing more than listing books that Mark Twain had owned," I mused. Needless to say, I was woefully short-sighted. I suspect I misunderstood Alan's reference book because of its very uniqueness. With nothing else to compare it to, I wasn't able to judge its usefulness. Soon, however, I had the wisdom to check out the volumes and take them home—where I kept them close by for more than two years.

When I finally published *Mark Twain A to Z*, its acknowledgments singled out *Mark Twain's Library* as one of the two finest reference works on Mark Twain yet published. That was only fair, as my own book would have been noticeably deficient if I had not always had Alan's volumes within easy reach while I was writing it. I later acquired my own set of *Mark Twain's Library* (not an easy task, by the way). Since then, my opinion of its value has only increased. *Mark Twain's Library* was in all ways such a remarkable and valuable reference tool that it almost boggles the mind to realize that we now have a revised and vastly expanded edition in *Mark Twain's Literary Resources: A Reconstruction of His Library and Reading.* No one studying Mark Twain seriously can afford to be without it.

R. Kent Rasmussen is the author of Critical Companion to Mark Twain, Mark Twain for Dog Lovers, *and many other books, articles, reviews, and contributions to Twain studies. He lives in Thousand Oaks, California.*

Preface

This study is a revised and enlarged edition of a work I published in 1980 as *Mark Twain's Library: A Reconstruction.* That initial version elicited favorable articles in the New York *Times* ("Image of Mark Twain as 'Eccentric' Reader Is Refuted in a Study") and the Los Angeles *Times*, and its merits were praised by scholarly journals. *American Literature* termed it "invaluable," *American Literary Realism* deemed it "a seminal study" and "one of the indispensable reference works," *Analytical and Enumerative Bibliography* called it "a phenomenal job on a monumental task," and *American Literary Scholarship, An Annual* declared it to be "a highly usable monument of research."

Despite these gratifying reviews, *Mark Twain's Library* went out of print within sixteen months. As the New York *Times* accurately noted, I had invested more than $15,000 in pursuing and describing the remnants of the Clemens family's library. Yet the resulting catalog mainly circulated in photocopied segments handed around among professors and graduate students, owing to the fact that only five hundred copies of *Mark Twain's Library* had ever been printed.

The 1980 edition owed its existence to the kind intervention of Thomas A. Tenney, who, learning that university presses were leery of tackling such a large project, convinced a commercial press to undertake its publication. After the resulting book had been out of print for several decades, Dr. Tenney encouraged me to return to the project to make the information available again while also inserting corrections and additions that could take the study closer to the ever-elusive goal of mapping Twain's intellectual background.

Starting Over: Revisits and Revisions

Bolstered by Tenney's assurances that the feat could be accomplished, I began the slow process of revamping and extending the original study. It is not often that a scholar gets the chance to improve upon an earlier version of his work, and I resolved to make the most of this opportunity.

To verify my entries, I revisited most of the collections that I had consulted in the 1970s. These included the Mark Twain Papers in the Bancroft Library at the University of California at Berkeley, the Hartford House and Museum, and the Mark Twain Library at Redding. Some of the sites and libraries, like the ones in Hartford, Connecticut and at the University of Texas at Austin and the University of Virginia in Charlottesville, had altered their names since 1980, and I revised the catalog to reflect these developments.

Then, too, hundreds of Clemens's formerly obscure literary references had been identified during the past few decades, either by individual scholars or by the editorial team at the Mark Twain Project in the Bancroft Library at the University of California at Berkeley. These discoveries have been woven into the Annotated Catalog with (I trust) due credit specified. In a number of cases I was able to add my own breakthroughs, including perhaps the last magazine article that Clemens read and marked, Charles William Wallace's "New Shakespeare Discoveries" in the March 1910 issue of *Harper's Monthly*.

A GRADUATE STUDENT'S RESEARCH ERROR: MEA CULPA

In reviewing my original Annotated Catalog, I realized to my embarrassment that as a graduate student researcher I had made a recurrent error that caused confusion in the rare book world. In my 1980 catalog I made unwarranted deductions about which edition the Clemenses owned or read; observing the book's dated inscription or other evidence, I identified its edition by relying entirely on the *National Union Catalog of Pre-1956 Imprints*, which I assumed to be an infallibly complete record of all editions. However, in cases where the Clemens family's association copies later surfaced after my *Mark Twain's Library* appeared, these books too often bore different imprints than the ones I had confidently assigned them. Scholars and booksellers

thereupon compounded the mistake by drawing the conclusion that Clemens or his family members must have owned other unrecorded editions of the same titles. I apologize for that misleading practice on my part, which I have tried my best to rectify in the corrected Annotated Catalog.

SAMUEL CLEMENS AS AN AUTODIDACT

This revised and expanded version brings us nearer to an idea of how truly comprehensive was Clemens's acquaintance with published materials, despite the fact that he had no formal education beyond grammar school. Obliged by his father's premature death in 1847 and the family's consequent poverty to give up his formal education in 1849, Clemens read so steadily and omnivorously that he remains one of the most striking examples of an autodidact among all American authors.[1] Other scholars have built upon my findings, and today's biographers are consequently far better acquainted with Clemens's literary, historical, philosophical, artistic, and scientific reading than anyone was when I first published articles on the topic more than forty years ago. Then, too, hundreds of additional books from Clemens's personal library have come to light, in part because of the publicity attending the publication of my 1980 book.

All of these new and disparate bits of information make the expanded catalog more enlightening in linking Clemens's reading with his writing and in understanding his complex mind and shifting interests. As a result, he will seem even less like an untutored, primitive genius and resemble more obviously the sophisticated citizen of his times that he in fact was.

Copy of doctoral dissertation on file at the University of California at Berkeley, 1974. Revised and enlarged, it became a 958-page book that was set in type by publisher G. K. Hall & Company.

TECHNOLOGY ASSISTS

Of course—and fortunately—there have been monumental shifts in technology since I pounded out the first version of this study on a Royal manual typewriter and then hired a typist who owned a state-of-the-art IBM Selectric II to prepare a manuscript for the publisher. Its subcontracted printer set the typescript pages in print with an aging Linotype machine (reportedly the operator was hospitalized after completing that huge key-stroking task).

BOOKS IN MOTION

An even more astonishing alteration in the intervening decades is the way Clemens's library books have moved around the country nearly as restlessly as Clemens himself did. Several of these startling relocations have involved large portions of his former library. Who would ever have imagined that a Catholic Archbishop would require St. John's Seminary in Camarillo, California, to sell the sixty volumes from Clemens's personal library that wealthy benefactor Estelle Doheny had donated to that institution? Christie's held auctions in 1987, 1988, and 1989 that scattered these books around the nation. An idea of the caliber of this collection can be conveyed by looking at just three of its books: Clemens's copies of Oliver Wendell Holmes's *Autocrat of the Breakfast-Table* (1858), Holmes's *Poems of Oliver Wendell Holmes* (1881), and Janet Ross's *Three Generations of English Women* (1903). These were priced at $6,000 each when resold by the Heritage Book Shop in Los Angeles. In another noteworthy development, the Mark Twain House and Museum in Hartford surprised the book world in 1997 by acquiring nearly three hundred books owned by Clemens and his family. These previously unexamined association copies had been sold at the 1951 Hollywood auction and included dozens of volumes containing Clemens's marginalia.

Nick Karanovich's immense collection of Twainiana, which contained hundreds of well-traveled association copies, had often been cited as the largest Mark Twain collection still in private hands, and it was long supposed that some favored university library—perhaps the Lilly Library at Indiana University, which had exhibited selections from the Karanovich holdings in 1991—would eventually receive its contents. Yet after Karanovich's untimely death the entire collection went up for sale in New York City on June 19, 2003, so that the results from his lifetime of collecting were set adrift once more. In Karanovich's place as the premier collector of Twainiana arose the prominent rare bookseller and learned scholar Kevin Mac Donnell of Austin, Texas; his collection of association copies (along with his thousands of other items pertaining to the author) now ranks as by far the largest in private ownership.

2003 Sotheby's catalog

Among academic libraries, the Mark Twain Papers in the Bancroft Library at the University of California at Berkeley has benefited the most from the major auctions and from collectors' donations of association copies. The already-significant assortment of books retained from the Clemens family's library by Clara Clemens Samossoud has continued to grow there.

No news connected with Mark Twain can compare with the epochal 1990 discovery of the first half of the holograph manuscript of *Adventures of*

Huckleberry Finn in a trunk in a Hollywood, California, attic, but the former contents of his library shelves have nonetheless produced stupendous surprises since I first cataloged them in 1980. The unexpected emergence of Clemens's annotated copy of Sir Thomas Malory's *Morte Darthur* was an astounding event when it was first displayed at a Mark Twain conference in 1997. Other remarkable developments involving Clemens's library books have nearly matched that find, such as the gift to Elmira College on October 11, 2008, of the long-sought copy of William C. Prime's *Tent Life in the Holy Land* that Clemens playfully annotated and then had fun lampooning in *The Innocents Abroad* (1869). Cyril Clemens's collection in Kirkwood, Missouri, included nine books from Samuel Clemens's library that went elsewhere before Cyril died in 1999. The death of Chester L. Davis in 1987 brought to an end his editorship of *The Twainian* and his oversight of the Mark Twain Research Foundation in Perry, Missouri, resulting in an auction at Christie's in New York City in 1991 of the association items he had collected. Equally notable has been the meteoric rise in prices for Mark Twain association copies, which have generally ascended toward the prohibitive for all but the most determined collector or library, especially for volumes that Clemens signed and annotated. Perhaps this lucrative demand accounts for the fact that several volumes have mysteriously vanished from the collections where they were formerly held.

Nearly ninety books that the Clemens family's housekeeper Katy Leary was allowed to select from Clemens's library as keepsakes after he died in 1910 had ended up in Rice Lake, Wisconsin, where her nephew Warren Leary, Sr. edited that town's newspaper. Their subsequent owners, Robert and Katharine Antenne, donated this collection to the Mark Twain Archive in the Gannett-Tripp Learning Center at Elmira College. The Mark Twain Archive at Elmira College additionally absorbed scores of books from the Quarry Farm library of Theodore and Susan Crane that inquisitive scholars discovered to contain Clemens's marginalia.

A LARGER, FULLER PICTURE

My Annotated Catalog introduces hundreds of new authors and titles to Clemens's range of contact and memory, corrects inadvertent errors in earlier entries, and considerably alters my 1980 inventory of the Clemens family's library and reading. Compiling this new reconstruction of their literary and intellectual life has been like solving a massive jigsaw puzzle: some of the pieces were initially upside down and unintelligible when they came out of the box; periodically I realized that I had wrongly placed a piece on my first guess; and frustrating gaps still remain in various areas. But as the individual pieces eventually take their proper locations, how satisfying it is to see discernible patterns fill in as the outlines of Clemens's reading take shape.

It turns out that Samuel Clemens as a reader enjoyed a notably wide compass of subjects. He knew by heart numerous passages of Shakespeare, venerated Tennyson's poems, and held in awe nearly every line written by Browning. But he also memorized the robust verses of Kipling and took pleasure in the fatalistic tone of FitzGerald's *Rubáiyát*. The sometimes baffling contradictions discernible in his own writings and personality are reflected in his library's contents as well. He relished collections of bawdy songs and off-color limericks, yet purchased only expurgated Shakespeare sets for his wife and daughters. In many respects a good judge of poetry, he nevertheless over-praised the products of his friends, especially the lacy effusions of the once-popular Thomas Bailey Aldrich. Loyal to his Nook Farm neighbors, he collected most of Harriet Beecher Stowe's and Charles Dudley Warner's writings. Dialect poems, stories, and novels about the Midwestern region where he grew up were almost certain to stir his interest and approbation, as his communications to James Whitcomb Riley attest. Charles Reade's and Dinah Muloch Craik's many popular novels took up a surprising amount of the family's book shelves, and he was familiar with most of the bestsellers of his day. He was often ready to lay everything else aside and take up any engrossing book that an author sent him, as he did with Edgar Watson Howe's first novel, *The Story of a Country Town*. The Scottish-born author and editor Robert Barr gave Clemens a copy of Barr's new novel, *A Woman Intervenes*, during a visit in Austria in 1897; the next day Clemens notified Barr that he had "read through to the end without stopping (& without skipping a line). And yet my custom is to skip liberally. . . . The story flows from the sources to the mouth without a break—& stays between the banks all the way, too." The book struck him as so polished that Clemens withdrew the "advice in the literary trade" he had imposed on Barr the previous day. "I take it back," he wrote. Though Clemens seemingly overlooked the writings of Herman Melville, Karl Marx, and

Sigmund Freud, we should always remember that far more than a thousand of the Clemenses' library books were given away to friends, went missing in their travels, were donated to libraries, or were lost in other ways without any record of their titles.

As Clemens's ability to visit acquaintances and enjoy outside experiences shrank in his final years, he became fixated on stylistic polish in books that he was sent or acquired; his marginalia increasingly struck out superfluous demonstrative pronouns and other unnecessary words and sternly corrected grammatical slips in the texts. He always had a tendency in this direction, but from around 1907 onward these irascible objections registered as his chief form of annotation in any books he picked up, a kind of armchair recreation for the aging author.

Whoever undertakes a full or partial biography of Clemens should allocate time to study his reading materials during the relevant periods, for the intellectual and literary stimulation he derived from books and periodicals was an integral part of his development as a writer and a thinker. He reacted to his reading almost viscerally, and from the late 1860s onward he typically held a pencil or pen in order to leave behind a transcript of his responses. *Mark Twain's Literary Resources* pays tribute to an easily underestimated facet of his life and personality: reading.

NOTES

1   This achievement is surveyed in more detail in my "Mark Twain's Lifelong Reading," *Mark Twain and Youth: Studies in His Life and Writings*, ed. Kevin Mac Donnell and R. Kent Rasmussen (London: Bloomsbury Academic, 2016), 30–43.

Acknowledgments

My sense of indebtedness is enormous for the assistance I have received since my *Mark Twain's Library: A Reconstruction* appeared. Scholars have passed me notes at academic conferences, sent me letters at my home and office, and (in recent decades) dropped me countless email messages. Rare book dealers and collectors have been extraordinarily cooperative and generous. Wherever feasible I have endeavored to specify each individual's contribution in the germane catalog entry.

Certain people's participation in the project was so substantive that I should name them here. I must first begin by thanking Kevin Mac Donnell, whose erudition about both Mark Twain and that era of American literature seems almost infinite. In a sense he has been my collaborator through the years, sending me snippets of information and urging me to persevere. He has played a large role in my scholarly life as a whole. I am also beholden to the late Nick Karanovich, whose generosity in sharing news and knowledge about the Clemens library was ceaseless until his death. In 1981, for instance, he sent me photocopies of early twentieth-century rare book auction catalogs that listed titles I could add to Clemens's library, and thereafter he kept up a steady stream of similarly useful materials. The late Thomas A. Tenney, too, never wavered in exhorting me to prepare an expanded edition of *Mark Twain's Library: A Reconstruction*. In every respect Tom Tenney must be viewed as the godfather to this study of Samuel Clemens's library and reading.

Kevin B. Mac Donnell

Frederick Anderson (1926–1979), editor of the Mark Twain
Papers and Mark Twain Project, 1964–1979

Among many favors, he deluged me over the years with photocopies of relevant letters, manuscripts, and scholarly studies that he laboriously annotated on my behalf.

Even before these debts, I owed much to the late Frederick Anderson, the former editor of the Mark Twain Papers in the Bancroft Library at the University of California at Berkeley, who immensely facilitated my progress in assembling what was then known about Clemens's library and reading. I could not have accomplished that first study without Fred Anderson's interest and guidance. Henry Nash Smith deserves mention for his willingness to direct the doctoral dissertation that led to many of these findings.

The current editor of the Mark Twain Papers and general editor of the Mark Twain Project, Dr. Robert H. Hirst, has likewise

fostered my research, and I am also grateful to the members of his staff, especially Victor Fischer, for their assistance whenever I visited the Bancroft Library. Paul Machlis was especially helpful to me with rare book auction catalogs in that collection. I trust that the Project's own labors will be somewhat lightened by the Annotated Catalog.

R. Kent Rasmussen has contributed to the fund of information at my disposal. Barbara Snedecor, former director of the Center for Mark Twain Studies at Elmira College, like her predecessors Gretchen Sharlow and the late Darryl Baskin, made me feel welcome during my periods of research and writing in Elmira. I must particularly single out the now-retired Mark Woodhouse, former curator of the Mark Twain Archive at Elmira College, for his patience and responsiveness.

His replacement, Nathaniel Ball, has been equally receptive to my inquiries. Marianne J. Curling, former curator at the Mark Twain House and Museum, went out of her way to be helpful, as did her successor Patti Philippon and her assistants, especially Mallory Howard. Diana Royce, former librarian of the Stowe-Day Library in Hartford, provided useful information. Beth Dominianni, the library director of the Mark Twain Library in Redding, Connecticut, was as obliging as her predecessors had been during my repeated visits to that lovely community and its vital library. Rare book dealer Robert T. Slotta shared his notes from the 1997 San Francisco auction as well as other valuable data. Barbara Schmidt generously conveyed a number of insightful contributions. The late Louis J. Budd sent multitudinous suggestions and reminders. Mary Boewe of Pittsboro, North Carolina, passed along numerous pieces of information. The late L. G. Crossman, professor emeritus at the University of Regina, added significantly to my list of literary allusions and made manifold corrections. The late Stanley Brodwin emerged as a staunch ally of my labors. The late Robert and Katharine Antenne of Rice Lake, Wisconsin, longtime custodians of the association items belonging to the Clemenses' housekeeper Katy Leary, became my close friends over the years. I am thankful to Auburn University at Montgomery for

endorsing my efforts to enlarge our understanding of Clemens's intellectual life. I also owe a great debt to NewSouth Books publisher Suzanne La Rosa and that firm's editor-in-chief Randall Williams for their commitment to bringing out *Mark Twain's Literary Resources.* Matthew Byrne assisted them ably in transitioning an unwieldy manuscript into print.

Irene Wong, as she did for the 1980 version of this work, accompanied me on my lengthy travels, figured out how to overcome every technical hurdle, and cheerfully predicted that it would be possible for her scholar-husband to complete this book.

Irene Wong and Alan Gribben, Austin, Texas, 1976

Introduction

Two intertwined stories explain the background of *Mark Twain's Literary Resources: A Reconstruction of His Library and Reading.* The first involves a providential occurrence in my scholarly life. In 1967 I had the good fortune to become employed by Frederick Anderson (1926–1979), the fifth editor of the Mark Twain Papers. I was to be one of his editorial assistants for the Mark Twain Project, a publishing series underway in the Bancroft Library at the University of California at Berkeley, the campus where I was studying for my doctorate degree in English. Two years later I had further cause to be grateful when I gained the eminent critic and scholar Henry Nash Smith (1906–1986) as the director of my doctoral dissertation. I chose its topic after much thought. During my editorial stint at the Mark Twain Project I made a point of inquiring of visiting scholars such as Walter Blair, Lewis Leary, Hamlin Hill, Robert Regan, John S. Tuckey, Edgar M. Branch, and Louis J. Budd about research topics that might benefit the field of Mark Twain studies. To a person, they answered: "*Please, someone*, undertake an inventory of Mark Twain's library and reading." They

explained that any scholar writing on Twain had to check dozens of disparate sources that revealed bits of his literary knowledge, but even after considerable effort the facts often proved elusive.

The immensity of this gap in Mark Twain scholarship denied commentators any accurate intellectual profile of his lifelong interests, periodic enthusiasms, and artistic evolution. Basically one had to rely on glimpses of his library shelves conveyed in Albert Bigelow Paine's biography (1912), followed by the tentative probing of Twain's reading in two master's theses by Henry A. Pochmann (1924) and Franklin L. Jensen (1964); three doctoral dissertations by George W. Feinstein (1945), Harold Aspiz (1949), and Sherwood Cummings (1950); and scattered references in scholarly articles (beginning with Olin H. Moore's "Mark Twain and Don Quixote" in 1922) and works of biography and criticism. By comparison, starting in the late 1940s meticulous studies had been initiated to identify the contents of other major American authors' libraries, so that within the next two decades published catalogs became available for the personal libraries of Emerson, Thoreau,

Melville, Dickinson, and other writers of stature. Stephen Crane's library proved to be one of the most difficult to trace. Determining what was in Hemingway's library required trips to Cuba, where many of his volumes had been left. F. Scott Fitzgerald's book collection, investigators learned with regret, had been largely lost as a result of his frequent moves.[1] Mark Twain' s library still remained relatively unexplored, providing an ideal opportunity for a graduate student who wanted to contribute something useful to the academic discipline he intended to enter.

The reasons that Twain's collection had resisted efforts to list its contents make up the second story to be summarized here.

Whatever books formed young Sam Clemens's library, nearly all have tumbled into the void, though a few clues point to titles such as Joseph Cundall's *Robin Hood and His Merry Foresters* (1841), a children's work quoted in *The Adventures of Tom Sawyer* (1876). In his teenage years Clemens read George Lippard's *Legends of the American Revolution; or, Washington and His Generals* (1847), a book that figures in *Adventures of Huckleberry Finn* (1885). Clemens would also recall the thrill he felt when by chance he ran across a scrap from a biography of Joan of Arc.[2]

Understandably Clemens could take very few books with

him on his subsequent travels as an itinerant printer, steamboat pilot, prospector, newspaper correspondent, and lecturer. Even then, however, his letters and notebooks began to record his reading in illuminating detail. By the mid-1870s a suddenly affluent Mark Twain was building a nineteen-room mansion in Hartford, Connecticut, and he indulged himself by incorporating into its plans a plushly furnished library room. He and his wife Olivia sat down and inscribed hundreds of volumes as they arrived from bookstores and publishers to stock their new library shelves. The family's library collection would grow to more than three thousand volumes

Alan Gribben, research editor, Mark Twain Project, Bancroft Library, 1971

as the years went by, but barely a third of these would still be extant and identifiable a century later. This depletion only partly resulted because of the post-1890 misfortunes of Clemens's roller-coaster life.

We need to view these losses with a measure of perspective. Only in the case of a hypothetical nineteenth-century author who kept a meticulous catalog of his book acquisitions, seldom traveled with books he owned, never changed residences, avoided bankruptcy and other life crises, refused to loan or make gifts of any books, resisted impulses to donate books to public libraries, and somehow possessed a foreknowledge that the books he signed, marked, or simply read would one day be tremendously valued—only for this unlikely individual could literary researchers rest assured of having a reliably complete record of his or her library. Not one of these criteria held true for Samuel Clemens, of course. By his testimony, for example, a large box containing his books went astray during the family's European travels. He accidentally left at least one book (Defoe's *Robinson Crusoe*)— and probably others in his lifetime—behind on a rail journey. He occasionally presented volumes he had annotated to people he met whom he thought might enjoy their subject matter. Clemens and his surviving daughter Clara made generous donations of more than two thousand books to a community library in Redding, Connecticut, where he spent his last years. In the nineteenth and early twentieth centuries the contents of an author's personal library collection, especially when he was principally known as a travel writer and humorist, were rarely transferred intact to an academic institution or private society

that might carefully preserve and catalog its contents and serve as a long-term custodian. It cannot be emphasized enough that, owing to the diverse fates of his library books, the record of Clemens's literary resources must always remain incomplete.

Less than a year after Clemens's death a large portion of his remaining library went up for sale at a New York City auction that only brought in an average of two or three dollars apiece for his annotated volumes of Montaigne, Voltaire, Emerson, Tennyson, his good friend William Dean Howells, and hundreds of others. Many of these books never surfaced again. That ill-advised auction was if anything overmatched forty years later by his daughter Clara's impromptu auction of most of the surviving library volumes at her estate in Hollywood. As a result of these catastrophes, by the late 1960s the Clemenses' library collection was widely dispersed and only fragmentarily documented.

A QUEST AND ITS DISCOVERIES

There was basically one way for an earnest graduate student in his late twenties to tackle this daunting project. After mounting a letter-writing campaign to libraries and book collectors, I climbed into a blue Volkswagen Beetle and logged 11,000 miles on a coast-to-coast odyssey in an effort to identify and examine the approximately 700 books that had seemingly survived these depredations. (Hundreds more would later come to light.)

To say the least, I had some incredible adventures. In Rice Lake, Wisconsin, I managed to track down the nearly ninety volumes that Katy Leary (1856–1934), the longtime housekeeper for the Clemenses, had been allowed to select as tangible mementos upon the death of her employer. However, when I arrived at the address of the current owner of these books, the widow of Leary's nephew, she had grown too gravely ill since my letters had arrived to give me admittance to her home. She informed me that she had nearly finished packing up her household and was moving to Florida to see if a change in climate might improve her health. She was clearly in excruciating pain. "Please do not bother me any further, Mr. Gribben," she said, firmly closing the door. (Mere months later she would pass away from a previously undiagnosed cancer.) Stymied by this refusal and left standing in dismay on the front porch, I glanced down at the sacks of books that (she had explained when I asked) her maid had set outside to be picked up by the truck for a charity thrift store. Curiosity overcoming me, I knelt down and peeked into the upright brown paper bags. I could hardly believe my eyes! Clemens's unmistakable signatures and marginalia were present in many of the volumes. The entire Leary collection was about to vanish. Returning to my car, I mulled over an urgent decision. I started my car and drove to the business district of the small town, looking for a public telephone booth (there were such things back in 1970). Scanning the pages of the local telephone directory, I began calling offices where someone might know if the ailing woman had any nearby relatives. My luck held, and at the Rice Lake *Chronotype* I located a daughter—Mrs. Katharine Antenne—who promptly joined me at the house and rescued the books before the truck arrived to collect the donations. Among these volumes were Clemens's copies of Edith Wharton's *The*

House of Mirth, Nathaniel Hawthorne's *The Scarlet Letter*, Walt Whitman's *Leaves of Grass*, Émile Zola's *Rome*, Harriet Beecher Stowe's *Uncle Tom's Cabin*, several studies of Shakespeare, Helen Keller's autobiography, Edward FitzGerald's *Rubáiyát of Omar Khayyám*, and an annotated volume of Rudyard Kipling's verse. Mrs. Antenne and her husband Robert, after retiring from a travel agency they later operated in Rice Lake, generously presented this Katy Leary collection to the Mark Twain Archive at Elmira College in installments between 1993 and 2002, having decided to give all Twain scholars access to the volumes.

I resolved at the outset of my quest that I would not pause or intrigue to collect any fragments of Twain's library for myself—even if a bargain might present itself. In those occasional situations when I uncovered a homeless association copy I contacted one of the established sites that had preserved Twain materials and alerted its director to this opportunity, as I did when I notified the Mark Twain House staff in Hartford that the bookseller Maxwell Hunley in Beverly Hills was offering a nice item, Eugene Campbell's *Poenamo: Sketches of the Early Days of New Zealand* (1881), inscribed by the author to Olivia Clemens in Auckland in 1895, for only $87.50. I likewise negotiated the transfer of Mark Twain association copies owned by Cyril Clemens to the Harry Ransom Center at the University of Texas at Austin. In another case I helped a Twain collector, Nick Karonovich, obtain volumes that had popped up in the Hollywood house where Clemens's daughter Clara once lived. Mainly I performed these services because I wanted people to be able to trust me—especially collectors, who were

At the beginning, I took notes on 3 x 5 cards. After these filled twenty-two cardboard file boxes, I obtained a wooden cabinet to give them more protection. Subsequent notes on 8 ½ x 11 sheets of paper occupied five drawers in a large metal cabinet.

instinctively wary of anyone assembling this much data about their holdings and somewhat suspicious about the entrance of a potential rival in the rare book market. If I resisted making any efforts to procure the Clemens library volumes still floating around the United States, I reasoned, then my motives would be transparent. That solemn oath also aided my sense of focus during the search; I wouldn't be distracted by the chance to chase down this or that association copy for the sake of personal benefit. This vow of bibliographic abstinence worked, and I enjoyed unstinting cooperation from book dealers, collectors, scholars, and librarians.[3]

My most arduous but rewarding week was spent poring over the books that Clemens and his daughter had contributed to the community library in Redding, Connecticut, his last place of residence. Most volumes had either been worn out by the patrons or sold in the early 1950s by a previous librarian endeavoring to make shelf space for newer titles. As a consequence of her decision, volumes bearing the purple "Mark Twain Library/Redding, Conn." stamp had entered the collections of research libraries and private collectors across the country. The remaining Clemens books had been temporarily shelved for their safety in a basement in the old library building, lit only by a single light bulb dangling from a wire. Determined to include all of them in my growing list, I sat in that dim basement for five long days to inspect each volume. A number of unsigned books, I discovered, were still upstairs on the lending shelves, filled with Clemens's marginalia. I commenced an Easter egg hunt of sorts for book spines that looked old enough to be likely candidates. Librarians Peggy Sanford and (later) Anne Cushman, together with library volunteers like Marge Webb, were eager for the Clemens collection to be assembled in one place and they assisted me in every possible way. During my several returns, Redding came to feel almost like a second home. Today all of those 240 Mark Twain association items have long since been transferred to secure bookcases in a modern building.

Lucky breaks continued throughout my hunt. Returning to the Berkeley campus, I ordered from the UCLA Library a copy of George Combe's *Notes on the United States of North America* (1841), curious about what Twain might have found of interest in that nineteenth-century travel book. To my astonishment and incredulity, I received from the Interlibrary Borrowing Service—and initially supposed that my eyes were playing tricks on me as I walked down the hallway and began leafing through the pages—Clemens's *own* copy, inscribed and annotated, inadvertently shelved in the UCLA Library stacks. Now, *what* were the odds for this coincidence? James D. Hart, director of the Bancroft Library at Berkeley, soon made arrangements for the volume to be transferred to the Mark Twain Papers.

I had another fortuitous advantage that could hardly be repeated today. In a more trusting, less security-conscious decade, the editor of the Mark Twain Papers, Frederick Anderson, loaned me a key to the rear door of that esteemed collection of books and manuscripts—meaning that I could work there without interruption until all hours of the night as well as every weekend. Many were the times that I didn't lock that door and leave the premises until three or four o'clock in the morning, even though it meant facing a lonely walk through a dark and deserted campus toward the side street where I had parked my car.

IMAGINING A NEW TYPE OF REFERENCE WORK

As my research notes gradually took shape I decided to design the format of my fast-expanding compendium as a *reference* book, an annotated catalog. This led to an emerging strain between my dissertation advisor and me, since Professor Smith had estimated that I would turn up no more than 400 or 500 titles and continued to insist that the "real" dissertation would be the preliminary chapters assessing the effects of Mark Twain's library and reading. Despite such predictions, I easily documented more than 600 titles within my first few months of industry—and, looking back, probably should have been encouraged at that juncture to break the thing into component parts and only submit a portion as my Ph.D. dissertation. But I was young and idealistic (and stubborn), and my distinguished director had relatively little interest in describing primary materials, his forte being the stylistic and thematic study of literary artistry. By contrast, I had supported my graduate studies since 1967 by hands-on editorial work in the Mark Twain Project at Berkeley. This experience in annotating Twain's previously unpublished notebooks, letters, and manuscripts had made me acutely aware of the usefulness of consolidating information to facilitate scholarly research. So I pushed on with the annotated catalog as well as five opening chapters. By dint of tremendous labor and periodic negotiations with Professor Smith, in 1974 I finally finished my dissertation—at 2,370 pages the longest ever filed there, or so the surprised clerk in the Graduate Office informed me.

Essentially I had created an entirely new, more integrated format for understanding an author's literary resources. Previous studies had either simply listed the extant books from writers' personal libraries or else had attempted to deduce their reading from textual evidence. My invention combined these approaches into more complex alphabetical entries, with all the information about book titles, inscriptions, marginalia, scholarly commentaries, and other facts conveniently assembled in one location. A "Finding List" assisted readers in locating the entries for which they might know a title but not its author. Yet despite the comprehensiveness and practicality of my doctoral dissertation, no university press was receptive to such a massive manuscript. That problem was further compounded in 1975 when a library volunteer at the Mark Twain Library in Redding, Connecticut found the long-missing accession record of the first book donations to that community collection. This document recorded 1,751 books that Mark Twain or his daughter Clara had contributed. I decided to incorporate all of these additional titles, despite the fact that

they extended the length of my manuscript by hundreds of pages.

IN PRINT AND SOON OUT OF PRINT

Then, in 1980, Thomas A. Tenney, an independent scholar in Charleston, South Carolina, turned up in my life and located a Boston publisher, G. K. Hall & Company, willing to take on the challenge. By that point I had produced nearly 5,000 entries for books, stories, poems, essays, plays, operas, songs, newspapers, and magazines; included were more than 2,500 book titles that Clemens and his family owned, read, or mentioned. Listing and describing them in *Mark Twain's Library: A Reconstruction* required two volumes and 958 pages of small print.

To my great disappointment the publisher, which had become a subsidiary of ITT, balked at reprinting my book after the first edition sold out within sixteen months. (A federal court tax ruling had abruptly rendered unsold books as taxable, making it costly for publishers to keep multi-volume works in stock.) The original editors who had accepted my manuscript and overseen its production—most notably Paul M. Wright—had moved on to another publishing firm, and thus there was no one left to champion the reprinting of my book. G. K. Hall & Company offered me the plates for my out-of-print book, but the $2,000 price was beyond what I could afford at the time on my salary as a recently promoted associate professor. The result was frustrating for an author who had spent ten years tracking down so many books and references, and it likewise became a problem for Twain scholars and students. *Mark Twain's Library: A Reconstruction* originally sold for

$75; twenty years later the two volumes were selling for prices up to $500, when they could be found, in rare book catalogs. (I myself, wanting extra copies, occasionally bid on sets offered by book dealers.) People wrote me ruefully to say that they had neglected to purchase *Mark Twain's Library* when it was first offered, and to inquire whether I knew of any copies that were for sale. Nonetheless, no publisher would ever reprint the lengthy monograph, despite the fact that three university presses requested copies for cost-estimates. Everyone concluded that it was one of the most unpublishable works ever to be in high demand in the scholarly market.

In 2002 Thomas Tenney, who had by then become editor of the *Mark Twain Journal*, stepped forward again. He offered to publish a new edition of my work under the imprint of his journal, and enlisted JoDee Benussi to assist in keystroking and looking up references. Although that noble effort on Dr. Tenney's and Ms. Benussi's part never came to fruition, owing to my time-consuming academic responsibilities as a department head, it did ultimately motivate me to dust off the file drawers of notes and photocopies I had collected over the years, undertake an OCR scan of the original 1980 text of my book, and begin inserting new information that had come to light. Ms. Benussi had spotted factual errors in the Annotated Catalog that could now be corrected, and she had also suggested some excellent additions. Over the years, beginning in 1972, I had published numerous articles in scholarly journals and books on the subject of Clemens's library and reading; I have now revised and updated nineteen of these essays for inclusion in this new book.

A press in the city where I had relocated in 1991, NewSouth Books, expressed an interest in taking on the project.

CONFRONTING MAJOR NEW DEVELOPMENTS

Of course the world of literary scholarship had changed in the intervening decades since *Mark Twain's Library* was issued. "Source studies," once so respected and plentiful, are today disparaged as simplistic misrepresentations of how literary genius absorbs and recycles reading materials. A new concept has gained currency—intertextuality, a more complicated interpretation. It is assumed that the artist virtually swims in a world of potential resources that need only be mentioned, not lined up and labeled as proofs of definite "influence." This critical trend made me glad that I had so seldom pressed the case for the direct impact of particular books on specific passages in Twain's works.

But in other respects I had made serious faux pas. For instance, I had erroneously guessed about the fate of Mark Twain's copy of Sir Thomas Malory's *Morte Darthur* [sic]. Twain had *not* cannibalized it in extracting passages to quote in his *A Connecticut Yankee in King Arthur's Court* (1889), as I had speculated. True, the Malory volume had been listed in neither the 1911 catalog nor the 1951 auction sheet, but nonetheless it had been sold by Clara Clemens Samossoud, probably in the late 1940s or early 1950s. In a stunning development the volume made its reappearance on 16 August 1997 at the third international "State of Mark Twain Studies Conference" at Elmira College, replete with Twain's annotations. I had to listen politely

Library in the former Jervis Langdon residence, c. 1900
(Courtesy of the Mark Twain House & Museum, Hartford, Connecticut)[4]

while younger Twain scholars at the confer-ence diplomatically alluded to my published miscalculation.

AN UNEXPECTED HARTFORD WINDFALL

Does the surfacing of the Malory book signal that possibly even Twain's long-miss-ing copy of Jonathan Swift's *Gulliver's Travels* might someday come to light? Perhaps that is too much to ask, but minor miracles do occur with regularity. In 1997, 271 volumes that had been sold at the 1951 sale and were long believed to have permanently disap-peared, unexpectedly made their way to the Butterfield & Butterfield auction block in San Francisco. An amateur collector had

purchased them at the Hollywood auction and stored them in barrels in Southern California. The Mark Twain House and Museum of Hartford raised enough funds to land the entire group for $200,500. Among these acquisitions were history and science books, Darwin's writings, Plutarch's *Lives*, a set of Shakespeare, Defoe's *Moll Flanders*, and Macaulay's *Essays*, along with titles by Hawthorne, Longfellow, Stowe, Howells, and Browning—even works by James Feni-more Cooper, whom Twain ridiculed. The acquisition of that huge trove ranks as one of the major events occurring since my original listing in 1980. The Hartford *Courant* hailed it as "a big piece of Mark Twain's life . . . coming back to Hartford" (17 July 1997) and expressed relief that "now the 271 volumes will be available to scholars and Twain fans, and not be dispersed into private hands" (22 July 1997). The New York *Times* of 1 August 1997 reported that "two collectors and a rare-book dealer had to be outbid," and that the new additions "tripled the number of volumes from Twain's personal library now in the museum's care." The *Times* quoted John Vincent Boyer, then the executive director of the Mark Twain House, who termed the acquisition "an extraordinary array showing the unusually wide and encyclopedic interests" of the Clemenses. Upon the books' arrival, Boyer said, "I knew intellectually what we were going to receive . . . And then you see the books and you recognize that these were things that Mark Twain fell asleep reading."

THE LANGDON FAMILY COLLECTIONS

Another revelation had occurred in Elmira, New York, where important volumes by Charles Dickens, Thomas Carlyle, W. E. H. Lecky, Thomas Macaulay, and other eminent authors, annotated in Clemens's hand, were discovered on the shelves of the library of Quarry Farm. Its owners Theodore (1831–1889) and Susan Crane (1836–1924) had made Clemens and his family comfortable there for nearly two dozen summers. However, that valuable library collection presented the compiler of this catalog with several formidable problems. First of all, a large number of the books at Quarry Farm originated from the personal library of Clemens's niece, Ida Langdon (1880–1964), the daughter of Charles Jervis and Ida Clark Langdon and a well-educated woman with a bachelor's degree from Bryn Mawr College and master's

and doctoral degrees in English from Cornell University. She taught at Bryn Mawr and Wellesley College before joining the faculty of Elmira College in 1920, where she taught until 1942, at one point serving as the department chair, and then in retirement was awarded the rank of professor emerita in 1945. (It was Ida Langdon who donated Clemens's octagonal study to Elmira College in 1952.) As one might suppose, this English professor was fond of marking her books, especially the literary texts, and this has caused the hearts of many visitors to Quarry Farm to skip a beat as they took down a random volume from the library bookshelves and discovered what they hoped to be another addition to Mark Twain's known marginalia. In a few cases it is a little difficult to determine which markings were by Ida and which by Clemens or his wife Olivia, but a closer inspection usually settles the matter. Still, this is a complicating factor, especially regarding the literary works that Ida Langdon did *not* sign or annotate; were they initially *her* possessions, or had they belonged to Theodore or Susan Crane at Quarry Farm, which might mean that Clemens had opportunities to read them?

Then, too, there is the sheer number of books that were shelved throughout the Langdons' house on East Hill. In the early 1980s, a book dealer in Horseheads, New York—Emily Schweizer Martinez—was retained (for a fee of $300, according to her note on the document about a check she received on 31 May) to inventory and assess the value of the Quarry Farm library. Presumably this was for tax purposes involving the donation in 1982 of Quarry Farm and 6.7 acres of its land to Elmira College by Jervis

*Quarry Farm parlor, c. 1890s (Mark Twain Archive, Elmira College); a renovation
in 1925 included a dedicated library where the Langdon and Crane
books were eventually shelved together.*

Langdon Jr. and his wife Irene. Ms. Martinez made a list of the 1,699 books she found on various shelves, upstairs and downstairs, and estimated their market value as used books at $21,966. A very substantial portion of the titles dated from the decades *after* Clemens's last visit to Quarry Farm in 1907; many of them had been purchased in the 1920s and 1930s and a few even as late as the 1960s. Her inventory was arranged alphabetically for each area and every shelf in the house where she found the volumes, making it difficult to look for any particular author or title. She did pause to record ownership inscriptions and the presence of Clemens's marginalia, but mainly she was interested in assessing the physical condition of the books in order to estimate their value. (The books heavily annotated by Clemens were appraised at $250 or less apiece.)

The core of the Langdon family library in the city of Elmira eventually migrated up East Hill to Quarry Farm. It consisted of volumes designated with numbered bookplates identifying the "J. Langdon Family Library" that the senior Jervis Langdon (1809–1870) had assembled. Some of the books have post-1870 publication dates, indicating that the family continued to employ that same bookplate for additional acquisitions after Jervis Langdon died. Many volumes with these bookplates are now housed in the Mark Twain Archive at Elmira College.

The enlarged Annotated Catalog in *Mark Twain's Literary Resources* contains most of the Crane and Langdon books displaying publication dates within the range of Clemens's visits to Quarry Farm, which ended in 1907. Certain volumes belonging to the household of Charles Jervis Langdon (1849–1916) and his wife Ida B. Clark (1849–1934) presumably remained separate from the Cranes' until after Clemens's death in 1910, but since he might have had access to the Langdons' collection whenever he visited their Elmira home a considerable percentage of its most promising contents are included. The catalog does exclude titles that Ida Langdon or other members of the Langdon family added after 1907 to the collection. These listings rely on my personal examination of the volumes in the Quarry Farm library and the Mark Twain Archive at Elmira College as well as information supplied by Mark Woodhouse, former archivist at Elmira College, the appraisal of the Quarry Farm library made in the early 1980s by the local book dealer Emily Schweizer Martinez, and an inventory prepared in June 2016 by Nathaniel Ball, archivist at Elmira College, of all books known to have belonged to the Langdons and the Cranes. Of course there can be no conclusive evidence that Clemens looked into every single work shelved at Quarry Farm or the Langdons' residence, but given his innate sense of curiosity it seems logical to consider them as accessible literary resources.

FORGERS FIND MARK TWAIN

Soaring sale prices have led to a steadily improving series of forgeries. In fact, I and other Twain experts have detected dozens of forged association copies, including a set of Twain's published works that purportedly contained his handwritten comments and had been purchased for a substantial price.[5] The instigator of this expensive hoax has not been traced. However, the majority of the "S. L. Clemens/(Mark Twain)" fake autographs bear the trademarks of Eugene Field II (1880–1947), the swindler son of the famous American poet, and his shady bookseller associate Harry Dayton Sickles, about whom little is known other than that he operated in the Chicago vicinity. A few other fraudulent signatures are thought to have originated from the pen of Mark Hofmann (b. 1954), the infamous Salt Lake City forger who murdered two people with bombs before he was brought to justice. Joseph Cosey, born in 1887 and believed to have died around 1950, long identified as a major manufacturer of alleged Poe and Lincoln manuscripts, periodically also employed his talents in producing "Mark Twain" items.

But there are other hands out there busily creating new Mark Twain materials, and all collectors and libraries should be on guard. It is quite tempting to unscrupulous people to take an otherwise-ordinary nineteenth-century volume and trace the name "Mark Twain" onto its front endpaper or one of its flyleaves. A critical eye can detect these usually (though not always) clumsy efforts to fool the unwary. Forgers of putative marginalia are quite capable of copying individual letters to compose a word whose separate elements resemble something Clemens might have written, yet there is what I like to term a "rhythm" belonging to his handwriting (and to all of ours, for that matter) that is almost impossible to duplicate even in a brief word or two, let alone in a sentence or paragraph. Booksellers and their customers fall prey to these counterfeit association copies because they *want* to believe they are handling a previously unrecorded addition to Mark Twain's reading, which always seems feasible in light of the chaotic dispersals of his family's library. In an attempt to keep the record straight regarding genuine versus spurious association copies, the new Annotated Catalog lists these suspected forgeries as a service to the book world. The dubious "autographs" that enhance their value will most likely keep them circulating indefinitely from buyer to buyer, and a proliferating number of questionable additions to Clemens's library will probably make their appearances in the decades ahead.

INSERTING NEW MATERIAL

It has been a satisfying pleasure to add to the shelves of Clemens's library. In the office at my residence over the past decades I assembled new catalog entries, many of them derived from recently noticed literary allusions, that fill five file cabinet drawers. Events have kept delivering new findings. In June 2003, for example, I traveled to New York City to observe, at Sotheby's, an auction of the collection of Nick Karanovich (1938–2003), who had devoted his entire life and a modest inheritance to the procuring of every item related to Mark Twain that came up for sale. When he passed away prematurely at the age of sixty-four, I and the world were finally able to see all that he had brought together in his home in Fort Wayne, Indiana. Clemens's heavily annotated copies of Robert Browning's *Parleyings with Certain People of Importance in Their Day*, George Otto Trevelyan's *Life and Letters of Lord Macaulay*, Thomas Higginson's recollections titled *Contemporaries*, Samuel Dill's

Alan Gribben at Department of Special Collections, Washington University Libraries, St. Louis, 2015

Roman Society in the Last Century of the Western Empire, William Still's exposé of slavery's evils titled *The Underground Rail Road*, and other association items re-entered the rare book market at this landmark sale. There at Sotheby's I watched as Ulysses S. Grant's memoirs, signed by Clemens, sold for $33,000. A volume of Robert Browning's verse went for $12,000, as did a book by Theodore Roosevelt. Moncure Conway's influential *Autobiography* sold for $19,200. Quite a few volumes never previously seen were gaveled down in this auction that realized the impressive sum of $1,427,400 for relatives to whom Mr. Karanovich wished to leave a substantial bequest.

From this brief chronicle one can see that the search for indications of Clemens's reading and his ever-drifting library volumes will be endless, but all the same this revised and expanded edition of my 1980 work significantly augments the ongoing inquiry.

NOTES

1 For a fuller survey of these developments, see my "Private Libraries of American Authors: Dispersal, Custody, and Description," *Journal of Library History* 21 (Spring 1986): 300–314; reprinted in *Libraries, Books & Culture*, ed. Donald G. Davis Jr. (Austin, Texas: Graduate School of Library and Information Science, University of Texas, 1986): 300–314.

2 This subject is treated more substantially in my essay, "Samuel Clemens's Earliest Reading Experiences," which is published in the present volume.

3 As evidence that virtue is sometimes rewarded, however, following the publication of *Mark Twain's Library: A Reconstruction* in 1980 three different individuals presented me—in fact, pressed on me—books they owned that had once belonged to Clemens. Each person remarked that I had "earned" the gift.

4 For more about the elegance of the Langdon home, see Walter G. Ritchie Jr., "The Jervis Langdon Residence in Elmira, New York," *Mark Twain Journal: The Author and His Era*, 56.1 (Spring 2018): 72–85.

5 See Ronald Wesley Hoag, "All That Glitters Is Not Mark Twain: The Case of the Riverdale '3,'" *Mark Twain Journal* 29.2 (Fall 1991): 2–9.

MARK TWAIN'S
LITERARY RESOURCES

VOLUME ONE

1

William Dean Howells's 'Most Unliterary' Author: Mark Twain

When the first version of this study—*Mark Twain's Library: A Reconstruction*—appeared in 1980, the New York *Times* reported that its author had "mixed ivory-tower research with tireless travel and extraordinary luck to uncover Mark Twain's masquerade as a man who did not read many books." Various scholars soon expressed surprise at the breadth and depth of Samuel Clemens's reading as well as their appreciation for such a convenient format to consult for specific authors and titles with which he was familiar. Several academic commentators acknowledged that they had greatly underestimated Clemens's acquaintance with literary works, both ancient and contemporary. This was to be expected, because Clemens had deliberately downplayed his erudition in interviews with reporters and conversations with acquaintances. He seems to have adopted this role of unlettered genius rather instinctively, as he saw how it fit with his image as a sardonic wisecracker and uninhibited observer of human affairs. To have revealed the true extent of his daily reading would have set him apart from a significant percentage of his demotic audience. Then, too, this pretense of being a sort of literary innocent protected him against random charges of imitation such as he had seen lodged against his one-time friend Bret Harte who had, many believed, emulated formulas employed by Charles Dickens.

"I don't know anything about anything, and never did," Clemens informed his designated biographer with pleasure in 1909.[1] This extreme statement about his lack of literary knowledge summarized a long series of similar disclaimers that intensified in the 1880s. Only a few of his acquaintances managed to penetrate and dispute this pose. Hartford journalist and editor Charles Hopkins Clark (1848–1926), who substantially assisted Twain in preparing *Mark Twain's Library of Humor* (1888), wrote a searching profile of him for the "Authors at Home" series that appeared in the 17 January 1885 issue of *The Critic*. In Clark's opinion, "for years past he has been an industrious and extensive reader and student in the broad field of general culture. He has a large library and a real familiarity with it, extending beyond our own language into the literatures of Germany and France. He seems to have been fully conscious of the obligations which the successful opening of his literary career laid upon him, and to have lived up to its opportunities by a conscientious and continuous course of reading and study which supplements the large knowledge of human nature that the vicissitudes of his early life brought with them. . . . His parlor-reading of Shakespeare is described as a masterly performance."[2]

Yet in an 1886 letter responding to an editor of *The Critic* who had asked him to name one hundred authors whom a person should read, Clemens professed literary ignorance, announcing: "If it be a confession, then let me confess to-wit: 1. All the romance [i.e., fiction] which I have read in twenty years would not over-crowd a couple of crown octavo volumes; 2. All the poetry which I have read in twenty years could be put between the lids of one octavo. I do not read anything but history & biography. . . . No, leave me out: My testimony would not be valuable."[3] To a correspondent in 1887 Clemens insisted, "I have no liking for novels or stories—none in the world; & so, whenever I read one—which is not oftener than once in two years, and even in these same cases I seldom read beyond the middle of the book—my distaste for the *vehicle* always taints my judgment of the literature itself."[4] "Personally I never care for fiction or story-books," he told Rudyard Kipling in 1889. "What I like to read about are facts and statistics of any kind."[5] "With modern writers of fiction I confess I have no very extensive acquaintance," Clemens assured a newspaper interviewer in 1895. 'I read little

but the 'heaviest' sort of literature—history, biography, travels. I have always had a fear that I should get into someone else's style if I dabbled among the modern writers too much, and I don't want to do that."[6] On other occasions he denied ever reading Le Sage's *Gil Blas* or Carlyle's *Sartor Resartus*[7] although there is much evidence to the contrary. These repeated avowals of ignorance are the principal source of the once-widely-accepted representation of him as a basically unread man, an affected pose which I and other scholars have inveighed against.[8]

One of the most frequently cited expressions of Clemens's views about literature occurred in a fragment that survives from a letter he wrote sometime between 1890 and 1893. There Mark Twain assured an inquisitive (and unidentified) correspondent that he could as easily have written adult novels instead of boys' fiction if he had so chosen, for "I surely have the equipment, a wide culture; & all of it real, none of it artificial, for I don't know anything about books."[9] This declaration comes into clearer focus when it is juxtaposed with his assertion in *Is Shakespeare Dead?* (1909) that Shakespeare, like any other writer, was incapable of mastering the terminology of a profession merely from reading books about it. "He will not, and cannot, get the trade-phrasings precisely and exactly right," Mark Twain argued. For this reason Twain lauded Richard Henry Dana's *Two Years Before the Mast* (in *Is Shakespeare Dead?*), since Dana "didn't learn his trade out of a book, he has *been* there!"[10] Anyone who quotes Mark Twain's contention that he learned little from books should realize that he was primarily trying, as a former journeyman printer, steamboat pilot, mining prospector, newspaper reporter, and travel correspondent, to differentiate between vicarious, second-hand knowledge and actual "field" experience. He made this distinction repeatedly, warning an aspiring writer in 1885: "The moment you venture outside your *own* experience, you are in peril. . . . What you have not lived you cannot write."[11] In Chapter 14 of Twain's *The American Claimant* (1892), Lord Berkeley is characterized as "a young fellow . . . who hasn't any culture but the artificial culture of books, which adorns but doesn't really educate."

By the 1930s a few critics had begun to question the truthfulness of Twain's purported disdain for *belles-lettres* and his claims of limited reading. Minnie M. Brashear proposed in 1934 that his disavowals should be construed as a "half-humorous" acknowledgment of "his sense of contrast between his equipment as a writer and that of Hawthorne, for instance, or his friend Brander Matthews." She perceived that Mark Twain's tendency to minimize his reading "was a part of the legend he deliberately created about himself, either because it pleased his vanity to believe that what he had read had been of small value in his development, or because he knew that he was more interesting to his American public in the role of an original, than as a man who had from boyhood extended his powers and his horizon by diligent reading."[12]

In 1962 Dewey Ganzel analyzed Mark Twain's pretense of having slight knowledge about literature with equal acuteness. Twain's "extravagant overstatement" of ignorance concerning books, Ganzel observed, "seems oddly incongruous with the novelist we know Clemens to have been, but it is characteristic

of the persona which he fabricated: Mark Twain was the 'natural man' of the frontier, self-taught and full of savvy, possessing an imagination uncluttered with literary analogues. This persona, useful to Clemens, is delightful to us, but it can be misleading."[13]

Scholars intent on looking behind the mask that Clemens constructed can find valuable comments in a biographical sketch for the May 1896 issue of *Harper's Magazine* written by Clemens's close friend Joseph H. Twichell. He recounted the impediments Clemens faced when he recognized that authorship would be his permanent career. "His qualification for it, in the ordinary reckoning, was small, as he perfectly well knew. He was not what is called an educated man. He had no formal literary culture. His acquaintance with books was limited" (p. 818). Twichell went on to explain that Twain's "deficiency he has, during the thirty years that have since elapsed, applied himself with large diligence to repair." The Nook Farm clergyman took obvious pride in reporting: "All that time he has been an eager, industrious reader and student. He has acquired French and German. . . . He has widely acquainted himself with literature—modern literature especially—in various departments." Moreover, "he does not in the least share the slighting regard of the learning of the schools which so-called self-made men are prone to entertain." Rather, on many occasions he has expressed "his sense of disadvantage without remedy in having been denied the opportunity of a classical training in his youth" (p. 822). Twichell's depiction of Clemens as a man who was continually aware of, and striving to compensate for, his educational shortcomings seems suspiciously like the self-image that some Nook Farm residents might have preferred Clemens to entertain. It is unintentionally an anomalous description of the author who purported to be utterly ignorant of books. But this portrayal as self-educated intellectual evidently did not satisfy Clemens; he was already advancing his poses as unsophisticated Westerner and obstructed student.

Conversations with associates were one means of achieving his desired public image. Carlyle Smythe, Clemens's companion during a portion of his global tour in 1895–96, promulgated the notion of Mark Twain as an incorrigibly fickle reader that endured for most of the next century. Inappropriately titled "The Real 'Mark Twain,'" Smythe's essay in the September 1898 issue of the *Pall Mall Magazine* paid careful attention to Twain's "curiously eccentric" yet "entirely serious" literary preferences. "He has a gluttonous appetite for books, but his taste is the despair of his family and friends," Smythe announced. "If he ever had a palate for poetry it has become atrophied, . . . and now the one poet whose works afford him any pleasure is Browning." As for fiction, "roughly speaking, I may say that he reads anything in prose that is clean and healthy, yet he has never been able to find a line in Thackeray which interested him. Addison and Goldsmith are thrown away upon him; and Meredith, perhaps not unnaturally, provokes him to laughter." Smythe repeated a remark by Clemens indicating his willingness to sanction this picture of uncouth ignorance: "I asked Mr. Clemens one day how he explained this indifference to the acknowledged master-craftsmen in his own trade. The explanation candidly given was, 'I

have no really literary taste, and never had.'" Smythe somewhat perceptively added, "Yet this is an explanation whose chief vice is that it fails to explain; for he is a thorough admirer of Stevenson, and reads Mr. Kipling . . . while I have heard him quote both Shakespeare and Tennyson" (pp. 30–31).

When Clemens died in 1910 his reading habits and tastes received an authoritative assessment that assured the survival of this concept of their minimal, eccentric nature. In *My Mark Twain* (1910) his friend William Dean Howells paused in his sketch of Mark Twain to recall the kinds of books he read. Somewhat oddly, Howells used himself as the standard for comparison, and matched his own literary knowledge against his friend's as though they had been rivals.

> If I mention my own greater bookishness, by which I mean his less quantitative reading, it is to give myself better occasion to note that he was always reading some vital book. It might be some out-of-the-way book, but it had the root of the human matter in it: a volume of great trials; one of the supreme autobiographies; a signal passage of history, a narrative of travel, a story of captivity, which gave him life at first-hand. As I remember, he did not care much for fiction, and in that sort he had certain distinct loathings. His prime abhorrence was my dear and honored prime favorite, Jane Austen. . . . He seemed not to have any preferences among novelists; or at least I never heard him express any. He used to read the modern novels I praised, in or out of print; but I do not think he much liked reading fiction. As for plays, he detested the theatre, and said he would as lief do a sum as

William Dean Howells and Mark Twain, Stormfield, 1909

follow a plot on the stage. He could not, or did not, give any reasons for his literary abhorrences, and perhaps he really had none. But he could have said very distinctly, if he had needed, why he liked the books he did. . . . Generally, I fancy his pleasure in poetry was not great, and I do not believe he cared much for the conventionally accepted masterpieces of literature. He liked to find out good things and great things for himself.[14]

Howells concluded his appraisal with the remark that was to become a mainstay of Mark Twain studies: "Of all the literary men I have known he was the most unliterary in his make and manner."

What Howells clearly intended to emphasize was the fact that Clemens's reading, though wide, was far less programmatic than that of a regular literary reviewer such as himself. But his many references to Clemens's literary dislikes had the effect of strengthening the image of Mark Twain as a writer very little influenced by his reading. Howells suggests that Clemens was comfortable only with biographies, vivid passages of history, and travel books, like an adolescent fascinated with faraway places and notable people. The summary dismissal of fiction, drama, and poetry as of little interest to Clemens seems to imply that they are beyond his grasp, and Howells's phrase, "some *vital* book," damns with faint praise, connoting as it does the simple and overcolored. All in all, it is a remarkably condescending passage for a tribute to an iconic author written in May 1910 shortly after his funeral.[15]

Had anyone other than Howells written of Clemens as an "unliterary" man, the label

might soon have been recognized as ludicrous. But Howells's eminence in American letters and his intimate relationship with Clemens deterred anyone at the time from challenging his judgment. In 1922, two years after Howells's own death, Olin H. Moore traced the doctrine of Mark Twain's supposed "ultra-originality" largely to Howells's comments about his reading.[16] Writing in 1934, Minnie M. Brashear found it strange that "even his friend Howells [should have] thought of him as an adventurer among literary men."[17] Yet the view that Clemens eschewed *belles-lettres* had been affirmed by another leading American critic. In "Memories of Mark Twain," an essay of 1919, Brander Matthews remarked: "I was not at all surprised when Mark promptly assured me that he had never read 'Gil Blas'; I knew he was not a bookish man. He was intensely interested in all the manifestation of life, but had no special fondness for fiction,—an attitude not uncommon among men of letters. He was a constant reader of history and autobiography, not caring overmuch for novels and getting far more enjoyment out of Suetonius or Carlyle than he did out of Scott or Thackeray."[18]

Matthews thus applied the final touches to a portrait already sketched by Albert Bigelow Paine in his *Mark Twain: A Biography* (1912) and *Mark Twain's Letters* (1917). Indeed, it was Clemens's designated biographer Paine who perhaps more than anyone else gave currency to the impression that Clemens's reading habits were quite focused and limited; in his biography Paine even reproduced in facsimile a written declaration by Clemens, dating it around the period of 1874: "I like history, biography, travels, curious facts &

strange happenings, & science. And I detest novels, poetry & theology" (p. 574). However, the envelope on which Clemens jotted this announcement survives in the Mark Twain Papers at Berkeley, and its handwriting, ink, and the accompanying book titles he added clearly attribute the note to November 1909, not 1874. Clemens's note seems to relate to the books he had just been reading and had listed there—an ephemeral novel, *The Agony Column*, two volumes on English surnames, a travel journal about Patagonia, and a collection of biographies of figures in the history of science—Galileo, Tycho Brahe, and Kepler. Paine implied that this was a view Clemens held throughout his lifetime, whereas the note belonged to a period at the very end of Clemens's life, when, increasingly ill and embittered, very little seemed to be pleasing him.[19] Of course there is no question that Clemens *did* indeed relish works of biography and history as well as books about singular facts and events, but we can now be certain that he had a keen taste for *belles-lettres*—fiction, poetry, drama—that included all centuries and a number of foreign languages and cultures.

CLEMENS'S RELIANCE ON LIBRARIES

The Annotated Catalog of *Mark Twain's Literary Resources* reveals how inadequate was this prevailing notion of Samuel Clemens as an unlettered humorist (or rather, it illustrates how effectively he promoted that useful image). The evidence has been derived mainly from an inventory of the books in his personal library, but also documented are instances when he drew upon the resources of public and private libraries in Hartford and elsewhere. It might be supposed, in light of Clemens's affluence, the ample size of his own library, and his familiarity with the major American and English publishers, that he would have found little occasion for using either lending libraries or private libraries. Yet on the contrary, he borrowed books frequently from public and private collections to supplement his own holdings. His consequent feeling of indebtedness, in fact, was great enough to move him, late in his life, to make extensive book donations to several libraries, including a community library in Redding, Connecticut primarily established with huge book donations from Clemens and his daughter Clara in addition to a monetary bequest he left its trustees.

CONTACTS WITH LIBRARIES

Clemens's interest in library collections dated from his boyhood, and his father was partially responsible. John Marshall Clemens helped found the Hannibal Library Institute in 1844; before that decade ended the organization had seventy stockholders and 425 books. At the time of the elder Clemens's death in 1847 he was its president and was authorized to call meetings of the stockholders. Twenty-eight-year-old Orion Clemens made efforts to revive its membership in 1853, shortly before his brother Sam left Hannibal permanently and Orion moved to Muscatine, Iowa.[20] The Institute fell on hard times after John Marshall Clemens's demise and lost most of its members and books, but young Sam Clemens may have taken advantage of his family's membership before the remnants of its collection were locked up for safekeeping until an attempt could be made at reorganization.

Clemens himself recalled that his first experience of libraries occurred in Sunday school, where—provided that he could repeat by heart a specified number of verses from the New Testament—he was allowed to check out books for one week.[21] Immersion in those highly moral story-books left him with a shrewd understanding of the Sunday-school writers' motives and techniques, which he would burlesque in early sketches such as "The Story of the Good Little Boy" (1870). Sunday-school books also contributed to the good boy/bad boy contrast he employed effectively in *The Adventures of Tom Sawyer* (1876), "Edward Mills and George Benton: A Tale" (1880), and other works of fiction.

In the course of his *Wanderjahr* in 1853–54 Clemens discovered the wealth of books available in urban libraries. On 31 August 1853 the seventeen-year-old typesetter wrote to his mother from New York to assuage her misgivings about his behavior in a large, unfamiliar city. In a postscript he added: "The printers have two libraries in town, entirely free to the craft; and in these I can spend my evenings most pleasantly. If books are not good company, where will I find it?"[22] Shortly thereafter he wrote to his sister Pamela: "You ask where I spend my evenings. Where would you suppose, with a free printers' library containing more than 4,000 volumes within a quarter of a mile of me, and nobody at home to talk to?"[23] He was referring to the Printers' Free Library and Reading Room of the New York Typographical Society, open nightly from six until ten p.m. for "all . . . connected with the book and newspaper business."[24]

Most respectable hotels in the nineteenth century had libraries, and early in his travels Clemens developed a habit of looking into them. At nineteen, when family errands necessitated a one-night stopover in 1855 in tiny Paris, Missouri, he disdainfully recorded in his first known notebook the two paltry volumes—*Jayne's Medical Almanac* and George Darley's *Lives of Beaumont and Fletcher*—that constituted the contents of the library room in the local hotel.[25] His complaint about the miscellaneous quality of reading fare at the Deming House in Keokuk, Iowa became a joke in his 19 April 1867 letter to the *Alta California*,[26] and later was developed further into an episode in Chapter 57 of *The Innocents Abroad* (1869). He noticed this detail throughout his life; a hotel's library was one of the criteria by which he judged it. On 21 September 1878, for instance, he observed in Notebook 16 that in Milan, Italy, "hotel libraries are only novels & hymn books."[27]

Clemens also took advantage of the libraries maintained on oceangoing vessels. He scoffed at the anemic collection he found aboard the *Quaker City* in 1867, recalling that the passengers were instructed beforehand to bring along a specified assortment of books to make up the ship library. "It was the rarest library that ever was seen," he wrote in his letter from Jerusalem. "As we neared Gibraltar we could hardly find out from any book on board whether Gibraltar was a rock, or an island, or a statue, or a piece of poetry. . . . We were bound for France, England, Italy, Germany, Switzerland, Greece, Turkey, Africa, Syria, Palestine, Egypt, and many a noted island in the sea, and yet all our library, almost, was made up of Holy Land, Plymouth Collection and Salvation by Grace!"[28]

He derived greater satisfaction from the books on board the ships that carried him across the Indian Ocean for his lecture tour in 1895 and 1896. On 8 January 1896 he noted that "on this voyage [from Sydney to Ceylon aboard the *Oceana*] I have read a number of novels," adding, "This is the best library I have seen in a ship yet."[29] A few months later, in April 1896, he commented again on how much reading added to his enjoyment of a voyage: "Seventeen days ago this ship sailed out of Calcutta; & ever since, barring a day or two in Ceylon, there has been nothing in sight but a tranquil blue sea & a cloudless blue sky. . . . Seventeen days of heaven. . . . One reads all day long in this delicious air, of course. To-day I have been storing up knowledge from Sir John Lubbock about the ant."[30]

Moreover, he liked to browse in the private libraries of his relatives and friends. When Clemens married into the Langdon family in 1870 he gained access, over the succeeding decades, to hundreds and hundreds of books that would not show up in his own library collection. The Langdons, especially Olivia's sister Susan Crane and her husband Theodore who lived at Quarry Farm on East Hill above Elmira, readily gave Clemens permission to rummage through their bookshelves at his leisure. The Cranes offered him twenty-two summertimes of convenient entree to nearly all of the standard authors of the day—Plutarch, Shakespeare, Milton, Scott, Dickens, Macaulay, Tennyson, Carlyle, Hawthorne, Thackeray, Darwin, Stevenson, Browning, Kipling, and many others—and also to works less venerated at the time such as those by Pepys, DeQuincey, Hugo, Zola, and Conrad, together with histories like those

of W. E. H. Lecky. When Rudyard Kipling went to Elmira in 1889 he discovered Clemens perusing the "Mathematics" entry in the *Encyclopaedia Britannica* in his in-laws' Quarry Farm library.[31] Numerous volumes from the Cranes' collection, signed by Theodore or Susan Crane, bear Clemens's unmistakable marginalia.

Grace King visited Frederick Church's Moorish Victorian mansion "Olana" in upstate New York with the Warners and the Clemenses in 1886. She observed that following dinner Clemens composedly "shuffled in amongst us in slippers with a big pipe in his mouth. . . . I came through the library after a while to hunt up the others & found Clemens reading some antique book."[32] The superbly drawn descriptions of parlor libraries in Mark Twain's published writings testify to the care with which he noted the books in homes that he visited. From the ante-bellum "house beautiful" he meticulously catalogued in Chapter 38 of *Life on the Mississippi* (1883), with its *Ivanhoe* and *Friendship's Offering*, to the volumes he recognized on parlor tables when he was a newspaper correspondent in Honolulu (Baxter's *Saints' Rest* and Tupper's *Proverbial Philosophy*) that he recalled in Chapter 3 of *Following the Equator*, Mark Twain showed how much he enjoyed the game of plucking from a few book titles the whole way of life of their owners.

As a dues-paying member of the Young Men's Association in Buffalo, New York from 1869 until 1872, Clemens had been entitled to use its 15,000-volume library at the corner of Main and Eagle Streets—the only large circulating library in that city.[33] During his subsequent years of residence in Hartford,

Clemens regularly supplemented his own book collection with materials from the Hartford Library Association, which in 1884 contained 36,000 volumes.[34] On 13 October 1884 he wrote to Caroline M. Hewins, the librarian since 1875, to request that the young Hartford sculptor Karl Gerhardt be allowed to charge out books on Clemens's subscription—provided that his quota had not yet been reached.[35] A receipt for Clemens's one-year fee is in the Mark Twain Papers, dated 9 June 1888. The "cash book" for the Hartford Library Association, now in the possession of its successor, the Hartford Public Library, reveals that Clemens paid a yearly $25 membership fee for the five members of his family routinely between 15 June 1881 and 12 June 1889.[36] Memberships entitled subscribers to withdraw ten books at a time. Unlike the carefully recorded borrowings by Nathaniel Hawthorne from the Salem Athenaeum,[37] Clemens's withdrawals are unknown to us. The Hartford Library book charge records for that period seem to have been discarded.

"A public library is the most enduring of memorials . . . for it, and it only, is respected by wars and revolutions, and survives them," he declared on 22 February 1894 in a letter to the officers of the Millicent Library, which had been built in Fairhaven, Massachusetts by his friend and financial advisor Henry Huttleston Rogers. Praising the furnishings and atmosphere of that community library, Clemens disparaged "the customary kind of public library, with its depressing austerities and severities of form and furniture and decoration." For the benefit of library patrons he called instead for "light and grace and sumptuous comfort."[38]

Clemens predictably utilized metropolitan libraries in the United States and London. In a speech at the Savage Club on 21 September 1872 he praised the "astounding" Library of the British Museum: "I have read there hours together, and hardly made an impression on it," he quipped. "I revere that library."[39] In his English journals of 1872 Clemens expressed unqualified gratitude: "I am wonderfully thankful for the British Museum. . . . All the room & all the light I want under this huge dome—no disturbing noises—& people standing ready to bring me a copy of pretty much any book that ever was printed under the sun."[40] He included "London Library" in his budget of anticipated weekly expenses after moving to Tedworth Square in September 1896, and he was delighted to find another library with liberal lending policies: "Chelsea free library. Only one book allowed to one name. But if you really *want* to read, they are glad to make it easy for you. They give you a hint. You take out about 3 cards—I took out 3—as artist, poet, & scientist."[41] Sometimes he directed his publishers to undertake library searches on his behalf; in 1901, planning a book about American lynchings, he asked Frank Bliss to dispatch a research assistant to "the Hartford library or the Boston Public" to obtain a biography of the abolitionist Owen Lovejoy.[42]

The importance he attached to circulating libraries is evident in his defense of them as vital instruments of self-education for the masses. In Clemens's view a city without libraries betrayed the mental indolence of its inhabitants; this was another thing for which he berated the French. "No circulating (public) libraries," he recalled disapprovingly.[43]

On the other hand he enthusiastically jotted down figures for the circulating collections of small libraries he passed on his lecture tour in 1895: Helena, Montana had 13,000 volumes; Tacoma, Washington reported 2,264.[44] In South Africa, too, he made a similar note: *"June 26* [1896], *Grahamstown.* Beautiful town. Is cultured; has a library."[45] He spoke encouragingly on 27 September 1900 when addressing the ceremonial opening of the Kensal Rise Library in northwest London, not far from where he had been living in Dollis Hill house: "A reading room is the proper introduction to a library, leading up through the newspapers and magazines to other literature."[46] He donated five of his own books to help this small London public library get its start.

This assistance to libraries became more extensive. Clemens informed Howells on 25 July 1903 that he had "sent a couple of bushels" of his library books "to the little Riverdale library" in preparation for moving his family to Italy (*MTHL*, p. 773). Did Clemens mean the Kingsbridge Free Library in Riverdale, which survived a fire in the city in October 1903, gained a new building in 1904, and ultimately became a branch of the New York Public Library system? I made repeated but unsuccessful efforts to locate the records of those donations—quite a few of them presumably signed and annotated by "S. L. Clemens," a name not recognizable to many, then as now. (It is also possible that Clemens instead gave the books to the other local library, a collection maintained by the Riverdale Library Association, but my attempts to locate any accession records from 1903 were unavailing there as well.)

In view of these attitudes, it is hardly surprising that in 1908 Clemens was instrumental in founding a lending library in Redding, Connecticut. He spoke at its opening ceremony on 28 October 1908, saying, "We have here at least the nucleus of a library and that should be a cause for satisfaction." After his daughter Jean died on Christmas Eve in 1909, Clemens decided to sell the small farm that he had given her and use the proceeds to enable the community to erect a building to house the book collection that he and others were donating. On 6 April 1910 he instructed his New York City attorney Charles T. Lark to oversee this arrangement and place the resulting money in the hands of three trustees—Albert Bigelow Paine, H. A. Lounsbury, and William E. Hazen.[47] Accordingly, a week before his death Clemens wrote a check for $6,000 (the equivalent of more than $150,000 today) to build and furnish this structure.[48] His generous financial gift vastly surpassed the contributions of other contemporary residents.[49] For him the proliferation of public libraries ranked among mankind's signal achievements in the nineteenth century. Where this repository of learning and the arts was lacking, the town seemed like his fictional Black Jack, Arkansas in "The Second Advent" (1881): "There are no newspapers, no railways, no factories, no library; ignorance, sloth and drowsiness prevail."[50]

ACCEPTING A WELL-READ TWAIN

The frequency with which Clemens patronized libraries is as impossible to reconcile with his public persona of an unbookish folk humorist as was his bibliophilistic attention to his personal library. The passing of time and the surfacing of new materials have enabled scholars to strip away portions of the fallacy perpetuated by William Dean Howells, Albert Bigelow Paine, and other biographical commentators. From the earliest books we now know Clemens to have read, such as George Lippard's *Legends of the American Revolution* (1847) and J. L. Comstock's *Elements of Geology* (1851), down to the book in which Clemens sought cures for Jean Clemens's epilepsy, John Quackenbos's *Hypnotic Therapeutics* (1908), his appetite for factual, expository writing never abated. But probably the last book he annotated was William Lyon Phelps's *Essays on Modern Novelists*, presented to Clemens on 2 March 1910, and among the books he read shortly before his death was Thomas Hardy's *Jude the Obscure.* These and other titles in the following Annotated Catalog of Clemens' library books and literary references reveal how much more widely Clemens read in *belles-lettres* than is generally realized.

Why Clemens instigated the ruse of literary ignorance is a question that partly involves his perceived relationship with his commercial audience. The author of *Innocents Abroad, Roughing It, Huckleberry Finn,* and other subscription books evidently doubted that his readers would identify with a well-read author.[51] In casting his persona as a common man, Twain was obliged to lower the admitted level of his sophistication about literature. It also gratified him that his public thought of his artistry as spontaneous and non-derivative. Gradually we are recognizing Clemens as a writer who viewed reading as an essential daily occupation, who subscribed perennially to numerous newspapers and magazines, and who inquisitively sifted a catholic range of reading materials. If his lifetime reading proves to be less purposeful than that of William Dean Howells, a professional literary reviewer, and if Clemens's investigations of various books were often impulsive, the diversity and extent of his acquaintance with books nonetheless represented an astounding achievement, even for a prominent writer who resided in the stimulating atmosphere of Nook Farm.

THE CLEMENSES' LITERARY CONNECTIONS

To reconstruct the library of Samuel L. Clemens and his family is, in a sense, to evoke the atmosphere in which they lived. Highly literate and intellectually curious individuals, they led lives that were to a great extent centered around books. Their correspondence is honeycombed with mentioned and recommended book titles, and Clemens's notebooks make countless references to his reading. Interior photographs of their homes reveal the immense space they devoted to bookshelves. A sizable percentage of these titles came from the Brown & Gross bookshop at 77 Asylum Street in Hartford. Hundreds of volumes with fondly worded inscriptions confirm that books of all types were their favorite gifts to each other to commemorate birthdays, Christmases, anniversaries, trips, and other events. Prominent authors regularly dined at their Hartford house. A catalog of their library collection becomes something of an index of their lives, a type of family biography. Novels, encyclopedias, Bibles, travel guides, etiquette manuals, collections of correspondence, cookbooks, gardening handbooks, essays, fashion magazines, foreign language grammars, field guides to birds and wildflowers, volumes of poetry, songbooks, health-care instructions, hymnals—scarcely any of the Clemenses' intellectual, social, and personal interests, whether significant or quotidian, eluded representation in their library collection. But documenting the contents of this library presented major obstacles. When Clemens died in 1910 his surviving library was "valued at . . . $2,000," a substantial sum in that era.[52] However, his collection had already been considerably dispersed by library donations during his lifetime and the remaining contents would be decimated by large auctions in 1911 and 1951 that left highly incomplete records of his and his family members' reading.

NOTES

1 Albert Bigelow Paine, *Mark Twain: A Biography* (New York: Harper & Brothers, 1912), p. 1500—hereafter cited as *MTB*.

2 *The Critic* 6.55 (17 January 1885): 26.

3 Clemens to Joseph B. Gilder, Hartford, 16 May 1886, *Sotheby's 2003*, lot 60. Now in the collection of Kevin Mac Donnell.

4 Clemens to Bruce Weston Munro, Hartford, 21 April 1886, *Sotheby's 2003*, lot 62.

5 "An Interview with Mark Twain," collected in *From Sea to Sea: Letters of Travel*. 2 vols. (New York: Doubleday and McClure, 1899), 2: 180.

6 "Visit of Mark Twain: Wit and Humour," Sydney [Australia] *Morning Herald*, 17 September 1895; *Mark Twain: The Complete Interviews*, ed. Gary Scharnhorst (Tuscaloosa: University of Alabama Press, 2006), p. 205—hereafter cited as *Complete Interviews*.

7 Clemens to David A. Munro, 8 February 1905; ALS in the Henry W. and Albert A. Berg Collection, New York Public Library. See also Brander Matthews, *The Tocsin of Revolt and Other Essays*

(New York: Charles Scribner's Sons, 1922), p. 267.

8 Beginning with Olin H. Moore's seminal essay in the June 1922 issue of *PMLA*, and including Friedrich Schöenemann, Minnie M. Brashear, Harold Aspiz, Gladys Bellamy, Albert E. Stone, Jr., Edward Wagenknecht, Walter Blair, Dewey Ganzel, Howard G. Baetzhold, and others. (See the Critical Bibliography.)

9 *Mark Twain's Letters*, ed. Albert Bigelow Paine (New York: Harper & Brothers, 1917), p. 543, corrected from the ALS in the Mark Twain Papers, Bancroft Library, University of California at Berkeley—hereafter cited as MTP.

10 *The Writings of Mark Twain*, Definitive Edition (New York: Gabriel Wells, 1922), 26: pp. 304, 336.

11 Clemens to Olivia Clemens, 11 January 1885, quoted in *The Love Letters of Mark Twain*, ed. Dixon Wecter (New York: Harper & Brothers, 1949), p. 228.

12 *Mark Twain: Son of Missouri* (Chapel Hill: University of North Carolina Press, 1934), p. 197.

13 "Samuel Clemens and Captain Marryat," *Anglia* 80 (January 1962): 405.

14 *My Mark Twain: Reminiscences and Criticisms*, ed. Marilyn Austin Baldwin (Baton Rouge: Louisiana State University Press, 1967), pp. 15, 16.

15 *Mark Twain-Howells Letters*, ed. Henry Nash Smith and William M. Gibson (Cambridge: Harvard University Press, Belknap Press, 1960), p. 854.

16 "Mark Twain and Don Quixote," *PMLA* 37.2 (June 1922): 324–325.

17 *Mark Twain: Son of Missouri*, p. 240.

18 *Tocsin of Revolt*, p. 267.

19 Paine's contribution is analyzed in my "'I Detest Novels, Poetry & Theology': Origin of a Fiction Concerning Mark Twain's Reading," *Tennessee Studies in Literature* 22 (1977): 154–161. (A revised version of this essay appears as a chapter in the present volume.)

20 *Mark Twain: Son of Missouri*, pp. 95–96, 104, 200, citing the Hannibal *Weekly Journal*, 31 March 1853. See additionally the 22 June 1854 issue of the Hannibal *Missouri Courier*, which recounts the history of the Hannibal Library Institute.

21 *Autobiography of Mark Twain*, ed. Harriet Elinor Smith. 3 vols. (Berkeley: University of California Press, 2010), 1: 418.

22 *Mark Twain's Letters, Volume 1, 1853–1866*, ed. Edgar Marquess Branch, Michael B. Frank, and

Kenneth M. Sanderson (Berkeley: University of California Press, 1988), 1: 10—hereafter cited as *MTLet*.

23 *MTLet* 1: 14.

24 *Rode's New York City Directory* (New York: Charles R. Rode, 1853), Appendix, p. 36.

25 *Mark Twain's Notebooks and Journals*, ed. Frederick Anderson, Michael B. Frank, and Kenneth M. Sanderson (Berkeley: University of California Press, 1975), 1: 37.

26 *Mark Twain's Travels with Mr. Brown*, ed. Franklin Walker and G. Ezra Dane (New York: Alfred A. Knopf, 1940), p. 153.

27 *Mark Twain's Notebooks and Journals*, ed. Frederick Anderson, Lin Salamo, and Bernard L. Stein (Berkeley: University of California Press, 1975), 2: 193.

28 *Traveling with the Innocents Abroad*, ed. D. M. McKeithan (Norman: University of Oklahoma Press, 1958), pp. 303–304.

29 Notebook 37, TS p. 3, MTP.

30 Notebook 37, TS p. 44, MTP.

31 Kipling, *From Sea to Sea: Letters of Travel* (1899) 2: 180.

32 Quoted by Robert Bush, "Grace King and Mark Twain," *American Literature* 44.1 (March 1972): 34.

33 William H. Loos, "Mark Twain and the Young Men's Association," *Buffalo & Erie County Public Library Bulletin* (December 1985): 4; Thomas J. Reigstad, *Scriblin' for a Livin': Mark Twain's Pivotal Period in Buffalo* (Amherst, New York: Prometheus Books, 2013), pp. 46, 88.

34 *The Memorial History of Hartford County Connecticut 1663–1884*, ed. J. Hammond Trumbull. 2 vols. (Boston: Edward L. Osgood, 1886), 1: 541–550.

35 ALS in Hartford Public Library.

36 Letter from Wilbur B. Crimmin, Acting Librarian of the Hartford Public Library, to Alan Gribben, 9 October 1973.

37 Marion L. Kesselring, *Hawthorne's Reading, 1828–1850: A Transcription nd Identification of Titles Recorded in the Charge-Books of the Salem Athenaeum* (New York: New York Public Library, 1949).

38 *Mark Twain Speaks for Himself*, ed. Paul Fatout (West Lafayette, Indiana: Purdue University Press, 1978, repr. 1997), p. 146.

39 *Mark Twain Speaking*, ed. Paul Fatout (Iowa City: University of Iowa Press, 1976), p. 71. He sent a draft of this speech to Moncure D. Conway on 22 September 1872 (*MTLet* 5: 174).

40 *MTLet* 5: 598.

41 Notebook 39, TS pp. 4, 13, MTP; one of Clemens's Chelsea Public Libraries cards was reproduced in the *Mark Twain Journal* 36.2 [Fall 1998]: 31.

42 ALS, 26 August 1901, Harry Ransom Center, University of Texas, Austin.

43 Notebook 34, TS p. 4, MTP.

44 Notebook 35, TS p. 27, MTP.

45 Notebook 38, TS p. 55, MTP.

46 *Mark Twain Speaking*, p. 341.

47 Brent M. Colley to the Mark Twain Forum, email, 27 August 2017, quoting Clemens's letter to Charles T. Lark. Clemens instructed Lark to have the documents ready for him to sign on 14 April 1910.

48 New York *Times*, 10 July 1910.

49 Ledger Book of the Mark Twain Library Trustees, 1910, Mark Twain Library, Redding, Connecticut.

50 *Mark Twain's Fables of Man*, ed. John S. Tuckey (Berkeley: University of California Press, 1972), p. 53.

51 Hamlin Hill analyzed the subscription-book readers ("mechanics and farmers") and Twain's popular persona ("a groundling with some literary aspirations") in "Mark Twain: Audience and Artistry," *American Quarterly* 15.1 (Spring 1963): 25–40.

52 New York *Times*, 27 October 1910. That would be about $50,000 today.

2

Friends Like These

Lavishing Faint Praise on Mark Twain

Hard as it may be to believe, the long-running controversies over the teachability of *Huckleberry Finn*, the arguments about whether Huck's voice was white or black, the diminishing claims about Twain's alleged homosexuality, and the disagreements about the racial logic of *Pudd'nhead Wilson* have not been the only subjects interesting those engaged in contemporary scholarly conversations about Mark Twain. His biographers have additionally been commenting on, and criticizing, the "proprietary" nature of the earliest chroniclers of Twain's life. Hamlin Hill led off this line of objections in 1973, complaining in *Mark Twain: God's Fool* that Albert Bigelow Paine, the Mark Twain Estate, and Harper & Brothers had orchestrated the careful packaging and marketing of a valuable and beloved commodity known as Mark Twain. Hill insisted that much of Paine's "editing of the writings of Mark Twain consisted of removing from the unpublished material what he considered to be blasphemies and vindictiveness. He [Paine] was also the officially chosen guardian of an image which Clara Clemens, her

father's only surviving daughter, believed the public expected of Mark Twain." Paine could get away with these liberties, according to Hill, because "one-third of Paine's biography presented his firsthand account" of the years "when Paine was in almost daily contact with his subject." Nearly a decade and a half after Paine had brought out his biography in 1912, Paine wrote to Harper & Brothers to caution Twain's official publisher: "I think on general principles it is a mistake to let any one else write about Mark Twain, as long as we can prevent it. . . . As soon as this is begun (writing about him at all, I mean) the Mark Twain that we have 'preserved'—the Mark Twain that we knew, the traditional Mark Twain— will begin to fade and change, and with that process the Harper Mark Twain property will depreciate." Aside from the lack of faith this advice shows in Twain's genius, the various biographers' intentions, and the American public's discrimination, the highhandedness and degree of calculation reflected in Paine's words were par for the course regarding the lucrative property that Samuel L. Clemens left behind in the resonance of his famous pen name.

Louis J. Budd took up this topic in a more jovial manner than Hill, reminding us in a study titled *Our Mark Twain* (1983) that "Mark Twain is all around us today" and elaborating on how Twain himself along with numerous collaborating writers as well as the American public all conspired to create the iconic image known as "Our Mark Twain." Budd wrote, "At the risk of sounding like Twain's official biographer, Albert Bigelow Paine, I proceed in the tone of gratitude that his posturing worked and gave us both his writings and his public personality. . . . Within and beyond his books Twain reinforced qualities crucial to the happiness and perhaps survival of humankind: delight in experience, emotional spontaneity, and irreverence toward pomposity, petrified ideas, injustice, and self-pride."

But Harold K. Bush Jr. reminded us that the often-employed phrase "Our Mark Twain" can in fact be traced beyond even Albert Bigelow Paine back to William Dean Howells, who called Twain "the Lincoln of literature" but who also had what Bush termed an "agenda" in so doing; that is, Howells presumably had a vested interest in protecting and enhancing the status of an author he had discovered, edited, and promoted for thirty-five years. Indeed, Augusta Rohrbach, reviewing Howells's career, refers to him as "American literature's middle manager" because of his championship of so many up-and-coming writers such as Twain once was.

On the other hand, it is a fact that Mark Twain was the originator of many of the contours of his well-known profile—his unbookish ways, his purported indolence, his propensity for smoking (this one was certainly true), his loathing of certain types of vain people, his caution toward and misjudging of animals, and so forth. I myself have remarked on this phenomenon, commenting in 1984 that "Clemens led the way in modern-day 'image making,' aided by advances in technology and mass communications," and asserting that "he had wanted, if possible, to ensure something more grandiose than the probability that he would merely be remembered in future ages; he craved a guarantee that his name and triumphs would be catalogued among the major features of American cultural and literary history." As Mark Twain he of course succeeded, and today "the trappings of a legend afloat in a commercial, urban society are awesome."

But I am equally interested in what I have termed "Twain's terrific possessiveness about his posthumous image." Orion Clemens received a letter from his brother in 1887 that emphasizes this attitude: "I have never yet allowed an interviewer or biography sketcher to get out of me any circumstance of my history which I thought might be worth putting some day into my biography," declared Twain. "I hate all public mention of my private history, anyway. It is none of the public's business. . . . I have been approached as many as five hundred times on the biographical-sketch lay, but they never got anything that was worth the printing." Accordingly, when a would-be biographer approached Clemens in 1900 to ask for permission to publish a book and some sketches about Mark Twain, the lionized author answered with a roar: "I am sorry to object, but I really must. Such books as you propose are not proper to publish during my lifetime. A man's history *is his own property* until the grave extinguishes his ownership in it. I am strenuously opposed to having books of a biographical character published about me while I am still alive." When the biographer persisted, Twain made arrangements to have a lawyer keep an eye on him: "I won't have it," Twain wrote. "Watch for advertisements of these books. . . . He is a ~~mere maggot who tries to feed on people while~~ they are still alive." It is similarly instructive to read the headnote that Twain wrote for a biographical sketch he furnished to precede his own selections in *Mark Twain's Library of Humor,* published in 1888; the headnote stated that *The Innocents Abroad* was "the result of his experience and observation . . . on the *Quaker City* in her famous cruise to the Holy Land. . . . His succeeding books *continue the story of his own life*, with more or less fullness and exactness" (emphasis added). Could the proprietary tone be any more explicit?

However easy it is to demonstrate that Twain himself sought to control and disseminate his preferred version of his life, this is not the point of the present essay. Rather, I want to suggest two other sources that contributed posthumously to Twain's image in ways we have come to take for granted. As Rufus Griswold demonstrated all too clearly in the case of Edgar Allan Poe, the reputation of an author can be affected, for better or ill, and perhaps permanently, by the initial impressions published by the writer's trusted friends. Mark Twain suffered no such gross slanders by his literary executor, but the biographical memoirs brought out within the first two years after Twain's death nonetheless set the stage for misconceptions and innuendoes that have surfaced and resurfaced in subsequent treatments of the author.

In 1910 William Dean Howells, acknowledging that he was writing "in a cloud of grief" owing to the successive deaths of his own wife Elinor as well as his longtime friend Clemens, appended a collection of past reviews and essays to a full-scale reminiscence that he brought out under the title *My Mark Twain.* An editor of a later edition of this work, Marilyn Austin Baldwin, praised Howells's boldness and "realistic writing" in his uncharacteristically frank naming of what she called Mark Twain's "shortcomings," explicit faults that ensured this picture of Twain "is not a eulogized mannequin." Among these "shortcomings" she cites are (1) Twain's "frenzies of resentment or suspicion," (2) his repeated and exaggerated censure of what Twain called the "Damned Human Race," and (3) his religious skepticism (whereas Paine would fudge on this sensitive matter, rationalizing that deep down Twain no doubt believed in immortality). Baldwin goes on to add examples of where Twain and Howells in her phrase "differed," without noting that most of these highlighted differences gave the distinct advantage to the more patient, forbearing, and cautious Howells. In an area that I have personally been very concerned in pursuing, Howells delicately mentions "my own greater bookishness, by which I mean his less quantitative reading," and then characterizes Twain's reading as mainly amounting to "out-of-the-way" books that had "the human matter" in them; volumes about great trials; "the supreme autobiographies"; "signal" passages of history; travel narratives; and stories of "captivity." Howells said of his recently deceased friend, "As I remember, he did not care much for fiction, and in that sort he had certain distinct loathings," specifically naming Goldsmith and "my dear and honored prime favorite, Jane Austen." Howells repeated again the basic theme that "he used to read the modern novels I praised, . . . but I do not think he much liked reading fiction." The differences between the two men mount as Howells's narrative progresses: "As for plays, he detested the theatre, and said he would as lief do a sum as follow a plot on the stage." Regarding other genres, "I fancy his pleasure in poetry was not great, and I do not believe he cared much for the conventionally accepted masterpieces of literature." As though striving to be fair, Howells pauses to concede that Twain did relish certain verses by Browning, John Hay, and William Morris.

The crowning assessment is one that echoed down the corridors of the ensuing century: "Of all the literary men I have known," concluded Howells, "he was the most unliterary in his make and manner." To support that thesis, Howells cites Twain's unfamiliarity with Latin, his literary expression ("his style was what we know, for good and for bad"), his lack of interest in proper "sequence," including "the construction of his sentences, and the arrangement of his chapters, and the ordering or disordering of his compilations," in connection with his utter lack of fear about the repetition of words and phrases.

Now, the most telling thing about Howells's recollections of Twain's reading habits, to take up the biographical topic I happen to know best, is that virtually all of them were utterly mistaken. Twain left behind a voluminous record of his pleasures in owning, reading, and annotating many hundreds of volumes in each of the genres Howells dismissed. So the question arises as to *why* Howells rushed these statements into print within months of his friend's demise. The implications of his judgments were decidedly if subtly injurious to the literary standing of his longtime close friend. True, these innuendoes aren't of the vengeful order of Hemingway's destructive little time bombs he left behind to explode under the reputations of F. Scott Fitzgerald and Gertrude Stein. Nonetheless, a famous person who made his living by writing and lecturing is here accounted to be at bottom "unliterary." Moreover, Olivia Clemens was his dictatorial ruler; he the abject subject—such was the picture painted by Howells. Twain he recalled as absolutely obsessed with telling "the story of his life, the inexhaustible, the fairy, the Arabian Nights story, which I could never tire of even when it began to be told over again." In Twain's pranks, his costumes (ranging from a sealskin coat to a white suit to the red Oxford gown), and his sometimes-insensitive imitations of African Americans and others, "he was a youth to the end of his days, . . . [with] the heart of a good boy, or a bad boy, but always a wilful boy, and wilfulest to show himself out at every time for just the boy he was." Howells, forgetting the *Library of American Humor* project of 1888, remembered all their joint endeavors as having been rank failures, which justified a prudence on Howells's part that purportedly saved him from the fate of others who had combined with Twain to their detriment.

This was because "he liked, beyond all things, to push an affair to the bitter end, and the end was never too bitter unless it brought grief or harm to another."

Howells opined that Twain "did not care much to meet people, as I fancied," which was just as well, Howells indicated, because most of Howells's Boston/Cambridge acquaintances "might not have appreciated him at, say, his transatlantic value. . . . In proportion as people thought themselves refined they questioned that quality which all recognize in him now. . . . I cannot say just why Clemens seemed not to hit the favor of our community of scribes and scholars, as Bret Harte had done, . . . but it is certain he did not, and I had better say so."

Other errors on Twain's part appear to multiply in this telling. The Whittier Birthday Dinner speech of 1877 is rehashed in the worst possible light; Howells recalls it as "the amazing mistake, the bewildering blunder, the cruel catastrophe." Howells belittled Twain's gullibility regarding "superstition, usually of a hygienic sort," illustrating it with the Plasmon episode. "I was not surprised to learn that 'the damned human race' was to be saved by plasmon, . . . and that my first duty was to. . . procure enough plasmon to secure my family against the ills it was heir to for evermore. . . . But . . . he had to do something with his money, and it was not his fault if he did not make a fortune out of plasmon." In the matter of holding grudges, Twain was supposedly in a class by himself: "Clemens did not forgive his dead enemies; their death seemed to deepen their crimes, like a base evasion, or a cowardly attempt to escape; he pursued them to the grave." Where

he felt taken advantage of, said Howells, "he was a fire of vengeance, a consuming flame of suspicion that no sprinkling of cool patience from others could quench; it had to burn itself out. . . . In his frenzies of resentment or suspicion he would not, and doubtless could not, listen to reason." Twain's ire with human follies was so great that it almost exhausted Howells's ingenuity of recounting.

Was it conceivably a long-suppressed jealousy on Howells's part toward a man whose subscription-publishing ventures and speaking engagements had brought him a substantial fortune that stirred these little calumnies? Howells somewhat brittlely recalled the year when Clemens built "the stately mansion in which he satisfied his love of magnificence . . . , and he was at the crest of the prosperity which enabled him to humor every whim or extravagance." This was the same period, Howells notes, when he and Charles Dudley Warner were obliged to "walk home in the frugal fashion by which we still thought it best to spare car fare; carriage fare we did not dream of."

I am not for a moment saying that Howells's effort qualified as any sort of biographical butcher-job. After all, in that same lengthy essay Howells passingly compares Mark Twain to Shakespeare, Cervantes, Swift, and Lincoln, which hardly placed him among poor company. Moreover, Howells also alludes to him as "the most consummate public performer I ever saw." And he credits Twain with using English "as if it were native to his own air, as if it had come up . . . out of Missourian ground." Rather, I am talking about the *implications* of this type of left-handed praise. It was a relationship that was more vexed (on both sides) than is often realized, a friendship containing tensions that surfaced in odd and unpredictable ways. For example, there were Twain's frequent and mischievous tweakings of Howells's favorite authors such as Jane Austen. One thing is certain: Howells's phraseology and impressions can be detected in virtually every subsequent biographical study, so trusted was he as an infallible authority. For instance, consider the frequency with which the phrase "the damned human race" echoes throughout Mark Twain scholarship, even though there seems to be no other source of this exact wording except Howells's recollections as voiced here. Harold K. Bush Jr. observed this phenomenon, noting that "Howells's preeminence as the key original Twain scholar still exerts influence almost a century later."

Albert Bigelow Paine, who had passed four years in Twain's company, nevertheless often deferred to the aptness of the delineations in Howells's *My Mark Twain*. Two years later, in 1912, Paine's biography would strike many of the same chords and employ similar language or make direct reference to Howells as the source. Of course it could obviously be argued that these two men knew Twain well enough so that they coincidentally came to the same conclusions about his temperament and habits. But I submit that Howells made an indelible impact on Paine and all the students of Twain who followed. In the first place, Paine sometimes quotes straight from Howells's memoir, as on page 1446 of Paine's biography. Howells was almost certainly Paine's model in saying that Twain's temper resembled lightning that could strike out of darkening clouds, as when he

missed his shots at billiards (p. 1328). Also, to take another example in the matter of Twain's reading, Paine insisted that Twain "had no general fondness for poetry," and that Twain's favorite books numbered "not more than dozen," most of which happened to be volumes of letters, memoirs, or history. The impression conveyed is that Twain read narrowly and usually out of curiosity about celebrated people. This distortion of the patterns of Twain's reading partially resulted from the fact that Paine accompanied Twain only during the final four years of his subject's life. Yet it can be proven that Paine manipulated the written evidence to substantiate Howells's earlier reports. On page 512 of Paine's biography he deliberately and *knowingly* misdated some jottings Twain made in or after November 1909—notes referring to specific works Twain had been reading at that time—and attributed them to the year 1874 and to his reading *in general*.

These acts of shaping (or reshaping) Twain's persona, of which I have primarily touched upon those related to his literary knowledge, bore results that can be detected in the subsequent biographies of Justin Kaplan, Everett Emerson, Andrew Hoffman, and others. Mark Twain probably trusted his final friends a little too much, in the sense that I cannot see *Twain* delivering such mixed encomiums about either Howells or Paine, had he survived *them*. But our later age has also perhaps relied on their firsthand impressions too credulously, without considering that they were mortal men, not video cameras, and that there was much about Mark Twain for them to envy.

WORKS CITED

Budd, Louis J. *Our Mark Twain: The Making of His Public Personality*. Philadelphia: University of Pennsylvania Press, 1983.

Bush, Harold K., Jr. "Our Mark Twain? Or, Some Thoughts on the 'Autobiographical Critic,'" *New England Quarterly* 73.1 (March 2000): 100–121.

Gribben, Alan. "Autobiography as Property: Mark Twain and His Legend," in *The Mythologizing of Mark Twain*, ed. Sara deSaussure Davis and Philip D. Beidler. Tuscaloosa: University of Alabama Press, 1984.

_____ "I Detest Novels, Poetry & Theology': Origin of a Fiction Concerning Mark Twain's Reading," *Tennessee Studies in Literature* 22 (1977): 154–61. (A revised version of this essay appears as a chapter in the present volume.)

Hill, Hamlin. *Mark Twain: God's Fool*. New York: Harper & Row, 1973.

Howells, William Dean. *My Mark Twain: Reminiscences and Criticisms*. Ed. Marilyn Austin Baldwin. Baton Rouge: Louisiana State University Press, 1967.

Paine, Albert Bigelow. *Mark Twain: A Biography*. New York: Harper & Brothers, 1912.

Rohrbach, Augusta. "'You're a Natural-Born Literary Man': Becoming William Dean Howells, Culture Maker and Cultural Marker," *New England Quarterly* 73.4 (December 2000): 625–653.

3

Samuel L. Clemens's Earliest
Literary Experiences

While most people would agree that a person's early literary experiences have some degree of lasting effect on an individual's intellectual development, there have been relatively few studies of American authors' childhood and adolescent reading. One of the obvious reasons is the extreme difficulty of documenting their initial encounters with literary materials. This is assuredly the case with Samuel Clemens. Hardly any of the books that Clemens read as a boy and a teenager have survived, mainly because he moved about so frequently. Not until he married and settled into his new home in Hartford did his book collection begin to take a permanent form. Thus we can only speculate about his youthful exposure to books, relying mainly on allusions in his writings and his late autobiographical reminiscences—along with the testimony of those who knew him in Hannibal and St. Louis, Missouri and Muscatine and Keokuk, Iowa, and who survived to give their impressions to his biographer Albert Bigelow Paine and other inquiring writers.

In Clemens's case we can begin any such inventory with two schoolroom textbooks in wide use in the 1840s, Samuel Kirkham's *English Grammar in Familiar Lessons* and Jesse Olney's *A Practical System of Modern Geography*. As an adult Clemens mentioned "Kirkham's *Grammar*" as having been part of his boyhood education, and an inscribed copy has been found that may have belonged to him. In 1907 he recorded the fact that he had "studied 'Olney's Geography' in school when I was a boy." (*McGuffey's Eclectic Reader*, another likely textbook, lacks this definite confirmation as one of his experiences.) We know how Clemens's first school teacher started each day's lessons; she read verses to the class from the New Testament. More than half a century later Clemens requested that the Clemens family's Bible be sent to him after his sister-in-law Mollie Clemens died in 1904. He asked her executor to send "my mother's old illustrated Bible, if it still exists." It did survive, with some annotations, and is today part of the Mark Twain Papers in Berkeley.

The other book title he requested after all members of his childhood family had passed away was what Mollie Clemens's legal will referred to as "the old Britannica which was their father's" and which Clemens described as "the *old* Cyclopedia (my father's—I do not care for any later one)." Written by William Nicholson and published in 1818 as the *American Edition of the British Encyclopedia, or Dictionary of Arts and Sciences. Comprising an Accurate and Popular View of the Present Improved State of Human Knowledge*, it would have furnished the Clemens children with a wide array of entries on diverse subjects.

John Marshall Clemens helped establish a lending library in Hannibal that augmented his very meager personal book collection. It would be desirable to know the holdings of that Hannibal Library Institute, but its contents of four or five hundred volumes were dispersed by 1853 without any extant records.

Another influence that entered the Clemens home—and a surprising one—was the family's subscription to *Peter Parley's Magazine*. Founded by Samuel Griswold Goodrich, who wrote under the pen name of Peter Parley, the magazine never enjoyed a large circulation. The numerous pen and ink drawings that adorned its stories and articles seemed to account for its survival during the era before the Transcontinental Railroad opened up vast new territories for literary journals. Nevertheless when Albert Bigelow Paine documented the Clemens family's circumstances, he was assured that John Marshall Clemens "subscribed for *Peter Parley's Magazine*, a marvel of delight to the older children."

Paine counted Sam's brothers Orion and Henry as far more serious readers than Sam, and indeed when Orion's Hannibal *Journal*

needed literary material to fill the spaces between news and advertisements, such eminent authors as Thackeray, Dickens (mainly his *Pickwick Papers*), Boswell, Frederick Marryat, Hawthorne, Harriet Beecher Stowe, Daniel Webster, Bulwer-Lytton, Thomas Macaulay, Trollope, Goldsmith, Pope, Burns, Hannah More, Edward Young, Thomas Gray, William Cowper, and Benjamin Franklin were called upon to plug the newspaper gaps. One presumes, then, that there were copies of those authors accessible there in the print shop for this purpose—and possibly for printing apprentices to glance at between locking up the heavy type forms.

But a young person cannot live on classics alone. A lurid 1839 crime novel by William Harrison Ainsworth, *Jack Sheppard: A Romance*, based on the life of a famous London thief, robber, and escape artist, definitely snagged Sam Clemens's boyish attention. By 1856 Clemens was making fun of Ainsworth's "instructive and entertaining" book but in doing so showing knowledge of its idealized plot. Jack Sheppard was eventually caught and hanged in 1724, a fact that the novel had to accommodate. We know that Clemens would own an 1862 copy of Ainsworth's *The Lord Mayor of London; or, City Life in the Last Century*, so he definitely remained intrigued by this British author.

In composing *Tom Sawyer*, Twain could still quote almost by heart a children's book about Robin Hood. Convinced that Tom Sawyer's Robin Hood play-acting with Joe Harper on Cardiff Hill had a specific literary source, I spent several months back in 1975 tracking down all copies of children's versions of the Robin Hood legend that would have been in print during Clemens's childhood. Finally—in the library of a religious seminary near the top of a steep hill in Berkeley—I ran across Stephen Percy's *Robin Hood and His Merry Foresters*, published in 1841 and often reprinted. It contained the exact line (with one spelling variant) that Tom Sawyer emphatically quotes to a confounded Joe Harper: "Robin Hood sprung up, and with one sudden back-handed stroke slew poor Guy of Gisborne upon the spot." As usual, Tom misconstrues what he has read and instead of administering a backhanded stroke he orders poor Joe to turn around and let him stab him in the back to comply with the text. Decades later, in 1883, Clemens would write about "the fascination" that the Robin Hood story held for him when he was a boy—"a fascination so great that it paled the interest of all other books & made them tame & colorless. . . . I have always regretted that I did not belong to Robin Hood's gang," he declared.

There is sufficient evidence to assert that Tom Sawyer's beloved "authorities" came from Sam Clemens's boyhood bookshelves. Tom's (and Sam's) readings definitely included the "wildcat" literature of Ned Buntline (the pseudonym of the alcoholic womanizer Edward Zane Carroll Judson). Buntline's *The Black Avenger of the Spanish Main; or, The Fiend of Blood* (1847) almost defies description in its outlandish plot twists and bizarre settings; suffice it to say that its subtitle was richly deserved. Clemens also made reference in a notebook to Buntline's *The Convict; or, The Conspirator's Victim*. As a boy he might have met Buntline in 1851 when the dime novelist lectured in Hannibal; in any event,

the two men corresponded in later years when Buntline sought Clemens's help in getting a subscription publisher.

However, Tom Sawyer's smattering of literary knowledge hardly provides an adequate picture of his creator's rapidly evolving tastes at the same age. One of Clemens's school classmates, for example, recalled that Sam Slick's comical sketches in *The Clockmaker* entertained Clemens immensely. Clemens himself would recall the sensation made in Hannibal by the French novelist Eugene Sue's best-selling *The Wandering Jew*, with its implicitly anti-Catholic message (and its direct attack on the Jesuit order). Sue basically used the Christian legend about a man who had taunted Christ and was cursed to wander the earth endlessly as a hook for the title; the novel's murkily Gothic plot barely made any reference to that medieval legend and instead depicted a family about to come into a fortune if the dastardly Jesuits can be blocked by the family's supernatural protectors. In *Following the Equator* Mark Twain remembered that this novel revived interest in the murderous Thugs of India "fifty years ago" in the Mississippi River Valley. Twain declared, "Then Eugene Sue's 'Wandering Jew' appeared, and made great talk for a while. One character in it was a chief of Thugs—'Feringhea'—a mysterious and terrible Indian who was as slippery and sly as a serpent, and as deadly; and he stirred up the Thug interest once more. But it did not last. It presently died again—this time to stay dead."

Firm evidence regarding Clemens's early reading is otherwise so scanty that the incontrovertible proof that he was familiar with George Lippard's patriotic book about

100 DOLLAR PRIZE TALE.

THE

BLACK AVENGER

OF THE SPANISH MAIN:

OR,

THE FIEND OF BLOOD.

A Thrilling Story of the Buccaneer Times.

BY NED BUNTLINE,

AUTHOR OF 'THE KING OF THE SEA,' ETC.

Ned Buntline's The Black Avenger of the Spanish Main; or, The Fiend of Blood *(Boston: F. Gleason, 1847) was one of Tom Sawyer's favorite books. (Ned Buntline was the pseudonym of Edward Zane Carroll Judson.)*

General George Washington's military feats, *Legends of the American Revolution; or, Washington and His Generals* (1847), is immensely welcome. Clemens wrote to his brother Orion in 1853 from Philadelphia to describe a recent sight-seeing excursion: "Geo. Lippard, in his 'Legends of Washington and his Generals,' has rendered the Wissahickon [River] sacred in my eyes," he announced. Lippard, a journalist, social reformer, and author of historical and gothic novels, was still living in Philadelphia when Clemens arrived there. Much later this same book figured significantly in Twain's *Huckleberry Finn*. In Chapter 5 of that novel, ordered by Pap Finn to prove he could read, Huck "took up a book and began something about General Washington and the wars." Huck's father, a devoted illiterate, responds furiously by giving "the book a whack with his hand and knocked it across the house." At least one scholar has contended that Clemens also knew Lippard's sensation novel *The Quaker City; or, The Monks of Monk Hall*, but that matter remains far from settled. Likewise Clemens's tale of finding a leaf from a book about Joan of Arc blowing down the street—an event that supposedly opened up for him the entire world of medieval history and religious persecution—must be left as an open question, inasmuch as his recitals of the incident differed (or were omitted entirely) from time to time. Recently his story has been gaining believers. More than anything this anecdote suggests young Clemens's receptiveness to new literary experiences.

Frederick Marryat is a name lost on today's readers, but in the first half of the nineteenth century he was prominent and often cited. Twainians mainly recall that Clemens owned and annotated an 1840 edition of Marryat's *Diary in America*, and that he would allude repeatedly to Captain Marryat's impressions of America and its rivers in *Life on the Mississippi*. It has been noted that Twain also drew without acknowledgment on Marryat's account of the brutal career of the outlaw John Murrell as well as Marryat's description of a religious revival meeting along the Mississippi. But it has not been recognized that Clemens owned an undated copy of Marryat's *The Pacha of Many Tales*, which he referred to in *A Tramp Abroad*. In "Villagers of 1840–3" Twain would designate Marryat as one of the favorite authors of Hannibal during his boyhood, which causes one to wonder if he did not encounter other titles that Marryat aimed at boy readers, such as *Snarleyyow; or,*

The Dog Fiend (1837) and *The Phantom Ship* (1839). Marryat's *The Children of the New Forest*, originally published in 1847, was one of the books that Clemens's daughters often requested him to read aloud to them.

Clemens would recall Lord Byron as one of the Hannibal idols in the 1840s, and he also seemed to link Shelley with that era. The influence of Walter Scott in that decade was even more palpable. One of the main steamboat companies serving the port of Hannibal, the St. Louis & Keokuk Packet Line, had named its vessels after the characters in Scott's novels. Indeed, many of the Romantic era writers against whom Twain later revolted were part of his literary vocabulary in the first decades of his life, including James Fenimore Cooper (whose Native Americans Twain would lampoon) and Edgar Allan Poe, whose works he alternately praised or disparaged.

To the list of printed literary materials should be added the endless parade of visiting shows that the steamboats brought to the Hannibal wharf. Siamese twins, wild animal displays, minstrel shows, circuses, mesmerists, phrenologists, and many other attractions made calls at the town. The list of minstrel songs with which Sam Clemens became familiar would make a lengthy study in its own right, beginning with "De Camptown Races," "Old Kentucky Home," "Swanee River," "Buffalo Gals," "Old Dan Tucker," and many others. Clemens would likewise recall the sheet music that adorned the parlor pianos in Hannibal—such sentimental songs as "The Larboard Watch," "A Life on the Ocean Wave," "Sweet Ellen Bayne," "Nelly Bly," "Oft in the Stilly Night," "The Last Link," "Bonny Doon," "Old Dog Tray," "The Last Rose of

Summer," "Bright Alforata," and dozens of other melancholy tunes.

We should never forget, either, the folk tales that he heard the gifted oral interpreter Uncle Dan'l narrate on his Uncle John Quarles's farm during Sam Clemens's summer sojourns in the hamlet of Florida, Missouri.

Two years before Clemens became an apprentice pilot he copied into his notebook entire pages of a volume about phrenology and the temperaments. This was George Sumner Weaver's *Lectures on Mental Science According to the Philosophy of Phrenology*. Some of Weaver's concepts and phrasing, especially the term "temperament," would cling to Clemens's thought throughout his lifetime. One of the most verifiable of the books owned by Clemens in the 1850s is J. L. Comstock's *Elements of Geology* (1851), which he signed "Samuel L. Clemens/1856./June 25th, 1856" while he was living in Keokuk, Iowa.

Jonathan Swift's *Gulliver's Travels* was another of Clemens's earliest reading experiences. He nicknamed a young playmate "Gull" after Lemuel Gulliver. In 1854, during a visit to Washington, D.C., Clemens wrote that the buildings are "strewed about in clusters. . . . They look as though they might have been emptied out of a sack by some Brobdignagian [*sic*] gentleman, and when falling, been scattered abroad by the winds." This image occurred to him in a different context while he was living on the West Coast; assessing the damage from a San Francisco earthquake he wrote about seeing "a brick warehouse mashed in as if some foreigner from Brobdignag [*sic*] had sat down on it." Writing to Olivia Langdon in 1869 while rereading Swift's masterpiece, Clemens admitted that he was

"much more charmed with it than I was when I read it last, in boyhood—for now I can see what a scathing satire it is upon the English government, whereas, before, I only gloated over its prodigies & its marvels." He warned his future wife, however, that "portions of it are very coarse & indelicate." Nearly two dozen allusions to *Gulliver's Travels* have been identified in Twain's various works, concluding with a reference he made to "Gulliver in Lilliput" in a 1906 Autobiographical Dictation. It seems likely that Mark Twain hoped to produce in *A Connecticut Yankee* a modern satire meriting comparison with both *Gulliver's Travels* and *Don Quixote*. It is a shame that we have never turned up Clemens's personal copy of Swift's classic, especially since his household records show that he purchased one copy in 1880 and his Notebook 25 indicates that he acquired another copy in 1885. (However, the tireless collector Kevin Mac Donnell located and acquired Jervis Langdon Sr.'s 1866 copy of *Gulliver's Travels*, replete with Clemens's unmistakable notes and markings. Clearly Clemens had access to this volume at some point in Theodore and Susan Crane's Quarry Farm library.)

It has been established that Clemens owned and annotated a nine-volume set of *The Letters of Horace Walpole* that was published in installments between 1861 and 1866. Only Volume 9 of this set appears to have survived, and it resides in the Beinecke Library at Yale. Quite likely he had read an earlier edition, though, because in a public speech in 1899 he included Walpole's letters among his early reading: "I . . . read the *Walpole Letters* when I was a boy. I absorbed them, gathered in their grace, wit, and humor, and put them away to be used by and by. One does that so unconsciously with things one really likes. I am reminded now of what use those letters have been to me."

Clemens's fascination with Daniel Defoe's fictional castaway began early and continued unabated throughout his lifetime. Hank Morgan, for instance, would compare himself to "Robinson Crusoe cast away on an uninhabited island." *The Arabian Nights* over Clemens's lifetime would become his second-most-cited literary source next to the Bible. The novels of Alexandre Dumas with their castle dungeons and ingenious prisoners— especially *The Count of Monte Cristo* and *The Man in the Iron Mask*—were seemingly etched into Clemens's memory during his youth and then would return in various manifestations throughout his writings, most notably in Tom Sawyer's detailed demands that plagued the hapless Jim in *Adventures of Huckleberry Finn.*

In St. Louis in the 1850s Clemens would be introduced to the novels of Thackeray and Disraeli. Although he later became critical of Charles Dickens's novels, he unmistakably knew many of them by the time he was prospecting and reporting in the Far West. He had additionally read works by Shakespeare, Cervantes, Voltaire, and Thomas Paine.

It could be said, then, that the foundations of Mark Twain's writing career were laid early and solidly by the range of his youthful curiosity about printed and oral materials. He had already gone through an ample library, both popular and classic literature, well before he undertook the profession of authorship.

———————

Individual entries in the Anotated Catalog provide the documentation for authors and books mentioned in this essay.

4

Samuel L. Clemens's Eclectic Reading

His Favorite Books

In 1924 a graduate student named Henry Pochmann, mainly relying on the testimony of Samuel Clemens's designated biographer, Albert Bigelow Paine, ventured to name the ten books that Clemens "read most and knew best": the Bible, Suetonius's *Lives of the Twelve Caesars*, Cervantes's *Don Quixote*, Malory's *Le Morte D'Arthur*, Lecky's *History of European Morals*, Carlyle's *French Revolution*, Greville's *Journal*, Pepys' *Diary*, Saint-Simon's *Memoirs*, and Casanova's *Memoirs*.[1] While Pochmann identified books that Clemens indisputably knew and venerated, he was unaware that Paine had chosen to emphasize works Clemens praised during his last years. Today the task of determining the titles that Clemens perused repeatedly throughout his lifetime is far less confounding than the author himself once humorously prophesied it would be in the year 2901. By that date, Mark Twain predicted in an uncompleted manuscript titled "The Secret History of Eddypus," owing to the erosions of factual knowledge he would be known erroneously as "The Father of History" and

few truths about his biography could be recovered. Researchers would absurdly conclude that "The Father of History was a great reader; but like all lovers of literature, he had a small and choice list of books which were his favorites, and it is plain . . . that he read these nearly all the time and deeply admired them. We do not know what their character was, for he does not say, and no shred of one of them now remains. . . . We have only the names: Innocents Abroad; Roughing It; Tramp Abroad; Pudd'nhead Wilson; Joan of Arc; Prince and Pauper—and so on; there are many. Who wrote these great books we shall never know."[2]

On 20 January 1887 Clemens himself made an effort to pin down his reading tastes. In a letter responding to questions posed by the Reverend Charles D. Crane of New Castle, Maine, Clemens identified eight of his favorite authors and books: Shakespeare's plays, Robert Browning's poetry, Thomas Carlyle's *The French Revolution*, Sir Thomas Malory's *Morte D'Arthur*, Francis Parkman's histories, *The Arabian Nights*,

James Boswell's *Life of Samuel Johnson*, and Benjamin Jowett's translation of Plato. Asked by Crane to recommend books for young people to read, Clemens suggested Thomas Macaulay's histories and essays, Plutarch's *Lives*, Ulysses S. Grant's *Memoirs*, Daniel Defoe's *Robinson Crusoe*, *The Arabian Nights*, Jonathan Swift's *Gulliver's Travels*, and Alfred Lord Tennyson's poetry.[3]

Any such list of Clemens's favorite authors and books must indeed include Thomas Macaulay, who wrote essays and English histories in which Clemens reveled. Thomas Carlyle, it is also true, became a cornerstone of his library. James Boswell's biography of Dr. Samuel Johnson earned his praise, as did Jowett's translation of Plato. Plutarch's *Lives* decidedly qualified as a favorite. Once Clemens discovered Sir Thomas Malory he became entranced with these legends rendered in prose. *Morte D'Arthur* furnished the plot line, language, and characters for Twain's *A Connecticut Yankee in King Arthur's Court*, and Twain was entirely sincere in applauding "the master hand of old Malory." Francis Parkman's North American histories held his attention during the 1880s and periodically thereafter. *The Arabian Nights* always maintained its appeal for him, beginning in his boyhood. In 1907 he named "Aladdin and the Wonderful Lamp" and "Ali Baba and the Forty Thieves" as his favorite tales of the collection. Daniel Defoe's *Robinson Crusoe* earned his lifelong loyalty. Jonathan Swift's *Gulliver's Travels*, Clemens wrote, was filled with "prodigies" and "marvels," but also contained "the full tide of his venom—the turbid sea of his matchless hate." The phrases of Shakespeare, whom he acknowledged as

"the world's great teacher," like the lines of Tennyson, echoed in Clemens's thoughts constantly.

Who would not have paid a large admission to witness Clemens reading Robert Browning's poetry at those Browning Society meetings in 1886 and 1887! What a spectacle it must have been to observe the tremendous anomaly of that champion of verbal clarity, possibly the most immediately comprehensible, luculent, and straightforward author of nineteenth-century America, who was playing the leading role in the development of an American colloquial style, manifesting his passion for the poetry of Browning, one of the most opaque English writers of that same century. In Twain's words, Browning's poetry reminded him of "a splendor of stars & suns [that] bursts upon you and fills the whole field with flame." Twain bragged, "I can read Browning so Browning himself can understand it. It sounds like stretching, but it's the cold truth." This adulation of Browning's veiled complexity was occurring during the decade when Twain was writing pellucid narratives such as *Life on the Mississippi*.

However, his book appetites were more varied and evolving than those hasty and abbreviated lists he made in 1887 might suggest. Fortunately, enough of Clemens's personal library and a sufficient number of references to his reading have survived to allow plausibly inclusive guesses about his preferences.[4]

Henry Pochmann was unquestionably correct in naming the Bible first. Clemens read every book of the New Testament repeatedly. The Old Testament he likewise revered, wondering in 1869, "Who taught those ancient writers their simplicity of language, their felicity of expression, their pathos, and, above all, their faculty of sinking themselves entirely out of sight of the reader and making the narrative stand out alone and seem to tell itself?" As Clemens grew older his allusions to biblical figures and his quotations from the text became somewhat less frequent, but at the same time he increasingly used the Bible as a basis for fictional writings about mankind's foibles. His attitude was seldom truly reverential—passages in *The Innocents Abroad* (1869) border on the sacrilegious, with the strict exception of sites and incidents relating to the life of Christ—but later in his life he viewed the Bible as a convenient collection of venerated myths with which his readers were familiar. "Extracts from Adam's Diary" and "Captain Stormfield's Visit to Heaven" typify the writings that resulted. This detached, intellectualized approach allowed him to return for source material again and again. The Bible, like many of the books in which Twain was interested over a considerable period of time, received varied treatments in his writings—often burlesque, sometimes caustic, but just as readily serious.

He never tired of Benvenuto Cellini's *Autobiography*, which he called "that most entertaining of books. . . . It will last as long as his beautiful Perseus." Clemens repeatedly referred to an episode in the first chapter of Benvenuto's book in which, when Cellini was five years old, his father boxed his ear so that he would remember a rarely seen salamander emerge from a log in their fireplace. As a companion to Cellini's and Franklin's autobiographies he would later add Moncure D. Conway's, which likely reinforced Twain's

idea of organizing his own autobiography by topic rather than by chronology. Dumas *père's* novels supplied him with absorbing entertainment. To his mind Richard Henry Dana's *Two Years Before the Mast* had no peer among tales of the sea.

U. S. Grant's *Memoirs*, which Clemens had solicited and published, he liked for literary reasons as well. Clemens could quote at length passages from the poetry of Percy Bysshe Shelley. This same man who loved the poetry of Robert Browning and led oral readings for Browning devotees in the 1880s simultaneously rained praise on the forgettably conventional verse of Thomas Bailey Aldrich. Even after Aldrich had died and his literary reputation was rapidly declining, Clemens stubbornly insisted that "his fame as a writer" would still be "based not upon his output of poetry as a whole but upon half a dozen small poems which are not surpassed in our language for exquisite grace and beauty and finish." Was Clemens blinded in this instance by friendship? By an allegiance to the New England literati? Or did he expect smaller accomplishments from American poets than those writing in England?

Albert Bigelow Paine was right in identifying Thomas Carlyle's *French Revolution* as a perennial bedside companion for Clemens, but he knew Carlyle's other works as well. The writings of Robert Louis Stevenson spoke to Clemens deeply. *The Rubáiyát of Omar Khayyám*, especially in Edward FitzGerald's translation, which struck him as flawless, deserves a special place in any listing of his most beloved works. Twain even wrote a comic imitation of this poem (burlesquing literary works being one of Twain's instinctive ways of paying tribute to them) about the downsides of aging, and he swore of *The Rubáiyát* that "no poem had ever given me so much pleasure before, and none has given me so much pleasure since; it is the only poem I have carried about with me." (Literate citizens of the nineteenth century often carried—in wallet or purse—pages of poetry that inspired or instructed them. Think of it as their equivalent of today's electronic tablet.) James Whitcomb Riley's homespun poetry pleased Twain immensely, despite its being such a far cry from the lines of Browning or Tennyson. Naturally Clemens's library had plenty of space on his shelves set aside for his good friend William Dean Howells, many of whose novels and plays Clemens took the time to extol and discuss in letters to Howells. "You are really my only author," he announced memorably to Howells in 1885. "I am restricted to you." William E. H. Lecky must make the list, to be sure, since he wrote the kind of history Clemens best liked to read, and Lecky's book on the history of European morals Clemens delighted in reading and arguing with in the margins of several copies.

The novelist W. W. Jacobs painted "with camelhair pencil" rather than a "whitewash brush," Clemens observed approvingly. He liked to read aloud from Joel Chandler Harris's "Uncle Remus" sketches. Clemens even visited Harris, whose tales, Clemens remarked, were so good that they were like "alligator pears—one eats them for the sake of the salad-dressing. . . . Uncle Remus. . . . and the little boy . . . are high and fine literature, and worthy to live, for their own

sakes." Dr. John Brown's books held a place in Clemens's heart. Booth Tarkington "has the true touch," commented Clemens. "His work always satisfies me." Anatole France appealed to Clemens late in his life, especially *The Crime of Sylvestre Bonnard*. Cervantes's *Don Quixote*, Clemens stated, "is one of the most exquisite books that was ever written, & to lose it from the world's literature would be as the wresting of a constellation from the symmetry & perfection of the firmament." Of François Rabelais he said in 1903, "If I had lived in the fifteenth century I should have been Rabelais. I know him from top to bottom."

All of this is to say that Samuel Clemens read omnivorously, memorized passages from a large number of literary classics, and stayed abreast of the fiction in his own era. Throughout his life he was a regular and eager patron of theatrical productions. He was a fully formed reader, and almost certainly more accomplished in this area of intellectual activity than the majority of his college-educated peers.

OMISSIONS IN CLEMENS'S READING

There were, however, from the point of view of twenty-first-century literary historians, three notable omissions in what we know of Clemens's reading. As far as can be determined, he never made the acquaintance of Herman Melville, Karl Marx, or Sigmund Freud. Melville seems a disappointing zero because Clemens visited the Sandwich Islands and possessed a curiosity about the South Pacific. Moreover, in general he liked books about ships (for example, he devoured and even wrote an imitation of William Clark

Russell's *The Wreck of the "Grosvenor,"* saying that it "has no superior in the literature of the sea"), yet he seems never to have read Melville's *Omoo* or *Typee*, let alone the then-neglected *Moby Dick*. Karl Marx is another strange blank. Clemens would hardly have admired his programmatic writing style, but Clemens was interested in economic theories and had various such studies in his library. Freud was not really in vogue in the United States until after Clemens died. A few scholars have speculated about their possibly having met in Vienna. Though Clemens wondered in 1895 why "the world is not full of books that scoff at the pitiful world, & the useless universe & the vile & contemptible human race,"[5] he would barely if at all acquaint himself with the writings of Stephen Crane, Frank Norris, Theodore Dreiser, and other American Naturalists who presented stark views of man' s existence and destiny. (He did read, and condemn, Émile Zola.)

ECLECTIC LITERARY TASTES

But Clemens's literary range was far greater and more complex than any compilation of "favorites" can suggest. Some of his most extensive programs of reading, for example, centered recurrently on authors for whom he professed a distaste—James Fenimore Cooper, Bret Harte, Walter Scott, George Eliot, and Jane Austen. He was entirely familiar with the novels of Charles Dickens, whose techniques he ultimately disparaged. Bret Harte's work he once admired, but owing to a suddenly mushrooming dislike for the man he began to belittle Harte's writings. Twain was well enough acquainted with Arthur Conan Doyle's detective pieces to attempt

at least one major burlesque of them. He purportedly despised Oliver Goldsmith's writings, but read them repeatedly. His ambivalent attitude toward Benjamin Franklin's *Autobiography* contained unmistakable elements of admiration. He detested Lord Byron's character but quoted his poems. He probably mastered the writings of Mary Baker Eddy more thoroughly than quite a few of her converts.

Clemens also read a large number of books because of personal friendships with their authors. Besides William Dean Howells, whose works he read as soon as they were issued, he knew and owned the writings of Thomas Bailey Aldrich, Charles Dudley Warner, John Hay, George Washington Cable, Harriet Beecher Stowe, and Dr. John Brown. A great many books and authors perhaps could not be termed "lifelong" favorites, yet he displayed intense interest in them at one point or another: Charles Ball's *Slavery in the United States*, George Standring, Jules Verne, Irving Bacheller, William Allen White, and James Branch Cabell, to cite some examples. During the 1880s and 1890s he became increasingly intrigued by the theories of Charles Darwin and John Lubbock.

For numerous other writers Clemens showed only slightly less partiality: James Russell Lowell, John Lothrop Motley, Hamlin Garland, Lewis Carroll, Poultney Bigelow, and Edward Bellamy. He could quote with equal facility the poetry of Holmes, Longfellow, Goethe, Heine, Coleridge, Burns, Schiller, and Emerson—or of Felicia Hemans, Reginald Heber and Thomas Gray. The witty librettos of William S. Gilbert consistently amused him.

The pronounced eclecticism of Clemens's literary taste is virtually impossible to categorize; his inquiring mind led him to sample an infinite variety of reading experiences: major writers of English literature from Chaucer to Boswell to Tennyson, travel narratives by Charles Dickens as well as the far inferior William C. Prime, obscure accounts of French court trials, novels by Hugo, Balzac, and the now-unknown John Habberton, operas by Wagner, and myriad works in science, religion, sociology, history, philosophy, and drama. His writings and the testimony of his acquaintances establish his affection for vulgar—even very bawdy—folk songs as well as the most ethereal poems and arias. He investigated but did not entirely approve of the writings of Bunyan, Fielding, Smollett, Lamb, Thackeray, and Ruskin. He devoured a great many books written by women; gender was clearly no barrier in his choice of reading matter. He read more books about African American slavery than one might expect of a former Southerner who in his younger years had agreed with its tenets. He gradually altered his unfavorable view of Native Americans, in part because of his reading on the subject. Empathetic reading was his portal to the lives of other inhabitants, past and present, of planet Earth.

CHILDREN'S LITERATURE

His opinion of most children's books scarcely stayed the same as he had expressed it in 1871 to Orion Clemens: "I never saw one that I thought was worth the ink it was written with."[6] Some works, such as Jacob Abbott's *Rollo Books*, Charlotte Yonge's histories for children, and Howard Pyle's illustrated volumes, he encountered in reading nightly to his daughters. Their intellectual development as readers was tremendously important to him. Clemens was grateful to George MacDonald's poignant *At the Back of the North Wind* (1871) on account of the pleasure it gave his children. He paid for a family subscription to the Hartford Public Library. He and Olivia constantly helped their daughters choose readings from the girls' well-stocked personal libraries that their parents provided. Unquestionably this practice kept him aware of trends in children's literature. In the 1880s Clemens additionally encouraged them to memorize and perform brief scenes by Shakespeare and other dramatists.

POETRY

In the case of poetry, Twain's numerous parodies of famous poems prove little concerning his attitude toward verse; that he burlesqued Gray, Moore, Byron, Wolfe, Campbell, Poe, Longfellow, religious hymns, and obituary verse simply means that he was a humorist who habitually looked for materials with which his audience was already familiar.[7] As George Feinstein observed, Clemens disparaged unnaturalness and insincerity, grandiloquence and attitudinizing among what he termed the "hogwash" poets, but this does not support the assumption that Clemens believed the presence of these faults in lesser poets "justifies his furtive suspicions about poetry in general."[8] Albert Bigelow Paine had promoted this impression by avowing that Clemens "had no general fondness for poetry"[9] and that remark influenced many subsequent commentators, yet Paine himself names exceptions to this prejudice—Omar Khayyám, Robert Browning, Rudyard Kipling, Willa Cather—and a host of others could be added, beginning with Shelley, Tennyson, Bryant, Longfellow, and Holmes. Kipling's poems might have been predicted to have caught Twain's fancy, and indeed Kipling held Twain's allegiance for years and his verse even entered some of Twain's public readings. Isabel Lyon, the secretary who lived in Clemens's household during the period when Paine was forming his views of Clemens's literary tastes, recorded Clemens's favorable excitement about works of serious poetry. On 25 February 1906 Clemens "paced the room" as he talked to Isabel Lyon and Witter Bynner "about the power of poetry to convey our thoughts in fittest form." On 7 October 1906 Lyon also recorded: "He has been giving us a lovely evening, for he has been reading poetry for more than an hour—the old English ballads, and war poems." [10]

Classics

We have substantial evidence that Clemens was not necessarily referring to his own inclinations when he devised (in Notebook 39 in 1896) and published (in Chapter 25 of *Following the Equator*) his famous maxim that a "classic" is "a book which people praise & don't read." In November 1900 he applied this same maxim to *Paradise Lost* in a speech to the Nineteenth Century Club: "It's a classic, just as Professor Winchester says, and it meets his definition of a classic—something that everybody wants to have read and nobody wants to read." [11] Yet however one defines "classics," Clemens had

read many of them: *Paradise Lost* (by at least 1858), *Pilgrim's Progress, Morte D'Arthur, Hamlet, The Decameron, In Memoriam, Canterbury Tales, The Deerslayer,* Goethe's *Faust, The Iliad, The Odyssey, Tom Jones, David Copperfield, Gulliver's Travels, Rime of the Ancient Mariner, The Scarlet Letter,* and a plethora of others. Books like Isaac Disraeli's six-volume compendium, *Curiosities of Literature,* enabled him to envision how literary works were shaped by their historical contexts.

Novels

With the current best-sellers of his day it was just the same. Mark Twain told an incredulous Rudyard Kipling in 1889: "'I never read novels myself,' said he, 'except when the popular persecution forces me to—when people plague me to know what I think of the last book that everyone is reading.'" Kipling then mentioned the currently popular *Robert Elsmere* (1888) by Mary Augusta Ward, and Twain conceded that he *had* read that work; in fact he had begun "a course of novel reading" as a result of liking *Robert Elsmere.* But he straightaway raised his unbookish mask again. His program of novel-reading had concluded, he said. "I have dropped it now. It did not amuse me." [12] The hundreds of contemporary novels in his personal library give the lie to these protests.

Quite likely Mark Twain had William Dean Howells specifically in mind when he wrote in "What Paul Bourget Thinks of Us" (1894): "There is only one expert who is qualified to examine the souls and the life of a people and make a valuable report—the native novelist." While in Twain's opinion not many other novelists measured up to Howells's performances, he was still willing to give their works a trial. Had Clemens bothered to keep a reading log, few of the hundred or so best-known contemporary British and American novelists would be unrepresented in its pages. *The Cloister and the Hearth* was only one of Charles Reade's various novels with which Clemens was familiar, for example. Clemens jotted both critical and complimentary marginalia in his copy of Sarah Grand's *The Heavenly Twins* in 1894. Olivia Clemens encouraged her husband to open the covers of a number of novels he might otherwise have passed up. Their predictability amused him. He assured a Mr. Benton in 1870 that he and Olivia were as happy in their new house in Buffalo "as if we were roosting in the closing chapter of a popular novel."[13] Some evidence suggests that the reading tastes of Clemens and his wife differed as diametrically as their respective sightseeing interests in Rome in November 1878, when Clemens informed the Reverend Joseph H. Twichell: "Livy & Clara [Spaulding] are having a royal time worshiping the old Masters, & I as good a time gritting my ineffectual teeth over them."[14] The adulation that Olivia and her daughters lavished on George Eliot finally proved to be too much, and Clemens launched sniping attacks on the object of such idolatry. Clemens's disagreement with his wife's literary judgments conceivably stimulated the half-finished burlesques of sentimental novels he attempted. Goldsmith's *Vicar of Wakefield*, for instance: could that perhaps have been one of Olivia's favorites? Olivia also enjoyed historical novels of the sort Clemens often

disapproved. Samuel E. Moffett received a letter from Clemens on 23 April 1900 from London: "Your aunt Livy is greatly in your debt for the list of historical novels."[15]

Clemens's repugnance for James' *The Bostonians* is fairly well known, but he may not have felt this way toward all of James' writings. As Clemens himself noted in 1891, "To see all that is good in a book, a person has got to read it just in the right time of his life—a year earlier or a year later would make a difference, ten years would make a really prodigious difference. I mean, with most books. There are great masterpieces to which the remark does not apply—perhaps."[16] James was one of the authors whom Clemens at least owned and read, whether or not he encountered James' novels in the "right time of his life." In 1900 he referred to James as "the master."[17]

Short Stories

Clemens unquestionably read many short stories, though he once claimed not to care for the genre. There was Edgar Allan Poe, whose tales he relished. Praising Grace King's "Earthlings" in 1888, Clemens wrote that he "*felt*" her novella, "whereas with me a story is usually a procession & I am an outsider watching it go by—& always with a dubious, & generally with a perishing interest. If I could have stories like this one to read, my prejudice against stories would die a swift death & I should be grateful."[18] Of course for Mark Twain exaggeration was reflexive in making a point at a given moment, so it is difficult to know precisely how to value this and similar comments. He was willing, as he remarked about good historians, to "enlarge the truth by diameters" in order to gain his audience's attention and impart an opinion that they might thus remember. Effect was more crucial than consistency, especially when he addressed personal friends. Still, the probability that Clemens did indeed view with disdain the narrative techniques of most short works of fiction seems likely.

HUMORISTS

Clemens was an expert on certain types of fiction. He knew the writings of American humorists sufficiently well that he planned in 1885 to write an essay about them and explain why "the West & South have produced the chief (lowcomedy) humorists."[19] The comic pieces of A. B. Longstreet, George Washington Harris, William Tappan Thompson, Thomas Bangs Thorpe, B. P. Shillaber, John Phoenix, Artemus Ward, and other American humorists were part of his heritage that he supplemented by reading the more contemporary literary comedians like Robert J. Burdette, Finley Peter Dunne, and George Ade. A score of John Kendrick Bangs' amusing books sat on Clemens's library shelves.

LETTERS

Albert Bigelow Paine correctly remembered that Clemens "would read any volume of letters or personal memoirs; none were too poor that had the throb of life in them, however slight."[20] In a note Clemens wrote to Olivia in her sickroom on 9 February [1903?] he told about reading a book describing Calcutta in an earlier period: "How wonderful are old letters in bringing a dead past back to life & filling it with movement & stir of figures clothed in ruddy flesh! It all seems more *real* & *present* than it does in a novel, & one *feels* it more & and is more a part *of* it."[21] Among many others, Clemens owned or read the collected correspondence of John Adams, Bismarck, Horace Bushnell, Thomas Carlyle, Caroline Fox, John Lothrop Motley, James Russell Lowell, Thomas Macaulay, the Mendelssohn family, Dorothy Osborne, Marie de Sévigné, George Ticknor, and Horace Walpole.

AUTOBIOGRAPHIES

Paine was indubitably accurate in stating that "Clemens had a passion for biography, and especially for autobiography, diaries, letters, and such intimate human history."[22] A good index of Clemens's best-loved diaries and autobiographies is the list of authors he jotted down in 1894 for inclusion in his projected (but never realized) "Back Number" magazine: Margravine Wilhelmina, Pepys, Saint-Simon, Benjamin Franklin, (especially) Benvenuto Cellini, Thomas Moore, Sir William Pembroke, Rousseau.[23] He could have added Marie DuBarry, P. T. Barnum, Philippe de Commynes, Marie Bashkirtseva, Mary Somerville, John Evelyn, Madame Desbordes-Valmore, and (later) Moncure D. Conway and Henri de Blowitz. Certain habits Clemens could not tolerate in diaries or letters: an author's tendencies to refer to events without describing them, to mention a remark without quoting it, or to allude to individuals without characterizing them. The diaries of George Ticknor and the letters of James Russell Lowell irked him on account of these shortcomings; as Clemens wrote to Howells after reading Ticknor's

Journals on 29 August 1877, Ticknor "*refers to too many good things when he could just as well have told them.*"[24] Mark Twain conscientiously tried to avoid these failings in his own *Autobiography*, which abounds in lengthy descriptions of events, entire letters inserted into the text, and opinionated characterizations of his acquaintances.

BIOGRAPHIES

Clemens's knowledge of biographies was truly encompassing. He seems to have read Walter Bagehot's *Biographical Studies*, Emma E. Brown's *Life of Oliver Wendell Holmes*, Moritz Busch's *Bismarck*, Henry Dirck's *Marquis of Worcester*, Edward Dowden's *Shelley*, Froude's *Carlyle* and *Short Studies on Great Subjects*, Edmund Gosse's *Thomas Gray*, Ferris Greenlet's *Thomas Bailey Aldrich*, Albert Bigelow Paine's *Captain Bill McDonald* and *Thomas Nast*, Justin McCarthy's *Queen Anne*, E. T. McLaren's *Dr. John Brown*, H. P. Mendes's *Earl of Beaconsfield*, Louis Nohl's *Liszt*, *Wagner*, and *Beethoven*, James Parton's *Voltaire*, Plutarch's *Lives*, Margaretha von Poschinger's *Emperor Frederick*, Janet Ross's *Three Generations of English Women*, Francis Thompson's *Shelley*, Otto Trevelyan's *Lord Macaulay*, and René Vallery-Radot's *Life of Pasteur*, among many others. At the same time, however, he adamantly resisted all blandishments to cooperate with prospective biographers for a book about himself. "I hate all public mention of my private history, anyway," he wrote to Orion Clemens on 8 December 1887. "It is none of the public's business."[25] Much later he tried to prevent Will M. Clemens from issuing a biographical study, insisting that only "the grave" ends a

man's ownership of his personal history.[26] Eventually, of course, Clemens selected Albert Bigelow Paine to produce a carefully crafted, official biography.

PLAYS

Most scholars have underestimated Clemens's attendance at dramatic performances. Henry Pochmann began this error in 1924 when, relying on the assessments of Howells and Paine, he observed: "Of the drama Mark Twain apparently knew very little."[27] This notion was certainly off base for 1889, when Clemens went to the theater so often that he had to set down two "Unalterable Laws" for himself: "No theatre & RR journey the same day" and "No matine & theatre the same day."[28] It apparently pleased Clemens to make public pronouncements contradictory to his habits; he once told a newspaper interviewer that he had experienced "a surfeit of theatres" while writing drama reviews for the San Francisco *Call*. "My family are fond of the play and go very often," he said, "but they don't enjoy themselves as much as they otherwise would when they persuade me to go with them."[29] Whether or not his family took pleasure in Clemens's company, the number of times he attended the theater during his lifetime is impressive even from the meager documentation that is available. "Get to Rices by 6:45. Julia Marlow's [*sic*] new play," reads one of his typical notebook entries during 1902, when he frequently came in from Riverdale to see plays.[30] He often took young girls to matinee performances during his last years; on one such occasion he criticized an unidentified stage production as "too frivolous & vaudevillish," and using "too much ballet & clothes & foolish songs."[31] The fact that his tastes in drama ran to serious "problem" plays and tragedies as well as comedies, and that he hoped the American stage would mature to the point where tragedies such as Adolph Wilbrandt's would be accepted, hardly accounts for the impression Clemens evidently gave Howells that he "detested the theatre."[32] During the 1880s Augustin Daly personally reserved seats for Clemens, his family, and his friends.[33] John Drew recalled that Clemens was among the prominent people who "became very closely interested in what went on at Daly's, and . . . usually tried to be present at the first night of a new play or the revival of an old one."[34] Daniel Frohman testified that Clemens "was a great friend of the theatre and often spoke at theatrical gatherings."[35]

Operas

Clemens's cavils against the opera, on the other hand, seem to express his genuine feelings. He was baffled and displeased by the rich combination of lyrics, melody, orchestra, dramatic gesture, scenery, and costume. "I know of no agony comparable to the listening to an unfamiliar Opera," he proclaimed in May 1878.[36] "To me an opera is the very climax & cap-stone of the absurd, the fantastic[,] the unjustifiable," he added in August 1878.[37] "I hate the opera," he stated plainly to Howells from Munich in January 1879.[38] "I dislike the opera because I want to love it and can't," he wrote in Chapter 24 of *A Tramp Abroad* (1880). The best explanation for his antipathy appeared in a newspaper interview he granted in 1901: "I think opera is spoiled by attempting to

combine instrumental and vocal effects. I love instrumental music and I love a good voice, but I don't like them together. It's too generous. I can't fully take it in."[39] Despite these opinions, however, Clemens was fond of certain standard musical pieces from operas, particularly overtures from the operas of Rossini and Wagner.

Travel Narratives

Clemens's interest in books of travel is also correctly recognized, and it is possible to detect his contact with well more than one hundred travel writings. For one thing, he never tired of investigating British opinions of America; his Colonel Sellers knows that whenever the English travel in the United States "they all keep diaries" and are afflicted "with the travelling Briton's everlasting disposition to generalize whole mountain ranges from single sample-grains of sand" (*The American Claimant*, Chapter 21). To justify his anti-British bias Clemens noted in February 1890 that "a thousand" Englishmen had criticized America in books—naming Charles Dickens, Frederick Marryat, Mrs. Trollope, Lepel Griffin, and Matthew Arnold.[40] When he himself traveled abroad, Clemens invariably obtained guidebooks to supply factual details, but he insisted that most such publications overstated the attributes of scenic views. Of the forts, mosques, and tombs in Delhi and Agra, Mark Twain writes: "By good fortune I had not read too much about them, and therefore was able to get a natural and rational focus upon them, with the result that they thrilled, blessed, and exalted me. But if I had previously overheated my imagination by drinking too much pestilential literary hot Scotch, I should have suffered disappointment and sorrow" (*Following the Equator*, Chapter 59).

HISTORY

Roger Salomon believed that Clemens's readings in history mainly consisted of memoirs such as Saint-Simon's or Casanova's, personalized narratives like Carlyle's *French Revolution*, and enormous compilations of human thought and conduct such as Lecky's *European Morals*.[41] Actually Clemens's views were also shaped by many less celebrated works; on the topic of American history, for instance, he owned or read (among many other volumes) surveys by Alexander Brown, William Cullen Bryant and Sydney Howard Gay, Andrew Carnegie, John Fiske, Thomas Higginson, Jean Nadaillac, Frederick Ober, (particularly) Francis Parkman, and Woodrow Wilson, as well as books on the Civil War written by John S. C. Abbott, George Henry Gordon, U. S. Grant, A. B. Hart, J. T. Headley, J. K. Hosmer, George McClellan, S. J. May, Louis Philippe d'Orleans Paris, Whitelaw Reid, and William Tecumseh Sherman. Thus Clemens's history sources consisted of many memoirs, but also included standard textbooks and reference works of his day. Salomon outlined Clemens's shift from the nineteenth-century doctrine of historical progress toward a theory of historical cycles. Nonetheless "one has the feeling when reading his marginalia," wrote Salomon, "that the chief source, early and late in life, of Twain's interest in history was as documentation for his conviction of the despicability of the human race."[42]

The quantity of Clemens's historical reading has never been doubted. Paine recorded on 25 October 1909: "I am constantly amazed at his knowledge of history—all history—religious, political, military. He seems to have read everything in the world concerning Rome, France, and England particularly."[43] Even the early Greek historian Herodotus was represented in his personal library. Yet on a small sheet of paper Clemens humbly noted: "History. Read more of it than anybody, yet don't know as much about it as I do about multipli'n table, & I never can say *that* without breaking down at 9 x 6 is 35."[44] When Mark Twain began *A Connecticut Yankee* in 1886 he informed Charles L. Webster that "I have saturated myself with the atmosphere of the day & the subject,"[45] his characteristic approach toward writing about a period in which he had not lived. This extensive reading gave him definite notions about historiography. While history that is "unembellished by fancy" often "insures irksome reading," he wrote in the preface to "Three Thousand Years Among the Microbes" (1905), any narrative of "bare facts" at least "insures useful reading" and is preferable to "pure History unrefreshed by fact."[46]

THE LITERATURE OF ANCIENT ROME

Although Clemens had been denied the high school and college education that would have given him an easy command of Latin, by the time he reached adulthood there were good English translations available for the major Roman authors. His bookshelves would hold copies of Caesar's *Commentaries*, Cicero's *Select Orations*, Ovid's *Art of Love*, Propertius's *Elegies*, Pliny the Younger's

Letters, Plutarch's *Lives*, Suetonius's *Lives of the Twelve Caesars*, and Petronius's *The Satyricon*, as well as works by Virgil, Tacitus, and Flavius Josephus. Thus he was at far less of a disadvantage in knowing the outlines of early Roman culture than might be supposed. He also owned certain volumes of Greek thinkers of that period such as *The Discourses of Epictetus* and Athenaeus's *The Deipnosophists; or, Banquet of the Learned.*

PHILOSOPHY

Clemens's acquaintance with the subject of philosophy has been treated only by speculative commentary, and really deserves additional research. Minnie M. Brashear conjectured that he was the heir of eighteenth-century thinkers, especially Hobbes, Locke, Hume, and Newton.[47] Coleman O. Parsons assumed that Clemens knew the moral-sense writers and the "selfish" moralists—Shaftesbury, John Clarke, Francis Hutcheson, Jeremy Bentham, Richard Whately, La Rochefoucauld.[48] Clemens himself left few explicit statements about his knowledge, except to deny to Sir John Adams on 12 April 1898 that he had ever read any of the "associationist" philosophers such as David Hartley, James Mills and John Stuart Mill, or Alexander Bain.[49] He and his daughter Clara annotated a volume of Arthur Schopenhauer's essays. Several studies have compared his mature views with those of Friedrich Nietzsche.[50]

RELIGION

That Clemens viewed mankind's history as a struggle between enlightening science and reactionary religion cannot be disputed, but the corollary presumption that he therefore avoided theological books is mistaken.[51] No one could rail against the Bible, Christianity, and God as Clemens did from the 1880s onward except someone for whom spiritual topics were palpably present and troublesome. He was always ready to read an argument on either side of a religious issue. Announcing that he was "devouring" Robert G. Ingersoll's religiously skeptical lectures, he added, "They have found a hungry place, and they content it & satisfy it." He investigated Andrew D. White's *Warfare of Science with Theology*, G. P. Merriam's *A Living Faith*, Rufus Noyes' *Views of Religion*, Ranke's *History of the Popes*, Oliver Lodge's *The Substance of Faith*, George Park Fisher's *Supernatural Origin of Christianity*, Renan's *The Apostles*, W. H. Rule's *History of the Inquisition*, Sienkiewicz's *Quo Vadis?*, Philip Vivian's *The Churches and Modern Thought*, T. W. Doane's *Bible Myths and Their Parallels in Other Religions*, Henry Drummond's *The Greatest Thing in the World* and *Pax Vobiscum*, Jonathan Edwards's *Freedom of the Will*, Sarah Titcomb's *Aryan Sun-Myths*, and numerous other volumes related to religion, hymns, sermons, witchcraft, and skepticism. What he most disliked, it would appear, was being *compelled* to read works on religion. The origins of this distaste for compulsory theology are presumably traceable to his childhood experiences. At any rate, he was enraged at the disproportion of subject matter he discovered in the library on a ship in which he crossed the Indian Ocean; on 8 April 1896, after leaving Ceylon, he observed: "The library of this ship is a curiosity, & is a fine example of the impudence which over-godliness is sure to breed." The "statistics issued by the great libraries," he recalled, indicate that sixty-five per cent of the general readers prefer fiction and only five per cent care for "theological & goody-goody." The Anglo-Indian owners of this ship were obviously indifferent to these desires. "What the public require in the way of fiction is 65 per cent of the bulk," yet they are furnished with "less than a sixth of that" (fifteen titles out of ninety-four); whereas the company placed six times the needed number of religious books in its library and then has the gall to charge "famine prices: a rupee for 3 weeks' gorging of these aids to indigestion."[52]

SCIENCE

Clemens's respect for scientific theories spanned his lifetime, as Hyatt Howe Waggoner[53] and Sherwood P. Cummings[54] have shown. Many of his readings cannot be precisely identified; while he was writing "Three Thousand Years Among the Microbes" in 1905, for instance, Isabel Lyon wrote to book firms on 2 June "for some little books on microbes,"[55] but he left clues to only a few of these titles. We know, however, that Clemens owned an entire set of Charles Darwin's works and looked into John Lubbock's writings, C. W. Saleeby's *Cycle of Life* and *Evolution the Master-Key*, Shobal Vail Clevenger's *Evolution of Man*, Nathaniel Shaler's *Aspects of the Earth*, Carl Snyder's *New Conceptions in Science*, Alexander Winchell's *Sketches of Creation*, G. S. Woodhead's *Bacteria*, and Maeterlinck's *Life of the Bee*, along with John Fiske's *A Century of Science*. As telescopes improved, astronomy attracted him more and more;

at least a dozen titles on this subject were in his library, including Simon Newcomb's *Side-Lights on Astronomy*, Samuel G. Bayne's *The Pith of Astronomy*, A. V. Guillemin's *The Sun* and *The Heavens*, Joseph Norman Lockyer's *Elementary Lessons in Astronomy*, Martha E. Martin's *The Friendly Stars*, Oliver J. Lodge's *The Ether of Space*, and G. P. Serviss's *Astronomy with the Naked Eye* and *Curiosities of the Sky*.

CRIMINAL TRIALS

Criminal trials held a special fascination for Clemens. He was acquainted with volumes about sensational cases bearing titles such as *Remarkable Trials of All Countries*, *Noted French Trials*, *Lives and Criminal Trials of Celebrated Men*, *Causes Célèbres*, *Gallick Reports; or, an Historical Collection of Criminal Cases*, *History of the Most Remarkable Tryals in Great Britain and Ireland*, and *Famous Cases of Circumstantial Evidence*.

MISCELLANEOUS READING

The miscellaneous topics in which Clemens educated himself deserve essays in themselves. Though Clemens apparently was ignorant of Freud's theories of psychology, he knew William James' *Principles of Psychology*, John Adams's *Herbartian Psychology*, James Mark Baldwin's *The Story of the Mind*, and other studies. Clemens became familiar with many writings on American and English government and developed a degree of expertise on the internal affairs of South Africa, the Philippines, China, Japan, and Russia, as well as the contemporary international relations of the United States. In the last decade of his life he consumed many books and pamphlets that fed his rage over the atrocities resulting from colonial imperialism. He sought out material that might now be classified as anthropology—studies of the social customs of Native Americans (Hubert Howe Bancroft and Richard Dodge), African tribes (J. G. Wood), Icelandic farmers (Jón Jónsson), Australian aborigines (James Stuart Laurie, Robert Brough Smyth), and other indigenous cultures. Louis Figuier's *Primitive Man* was in Clemens's library. His use of reference tools was diligent; he typically began his research on a topic with the bibliography supplied in the *Encyclopedia Britannica*, and he often relied on Appleton's *American Annual Cyclopaedia*. "A Dictionary *is* the most awe-inspiring of all books, it knows so much," he commented in 1891,[56] and he owned the Merriam-Webster dictionary and the *Standard Dictionary*. He used many literary reference guides such as Charles Anthon's *Classical Dictionary* and E. Cobham Brewer's *Reader's Handbook*, *Dictionary of Miracles*, and *Dictionary of Phrase and Fable*. He knew various standard works of art history. He read considerably in French and German.

MAGAZINES

Much of Clemens's general knowledge came from magazines, which he read avidly. Even when he traveled abroad he arranged for regular receipt of American journals. For instance, he wrote to Franklin G. Whitmore from Florence on 2 November 1892: "Please notify our magazines & newspapers to stop sending through Paris (which costs money & time,) & mail direct to our Florence address."[57] His reliance on periodicals did not

mean he was content with their editors, however. "There is no magazine in existence which ever contains three articles which can be depended upon to interest the reader," he stated grumpily in his Autobiographical Dictation of 17 January 1906.[58] But he regularly scanned the issues of *Atlantic Monthly*, *Harper's Weekly* and *Monthly*, *Cosmopolitan*, *Century*, *McClure's*, *North American Review*, and other journals for those few engaging essays, stories, or poems.

NEWSPAPERS

Newspapers were his constant diversion and his frequent despair. The American press, he said in an Autobiographical Dictation of 27 April 1908 "is a singular product." Its editorial page is "morally clean," with commendable ideals, but the other pages of news are simply "poisonous dirt" that make the American newspaper resemble "a temple with only one angel in it—the other idols are devils." He charged that American newspapers "publish every loathsome thing they can get hold of"; with 2,500 daily newspapers in the nation, he said, he could think of "only six" whose conduct was not a "damaging influence."[59] Yet Isabel Lyon noted that in cleaning Clemens's room on 15 June 1907 while he was in England receiving his honorary Oxford degree, she looked into "his drawers of mss. and dear little clippings and pipes and things that he takes interest in. Usually the clippings are of the most violentest [*sic*] crimes. Oh terrible things that are 'permitted by a just God,' and usually there is a comment in the King's [Clemens's] handwriting on the margin."[60] Clemens's notebooks and scrapbooks teem with references to sensational crimes and trials about which he read in newspapers. In his later years he often took a newspaper article as the text for one of his daily Autobiographical Dictations.

Carlyle Smythe, who had accompanied Clemens during a part of his world tour, thought that "the reading of newspapers, to which he is addicted almost as much as to smoking bad cigars," might account for "why commonly he fails so hopelessly to appreciate the masters of literature" such as Goldsmith, Thackeray, and Meredith.[61] At one time or another Clemens regularly read the New York *Herald*, *Post*, *Sun*, *Times*, and *Tribune*, the Hartford *Courant*, the Boston *Transcript*, and *Galignani's Messenger* (Paris), and he also saw issues of other major newspapers. A former newspaperman, Clemens felt qualified to criticize the American press (in his Autobiographical Dictation of 7 September 1906 he blamed it for prompting the advent of Yellow Journalism in European newspapers)[62] and to commend it, especially for its "irreverence," the "only sure defence" of liberty.[63] It was a sign of Clemens's worsening health when he noticed in Bermuda on 6 December 1909 that his hunger for newspaper coverage of human affairs was finally subsiding. To Jean he wrote: "As for news of the great world, it does not interest me. The Times & the Herald have lain at my elbow 2 days, now—unopened. The sight of a newspaper stirs not a single quiver of interest in me."[64]

CLEMENS'S BREADTH OF READING

As Albert E. Stone Jr. has noted, Mark Twain's identification with the precocious Marjorie Fleming described by Dr. John Brown of Edinburgh is especially revealing in connection with his admiration of her zest for reading.[65] In "Marjorie Fleming, the Wonder Child" (1909) Mark Twain mused: "She reads philosophies, novels, baby books, histories, the mighty poets—reads them with burning interest, and frankly and freely criticizes them all."[66] This statement is a far more accurate appraisal of Clemens's own reading tendencies than those proposed by William Dean Howells or Albert Bigelow Paine—or even the misleading ones advanced by Clemens for himself.

NOTES

1. "The Mind of Mark Twain," master's thesis, University of Texas at Austin, 1924, p. 6. The earliest guide to Clemens's reading, this is also an illuminating collection of curious and disparate items which fell within Clemens's notice. Pochmann gathered references to Clemens's reading and his knowledge of folklore, nature, and various other topics with such system and erudition that this master's thesis continued to set an example for Mark Twain scholarship.

2. *Mark Twain's Fables of Man*, ed. John S. Tuckey (Berkeley: University of California Press, 1972) p. 338. Twain's manuscript dates from 1901 and 1902.

3. Shapell Manuscript Library, Beverly Hills, California. Clemens's letter to the Reverend Crane mentioned that his effort was rushed by the need to depart from Hartford and that he was merely trying to "take a shot on the wing."

4. The true scope of Clemens's knowledge of books, plays, and periodicals can at best only be suggested here. Detailed documentation of Clemens's familiarity with the following titles is supplied in the Annotated Catalog of Clemens's library books and literary references.

5. Notebook 34, TS pp. 34–35, MTP.

6. Letter dated 15 March 1871, quoted by Albert E. Stone Jr. in *The Innocent Eye: Childhood in Mark Twain's Imagination* (New Haven: Yale University Press, 1961), pp. 51–52.

7. Harold Aspiz listed Mark Twain's parodies of poets in Chapter 3 of "Mark Twain's Reading—A Critical Study," Doctoral dissertation, University of California, Los Angeles, 1949. Most of these examples were published by Arthur Scott in *On the Poetry of Mark Twain, with Selections from His Verse* (Urbana: University of Illinois Press, 1966).

8. "Mark Twain's Literary Opinions," Doctoral dissertation (University of Iowa, 1945), p. xlvi.

9. *Mark Twain: A Biography* (New York: Harper & Brothers, 1912), p. 1295—hereafter cited as *MTB*.

10. Isabel V. Lyon Journals, TS pp. 138, 191, Mark Twain Papers, Bancroft Library, University of California, Berkeley. Manuscripts and letters in the Mark Twain Papers are hereafter cited as belonging to MTP.

11. Paine, *MTB*, p. 1120.

12. "An Interview with Mark Twain," collected in *From Sea to Sea: Letters of Travel*. 2 vols. (New York: Doubleday and McClure, 1899), 2: 180.

13. ALS, Vassar College.

14. *The Letters of Mark Twain and Joseph Hopkins Twichell*, ed. Harold K. Bush, Steve Courtney, and Peter Messent (Athens: University of Georgia Press, 2017), p. 81.

15. Albert and Shirley Small Special Collection Library, University of Virginia, Charlottesville.

16. Notebook 31, TS p. 17, MTP.

17. Clemens to T. Douglas Murray, ALS, MTP.

18. Quoted by Robert Bush in "Grace King and Mark Twain," *American Literature* 44.1 (March 1972): 42.

19. Notebook 24, *N&J* 3: 156.

20. Paine, *MTB*, p. 1540.

21. ALS, MTP.

22. Paine, *MTB*, p. 1539.

23. Notebook 33, TS p. 46, MTP.

24. *Mark Twain-Howells Letters*, ed. Henry Nash Smith and William M. Gibson (Cambridge: Harvard University Press, Belknap Press, 1960), p. 200.

25. *Mark Twain, Business Man*, ed. Samuel C. Webster (Boston: Little, Brown, and Co., 1946) p. 389.

26. ALS dated 6 June 1900, Henry W. and Albert A. Berg Collection, New York Public Library, Astor, Lenox and Tilden Foundations.

27. "Mind of Mark Twain," p. 43.

28. Notebook 29, *N&J* 3: 484.

29. New York *World*, 14 October 1900; *Mark Twain: The Complete Interviews*, ed. Gary Scharnhorst (Tuscaloosa: University of Alabama, 2006), p. 348.

30. Notebook 45, TS p. 34, MTP.

31. Clemens to Dorothy Quick, 9 May 1908, MTP.

32. *My Mark Twain: Reminiscences and Criticisms*, ed. Marilyn Austin Baldwin (Baton Rouge: Louisiana State University Press, 1967), p. 16.

33. Clemens to Daly, 30 November 1888; two undated letters, 1880, Houghton Library, Harvard University.

34. *My Years on the Stage* (New York: E. P. Dutton and Co., 1922), p 106.

35. *Daniel Frohman Presents: An Autobiography* (New York: Claude Kendall & Willoughby Sharp, 1935), p. 141.

36. Notebook 14, *N&J* 2: 93.

37. Notebook 15, *N&J* 2: 139.

38   *Mark Twain-Howells Letters*, p. 248.

39   "Mark Twain Bearded in His New York Den," New York *Herald*, 20 January 1901.

40   Notebook 29, *N&J* 3: 541.

41   *Twain and the Image of History* (New Haven: Yale University Press, 1961), p. 22.

42   *Twain and the Image of History*, p. 22.

43   Paine, *MTB*, p. 1533.

44   Sotheby's sale, 19 June 2003, lot 230.

45   *Mark Twain, Business Man*, p. 355.

46   *Mark Twain's Which Was the Dream? and Other Symbolic Writings of the Later Years*, ed. John S. Tuckey (Berkeley: University of California Press, 1967), p. 433.

47   *Mark Twain: Son of Missouri* (Chapel Hill: University of North Carolina Press, 1934), pp. 248–251.

48   "The Background of *The Mysterious Stranger*," *American Literature* 32.1 (March 1960): 70 n. 41.

49   Quoted by Lawrence Clark Powell in "An Unpublished Mark Twain Letter," *American Literature* 13.4 (January 1942): 406.

50   See, for example, Philip E. Davis, "Mark Twain's Dream Life," *Mark Twain Journal* 51.1–2 (2013): 50–65; Michael Crews, "Mark Twain's Cheerful Determinist: Good News in *What Is Man?*," *Mark Twain Journal* 52.1 (Spring 2014): 61–80; and Patrick K. Dooley, "Mark Twain's Conscience as the 'Mysterious Autocrat': Why Moral Philosophers Need Literature," *Mark Twain Journal* 52.1 (Spring 2014): 81–90.

51   See, among other treatments of Clemens's abiding interest in theology, Joe B. Fulton's *The Reverend Mark Twain: Theological Burlesque, Form, and Content* (Athens: Ohio State University Press, 2006); Harold K. Bush Jr.'s *Mark Twain and the Spiritual Crisis of His Age* (Tuscaloosa: University of Alabama, Press, 2007); and Lawrence I. Berkove and Joseph Csicsila, *Heretical Fictions: Religion in the Literature of Mark Twain* (Iowa City: University of Iowa Press, 2012).

52   Notebook 37, TS pp. 30–31, MTP.

53   "Science in the Thought of Mark Twain," *American Literature* 8.4 (January 1937): 357–370.

54   "Mark Twain and Science," Doctoral dissertation, University of Wisconsin, 1950; "Mark Twain's Social Darwinism," *Huntington Library Quarterly* 2 (February 1957): 163–175; "Science and Mark Twain's Theory of Fiction," *Philological Quarterly* 37 (January 1958): 26–33; "Mark Twain's Acceptance of Science," *Centennial Review* 6.2 (Spring 1962): 245–261; "*What Is Man?*: The Scientific Sources," in *Essays on Determinism in American Literature*, ed. Sydney J. Krause, *Kent Studies in English* 1 (1964): 108–116; *Mark Twain and Science: Adventures of a Mind* (Baton Rouge: Louisiana State University Press, 1988.

55   Isabel V. Lyon Journal, now in the Mark Twain Archive, Elmira College, Elmira, New York; formerly in the Antenne Collection, Rice Lake, Wisconsin.

56   Quoted by C. Merton Babcock, "Mark Twain and the Dictionary," *Word Study* 42.1 (October 1966): 5.

57   ALS, Mark Twain House and Museum, Hartford, Connecticut.

58   *Autobiography of Mark Twain, Volume 1*, ed. Harriet Elinor Smith (Berkeley: University of California Press, 2010), 1: 287.

59   *Autobiography of Mark Twain, Volume 3*, ed. Benjamin Griffin and Harriet Elinor Smith (Berkeley: University of California Press, 2015), 3: 223–224.

60   Isabel V. Lyon Journals, TS pp. 252–253, MTP.

61   "The Real 'Mark Twain,'" *Pall Mall Magazine* (London) 16.65 (September 1898): 31.

62   *Autobiography of Mark Twain, Volume 2*, ed. Benjamin Griffin and Harriet Elinor Smith (Berkeley: University of California Press, 2013), 2: 227.

63   Notebook 27 (1888), *N&J* 3: 392.

64   ALS in MTP.

65   *The Innocent Eye*, pp. 262–263.

66   MS in MTP, Box 27, quoted by Stone, *The Innocent Eye*, p. 262.

5

Reading Mark Twain Reading

Although Mark Twain became determined to mask the scope of his reading, a Pittsburgh reporter caught him off guard in 1884 while he was getting a haircut during his platform tour with George Washington Cable and succeeded in enticing him to rattle on about Oliver Wendell Holmes, Nathaniel Hawthorne, Henry Wadsworth Longfellow, Charles Dudley Warner, Henry Irving, Edgar Allan Poe, Thomas Bailey Aldrich, William Dean Howells's *Silas Lapham*, Henry James's *Daisy Miller*, R. D. Blackmore's *Lorna Doone*, and Charlotte Bronte's *Jane Eyre*. Then Twain suddenly caught himself and quickly added that "I am not a careful reader of novels," that "much of my opinion is based upon what I hear from men and women of sound judgment who I know intimately," and that "my taste has a strong bent to history and biography."[1] Interviewed by another enterprising reporter in 1901 while he was summering on Lake Saranac in the Adirondacks, Twain acknowledged that he wrote only four hours a day, usually ending at 2 p.m., and then "very frequently his afternoon is spent with some favorite book by the lakeside. Here, sitting on some old moss-grown log, he will spend hour after hour."[2] An inquisitive newspaper interviewer and a photographer who tracked Twain down in Riverdale-on-Hudson during the winter of 1902 were "piloted" by Twain "into a little room in one corner of the house" that was "filled with books, piles of newspapers, boxes of cigars, corncob pipes, cans of tobacco and matches in about equal proportion."[3]

Despite such peeks into his actual habits, the impression of Twain persisted as a self-taught, improvisational literary artist who read only desultorily in unconventional works rather than as a writer committed to reading as a daily activity, a regular subscriber to newspapers and national magazines, and—even for Nook Farm, Elmira, or Redding—an unusually inquisitive explorer of the fiction, poetry, drama, and theology that Albert Bigelow Paine and others believed he ignored or disliked.[4]

There could be a number of reasons for his inclination to minimize his familiarity with books. To begin with, Twain was one of the earliest authors to become conscious of techniques for packaging and marketing his public persona (an ability that would

49

eventually lead him to adopt a white suit complementing his mane of white hair, bristling eyebrows, and drooping mustache). Clearly he perceived early on the usefulness of projecting the image of a self-taught American original uninfluenced by literary models. In his later years, when his name and talents were legendary, he liked to receive newspaper and magazine reporters while lying abed in his nightgown, puffing lazily on a cigar and feigning utter indolence. Twain would gratify them by delivering what they came for—a pungent commentary on the day's news—but all too often the reporters failed to notice one significant detail visible in their accompanying photographs: a formidable stack of books on Twain's bedstand.

Then, too, Clemens seems to have genuinely classified reading as one of his mildly deplorable vices, associating it with aromatic tobacco and unproductive idleness.[5] This notion manifested itself early; he reminded Olivia Clemens on 12 October 1872, writing from London, "You may have observed that I do dearly love to go to bed & lie there steeped in the comfort of reading. . . . Here, I lie & read every night til 1 or 2 oclock. It would be perfect bliss if you were at my side."[6] "How little confirmed invalids appreciate their advantages," wrote an ill Clemens to William Dean Howells on 26 January 1875. "I was able to read the English edition of the Greville Memoirs through without interruption, take my meals in bed, neglect all business without a pang, & smoke 18 cigars a day."[7] In August 1891 he looked forward to a boat excursion on the Rhône River in France that would offer "lazy repose, with opportunity to smoke, read, doze, talk, accumulate comfort,

get fat" and "avoid "the world and its concerns."[8] Also typical of this view of reading as a sign of dilatoriness was the sentiment he expressed in a letter of 28 July 1908 to his daughter Jean: "I am doing very very very very little work. . . . I seem to greatly prefer cards, & billiards, & reading, & smoking, & lying around in the shade."[9]

Another consideration was that he did not want to risk imputations of undue influence. It is conceivable, too, that Clemens mentally measured his rate of reading against that of William Dean Howells, who earned his living partly by writing book reviews for magazines. The rapidity of Howells's march through reading materials was enough to make anyone feel intellectually inadequate. In addition to these possibilities, we should remember that early on Mark Twain came to value and praise hands-on experience in preference to "book" knowledge. This belief militated against Clemens's revealing his bookishness.

There may also have existed in Twain a latent defensiveness about his lack of formal education. The Reverend Joseph H. Twichell noted in 1896 that on many occasions he had heard Clemens voice "his sense of disadvantage without remedy in having been denied the opportunity of a classical training in his youth." Of course numerous other male writers of that period likewise lacked the college background enjoyed by, say, Charles Dudley Warner—including Thomas Bailey Aldrich, William Dean Howells, Joel Chandler Harris, Harold Frederic, and Hamlin Garland—but Clemens seemed hypersensitive about having been taken from school in his early teens and put to work in a print shop. Wearing his Oxford University gown (from the ceremony that had bestowed an honorary degree on him in 1907) at every conceivable opportunity became his final defense against the lifelong deficiency he had always felt.

Gaining an awareness of Clemens's bookish proclivities hardly erodes our respect for his achievements, but on the contrary teaches us to applaud his unending curiosity. There were discernible stages of this proclivity. In his younger Hannibal years and in his wandering phase, he devoured James Fenimore Cooper, Charles Dickens, Walter Scott, and other authors whom he would later discount or disparage. It was during his marital courtship period, when he was mailing annotated books to Olivia Langdon, that he first perceived book margins as another area where his comic genius for repartee could flourish. Furnishing their Hartford house in the 1870s gave Clemens and his wife Olivia an opportunity to assemble a substantial family library in a sumptuous room on its first floor. Eventually it would consist of more than three thousand volumes. As a recreation Clemens took malicious pleasure in selecting his specially designated "Library of Literary Hogwash," examples of bad literature toward which he vented his scorn for amateurishness in employing words.

Authors who were more competent earned his respect in the form of prickly debates with them that he conducted in the margins of their books. The dialogues that he established with Thomas Carlyle, W. E. H. Lecky, Thomas Macaulay, and other historians of human behavior were examples of this vigorous give-and-take. During his final phase of literary connoisseurship in the 1900s, oral readings of material became his *sine qua non* test for both ideas and style. He refused to pass judgment on any work that he had not read aloud or had not listened to its being read orally.

At each stage of his writing career, books on certain topics—such as William Prime's *Tent Life in the Holy Land* or Edward Whymper's *Scrambles Amongst the Alps*—attracted him as momentary literary targets; at other junctures, the monumental accomplishments of Sir Thomas Malory, Cervantes, Daniel Defoe, and Jonathan Swift challenged and galvanized his own writing talents. Reading along with Twain in his intellectual journeys provides another avenue for comprehending his genius.

It is possible to see, judging from the pages of the more than 1,000 books surviving from Clemens's personal library—which represent less than a third of his family's lifetime collection—that he employed a number of volumes as literary resources, some books as quasi-notebooks, others, like the works of W. E. H. Lecky, as learned mentor-opponents to argue with good-naturedly, and still others as either inspirations for notes of admiration to their authors or as objects of private ridicule. In 1903 Edith Wharton posed a question to all readers that applies here: "What is reading, in the last analysis, but an interchange of thought between writer and reader? If the book enters the reader's mind just as it left the writer's—without any of the additions and modifications inevitably produced by contact with a new body of thought—it has been read to no purpose." She deplored "the mechanical reader" who "is like a tourist who drives from one 'sight' to another without looking at anything that is not set down in Baedeker."[10]

There was definitely nothing mechanical or passive for Clemens about the activity of reading; he tended to react instantly to each phrase, sentence, and paragraph. The margins in a large percentage of his books are decorated with his trademark witticisms, as though he were personally interrogating the authors as well as showing off for future readers. This habit he had acquired while courting Olivia Langdon and sending her amusingly annotated volumes, and he continued it after their marriage, as her letter to him of 7 January 1872 from Hartford makes clear: "I wonder you did not mark it still more than you have, but I am so very glad you marked it at all, I do so heartily enjoy the books that you have marked," she assured him after he sent her a copy of Longfellow's *The Golden Legend*. "I cannot afford to lose any thing that you have marked."[11] In a copy of Samuel Fowler's *Salem Witchcraft*, Clemens observed: "Well, their infamies covered but one year, & were heartily confessed & repented of, whereas Europe's iniquities in the same line covered eight centuries." Along the pages of *The Memoirs of the Duke of Saint-Simon on the Reign of Louis XIV* Clemens characterized the Court as "gilded lice" and scoffed that "persistence in making French people is but little creditable to God." Marie Sévigné's *Letters*, which recounted her life in the French court, exasperated Clemens: "These letters have not even the common French merit of being indecent." In a bestselling novel, Sarah Grand's *The Heavenly Twins*, Clemens groused that "these disgusting creatures talk like Dr. Samuel Johnson and act like idiots." Impatient with a translator of his adored Suetonius's *Lives of the Caesars*, Clemens complained about its

"Cowboy English." Clemens chaffed over the small fortune that Lewis Wallace made with his *Ben-Hur, A Tale of the Christ* (1880) and numerous spin-off editions concocted from extracts of the novel. In Wallace's pious preface to *The First Christmas, from Ben-Hur* (1902), Clemens wrote sarcastically, "Ah—the finger of God in it. How nice."

While a number of initially surviving books from his library have mysteriously vanished since my earlier survey appeared in 1980, many others, assumed to have been lost forever, have amazingly materialized. Clemens's never-before-seen comments in Carlyle's sweeping chronicle, *The French Revolution*, after hiding themselves for a century, have now been catalogued by Joe B. Fulton. Mary Boewe similarly transcribed Clemens's notes in several sets of the historian W. E. H. Lecky. A set of Charles Dickens that he consulted is now at Elmira College, having also turned up in Elmira. What other association copies are still lying around somewhere, awaiting their discovery?

Clemens's list of *un*favorites among notable literary names is quite possible to compile: Jane Austen and James Fenimore Cooper, for starters. *The Bostonians* "was unspeakably dreary," he wrote. "I dragged along half-way through it & gave it up in despair." To Howells he swore, "as for the Bostonians, I would rather be damned to John Bunyan's heaven than read that." George Meredith's characters Clemens found to be "artificialities—ingeniously contrived puppets rather than human beings." Oliver Goldsmith irked Clemens in 1894: "Perhaps it may be forgivable to write a really honest review of the Vicar of Wakefield & try to find out what our fathers found in it to admire, & what not to scoff at." Later he added that the novel has "the touch that makes an intentionally humorous episode pathetic and an intentionally pathetic one funny." William Makepeace Thackeray and Bret Harte attained prominent places in Clemens's book-hell. Charles Dickens came to be out of favor, too, but only after Clemens grew to be a recognized writer himself; in his teens he was known to carry around volumes of Dickens under his arm, by his twenties he knew various Dickens novels by heart, and later he both borrowed and owned entire sets of Dickens's works. Yet Clemens nevertheless averred, in the year before his death, "My brother used to try to get me to read Dickens, long ago. I couldn't do it." Charles Lamb was lost on him. Clemens held contradictory views of Nathaniel Hawthorne, admiring his eloquent prose but abhorring his plot strategies. "I can't stand George Eliot, & Hawthorne & those people; I see what they are at, a hundred years before they get to it, & they just tire me to death," he confided to Howells in 1885. Arthur Conan Doyle's "pompous sentimental 'extraordinary man' with his cheap & ineffectual ingenuities" did not seem to Clemens to merit the amount of adulation he received. Above all others, George Eliot resided in Clemens's literary doghouse. Eliot's novel *Daniel Deronda* was the subject of Clemens's complaints to Howells in 1885: "I dragged through three chapters, losing flesh all the time, & then was honest enough to quit, & confess to myself that I haven't *any* romance-literature appetite, as far as I can see." Just as bad was *Middlemarch*, which Twain had "bored through . . . with its labored & tedious analyses of feelings & motives, its

paltry & tiresome people, its unexciting & uninteresting story, & its frequent blinding flashes of single-sentence poetry." The result was that he "nearly died from the over-work. I wouldn't read another of those books for a farm." Twain's contempt for Sir Walter Scott has become legendary, and is currently a classroom touchstone for illustrating the shift from Romanticism to Realism in literature. Twain even went so far as to blame Scott's "showy rubbish" for defeating "the good work done by Cervantes" and for doing to the American South "more real and lasting harm, perhaps, than any other individual that ever wrote." To Brander Matthews, a champion of Scott, Clemens wrote in 1903 upon endeavoring to reread Scott: "Brander, I lie here dying, slowly dying, under the blight of Sir Walter."

Clearly in certain cases personal and contemporary prejudices were interfering with Clemens's critical judgments. He seemed to reject works whose pace was deliberately slow, whose characters were only gradually revealed, whose dialogue rang less than lifelike, and whose motives and morals were too apparent. There was also, in several of these put-downs, a subtle sense of competitiveness; whether dead or still living, these predecessors perhaps struck Clemens as rivals worth impugning.

Despite Clemens's long-term efforts to downplay his acquaintance with other writers' books, scholarship has revealed the wide breadth of his reading experiences and the ample size of his personal library. To a large degree we are finally capable of reading Clemens reading, of catching him in the act, of studying his predilections. He would not have liked that very much.

NOTES

1 *Mark Twain: The Complete Interviews*, ed. Gary Scharnhorst (Tuscaloosa: University of Alabama, 2006), pp. 62–64.

2 Scharnhorst, *Complete Interviews*, p. 397.

3 Scharnhorst, *Complete Interviews*, p. 476.

4 I endeavored to dislodge part of this impression in my "'I Detest Novels, Poetry & Theology': Origin of a Fiction Concerning Mark Twain's Reading," *Tennessee Studies in Literature* 22 (1977): 154–161. (A revised version of this essay appears as a chapter in the present volume.)

5 I have elaborated on this concept in "'Good Books & A Sleepy Conscience': Mark Twain's Reading Habits," *American Literary Realism* 9.4 (Autumn 1976): 295–306. (A revised version of this essay appears as a chapter in the present volume.)

6 *Mark Twain's Letters, Volume 5, 1872–1873*, ed. Lin Salamo and Harriet Elinor Smith (Berkeley: University of California Press, 1997), 5: 196—hereafter cited as *MTLet.*

7 *MTLet* 6: 357.

8 "Down the Rhône," published posthumously in 1923.

9 Christie's, 11 May 1987 auction, lot 38. TS in MTP.

10 Edith Wharton, "The Vice of Reading," *North American* Review 177.563 (October 1903): 513, 516.

11 *MTLet* 5: 17.

6

The Formation of
Samuel L. Clemens's Library

In 1879 a newspaper article about the misfortune of Dr. William Dindorf, a learned man compelled by a reversal of fortunes to sell his private library in Leipzig, caught the attention of Samuel Clemens; he clipped the story and pinned it to the rear endpaper of the notebook he was then using. This same document, Notebook 17, contains his notes for a tale about "the auction of a poor scholar's library."[1] Appendix F of *A Tramp Abroad* (1880) is the apparent result: there Mark Twain relates a mock German legend concerning the threatened library of Dr. Franz Reikmann, a "venerable scholar" who "had been all his life collecting his library, book by book, and he loved it as a miser loves his hoarded gold." In the denouement, two benevolent twin brothers—a pair of Mark Twain's recurrent mysterious strangers—intervene to rescue the books by inflating the bidding and then presenting both the library and the money to an astounded Reikmann.

That a newspaper clipping could stir such empathy within Clemens suggests the value he placed upon his own library. Though he certainly did not imagine himself a scholar, he nonetheless knew the thrill of procuring a long-sought-after volume. "Use with care, for it is a scarce book," he admonished on the title page of Henry H. Breen's *Modern English Literature: Its Blemishes & Defects* (London, 1857) in a note penciled in 1876. "England had to be ransacked in order to get this copy—or the bookseller speaketh falsely"[2] In 1877 he signed and dated Edward William Lane's translation of *The Thousand and One Nights* (London, 1839–41), adding, "A rare and valuable copy."[3] A flyleaf in *Memoirs of Hans Hendrik, the Arctic Traveller* (London, 1878) displays a similar inscription: "S. L. Clemens/Munich, Bavaria,/January, 1879./A very valuable book/—& unique."[4]

Clemens's peregrinations until 1870 evidently discouraged his book collecting impulses, however; only a few extant volumes appear to have been owned by him before his marriage. Among those surviving are his copies of J. L. Comstock's *Elements of Geology* (New York, 1851), signed in 1856,[5] *The New Testament* (New York, 1859), signed in a round, youthful hand,[6] James J. Jarves's *History of the Hawaiian or Sandwich Islands*, 2nd ed. (Boston, 1844), used in letters Mark Twain wrote in 1866;[7] and *The Holy Bible* (London, 1866), signed in 1867 and profusely annotated.[8] Clemens's desire for a permanent book collection housed in a special room is implicit in the letter he wrote to his future wife on 27 February 1869, in which he promised Olivia a place for them "apart from the jangling elements of the outside world, reading & studying together when the day's duties are done."[9] This dream was gratified in November 1874 when the Clemenses moved into their newly built nineteen-room house in Hartford; a large and opulent library was easily accessible on the first floor. At one side of the library a glass conservatory offered a view of muted sunlight and verdant foliage.

No doubt the pleasure Clemens was finding in his own library inspired his description of Francis Lightfoot Lee's literary life in a biographical sketch Clemens produced in July 1875: Lee "was educated. He was more than that—he was finely cultivated. He loved books; he had a good library, & no place had so great a charm for him as that. . . . Over their port & walnuts he & his friends of the gentry discussed a literature which is dead & forgotten, now."[10] Nine years later Clemens and George Washington Cable, two of the foremost American men of letters of their day, talked about literature in Clemens's library for nearly four hours one day in February 1884.[11] There in 1886 and 1887 Clemens also conducted a Robert Browning study group for Hartford women. Mary Bushnell Cheney recalled going to Clemens's Nook Farm residence to hear him read from Browning's works

at one of these meetings She was particularly impressed by the book-lined room where the gatherings were held, with its "carved black oak panelling of the walls." As she gazed about her it seemed that "the place was in itself a sort of revelation of poetic meanings," especially with the nearby "flowers and filtered sunshine of the little conservatory."[12] The elaborate Hartford house library well suited its owners, for the Clemens family venerated books. Indeed, books were the mainstay of the Nook Farm society; writing, revising, editing, publishing, reading, and reviewing were interwoven through the fabric of everyday life in that community. Like Clemens, neighbors such as Harriet Beecher Stowe and Charles Dudley Warner depended upon the publishing industry for their livelihood.

A large proportion of Clemens's library volumes were acquired between 1874 and 1877 when he and Olivia first had the income and the leisure to stock their new library shelves. Commercial stickers in Clemens's library books and extant sales receipts indicate that he bought from bookstores in Hartford, Elmira, Boston, and New York City. Brown & Gross,[13] booksellers at 77 Asylum Street in Hartford, billed him on 1 January 1881 for sixteen titles purchased during the preceding months; these included Albion W. Tourgee's *Bricks Without Straw*, Sidney Lanier's edition of *The Boy's King Arthur*,[14] Isa Craig Knox's *The Little Folks' History of England*, William Hamilton Gibson's *Pastoral Days*, Thomas Wentworth Higginson's *Young Folks' History of the United States*, August Rodney Macdonough's translation of *The Lovers of Provence, Aucassin and Nicolette*, Henriette E. (Guizot) Witt's *Monsieur Guizot in Private Life*, and several reference books.[15]

Nevertheless, throughout his professional life Mark Twain disliked retail bookstores, a prejudice likely deriving from the competition between subscription publishers, who employed canvassing agents to sell directly to customers, and the retail book trade. More than once Mark Twain was convinced that retail bookstores were surreptitiously hurting his profits as author and publisher by purchasing his books from unscrupulous agents and selling them over their counters. His disdain for the retail book trade shows through forcefully in Chapter 36 of *The Gilded Age* (1873) in which Laura Hawkins upbraids an impudent bookstore clerk who recommends only sensation novels: "What a bookseller—or perhaps his clerk—knows about literature *as* literature, in contradistinction to its character as merchandise, would hardly be of much assistance to a person—that is, to an adult, of course—in the selection of food for the mind."[16]

Confident of his own literary judgment and eager to avail himself of the privileges accorded to authors by the book trade, Clemens mainly built up his book collection by ordering from publishing houses. In the nineteenth century many American publishers also functioned as wholesalers for books issued by the other publishing firms; some publishers even went so far as to fill orders for rare and out-of-print volumes as well. Therefore, Clemens was able to request books with various imprints from a single firm. He seems to have seldom paid the full retail price, either; generally he received a special author's discount in addition to the reduced price offered by the wholesaler. Thus on 23 March 1873, Clemens simply dispatched a list of titles to an unnamed

publishing firm with the note, "Please send me per express, all these books, with bill for same." He requested an author's discount on the order.[17] Frequently he ordered from Boston and New York City firms. On 16 May 1874, for instance, Estes & Lauriat, Boston publishers and booksellers, credited Clemens for payments toward Guizot's *A Popular History of France*, then issuing in installments. The same firm billed Clemens for $50.55 on 14 July 1880 after shipping twenty-one books, including *Gulliver's Travels*, Dumas's *The Iron Mask*, Boswell's *Johnson*, Madame de Sévigné's *Letters*, Plutarch's *Lives*, and Brewer's *Phrase and Fable*.[18] In November 1877 James R. Osgood & Company of Boston billed him for nineteen titles purchased during the year, including Richard Irving Dodge's *The Plains of the Great West*, *The Chronicle of Henry of Huntingdon*, *Ingulph's Chronicle of the Abbey of Croyland*, and *Chronicles of the Crusades*.[19]

Clemens also levied heavily on the goodwill of his own publishers, ordering many volumes through their sales departments. This habit commenced with Elisha Bliss Jr.'s American Publishing Company; thereafter he routinely expected his successive publishers to attend to his library needs. "Yes, send me a collection of etiquette books," he replied casually to James R. Osgood on 7 March 1881—a period when he was working on the never-completed "Burlesque of Books on Etiquette."[20] On 22 July 1882 an employee of James R. Osgood & Company, responding to another of Clemens's requests, described and priced three editions of Thomas Carlyle's *Works* that included Carlyle's *Cromwell*. The same employee also sent "a lot of books relating to travels in the U.S. by English people in the first half of the century; twenty-five volumes in all. They include Mrs. Trollope, Basil Hall and Marryatt, &c., &c. Their average price is about a dollar per *volume*. Please return any you do not wish for."[21] During the years Clemens himself engaged in publishing, he often saddled Charles L. Webster and later Frederick J. Hall with this responsibility of book searches. In a 6 July 1884 letter, as one example, Clemens instructed Webster to send him "*personal narratives* of life & adventure out yonder on the Plains & in the Mountains."[22]

While engaged in writing *Following the Equator* at a London address, Clemens notified Chatto & Windus on 13 November 1896 that he needed a copy of Frederick G. Aflalo's *A Sketch of the Natural History of Australia* (London: Macmillan and Co., 1896).[23] Similarly, on 16 February 1902 he wrote to the general manager of Harper & Brothers, Frederick A. Duneka, to request a copy of Andrew D. White's *History of the Warfare of Science with Theology*, together with "any up-to-date books" describing "the *half-dozen great sciences*, by experts. Not *big* books, but condensations or small school-textbooks."[24] A busy Duneka could hardly have welcomed this task, but by then Clemens's habit of depending on his publishers for research and library services was thoroughly ingrained.

Clemens's antipathy toward retail bookstores did not extend to those that dealt in used books. In July 1877 Clemens entered a memorandum in Notebook 13 while in New York City: "2d hand bookstore—get full Harper Monthly for Sue [Crane], & some miscellaneous books."[25] Related entries reveal that he intended to purchase German

and French language books and a copy of *The Arabian Nights*. Two years later he jotted a similar entry ("Second-hand books") in Notebook 18 to remind himself of an errand in New York City.[26]

However, Clemens did frequent bookshops selling new retail stock wherever he traveled in Europe. If he was lonely or bored these stores provided intellectual stimulation; in one undated note he recalls a day he spent in London in the 1870s: "Nobody in town. Bought [John] Timbs—[Augustus J. C. Hare's] Walks [*in London*]—[John] Stow—Leigh Hunt, & a lot of other authorities & read about a thing, then went leisurely to see it."[27] One of these books may have been John Heneage Jesse's *London: Its Celebrated Characters and Remarkable Places* (3 vols., 1871), the flyleaf of which Clemens signed in London in 1873.[28]

Numerous volumes also entered his library collection as gifts acquired during his travels, especially on his world tour in 1895–96. In Sydney, Louis Becke gave him a copy of *By Reef and Palm*. In Dunedin, New Zealand, Malcolm Ross furnished copies of Frederick E. Maning's *Old New Zealand* (London, 1887) and other "very valuable books" (Notebook 34, TS p. 32). When Clemens left Sydney to sail for Ceylon, "H. S. Chipman gave me a great illustrated Australia," he noted in December 1895.[29] In Jeypore, "Mr. Aklom looked in, this morning, from Ajmere. . . . Brought an armful of books."[30] Meherjibhai Nosherwanji Kuka, compiler and translator of *The Wit and Humour of the Persians* (1894), presented Clemens with a copy in Bombay in 1896.[31] Indeed, Mark Twain extracted a significant portion of *Following the Equator*

(1897) from gift books that described the geography, history, and literature of the regions he visited.

Literally hundreds of other books arrived at Mark Twain's doorstep as unsolicited offerings from their authors. Many came from fledglings who hoped to attract praise from an established writer. "To Mark Twain,/The First Missourian,/from Robertus Love,/one of the latest," reads a typical inscription—this one written in 1906 on the title-page of *Poems All the Way from Pike* (1904).[32] Publishers often sent complimentary copies. John S. Phillips of McClure, Phillips & Company wrote to Clemens on 14 April 1905: "We sent you a little while ago a copy of 'The Troll Garden' by Miss Willa Sibert Cather. . . . We are venturing to call it to the attention of a few people, like yourself, of discernment and appreciation of the better sort of thing."[33] "As a rule, people don't send me books which I can thank them for," Clemens explained to Louis Pendleton on 4 August 1888, "and so I say nothing—which looks discourteous."[34] Years later, while abroad, he emphatically instructed his business agent, Frank G. Whitmore: "I seldom want the books that are sent me by strangers."[35] Yet despite such comments—and in spite of his giving away many of these presentation copies—Clemens's library contained a vast number of books inscribed by their authors. Many—like William Dean Howells's *A Chance Acquaintance* (inscribed "To S. L. Clemens with ever so much friendship"); George Washington Cable's *Old Creole Days, The Grandissimes*, and *Madame Delphine*; Joel Chandler Harris's *Free Joe and Other Georgian Sketches*; Thomas Bailey Aldrich's *Cloth of Gold*; Irving Bacheller's *Silas*

Strong, Emperor of the Woods—were welcome presents from Clemens's personal friends. Other volumes earned a place on Clemens's bookshelves after a perusal: P. T. Barnum's *Struggles and Triumphs* and *Dollars and Sense*, Hubert Howe Bancroft's *The Native Races of the Pacific States*, and Sir John Adams's *Herbartian Psychology*. Some books—like James Mark Baldwin's *The Story of the Mind* (1899) and a work by the American humorist Henry Clay Lukens ("Erratic Enrique"), *Jets and Flashes* (1883)—interested Clemens initially, but later were among the many hundreds of volumes he donated to the Mark Twain Library at Redding beginning in 1908.

Clemens's library shelves contained relatively few volumes considered "old" or "rare" in his day. As a matter of fact he scoffed at people who "collect rare books, at war prices, which they don't read, and which they wouldn't value if a page were lacking."[36] Although Clemens's criteria for acquisition were practical, he did occasionally buy such rarities as the Abbotsford Edition of Sir Walter Scott's works that he combed Edinburgh for ten days to find in 1873, and an 1860 reprint of Audubon's folio *Birds of America* for which he paid $150.[37] Even the Audubon was used, however; George Washington Cable reported from Hartford on 13 February 1884 about a day he passed with Clemens in Hartford: "Part of the time . . . was spent in consulting Audubon to identify a strange & beautiful bird that we had seen at breakfast time from the window of the library."[38] Books that would now be valuable, such as the travel volumes by Trollope, Combe, Fearon, Hall, and others that Clemens obtained in 1882 for research on English visitors to America, were then only fifty or sixty years old and did not have the "rare" status they possess today; Clemens marked passages and wrote in their margins as casually as if they were just off the press. He allowed himself one extravagance in selecting his library books, however: a sizable portion of his collection consisted of copiously illustrated works, particularly Gustave Doré's editions of such literary classics as *The Rime of the Ancient Mariner*.

To avoid losing books from his own library (and as though to leave behind a permanent record of his collection), Clemens tried to see to it that his own name or that of a family member appeared in volumes belonging to his household. Somewhat

A Gustave Doré engraving in The Rime of the Ancient Mariner

surprisingly—considering his preference for custom-made notebooks and his experimentation with printing methods and products—Clemens made no use of bookplates, at least in the volumes known to survive from his library. (Reports of bookplates turn out to be misinterpretations of sale labels from the auctions of 1911 and 1951, pasted on the front endpapers of volumes to authenticate their provenance.) Instead, Clemens preferred to sign the books he acquired, often providing the location, date, and donor. His inscription in Moritz Busch's *Bismarck in the Franco-German War* specifies: "SL. Clemens/ Dec. Xmas, 1879./From S. E. Moffett." That in Richard Henry Dana's *To Cuba and Back* is likewise typical: "Saml. L. Clemens/Hartford 1876." In 1876 he began sometimes signing his initials instead of the abbreviated form of Samuel Langhorne ("Saml. L.") that he had previously employed; by 1877, "S. L. Clemens" had become the customary form of his signature in books. "S. L. Clemens./1895./ From J. Henry Harper," he wrote routinely in the second volume of *Memoirs of Barras, Member of the Directorate*. In the final decade of his life he tended to omit the first period, linking the first two initials together as in the "SL. Clemens/1906" inscription which appears in Alleyne Ireland's *The Far Eastern Tropics*, or else merely signing his last name, like the "Clemens/1902" form he scrawled carelessly in Marshall M. Kirkman's *The Romance of Gilbert Holmes: An Historical Novel.*

Clemens frequently inscribed the names of his wife or children in their books; evidently he was more concerned with establishing ownership than the rest of his family, though Olivia did her share of designating the volumes. He

commenced this habit within a few years of his marriage: a copy of Alan Grant's *Love in Letters, Illustrated in the Correspondence of Eminent Persons* contains an inscription ("Livy Clemens/1872") in Clemens's hand. Occasionally he expanded his inscription, as he did in the copy of *The Holy Bible* (London, 1866) he took with him on the *Quaker City* excursion: "Saml. Clemens./Constantinople,/Sept. 2, 1867. Please return this book to stateroom No. 10, in case you happen to borrow it," he wrote somewhat accusingly on the flyleaf opposite the title page.[39] Clemens's signatures appear most frequently on the front free endpapers or (especially after 1900) on the front pastedown endpapers. Occasionally he signed one of the flyleaves, the half-title page, or the verso of a frontispiece portrait leaf. Although exceptions occurred, he characteristically used pencils to sign his acquisitions during the 1870s and earlier; thereafter he generally signed with ink—violet, blue, brown (quite probably a shade of oxidized black ink), or black. He increasingly employed black ink in the post-1900 period. Clemens virtually never signed his pseudonym in books belonging to his personal library, reserving "Mark Twain" for autographing the books he wrote himself. These minor bibliographical facts become crucial in detecting forgeries. Libraries and private collections in the United States and Canada already possess dozens of spurious association copies.

Upon departing with his family for Europe, Clemens mentioned to an unidentified correspondent, possibly Charles Dudley Warner, that by 20 March 1878 his family's books and furniture had been placed in a storage warehouse "for two or three years."[40] During their years abroad the Clemenses purchased numerous foreign language books—especially German novels. Olivia Clemens's account ledger for their European tour of 1878 and 1879[41] records numerous expenditures in bookstores; buying books for themselves and their relatives was one of their chief pastimes on the Continent. Clemens wasn't always pleased with the books he purchased. Though he had complained to Thomas Bailey Aldrich on 24 March 1874 about the "wretched paper & vile engravings" used in American subscription volumes,[42] in Europe he learned to value the bulky American subscription tomes with leather bindings and thick paper. He was disgusted to discover that "German books fall to pieces when you open them."[43] Nevertheless he obtained copies of works by Gottfried Keller, Johanna Kinkel, Elisabeth Bürstenbinder, Adelbert von Chamisso, Paul von Heyse, Gotthold Ephraim Lessing, and other writers. Upon his return to Hartford, Clemens promptly had the German-language volumes (now in the Mark Twain Papers at Berkeley) rebound in uniform three-quarters morocco covers by Case, Lockwood & Brainard, a local bookbindery; he saw to it that Yankee craftsmanship repaired the shoddy products of the German book industry.

Clemens derived profound enjoyment from his library room during the 1880s, and he was solicitous about its condition. On 25 October 1884 he reminded himself to "fix damp place in library shelves."[44] As his daughters matured he and Olivia encouraged them to choose and read books from the library. He and his wife had read to the girls almost daily when they were children, and now they hoped that Susy, Clara, and Jean would take as much

pleasure in the serenity of the library room as their parents did. On 16 July 1889 Clemens wrote to Susy: "For forty years Macaulay's England has been a fascinator of mine, from the stately opening sentence to the massacre at Glencoe. I am glad you are reading it. And I hope it is aloud, to Mamma."[45]

Unfortunately, however, Clemens's personal library shared the vicissitudes of his financial fortunes. He never was compelled to auction off its contents like the hapless Franz Reikmann of A *Tramp Abroad* (though he may have feared it could come to that), but as his financial stability melted away in the mid-nineties he lost access to his books. Clemens and his family left their Hartford home in the summer of 1891 to begin searching for economic relief and (later) climates and treatments that would benefit the health of Olivia and Jean. They initially hoped to devise a style of living that might ease their yearly expenses. As things turned out, they never returned to live in the Hartford house. Clemens's books were evidently still in Hartford when he began his round-the-world lecture tour in 1895. Quite likely Clemens thought about arranging for some of his books to rejoin him in London at the conclusion of his tour in 1896; there he attempted to establish a quasi-permanent home. But he wrote to T. S. Frisbie from Vienna on 25 October 1897: "Never mind the bookcase—I haven't any books now anymore."[46] At the turn of the century he took up residence in New York City, and he had definitely regained physical possession of his books by 1901 when he and his family settled into a rented mansion in Riverdale-on-the-Hudson, New York.

Olivia's health began to deteriorate,

however, and when her doctors recommended that the family relocate to Italy in 1903, Clemens, no doubt realizing that he could never again recreate the atmosphere of the library room in the Hartford house, gave up his efforts to maintain the collection intact. On 25 July 1903 he mentioned to Howells that he had contributed a portion of his library to a local institution: "All our books are packed & gone into storage for Italy. . . . We sent a couple of bushels to the little Riverdale library."[47] The whereabouts of this donation is not now known.

He soon longed for his own library books. The book collection he found in the Villa di Quarto near Florence, which he rented from the Countess Massiglia, offended his sense of nomenclature. One day in January 1904 he set aside a portion of his Autobiographical Dictation to berate the scarcity of reading matter in the room the Countess grandly designated as her "library." Its sole qualification for the name, he sneered, was a lonely glass-fronted bookcase containing four shelves of miscellaneous volumes, three-quarters of which were bound volumes of *Blackwood's Edinburgh Magazine* and books about Christian Science and spiritualism.[48]

When his sister-in-law Mollie Clemens died in 1904 (Orion had died in 1897), Clemens specifically reserved for himself only two books from her estate—his father's copy of *Nicholson's Encyclopedia* and his mother's favorite Bible—and then requested other books only if Mollie's relatives in Keokuk did not want them. To Susan Crane he wrote from Florence on 15 February 1904: "I have selected from Orion's library 175 or 200 books & requested that they be shipped to

you. . . . You can put the boxes in my study or in the barn."[49] Thus Clemens's library in the end contained a number of books from his brother's library, possibly ones he had read or glanced through previously in Orion's home.

After Olivia Clemens died on 5 June 1904, Clemens returned to America. Isabel V. Lyon, the secretary who had joined his household staff in 1902, took on the duties of unofficial librarian for her employer—stocking his bookshelves, suggesting titles for his reading and acquisition, selecting promising works from among the new books sent to him. It was Lyon who took Richard Le Gallienne's *Painted Shadows* (1904) to Clemens's bedroom on 6 January 1905 and recorded his comment that this was an "ever so charming" book by "an able cuss who writes deliciously."[50] She assumed these responsibilities as a matter of course because she was also Clemens's rapt audience when he read aloud passages from his day's reading. Some idea of how carefully she performed her chores in this line can be gained from her private journal entries following Clemens's move into 21 Fifth Avenue in New York City. On Monday, 2 January 1905, she remarked: "Much of today has been spent in trying to find places for the books that are scattered—piled—on the library floor."[51] Another entry made on the next Wednesday noted that "I have spent many hours working among the books collected from many quarters of the world." Two years later, on 13 July 1907, she recorded that she occasionally busied herself in "dusting books in the Library."[52]

Shortly before Clemens moved into Stormfield, his Italianate villa-style mansion near Redding, Connecticut, he parted with a significant portion of his library. The "four or five hundred old books" he donated to the Mark Twain Library at Redding in June 1908 included numerous volumes signed and annotated by Clemens, his wife, and his children. Possibly he wished to unburden himself of these reminders of Olivia and Susy and their Hartford home. Isabel Lyon recorded the fact that she began unpacking Clemens's books at Stormfield on 29 August 1908.[53] The volumes that remained for her to place on the shelves in his library there (minus the enormous number that Clemens or Jean later removed for additional donations to the community library) were essentially the remnants that composed Clemens's private library at the time of his death in 1910.[54]

NOTES

1. *Mark Twain's Notebooks & Journals, Volume II*, ed. Frederick Anderson, Lin Salamo, and Bernard L. Stein (Berkeley: University of California Press, 1975), 2: 276–77. Hereafter referred to as *N&J*.

2. Volume in the Mark Twain Papers, Bancroft Library, University of California, Berkeley—hereafter this collection is cited as "MTP."

3. "Books from the Library of Mark Twain . . . Purchased at the Sale of the Library of His Daughter Clara Clemens Samossoud," Zeitlin & Ver Brugge, Booksellers, List No. 132 (May 1951), Los Angeles, California, item #29.

4. Mark Twain Library, Redding, Connecticut.

5. Beinecke Library, Yale University.

6. Small Special Collections Library, University of Virginia, Charlottesville.

7. MTP.

8. Harry Ransom Center, University of Texas at Austin.

9. *Mark Twain's Letters, Volume 3, 1869*, ed. Victor Fischer and Michael B. Frank (Berkeley: University of California, 1992), p. 117.

10. Historical Society of Pennsylvania.

11. *Mark Twain-Howells Letters*, ed. Henry Nash Smith and William M. Gibson (Cambridge: Harvard University Press, 1960), p. 471—hereafter referred to as *MTHL*.

12. "Mark Twain as a Reader," *Harper's Weekly* 55.2820 (7 January 1911): 6.

13. Israel Witkower became proprietor of the successor to this firm in the second quarter of the twentieth century. This fact explains why Hellmut Lehmann-Haupt—The *Book in America: A History of the Making and Selling of Books in the United States*, 2nd ed. (New York: R. R. Bowker, 1952), pp. 243–44—reports that Clemens was one of the "regular customers" of Israel Witkower's bookstore in Hartford.

14. *The Boy's King Arthur; Being Sir Thomas Malory's History of King Arthur and the Knights of the Round Table*, ed. Sidney Lanier (New York: Scribner's, 1880). Clemens's introduction to Malory's heroes of the Round Table seemingly took place with this children's book, a previously overlooked source for *A Connecticut Yankee* (1889). See "'The Master Hand of Old Malory': Mark Twain's Acquaintance with *Le Morte D'Arthur*," *English Language Notes* 16.1 (September 1978): 32–40. (A revised version of this essay appears as a chapter in the present volume.)

15. Receipt in MTP.

16. Bryant Morey French—Mark *Twain and the Gilded Age* (Dallas: Southern Methodist University Press, 1965), p. 62—lists Chapter 36 among those written by Mark Twain without Charles Dudley Warner's collaboration.

17. Historical Society of Pennsylvania.

18. Receipts in MTP.

19. Receipt in Scrapbook #10, p. 69, MTP.

20. *MTHL*, pp. 360 n. 2, 362.

21. W. Rowlands to Clemens, ALS in MTP.

22. *Mark Twain, Business Man*, ed. Samuel Charles Webster (Boston: Little Brown, 1946), p. 265.

23. ALS in Berg Collection, New York Public Library.

24. TS in MTP.

25. *N&J* 2: 38.

26. *N&J* 2: 342.

27. MTP, DV15.

28. Huntington Library, San Marino, California.

29. Notebook 36, TS p. 10.

30. Notebook 36, TS p. 55.

31. MTP.

32. Mark Twain Library, Redding, Connecticut.

33. TLS in MTP.

34. *Mark Twain's Letters*, ed. Albert Bigelow Paine

(New York: Harper, 1917), p. 497—subsequently cited as *MTL*.

35 1 October 1903, TS in MTP.

36 Autobiographical Dictation, 12 February 1908; *Autobiography of Mark Twain, Volume 3*, ed. Benjamin Griffin and Harriet Elinor Smith (Berkeley, California: University of California Press, 2015), 3: 202.

37 Clemens to Mrs. Jervis Langdon, 2 August 1873, ALS, Mark Twain House and Museum, Hartford, Connecticut. The receipt for the Audubon volumes (dated 25 August 1880) is in MTP.

38 Quoted in Arlin Turner, *Mark Twain and George W. Cable: The Record of a Literary Friendship* (East Lansing: Michigan State University Press, 1960), p. 32.

39 Harry Ransom Center, University of Texas at Austin.

40 Buffalo and Erie County Public Library, Buffalo, New York.

41 MTP.

42 *Mark Twain's Letters, Volume 6, 1874–1875*, ed. Michael B. Frank and Harriet Elinor Smith (Berkeley: University of California, 2002), 6: 89—hereafter cited as *MTLet*.

43 *N&J* 2: 292.

44 Notebook 23, *N&J* 3: 75.

45 TS in MTP. Clemens was insistent about the advantages of interpreting literature orally; see "'It is Unsatisfactory to Read to One's Self': Mark Twain's Informal Readings," *Quarterly Journal of Speech* 62.1 (February 1976): 22–30. (A revised version of this essay appears as a chapter in the present volume.)

46 ALS, Lehigh University.

47 *MTHL*, p. 773.

48 *Autobiography of Mark Twain. Volume 1*, ed. Harriet Elinor Smith (Berkeley: University of California Press, 2010), 1: 235.

49 MTP.

50 Isabel Lyon's Journal, TS pp. 36, 77, MTP; Isabel Lyon to Mrs. Franklin Whitmore, 8 January 1905, ALS, Mark Twain House and Museum.

51 MTP, TS p. 34.

52 MTP, TS p. 262.

53 IVL Journal, TS p. 329, MTP.

54 "I describe their subsequent fate in "The Dispersal of Samuel L. Clemens's Library Books," *Resources for American Literary Study* 5.2 (Autumn 1975): 147–165. (A revised version of this essay appears as a chapter in the present volume.)

An earlier version of this chapter appeared in Studies in American Humor *2.3 (January 1976): 171–182.*

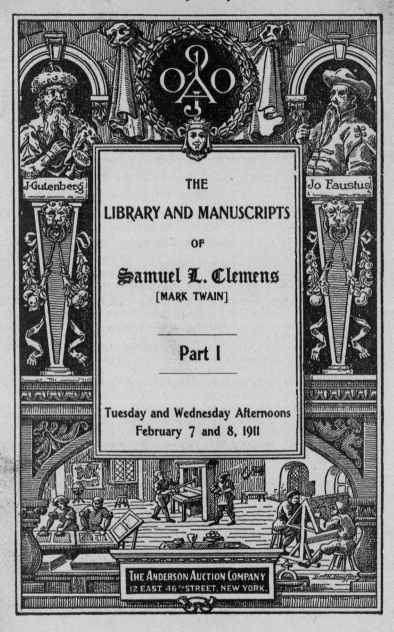

No. 892—1911

THE
LIBRARY AND MANUSCRIPTS
OF
𝔖𝔞𝔪𝔲𝔢𝔩 𝔏. ℭ𝔩𝔢𝔪𝔢𝔫𝔰
[MARK TWAIN]

Part I

Tuesday and Wednesday Afternoons
February 7 and 8, 1911

THE ANDERSON AUCTION COMPANY
12 EAST 46TH STREET, NEW YORK.

J·Gutenberg   Jo Faustus

1911 auction catalog, New York City

7

The Dispersal of
Samuel L. Clemens's Library Books

When Samuel L. Clemens died in 1910 his personal library seemingly still contained at least several thousand books. He had donated an unknown number ("a couple of bushels") to a lending library at Riverdale-on-the-Hudson, New York, in 1903[1] and had granted the newly formed Mark Twain Library in Redding, Connecticut, "four or five hundred old books" in 1908. (He and his daughter Clara subsequently sent several thousand more volumes from his Redding residence to that community library.) Inevitably he had lost some books in transit during his global travels. On September 24, 1892, he appealed from Florence to William Walter Phelps, U. S. minister to Germany, for assistance in locating a "big rough box filled with valuable books" that had been misdirected by a storage firm when the Clemens family left Berlin.[2] The crate was still lost on October 14, according to Clemens's letter to his daughter Clara,[3] and there is no sign that it was ever recovered.

A significant number of volumes also left his possession as presents to friends. Surely a few were accidentally misplaced in railway cars, ships, and hotel rooms during his frequent journeys. On January 6, 1870, Clemens good-naturedly reported to Olivia Langdon about losing a book during a rail journey to New York City: "I read 3 pages of Robinson Crusoe, lost & found the book some twelve or fifteen times, & finally lost it for good a couple of hours ago."[4]

Some books he presumably discarded after cannibalizing their pages for lengthy quotations in his published works. But other strangely absent books are less easy to account for. The fate of many volumes he is known to have owned and alluded to—*Tom Jones, Roderick Random, Gulliver's Travels*, Benvenuto Cellini's *Autobiography*, Aldrich's *The Story of a Bad Boy*, and many others—is a mystery. Conceivably they may have been removed from his library soon after he died by someone who appreciated their value, but the likelihood of this possibility decreases as each year passes without their coming to the surface. Yet despite this considerable attrition, a great many volumes passed into the possession of Clara Clemens Gabrilowitsch and the Mark Twain Estate in 1910.

THE 1911 AUCTION, NEW YORK CITY

For reasons that now seem shortsighted, an auction was held within a year to dispose of a substantial part of the remaining library. The Anderson Auction Company of New York City listed the collection in Catalogue No. 892, "The Library and Manuscripts of Samuel L. Clemens (Mark Twain)," and sold the 483 books on Tuesday and Wednesday, February 7 and 8, 1911, at their offices at 12 East 46th Street. Albert Bigelow Paine, who had begun to function as Clemens's literary executor, assisted by selecting minor manuscript and holograph fragments for inclusion in the volumes to enhance their value and by signing sales labels that were affixed to the front endpapers to authenticate the books' provenance. The auction also disposed of decorative furnishings from Clemens's Stormfield estate in Redding, including vases and a pair of Japanese bronze cranes. Not all of the books sold during those two days were listed in the seventy-four-page catalog issued by the Anderson Auction Company, since others would turn up over the years with sale labels signed by Paine that do not appear to have been forged. The timing of this sale seems ill-advised in retrospect, even if one accepts the notion that an author's book collection ought to be auctioned off piecemeal to anonymous buyers instead of being preserved intact as a monument to this thought and literature. Successful bids were ludicrously low for a writer of Clemens's stature, even in 1911; many volumes brought less than a dollar apiece, and prices seldom went above

$5.50—even for annotated copies. Books knocked down at only $1.25,[5] for example, included a copy of Balzac's *Une Fille d'Eve*, signed by Clemens; Emerson's *Essays*, signed and marked; an annotated copy of Basil Hall's *Travels in North America* (1829); and Charles Ball's *Slavery in the United States* (1837), an influential source for *A Connecticut Yankee*. Within a short time after the auction one of the most active bidders, the Lexington Book Shop of New York City, prepared a special catalog (No. 19) to resell the twenty-nine books they had purchased. Their prices in 1912 were exactly twice the sums they had paid the previous year.

Most of the auction items have never subsequently reappeared. One supposes that in passing from generation to generation their provenance became obscure, and that many—in spite of those signatures by "S. L. Clemens" and Paine's authenticating labels—were discarded or somehow lost. A few turn up periodically in rare booksellers' catalogs, but the disappearance of the majority is cause for regret, especially since the Anderson Auction Catalogue entries fall far short of modern bibliographic standards for book descriptions. Scores of books cannot now be identified by their author or edition from these sometimes paltry notes.

THE MARK TWAIN LIBRARY, REDDING, CONNECTICUT

Shortly before he moved into his Italianate villa-style mansion near Redding, Connecticut—"Stormfield"—Clemens parted with a significant portion of his library. He was to take possession of the Redding house on June 18, 1908; on June 5, 1908, he started to write to Jean about his generosity toward a neighborhood library near his new residence, but changed his mind and canceled the information, presumably fearing Jean might be alarmed that he and his secretary Isabel V. Lyon had designated the books too hurriedly during the packing-and-moving process at 21 Fifth Avenue. He wrote: "We have started a village library up yonder, & the people have named it for me. <We have dug four or five hundred old books out of our over-burdened shelves & inflicted them upon that library>."[6] Evidently Jean deciphered the cancellation or guessed its import, for she apparently wrote from where she was staying in Gloucester, Massachusetts, to protest against the decision. On June 14, 1908, Clemens reassured her: "Do not trouble about the books I am giving to the village library. There's none that you would wish to with-hold."[7] Albert Bigelow Paine dismissed Clemens's contribution in a similar manner in *Mark Twain: A Biography*:[8] "He had been for years flooded with books by authors and publishers, and there was a heavy surplus at his home in the city. When these began to arrive he had a large number of volumes set aside as the nucleus of a public library. . . . And so the Mark Twain Library of Redding was duly established."[9]

In point of fact the books Clemens donated to the Mark Twain Library at Redding included numerous volumes with family associations, many signed and annotated by either Clemens or his wife and children. The Mark Twain Library still contains Clemens's annotated copies of Robert Browning's *Poetic and Dramatic Works* (1887), T. W. Doane's *Bible Myths* (1882), Harriet Martineau's *Society in America* (1837), Parkman's *Montcalm*

and Wolfe (1885), Emmeline Stuart Wortley's *Travels in the United States* (1851), Thackeray's *Lectures* (1868), and James Baldwin's *The Story of the Mind* (1899). The collection also includes Olivia Clemens's copies of Charles Kingsley's *The Water-Babies* (1870), Joaquin Miller's *Songs of the Sierras* (1871), Lubke's *Outlines of the History of Art* (1881), Robert Browning's *Ferishtah's Fancies* (1887), and a copy of La Motte-Fouqué's *Undine* (1879) presented by Olivia to her daughter Susy. Clemens additionally contributed Susy's copies of *Young Folk's History of England* (1878) by Charlotte M. Yonge, Alvan Bond's *Young Folk's Illustrated Bible* (1878), and George Craik's *Manual of English Literature* (1888); Jean's copies of Margaret Farrington's *Tales of King Arthur* (1888) and Charles Kingsley's *Madame How* (1888); and Clara's copies of Louis Nohl's *Life of Beethoven* (1888) and W. Clark Russell's *Representative Actors* (1895). Possibly he wished to unburden himself of these reminders of Olivia and Susy and their Hartford home, or perhaps he simply felt that no one still in his family would be interested in these books. Jean herself may have become an advocate of the project after she moved into Stormfield in April 1909. In Katy Leary's later account of the founding of the library at Redding, she gave much of the credit to Jean, who (according to Katy's often unreliable narrative) sold her own small plot of farmland and contributed the proceeds to the Mark Twain Library. "She was always chasin' around after books for it. You know, she almost stripped the library at home to get books to put into the new one," recalled the Clemenses' housekeeper.[10]

Several researchers have studied the

Clemens books in the Mark Twain Library. In 1939, Coley B. Taylor edited a monograph on the marginal comments he found in Clemens's copy of William Makepeace Thackeray's *Lectures on English Humorists*.[11] An article by Edgar H. Hemminghaus listed the German-language volumes that were in the Mark Twain Library in 1945.[12] Albert E. Stone Jr. compiled a card catalog of 299 books in the Redding library in 1955 that he believed had once belonged to Clemens.[13] The problem of identifying these volumes is complicated. For the first fifty years of its existence the library treated the books donated by Clemens precisely like those given by other Redding residents; they were assigned call numbers and charge cards, imprinted with a large oval stamp reading "THE MARK TWAIN LIBRARY, REDDING, CONN." in purple ink on the endpapers and on random pages, and shelved for the use of patrons. Serious damage resulted to the most-often circulated books from this ordinary library usage. A large percentage of the volumes now lack the flyleaves inscribed by Clemens or members of his family. It is possible that Clemens, his secretary Isabel Lyon, or his daughter Clara may have removed a few flyleaves containing signatures or intimate family inscriptions when they selected the volumes for consignment to the lending library; two loose flyleaves from books inscribed by Olivia are in the Mark Twain Papers, evidently retained by her husband as mementoes. Yet in view of Clemens's normal respect for books as manufactured artifacts, as products of craftsmanship in papermaking, printing, and bookbinding, any systematic defacement does not seem likely to have been authorized

or perpetrated by him. One suspects that the signatures and inscriptions presented tempting prizes for souvenir-hunters and autograph collectors in the 1940s, 1950s, and 1960s. Clemens's books thus mutilated are usually indistinguishable from other volumes except for his marginalia (if any were present) and the evidence of absent flyleaves, whose frayed stubs often offer the most tangible indications of Clemens's former ownership.

Today the Mark Twain Library at Redding possesses approximately 240 volumes that can be identified as books Clemens and his daughter donated. The loss of the others is a fascinating footnote to the history of library management. In 1952 a librarian elected to solve a shortage of shelf-space by discarding volumes that had not been withdrawn by patrons within recent years. (She had recently attended a librarians' conference that advocated this practice of culling less-popular titles.) A book-dealer was offered these unwanted books if he would haul them away and make a small cash donation. The dealer soon recognized the actual value of the numerous Samuel L. Clemens association copies that were intermixed with miscellaneous books in the "truckload" of volumes he hauled away from the rural library for twenty dollars. Fortunately he passed along the identifiable Clemens items to a rare book expert; sixty-three of these books were shortly advertised in "A Mark Twain Catalogue" (1952), issued by Howard S. Mott, a New York City antiquarian bookdealer. Mott was not the bookman who made the almost unbelievable purchase at Redding, but he arranged the sale of those he listed in his catalog and many others as well. Today volumes that bear prominent

"MARK TWAIN LIBRARY" stamps on their pages are scattered throughout rare book collections around the nation. One wonders, though, how many hundreds of unsigned volumes, with or without marginalia, were not recognized as association copies and were cast adrift in this 1952 transaction.

A decade later the Mark Twain Library at Redding fortunately recognized the importance of Clemens's gift. Another librarian set about the task of retrieving Twain's volumes from the circulating collection. Those that have been recovered are now assembled in special bookcases in an air-conditioned facility. Students of Mark Twain may consult his marginalia under supervision. Using Alan Gribben's *Mark Twain's Library: A Reconstruction* as a guide, the New York *Times* published a list of the entire Redding collection in 2010.[14] Although the books would now sell for many thousands, the board of directors is determined to preserve the remaining volumes as permanent links with the writer who founded and lent his name to the library. Twain's gift to establish a community library has had a lasting effect. To access the activities at the Mark Twain Library, visit their website: www.marktwainlibrary.org.

THE 1951 HOLLYWOOD SALE, CALIFORNIA

Strange as the thoughtless discarding of so many association copies seems, a more bizarre event involving another portion of Clemens's library occurred across the continent at approximately the same time. In the spring of 1951, Clara Clemens Samossoud decided to sell her home at 2005 North La Brea Terrace in Hollywood, and along with it—at the same

auction—hundreds of the volumes that had remained in her possession after the first sale in 1911. These included a few books listed but not sold at the original sale, presumably because the bids were insufficient. From this collection she had already sold dozens of volumes privately in the 1940s through Maxwell Hunley's bookstore in Beverly Hills.

Of all the indignities that Clemens's library incurred following his death, the 1951 sale is unquestionably the most striking. Instead of entrusting the book auction to one of the reputable and experienced bookdealers in the Los Angeles area, Clara opted for the same auctioneers she retained to dispose of her home and its furnishings—presumably hoping thereby to hasten the proceedings. The two-page catalog that resulted is surely one of the more curious documents ever associated with the dispersal of a major author's personal library. Titled "Mark Twain Library Auction," it was apparently compiled by the auction manager, E. F. Whitman, and the auctioneer, Frank O'Connor, whose names appear at the top of the sheet. The catalog simply states that the auction would take place on April 10, 1951 and supplies the address of Mrs. Samossoud's residence. The additional information is minimal. Those who inventoried the book collection made no effort to determine the names of authors, places of publication, publishers, or dates; frequently the titles themselves are rendered in such an abbreviated or confusing form that identifications of the books are now impossible. Volumes were merely listed by numbers and shortened versions of the title or subtitle. With this perfunctory preparation—forty years after another portion of

Clemens's library had hurriedly gone under the gavel—the majority of the surviving books also went up for bids in a city that Clemens had never seen.

The unprecedented auction was long a favorite topic of conversation among bookdealers in Southern California. Its suddenness and Clara's desire for privacy in her home precluded the customary exhibition that normally precedes such an event. In fact, many dealers and book collectors across the nation learned about the sale only after it had already taken place. Those who noticed the newspaper advertisements placed by the auctioneering firm found it difficult to be present on such short notice. Representatives from academic institutions and research libraries were notably absent. The Mark Twain Papers at Berkeley, which might have been one of the most interested participants in the proceedings, was temporarily closed. Its editor, Dixon Wecter, had died unexpectedly on June 24, 1950, and his successor had not yet been appointed. Considering these circumstances—the haste of arrangements, the preparation of a catalog by people whose experience was furniture auctioneering, the lack of national advertising and notification of potential buyers—it hardly seems surprising that the prices brought by the books were again amazingly low. Clemens's heavily annotated copy of William Edward Hartpole Lecky's *History of European Morals* was sold for $50; his copy of Francis Parkman's *Jesuits of North America*, filled with marginalia, went for $35. Only one of his books—a copy of Bret Harte's *The Luck of Roaring Camp, and Other Sketches*, rich with caustic notes throughout—brought $200;

few of the others earned sums above $100 (Andrew D. White's *History of the Warfare of Science with Theology* did so); the average price paid was around $20.[15] The Associated Press estimated that "3,000 volumes" were sold, though the auctioneer's list contains nowhere near that figure. Numerous books have turned up in the intervening years that bear labels identifying them as originating from the 1951 auction and yet they were not listed among the sale items. Others have surfaced that lack this 1951 label and yet have credible price markings which tie them to the infamous auction. (The small, simple label, by the way, was quite possibly pasted in the volumes by Jake Zeitlin or another Southern California bookseller who attended the sale and made numerous purchases; it seems unlikely that the auctioneer firm had either the time or inclination to think of this kind of detail.)

Owing to the peculiar arrangements for the auction, a large number of volumes were purchased by amateur book collectors who resided in the Los Angeles area. As a consequence, certain households in that vicinity still contain volumes from Clemens's library. These books are not always identifiable to those unfamiliar with Samuel L. Clemens's name and signature, for although certification labels (possibly inserted by one or more of the book dealers who resold them) authenticated many books sold at the auction, a significant percentage never received these labels. Books in this condition can be passed from generation to generation within families until their association value becomes obscured.

Such a situation poses insoluble obstacles for the scholar who might wish to examine these volumes, but it can offer tangible rewards for alert bookstore browsers in Southern California. In May 1972, Mrs. Louise Halley of Santa Barbara passed an hour one morning in a secondhand "junk" store near her home and casually leafed through the miscellaneous books displayed in a battered bookcase at the front of the store. She was astonished to run across a copy of H. A. Taine's *Notes on England* that was signed by both Samuel L. Clemens and Olivia L. Clemens on consecutive flyleaves. The volume seemed well worth its marked price—fifty cents—so she promptly purchased it from the nodding store owner. Taine's *Notes* had sold for $13 at the Hollywood auction in 1951; the Mark Twain Papers in Berkeley purchased this copy from Mrs. Halley for considerably more than that amount. No doubt the Clemenses' books will continue to appear in used bookstores and secondhand charity outlets in the Los Angeles area.

Not all of the bidders at the 1951 sale were amateur collectors or curious spectators, of course. Maxwell Hunley of Beverly Hills was perhaps the only antiquarian bookdealer permitted by Mrs. Samossoud to inspect the sale items before the auction commenced. He used this advance information to bid knowledgeably on more than a hundred items, and he was generally successful. In June 1958 he issued a catalog offering many of these volumes for sale, "Mark Twain: A Collection of First Editions, Association Copies, Biographies and Books from His Library." Among Hunley's competitors at the sale was the well-known Los Angeles bookdealer, Jake Zeitlin. The firm of Zeitlin & Ver Brugge, Booksellers, issued List No. 132, "Books from the Library

of Mark Twain . . . Purchased at the Sale of the Library of His Daughter," in May 1951, only a month after the auction. The catalog listed forty-six volumes.

St. John's Seminary, Camarillo, California

Maxwell Hunley turned over many books he bought at the auction (those which he did not list in his 1958 catalog) to Mrs. Estelle Doheny, for whom he essentially acted as an agent at the sale. Mrs. Doheny donated them to the Edward Laurence Doheny Memorial Library at St. John's Seminary in Camarillo, California. In the Estelle Doheny Collection such books as William Still's *The Underground Railroad* and the *Memoirs of Wilhelmine, Margravine of Baireuth* joined other books purchased by Mrs. Doheny in 1940 from Clara Clemens Samossoud through Maxwell Hunley. This collection of sixty books from Clemens's library was eventually sold by St. John's Seminary at auctions conducted by Christie's in 1988 and 1989.

Mark Twain Papers, Bancroft Library, U. of California, Berkeley

More than a hundred books that had been kept as part of the Mark Twain Estate were spared from Mrs. Samossoud's precipitous auction in Hollywood. These became the nucleus of a portion of Clemens's library reassembled in the Mark Twain Papers, the extensive collection of manuscripts, letters, notebooks, and library volumes that she bequeathed to the University of California at Berkeley in 1965. To that core of association volumes were later added eight volumes purchased by the University of California at Los Angeles from the 1951 auction. The Special Collections librarian at UCLA, Wilbur J. Smith, believed that these books should properly join the large holdings of Mark Twain materials already established in Berkeley. Three successive editors of the Mark Twain Papers, Henry Nash Smith, Frederick Anderson, and Robert H. Hirst added additional volumes by bidding when they appeared on the rare book market; others have been given to the collection by various donors. The Mark Twain Papers now possesses more than 150 volumes that once belonged to Clemens's library. These include four annotated volumes of Bret Harte's stories; a copy of Cotton Mather's *Wonders of the Invisible World*, with profuse marginalia; and Clemens's three-volume set of Saint-Simon's *Memoirs*, heavily marked and noted. Robert H. Hirst, who became the editor of the Mark Twain Papers in 1980, has also overseen the publication of Mark Twain's works by the Mark Twain Project. The website for the Mark Twain Project, www.marktwainproject.org, accesses the possessions of the Mark Twain Papers.

THE MARK TWAIN HOUSE AND MUSEUM, HARTFORD, CONNECTICUT

By 1974, a "facsimile" library containing duplicate copies of books Clemens owned in his former house in Hartford, Connecticut, was assembled after the house had been restored and opened for public tours. With great care the Mark Twain House and Museum (formerly the Mark Twain Memorial) recreated Clemens's library with fidelity to its one-time appearance and contents. Albert E. Stone Jr., under the direction of Professor

Norman Holmes Pearson of Yale, assisted by compiling a tentative catalog of the library as it might have existed in 1892 (the year in which Clemenses permanently left their Hartford house). Hundreds of volumes were acquired for this project and arranged on the bookshelves of Clemens's library room. Although not primarily intended for use by scholars (mainly they are meant to restore the room to its original appearance for the benefit of touring visitors), these books and a catalog may be consulted upon request. Of equal importance, the Mark Twain House and Museum possesses more than three hundred volumes actually owned and, in many cases, annotated by Clemens or his family members. The results of a massive purchase at a 1997 auction as well as gifts from benefactors, these books are not normally on display to the public but are available to scholars. Among the books are Clemens's copy of Harriet Beecher Stowe's *Lady Byron Vindicated* (1870), Henry Bradshaw Fearon's *Sketches of America* (1819), and Nathaniel S. Shaler's *Aspects of the Earth* (1904), all containing substantial marginalia.

MARK TWAIN RESEARCH FOUNDATION, PERRY, MISSOURI (1939–1987)

Probably the best-known books from Clemens's library were owned by the Mark Twain Research Foundation, an organization chartered by George Hiram Brownell in 1947 as the successor to the Mark Twain Association, a group with national membership formed in 1941. Brownell had issued a newsletter called *The Twainian* since 1939, and this became the official publication of his Mark Twain Research Foundation, edited from his home in

Elkhorn, Wisconsin. Upon Brownell's death in 1950, Chester L. Davis of Perry, Missouri became the "Executive-Secretary" of the Mark Twain Research Foundation when he acquired most of the Brownell collection and moved it to Perry. Davis issued *The Twainian* from his law office in Perry.

Three local Perry supporters of the Foundation, Mrs. Burney L. Fishback and Mr. and Mrs. L. D. Norris, journeyed to Hollywood in April 1951 after Davis was notified of the forthcoming auction by Clara Clemens Samossoud. Although limited in funds for bidding, they managed to bring back to Perry a dozen volumes from the sale. Davis, who did not attend the auction, promised in the columns of *The Twainian* to "feed out material from time to time" from Clemens's marginalia.[16] He sporadically quoted from Clemens's annotations in his bi-monthly newsletter. Davis declined to allow anyone to examine the books he had not already described and quoted from in *The Twainian*. His obtrusive editorial mannerisms were sometimes annoying, but it was fortunate nonetheless that the books on which he reported did not simply vanish, as so many of their fellow volumes did after the 1951 sale. Davis's collection included Lecky's *History of European Morals* (1874), George S. Hillard's *Life, Letter, and Journals of George Ticknor* (1876), Moncure Daniel Conway's *Autobiography* (1904), E. W. Howe's *Story of a Country Town* (1883), and an edition of *The Thousand and One Nights*. Although Davis expressed his intention eventually to donate all of these books to the nearby (then-named) Mark Twain Birthplace Memorial Shrine, a state-funded museum and library in Florida, Missouri, his Twain

books were dispersed through an auction at Christie's in New York City after Davis passed away in 1987.

ANTENNE COLLECTION, MARK TWAIN ARCHIVE, ELMIRA COLLEGE

An exciting cache (known as the Antenne-Dorrance Collection) of books from Clemens's library came to light in 1966, when Anne Cameron Harvey, a graduate student at the University of Iowa in Iowa City, compiled a checklist of volumes then owned by Mrs. Irene Leary Stinn of Rice Lake, Wisconsin. Harvey sent a copy of her discovery to the Mark Twain Papers, and the titles thus became known for the first time to Mark Twain scholars. The provenance of the books began with Katy (Catherine) Leary (1856–1934), the housekeeper employed by Clemens from 1880 until his death. Katy Leary retired when Clemens died in 1910, and at that time Clara Clemens Gabrilowitsch granted her request to select approximately ninety volumes from her employer's library. (A note that Clemens's secretary, Isabel Lyon, had jotted in her journal on January 20, 1907 seems relevant to Katy Leary's desiring these books. Isabel Lyon recorded that Clemens was accustomed to calling Katy "The Librarian" while he was living at 21 Fifth Avenue, apparently because Katy often dusted his bookshelves.)[17] No record had been kept of these gifts and their very existence was unknown except to Katy Leary's relatives.

Mrs. Stinn's first husband, Warren Leary Sr., inherited the collection from his "Aunt Kate" in 1934. Mr. Leary had met Mark Twain, who presented him with an inscribed copy of *Tom Sawyer* in 1900 and once gave him a letter of recommendation. Katy Leary's nephew Warren, editor of the Rice Lake *Chronotype,* died in 1959 in Rice Lake; his widow later married Frank Stinn. Mrs. Stinn died in 1970, bequeathing the books jointly to her two daughters, Mrs. Katharine Antenne and Mrs. Mary Dorrance, both residents of Rice Lake. This is the collection that I rescued from a front porch in 1970.

Beginning in 1993, Robert and Katharine Antenne, who had become custodians of the collection, made periodic donations of volumes to Elmira College until 2002, when the last of the Katy Leary books were given. The Mark Twain Archive in the Gannett-Tripp Library at Elmira College now houses the Antenne Collection. More information is available at www.elmira.edu.

LOCATIONS OF BOOKS FROM THE CLEMENS FAMILY'S LIBRARY

The two auctions of 1911 and 1951 and the book donations by Clemens and his daughter widely disseminated his library collection across the United States. More than two-thirds of its contents have not reappeared. The following universities and libraries (and one private collection) own books from the Clemenses' family library. A few other individuals are omitted by request.

CALIFORNIA:
Mark Twain Papers, Bancroft Library, University of California at Berkeley

Research Library, North Campus, Special Collections, University of California at Los Angeles (10-volume set of Casanova's *Mémoires*)

Henry E. Huntington Library, San Marino

CONNECTICUT:
Mark Twain House and Museum, Hartford

Beinecke Rare Book and Manuscript Library, Yale University, New Haven

Mark Twain Library, Redding

ILLINOIS:
Rare Book and Manuscript Library, University of Illinois at Urbana-Champaign

Newberry Library, Chicago

MISSOURI:
Mark Twain Boyhood Home and Museum, Hannibal

Department of Special Collections, Washington University Libraries, St. Louis

NEVADA:
Special Collections, University Library, University of Nevada at Reno

NEW YORK:
Antenne Collection and Langdon Family Library, Mark Twain Archive, Elmira College, Elmira

Henry W. and Albert A. Berg Collection, New York Public Library, New York

Jean Webster McKinney Papers, Special Collections, Vassar College Library, Vassar College, Poughkeepsie

NORTH CAROLINA:
Wake Forest University, Winston-Salem

TEXAS:
Harry Ransom Center, University of Texas at Austin

Kevin Mac Donnell Collection, Austin

VIRGINIA:
Albert and Shirley Small Special Collections Library, University of Virginia, Charlottesville

NOTES

1   *Mark Twain-Howells Letters,* ed. Henry Nash Smith and William M. Gibson (Cambridge, Massachusetts: Harvard University Press, Belknap Press, 1960), p. 773.

2   ALS, Huntington Library, San Marino, California.

3   ALS, Mark Twain Papers, Bancroft Library, University of California, Berkeley—hereafter cited as MTP.

4   *Mark Twain's Letters, Volume 4, 1870–1871,* ed. Victor Fischer and Michael B. Frank (Berkeley: University of California, 1995), p. 1.

5   According to records in MTP.

6   TS in MTP.

7   TS in MTP.

8   New York: Harper & Brothers, 1912.

9   Paine, *Mark Twain: A Biography* (New York: Harper & Brothers, 1912), pp. 1471–72.

10 Mary Lawton, *A Lifetime with Mark Twain. The Memories of Katy Leary, for Thirty Years His Faithful and Devoted Servant* (New York: Harcourt, Brace and Co., 1925), p. 307.

11 *Mark Twain's Margins on Thackeray's "Swift"* (New York: Gotham House, 1935), published in a limited edition of 1,000 copies.

12 "Mark Twain's German Provenience," *Modern Language Quarterly* 6.4 (December 1945): 459–478.

13 The Mark Twain Library at Redding possesses a copy of Stone's catalog.

14 New York *Times,* "Twain's Bookshelf," 19 April 2010, p. A-17.

15 Auction records consulted in MTP and the Mark Twain Boyhood Home and Museum, Hannibal, Missouri.

16 *The Twainian* (May-June 1951): 2.

17 TS p. 219, MTP.

An earlier version of this chapter appeared in Resources for American Literary Study *5.2 (Autumn 1975): 147–165.*

Portrait of Samuel L. Clemens Reading, 1907 (Courtesy of the Mark Twain Papers, Bancroft Library, University of California, Berkeley)

8

'Good Books & a Sleepy Conscience'

Mark Twain's Reading Habits

Upon returning to his 21 Fifth Avenue residence from Dublin, New Hampshire in the autumn of 1906, Samuel Clemens amiably posed for a "gag" photograph that visually epitomized his attitude toward reading. Propped up in his magnificent bedstead imported from Italy, a cigar protruding from beneath his mustache and wire-rim spectacles hanging halfway down his nose, he lay indolently attired in nightclothes and pretended to contemplate the July 1906 issue of *The World's Work*.[1] A chronic idler delights in reading of others' labors, he seems to say.

THE BEDSIDE BOOKS

In truth Clemens did customarily read in bed, a habit that contributed to his lifelong conviction that he was relaxing rather than working by reading books. Apparently he acquired this preference for horizontal reading early in his adulthood. In "Concerning Chambermaids," a sketch written in 1866, he railed against hotel maids who "always put the pillows at the opposite end of the bed from the gas-burner, so that while you read and smoke before sleeping (as is the ancient and honored custom of bachelors), you have to hold your book aloft, in an uncomfortable position, to keep the light from dazzling your eyes."[2]

He kept up this "honored custom" during his intensive courtship of Olivia Langdon in 1869, as he confided to his friend Mrs. Fairbanks: "I have been in bed, reading & smoking, two or three hours, but I do not yet discover any inclination to go to sleep. I suppose it is because I am waiting for the morning to come, so that I can see Livy."[3] The soothing combination of reading and smoking in bed did not end with his marriage. On 15 April 1879 he informed William Dean Howells from Paris of his intention that evening "to turn in, immediately, & read & smoke."[4] He found at least one drawback to the practice about which he complained in Chapter 35 of *A Tramp Abroad* (1880): "When one is reading in bed, and lays his paper-knife down, he cannot find it again if it is smaller than a saber."

But such irritations seemed minor in comparison with the nocturnal relaxation his bedtime reading afforded; indeed, the indulgence was so pleasurable that he began to look for excuses to extend his hours in bed. On 29 August 1880, suffering from an abscess in his ear, he informed Joseph H. Twichell that "I take advantage of it to lie abed most of the day, & read & smoke & scribble & have a good time."[5] Sheer exhaustion provided another valid reason for lying about with a good book in daylight. He resorted to this recreation during one of his stints of composing the manuscript of *Huckleberry Finn*. "When I get fagged out," he wrote to Howells on 20 July 1883, "I lie abed [at Quarry Farm] a couple of days & read & smoke, & then go it again for 6 or 7 days."[6]

In the last fifteen years of his life Clemens cultivated the public image of himself as an unpretentious man who languidly conducted his literary, business, and personal affairs from his bedchamber. More and more often he received newspaper interviewers and posed for photographs in his ornate bed. His distant cousin Dr. James Ross Clemens, who met him in London in 1897 while pursuing postgraduate medical study, recorded an impression of the appearance Mark Twain evidently liked to present: "Entering his bedroom long past the hour of noon I found him in bed, luxuriously propped up on pillows and busily skimming through a crowd of books he had intrenched himself among."[7] Mark Twain told his relative he was preparing an after-dinner speech to be delivered that evening. After Clemens's return to the United States he was visited in 1900 or 1901 by William W. Ellsworth of the Century Company, who gave a vivid description: "It was Sunday afternoon; he was lying in his big, carved mahogany bed, surrounded with books and cigars, a beautiful figure with his great towering mass of white hair, his keen dark eyes and overhanging brows, his plain white nightshirt."[8] Ellsworth's thumbnail sketch accurately matches the series of photographs Albert Bigelow Paine took of Clemens in bed in 1906 at 21 Fifth Avenue; several of Paine's pictures show Clemens reading.

The testimony of Clemens's physician who treated him in the 1890s and 1900s makes it clear that this therapy usually was Clemens's own idea. Dr. Clarence C. Rice recalled in 1924 that his patient "was never ill—just colds. Sometimes he stayed in bed all day because he enjoyed reading and writing lying down. He was always reading, and seemed to enjoy any kind of printed page, from a child's school book to an almanac."[9] Dr. Rice may not have treated Clemens in his last years when he suffered genuine illnesses, but even then Clemens simply looked upon his sufferings as excuses for unbroken tranquility in which to read. Bedridden with bronchitis on 4 May 1903, he grumbled about Walter Scott's novels to Brander Matthews, explaining, "I haven't been out of my bed for 4 weeks, but—well, I have been reading, a good deal."[10] Paine reported that the books Clemens chiefly valued in his last years he normally kept "on the table by him, and on his bed, and in the billiard-room shelves."[11]

His early experience as a traveling correspondent also offered him another excuse besides overwork or illness for leisurely literary browsing. On 16 December 1866 Clemens noted in his journal of the voyage from San Francisco to New York on the S. S. *America*: "This is a long, long night. I occupy lower berth & read & smoke by a ship's lantern borrowed from the steward."[12] He may have picked up this habit during his off-watch hours while piloting Mississippi steamboats. At any rate it became a permanent part of his ocean regimen—though not without minor mishaps such as he mentioned on 14 June 1867 in Notebook 8: "Shipped a sea [aboard the *Quaker City*] through the open dead-light that damaged cigars, books, &c—comes of being careless when room is on weather side of the ship."[13]

In November 1873, three days out of New York en route to England, he wrote Olivia Clemens about his satisfaction with his quarters on the S. S. *Batavia*: "My port is so large that I can lie in my berth (on a delicious spring mattrass) & read as if out of doors. At night I can read with perfect ease (& all night long,) for a swinging lamp hangs above my head." Four days later he added in another letter, "I have read all during this weather—sleep would only tire me."[14] His friends usually took precautions to ensure that he boarded Atlantic vessels with diverting reading materials. Upon leaving the Murray Hill Hotel in New York City on 12 May 1893 he informed Howells, "You have given me a book, Annie Trumbull has sent me her book, I bought a couple of books, Mr. Hall gave me a choice German book, Laffan gave me two bottles of whisky & a box of cigars—I go to sea nobly equipped."[15] The next year he wrote to another correspondent following a voyage to France, "I thank you ever so much for the noble supply of books which I found in my stateroom."[16] When no such gifts were expected, he made his own advance arrangements. On 21 October 1903, for instance, he instructed Frank Duneka of Harper & Brothers to be certain that *Madame Bovary*

and Poultney Bigelow's *History of the German Struggle for Liberty* were both placed aboard the S.S. *Princess Irene* before his departure for Italy.[17]

Reading as a Guilty Pleasure

The same leisure that ocean voyages imposed upon Clemens he also found in railroad cars and hotel rooms—but the fact that he primarily associated reading with enforced physical inactivity explains the other indulgences it seemingly connoted for him: smoking cigars or pipes, drinking whiskey or beer, and luxuriating in idle comfort. When on 31 August 1885 he turned down an invitation to visit Dean Sage at his summer home, Clemens regretted typically that they could not "smoke and talk and scour the old books."[18] He was explicit about the purpose of his trip down the Rhône in August 1891; he sought "lazy repose, with opportunity to smoke, read, doze, talk, accumulate comfort, get fat," and avoid "the world and its concerns."[19] His attitude was summed up by a maxim that he set down in 1898 in Notebook 42: "Good friends, good books & a sleepy conscience: this is the ideal life." He was so pleased with the sentiment that he repeated it in the same notebook and used it to inscribe at least one presentation copy of *Following the Equator*.[20] In a sketch written the same year, Clemens reports that his wife complained about his behavior: "He didn't do a stroke of work the whole day," she supposedly fretted to a servant, "but sat in the balcony smoking & reading."[21] A tone of genuine self-reproach shows through the little joke that his wife was mainly irritated because he was "reading his own books." Clearly Clemens considered reading to be completely separate from "work," that is, writing—a curious attitude to find in a literary man of Clemens's stature.

Nor did he alter this concept when he passed the age of normal retirement from vocational labor. A note slipped to his ailing wife in her sickroom seclusion stated, "The day is done, it is time for reading, smoking, reflection, sleep."[22] Another note to her in 1904 mentioned that after "another full day's work" he has been "reading & dozing since."[23] He boasted of shameless indolence in a letter to his daughter Jean written on 28 July 1908: "I have ceased from having a liking for efforts. I seem to greatly prefer cards, & billiards, & reading, & smoking, & lying around in the shade. However, I worked 60 years, & if I am ever going to take a holiday it is time I was at it" (TS in MTP) The mental act of reading—no matter what the subject—apparently never struck him as intellectual effort. Weary from his battles with persistent ill health, he bragged nonetheless to Elizabeth Wallace on 27 August 1909: "I read, and read, and read, and smoke, and smoke, and smoke *all* the time (as formerly), and it's a contented and comfortable life."[24]

His reasons for linking books with forbidden dissipations may never be guessed. Conceivably he sensed parental disapproval for his preoccupation with popular romances as a youth in Hannibal. Jane Clemens has been praised by biographers for her plucky spirit and determination, but none has detected a literary side to her character. From everything that we know, she read little besides her Bible, local newspapers, and an occasional magazine. John Marshall Clemens's personal library indicates that he sought only books

that were practical or "improving."[25] As a young printer in New York City, as a river pilot, as a prospector, as a journalist, young Clemens probably rejoiced at opportunities to satiate his craving for books, unhindered by rebukes about his laziness. Such speculations have only the tendencies of Clemens and his parents as their basis; still it is worth considering how a professional writer came to associate—whether jocularly or seriously—reading books with embarrassing "vices" such as liquor, tobacco, cards, idleness, billiards, and sham illness. At some level of his psyche he equated the inaction required for reading with true laziness.

Clemens often read at night after his day's work was over, but for sustained programs of reading he preferred those periods when his mind was free from authorial preoccupations. He informed an importunate writer who sought his critical opinion in 1886: "I wish I could, but I can't. I never venture to read when I am writing anything, lest I get my attention diverted from my work, & have a long, hard pull of it getting back into the swing again."[26] Ideally, it seems, reading was a reward for his own literary labors. Obviously he made exceptions to this policy when he consulted travel books for *The Innocents Abroad, Life on the Mississippi*, and *Following the Equator*, or when he immersed himself in reference works and histories to produce *The Prince and the Pauper, A Connecticut Yankee*, and *Joan of Arc*. In these instances, however, he was reading for a definite purpose.

CLEMENS'S HABITS OF INDICATING OWNERSHIP OF BOOKS

Spurious association copies have usually

been easy to recognize; Clemens rarely signed his pseudonym to identify books belonging to his personal library, normally reserving "Mark Twain" as an autograph for his own literary writings. Only a few exceptions—Richard Grant White's *Words and Their Uses*, for example, signed "Mark Twain, 1873" in one place and "Saml. L. Clemens" in two others, and Dan Beard's *Moonblight*, evidently autographed by "Mark Twain" in 1905—appear to be authentic.

Sometime during young Clemens's stint as an apprentice printer in Hannibal he proudly typeset his own bookplate. A specimen of it was discovered in 1984 in the Clemens family Bible: "This BOOK belongs to/Samuel Clemens. Hannibal, Mo."[27] That was the only period when he utilized this means of designating a book's ownership; thereafter he either signed the books in his personal library or left them uninscribed. Inasmuch as Clemens esteemed the products of the printing press and employed custom-made notebooks, it does seem odd that he never pasted any other bookplates in his library volumes. However, he was meticulous about designating the ownership of books belonging to members of his household. Around 1877 Clemens began signing his library books with initials ("S. L. Clemens") rather than the "Saml. L. Clemens" form he previously preferred. During the last decade and a half of his life he usually omitted the first period, linking the initials together with a single stroke of his pen. Sometimes the second period got omitted as well. Pencil predominated in the signatures and inscriptions written in the 1870s and earlier; thereafter he generally used ink—violet, blue, brown (brown now, that is),

or black—until the post-1900 period, when he definitely favored black ink. Knowing these habits can provide rough dates of probable acquisition for the books Clemens signed.

He tended to avoid signing or annotating the pre-1820 volumes in his collection, out of deference to their antiquity, though there were exceptions. While he did not sign Samuel Clarke's *A Mirror or Looking-Glass Both for Saints & Sinners* (London, 1671), he could not resist marking its contents and commenting in its margins. Normally he also left very expensive sets or elaborately illustrated editions uninscribed and unmarked. Here, too, however, his enthusiasm sometimes got the better of him, as when he inscribed an edition of Coleridge's *The Rime of the Ancient Mariner* illustrated by Gustave Doré "To Livy L. Clemens/Nov. 27, 1876. From S. L. Clemens." But these were rare occurrences.

MAKING NOTES AND MARKS IN THE MARGINS

The first concrete evidence of Clemens's habit of margin-noting appeared during his courtship of Olivia Langdon; a heavily annotated copy of *The Autocrat of the Breakfast Table* survives as the prime example of the marginalia with which he amused her. On 27 February 1869 he wrote to his fiancée, "I am glad I marked those books for you, since the marking gives you pleasure, but I remember that the pencilings are very meagre—for which I am sorry. I have marked many a book for you, in the [railroad] cars [during his lecture tour]—& thrown them away afterward, not appreciating that I was taking a pleasure of any great moment from you. I will do better hereafter, my precious little wife."[28]

Above and opposite: Marginalia in dark blue ink and blue pencil in Francis Parkman's The Jesuits in North America in the Seventeenth Century *(15th edition, Boston: Little, Brown, and Co., 1880). Clemens signed the front free endpaper, "S. L. Clemens/Hartford, 1881" (Mark Twain Papers, Bancroft Library, Univ. of California, Berkeley; copyright 2019).*

Olivia's delight in his marginalia provided the sense of audience approval that he needed, and he continued to write in books he owned for the rest of his life. The tone of his later notes, like his marginal comments for his fiancée, suggests that they were intended for other eyes than his own. "The next hundred pages of this book are tolerably dull, *I* think," he jotted on page 137 of *Thackeray's Lectures.*[29] At times his wit gleams in a brief note, as when he scoffed at Alexander Thomson's translation of *The Lives of the Twelve Caesars*: "He reels from tense to tense like a Scot going home from a Burns banquet."[30] He seemed to relish the scant space offered by most margins, which required him to pare his comments down to the most economical expression possible. As his daughters grew older they joined Olivia in admiring his marginalia, although they sometimes faltered in guessing his meaning. Clemens mirthfully recorded the difficulties nine-year-old Clara had in deciphering a note on 8 June 1883:

Clara picked up a book—"Daniel Boone, by John S. C. Abbott" & found on the fly-leaf

lxxxii INTRODUCTION

voices of the disembodied children driving birds from their corn-fields.[1] An endless variety of incoherent fancies is connected with the Indian idea of a future life. They commonly owe their origin to dreams, often to the dreams of those in extreme sickness, who, on awaking, supposed that they had visited the other world, and related to the wondering bystanders what they had seen.

The Indian land of souls is not always a region of shadows and gloom. The Hurons sometimes represented the souls of their dead — those of their dogs included — as dancing joyously in the presence of Ataentsic and Jouskeha. According to some Algonquin traditions, heaven was a scene of endless festivity, the ghosts dancing to the sound of the rattle and the drum, and greeting with hospitable welcome the occasional visitor from the living world: for the spirit-land was not far off, and roving hunters sometimes passed its confines unawares.

Most of the traditions agree, however, that the spirits, on their journey heavenward, were beset with difficulties and perils. There was a swift river which must be crossed on a log that shook beneath their feet, while a ferocious dog opposed their passage, and drove many into the abyss. This river was full of sturgeon and other fish, which the ghosts speared for their subsistence. Beyond was a narrow path between moving rocks, which each instant crashed together, grinding to atoms the less nimble of the pilgrims who essayed to pass. The Hurons believed that a personage named Oscotarach, or the Head-Piercer, dwelt in a bark house beside the path, and that it was his office to remove the brains from the heads of all who went by, as a necessary preparation for immor-

[1] Brébeuf, Relation des Hurons, 1636, 99 (Cramoisy).

In our time this is done as a necessary preparation for the reception of religion.

DREAMS. lxxxiii

tality. This singular idea is found also in some Algonquin traditions, according to which, however, the brain is afterwards restored to its owner.[1]

Dreams were to the Indian a universal oracle. They revealed to him his guardian spirit, taught him the cure of his diseases, warned him of the devices of sorcerers, guided him to the lurking-places of his enemy or the haunts of game, and unfolded the secrets of good and evil destiny. The dream was a mysterious and inexorable power, whose least behests must be obeyed to the letter, — a source, in every Indian town, of endless mischief and abomination. There were professed dreamers, and professed interpreters of dreams. One of the most noted festivals among the Hurons and Iroquois was the Dream Feast, a scene of frenzy, where the actors counter-

[1] On Indian ideas of another life, compare Sagard, the Jesuit Relations, Perrot, Charlevoix, and Lafitau, with Tanner, James, Schoolcraft, and the Appendix to Morse's Indian Report.

Le Clerc recounts a singular story, current in his time among the Algonquins of Gaspé and Northern New Brunswick. The favorite son of an old Indian died; whereupon the father, with a party of friends, set out for the land of souls to recover him. It was only necessary to wade through a shallow lake, several days' journey in extent. This they did, sleeping at night on platforms of poles which supported them above the water. At length they arrived, and were met by Papkootparout, the Indian Pluto, who rushed on them in a rage, with his war-club upraised; but, presently relenting, changed his mind, and challenged them to a game of ball. They proved the victors, and won the stakes, consisting of corn, tobacco, and certain fruits, which thus became known to mankind. The bereaved father now begged hard for his son's soul, and Papkootparout at last gave it to him, in the form and size of a nut, which, by pressing it hard between his hands, he forced into a small leather bag. The delighted parent carried it back to earth, with instructions to insert it in the body of his son, who would thereupon return to life. When the adventurers reached home, and reported the happy issue of their journey, there was a dance of rejoicing; and the father, wishing to take part in it, gave his son's soul to the keeping of a squaw who stood by. Being curious to see it, she opened the bag; on which it escaped at once, and took flight for the realms of Papkootparout, preferring them to the abodes of the living. — Le Clerc, Nouvelle Relation de la Gaspésie, 310–328.

Notations written in blue pencil and dark blue ink in Francis Parkman's JESUITS IN NORTH AMERICA (Mark Twain Papers at Berkeley; copyright © 1976, Mark Twain Company).

a comment of mine, in pencil; puzzled over it, couldn't quite make it out; her mother took it & read it to her, as follows: "A poor slovenly book; a mess of sappy drivel & bad grammar." Clara said, with entire seriousness (not comprehending the meaning but charmed with the sound of the words,) "O, that must be lovely!" & carried the book away & buried herself in it.[31]

His closest friends were also allowed to enjoy his marginalia; one who surely knew about his reading notes was Howells, to whom Clemens wrote at 3 a.m. on 17 April 1909 to say that he was passing a sleepless night perusing James Russell Lowell's *Letters*. He mentioned to Howells that "on page 305, vol I, I have just margined a note" in amusement at Lowell's long-ago reference to "young" Howells.[32] Toward the end of his life Clemens could have anticipated that posterity might be interested in his reactions to his reading, but primarily one suspects that he himself took more pleasure than anyone else in reviewing what he had previously written in book margins.

Clemens devised a simple system of annotating those books that he expected to reread. Primarily he used plain vertical lines in the margin to draw his attention to significant passages. These lines were multiplied to express special interest; double lines are common in his books, and occasionally he scored specific passages with as many as three or four parallel vertical marks. Where his annotation is extensive on consecutive pages he sometimes alternated these vertical lines with curved brackets, which he also doubled, tripled, or quadrupled to signify a sentence or paragraph especially worth rereading. His tendency to make brackets with small hooks at the top and bottom sometimes helps distinguish his markings from those of other readers who may have added similar marginalia to a book. Near a passage that he had marked with a line or a bracket he often added a note—squeezing it into whatever space the page allowed. These comments occur about equally in the top, bottom, and side margins; in the latter case he would turn the book and write lengthwise along the page. In a typical instance of annotation in his copy of Francis Parkman's *The Jesuits in North America*,[33] for example, he underscored a sentence that described the Algonquin Indians, drew two brackets in curves which set off the entire paragraph, and wrote in the bottom margin beneath the passage: "Plainly these are not Indians of the Cooper style."[34] But such underlining of sentences he reserved for only the choicest passages; he seldom underlined more than three or four sentences in an entire chapter, whether he was reading fiction or non-fiction. Vertical lines and brackets, often elongated to encompass an entire passage or paragraph, composed the majority of his markings.

In making his annotations Clemens used pencil most frequently (sometimes almost exclusively) in the period up to 1880, but one also encounters penciled marginalia in books from later years. In reading, rereading, and reading again certain volumes he left behind alternating pencil and ink marginalia from each perusal; different colors of ink—violet, blue, brown, or black—also testify to his repeated appraisals of specific passages. Of course his methods and extent of marking varied with his moods and the subject matter; in John Fiske's *A Century of Science and Other Essays*[35] he annotated each paragraph of the first twenty-eight pages very heavily, but only three subsequent pages contain any marks whatever. Except for those volumes that became his favorites, the annotation is generally heaviest in the first fifty pages; often there is very little thereafter.

Clemens's preoccupation with prose style accounts for the largest number of his notes. He was compulsive about grammatical corrections, pausing to change stylistic slips as frequently in books that he admired as in those he abhorred. His concern with the most minor lapses is illustrated in Sarah Grand's *The Heavenly Twins*,[36] where on page 336 alone he changed "may" to "might," "is" to "was," and "to go less to" into "to go less frequently to." Likewise he revised "I should like to have suggested" to read "I should have liked to suggest"[37] and changed "we should like to have seen" into "should have liked to see."[38] Scores of similar editorial corrections dot the margins of his other books. It would seem that he simply could not pass over grammatical errors without substituting more proper forms. Those who accept the popular assumption that Mark Twain cared little about proofreading and revising his own manuscripts should inspect the painstakingly edited books in his library. These corrections also show his early training as a printer; generally the offending word or phrase is completely deleted and a heavy line leads the eye to the margin of the page where a new version is proposed.

Often Clemens's objection hinged on usages that were not grammatically wrong, but merely struck him as improvable. In Bret Harte's *The Twins of Table Mountain* Clemens canceled one word in the phrase "beat time with her feet" and substituted "beat time with her foot."[39] He objected to the polite diction of the stagecoach driver in Harte's story entitled "A Lonely Ride" in *The Luck of Roaring Camp and Other Sketches*, insisting that "one of those brutal Californian stage-drivers could not be polite to a passenger,—& not one of the guild ever 'sir'd' *anybody*."[40] He ridiculed the fastidious language Bayle St. John employed in his translation of Saint-Simon's *Memoirs*[41] by suggesting that in one place the word "love" actually meant "adultery" and in another instance "an unprintable relationship" between two men was inadequately implied.[42] After canceling many relative pronouns in James Russell Lowell's *Letters*, Clemens finally observed, "He is much too 'thatful' for me—it annoys a body."

The Maverick Reader

Clemens considered himself an unorthodox reader. In a letter to Edward H. House on 14 January 1884 he replied to House's request for reading suggestions by listing thirteen titles he had recently read, but he warned House, "I'm not a good person to apply to, because I seldom or never read anything that is new, & never read anything *through*, be it new or old."[43] Unquestionably Clemens did pay less attention to current best-sellers than his wife and her circle of friends. In his view a fifty-year-old book was potentially interesting for the opportunity it afforded to compare present with former social conventions; one could also judge whether the author possessed attributes that lasted. He never held the age of

a book against it as he first opened its covers. His observation to House appears overstated nonetheless, for he read a great many contemporary books. In making such pronouncements Clemens sometimes mistook what he was practicing at the time for the pattern of behavior he *always* followed. Certainly he was exaggerating for effect when he said that he "never read anything *through*," since scores of volumes survive with his markings scattered throughout their entirety. Judging from these same marginal comments, however, it seems true that he was apt to lay a book aside if it failed to secure his interest within the space of twenty, thirty, or forty pages.

All the same, his multitudinous marginal notes suggest the finical thoroughness with which Clemens picked his way through hundreds of his books. His actual reading habits were thus at variance with the image of himself that he presented in Chapter 59 of *Following the Equator*. There he confesses disappointment in the Taj Mahal as a consequence of his having read so many accounts of it in travel books:

I am a careless reader, I suppose—an *impressionist* reader; an impressionist reader of what is *not* an impressionist picture; a reader who overlooks the informing details or masses their sum improperly, and gets only a large, splashy, general effect—an effect which is not correct, and which is not warranted by the particulars placed before me—particulars which I did not examine, and whose meanings I did not cautiously and carefully estimate. It is an effect which is some thirty-five or forty times finer than the reality, and is therefore a great deal better and more valuable than the reality; and so, I ought never to hunt up the reality, but stay miles away from it, and thus preserve undamaged my own private mighty Niagara tumbling out of the vault of heaven, and my own ineffable Taj, built of tinted mists upon jeweled arches of rainbows supported by colonnades of moonlight.

To prevent such misapprehensions, Mark Twain suggests substituting numbers in place of adjectives to determine the true values of words and phrases. "Language is a treacherous thing, a most unsure vehicle, and it can seldom arrange descriptive words in such a way that they will not inflate the facts—by help of the reader's imagination." Twain's levity is plain enough, yet several critics have quoted his words out of their humorous context and have referred to Clemens as a self-professed "careless" and "impressionist" reader solely on the basis of this passage.

Instead of thinking of himself as one who skimmed books heedlessly, Clemens believed that his reading speed was below average. He informed Hamlin Garland on 30 June 1905 that he had put in an entire day and night ("up to 2 this morning") reading Garland's 438-page novel, *The Tyranny of the Dark*; though Clemens liked the book, he thought the pleasant expenditure of so many hours to be "criminal dissipations for a laboring man & slow reader."[44] He once recorded the time he required to analyze a moderately difficult scientific treatise. From the Hotel Krantz in Vienna Clemens wrote on 5 December 1898 to John Adams, author of *The Herbartian Psychology*, to report his rate of comprehension and annotation: "My wife had ordered me to stop work and spend the day in bed, and rest up," he explained. "And so, between 10 yesterday morning and 12 at night I was able to read to page 232 without a break—an uninterrupted view: a good thing, that. It is not fast reading, but then I cannot take things in swiftly if I wish to understand them—and also make marginal notes."[45] Here are summed up several elements Clemens required in order to enjoy himself: an entire day in bed, earned by unstinting overwork; the express sanction of his wife, the figurehead authority he appointed as his taskmaster, for this horizontal holiday; and the unbroken tranquility in which to engage a challenging book and unravel its mysteries with careful annotation. He scarcely needed to mention the supply of cigars and the glass of whiskey that were no doubt at his bedside.

Notes

1   The photograph was used for an advertising broadside, of which a copy exists in the Mark Twain Papers, Bancroft Library, University of California, Berkeley—hereafter cited as MTP. It appears to belong to the sequence of eight other photographs taken of Clemens in bed in 1906 by Albert Bigelow Paine at 21 Fifth Avenue; negatives and prints of these pictures are also in the Mark Twain Papers .

2   *Mark Twain's Sketches, New and Old* (Hartford: American Publishing, 1875), p. 250.

3   Clemens to Mrs. Fairbanks, 4 June 1869, published in *Mark Twain's Letters, Volume 3*, ed. Victor Fischer and Michael B. Frank (Berkeley: University of California Press, 1999), pp. 261–262—hereafter cited as *MTLet*.

4   *Mark Twain-Howells Letters*, ed. Henry Nash Smith and William M. Gibson (Cambridge: Harvard University Press, Belknap Press, 1960), p. 259—hereafter cited as *MTHL*.

5   *The Letters of Mark Twain and Joseph Hopkins Twichell*, ed. Harold K. Bush, Steve Courtney, and Peter Messent (Athens: University of Georgia Press, 2017), p. 101.

6   *MTHL*, p. 435.

7   "Reminiscences of Mark Twain," *Overland* 87 (April 1929): 105.

8   *A Golden Age of Authors: A Publisher's Recollection* (Boston: Houghton Mifflin, 1919), pp. 225–226.

9   "Mark Twain as His Physician Knew Him," *Mentor* 12 (May 1924): 48–49.

10 ALS, Columbia University.

11 *Mark Twain: A Biography* (New York: Harper, 1912), p. 1536.

12 Notebook 7, *Mark Twain's Notebooks & Journals, Volume I*, ed. Frederick Anderson, Michael B. Frank, Kenneth N. Sanderson (Berkeley: University of California Press, 1975), 1: 246—hereafter cited as *N&J*.

13 *N&J* 1: 335.

14 *Mark Twain's Letters, Volume 5, 1872–1873*, ed. Lin Salamo and Harriet Elinor Smith (Berkeley: University of California Press, 1997), 5: 473, 475—hereafter referred to as *MTLet*.

15 *MTHL*, pp. 652–653.

16 Clemens to Joseph Henry Harper, 11 September 1894, ALS in the Albert and Shirley Small Special Collections Library, University of Virginia, Charlottesville.

17 TS in MTP.

18 ALS in the collection of Mrs. Meredith Hare, Palisades, New York, TS in MTP.

19 "Down the Rhône," *The Writings of Mark Twain*, Definitive Edition (New York: Gabriel Wells, 1922), 29: 129

20 Mark Twain so inscribed a copy to James H. Scott in Vienna on 10 April 1898; the volume was formerly in the Estelle Doheny Collection of the Edward Laurence Doheny Memorial Library, St. John's Seminary, Camarillo, California.

21 "Wuthering Heights," DV236 in MTP.

22 Dated 27 February [1903], MTP.

23 ALS in MTP.

24 TS in MTP, quoted in Elizabeth Wallace's *Mark Twain and the Happy Island* (Chicago: A. C. McClurg, 1913), p. 131.

25 John Francis McDermott listed the contents of John Marshall Clemens's small library, as revealed by the appraisal of his property filed after his death in 1847, in "Mark Twain and the Bible," *Papers on Language & Literature* 4 (Spring 1968): 198. The elder Clemens owned only twenty-five or thirty books, mostly volumes of Missouri law cases.

26 Clemens to J. M. G. Wood, 8 September 1886, ALS, State University of New York at Buffalo.

27 MTP.

28 *MTLet* 3: 116. Clemens's copy of *The Autocrat* was formerly in the Estelle Doheny Collection of the Edward Laurence Doheny Memorial Library, St. John's Seminary, Camarillo, California. Bradford A. Booth reproduced the marginalia in "Mark Twain's Comments on Holmes's *Autocrat*," *American Literature* 21.4 (January 1950): 456–463.

29 Clemens's copy of this volume is in the Mark Twain Library, Redding, Connecticut. Coley B. Taylor published Clemens's marginalia in *Mark Twain's Margins on Thackeray's "Swift."* Limited edition: 1,000 copies (New York: Gotham House, 1935).

30 *The Lives of the Twelve Caesars*, p. 150, MTP.

31 "A Record of the Small Foolishnesses of Susie & 'Bay' Clemens (Infants)," MS p. 101, the Albert and Shirley Small Special Collections Library, University of Virginia, Charlottesville. Published in *A Family Sketch and Other Private Writings*, ed. Benjamin Griffin (Oakland, California: University of California Press, 2014), p. 88.

32 *MTHL*, p. 843.

33 The book is in MTP.

34 Parkman, *The Jesuits in North America*, p. 31.

35 In MTP.

36 Now in the Henry W. and Albert A. Berg Collection, New York Public Library, Astor, Lenox and Tilden Foundations.

37 Grand, *The Heavenly Twins*, p. 641.

38 Grand, *The Heavenly Twins*, p. 666.

39 Harte, *The Twins of Table Mountain*, p. 35.

40 Harte, *The Luck of Roaring Camp and Other Sketches*, p. 112.

41 This book and the two Bret Harte volumes are now in MTP.

42 Saint-Simon, *Memoirs*, 1: 137, 225.

43 ALS, Albert and Shirley Small Special Collections Library, University of Virginia, Charlottesville.

44 ALS, American Academy of Arts and Letters.

45 Quoted by Lawrence Clark Powell in "An Unpublished Mark Twain Letter," *American Literature* 13.4 (January 1942): 405–406.

An earlier version of this chapter appeared in American Literary Realism *9.4 (Autumn 1976): 295–306.*

9

'I Kind of Love Small Game'

Mark Twain's Library of Literary Hogwash

For Samuel Clemens the act of reading meant making judgments about what he read, and he did this almost by reflex, as the margins of books from his library frequently testify. Indeed, Clemens's "unliterary" image may flourish so persistently partly because his unfavorable remarks about books and authors very nearly outweigh his praise. But he seldom commented on anyone's writing at length; Sydney Krause pointed out that he left behind not a single fully rounded book review.[1]

From the miscellaneous opinions about literature that Clemens did set down, however, commentators have attempted to ascertain his critical standards. DeLancey Ferguson noted in 1943 that "pretentiousness, overwriting, inaccuracy of expression he detested. . . . His interest was always in the style, rather than the story."[2] Howard G. Baetzhold added that Clemens generally disliked absurdly romantic situations, excessive sentimentality, dearth of "interest," and the lack of believable or likable characters.[3] Yet Clemens's marginalia from 1894 in his copy of Sarah Grand's *The Heavenly Twins*[4] show his willingness on occasion

to overlook objectionable plot conventions and bizarre characterizations provided that the prose style was succinct, the syntax clear, the diction appropriate.

Edgar M. Branch identified criteria Clemens applied in his literary criticism between 1864 and 1866 that seem to hold true for his later criticism as well: "clarity, exactitude, simplicity, honesty—all implied in his hatred for literary pretension or ambiguity."[5] Clemens demanded the same high standards for those translating classical or foreign languages into English; inept renderings, as he remonstrated in their margins, could betray the original authors' thoughts and discourage even dedicated readers. Often as not this search for precision in style largely came down to a matter of diction. In 1905 Clemens explained that in written prose "phrasing is everything, almost. Oh, yes, phrasing is a kind of photography: out of focus, a blurred picture; in focus, a sharp one."[6]

Apparently it was less effort for Clemens to discern and comment on examples of words used ineffectively, a practice that appealed strongly to his instincts as a humorist, than to distinguish excellent passages. So adept did he consider himself at discovering specimens of atrocious writing, in fact, that he invented a sinister little sideline, an ever-growing hypothetical collection of truly execrable writings he maliciously labeled his "Library of Literary Hogwash" and reserved for particularly delectable examples. Nearly all of these volumes of prose and verse were neglected in their own day and would have been forgotten had not Clemens's attention fallen upon them. As he confided to General Bryce on 13 October 1894 in another connection (concerning Bourget's *Outre-Mer*): "Paul's book is wretchedly small game, & not much short of idiotic; but I kind of love small game."[7] This preference for easy targets involved the type of perverse pleasure-seeking that Clemens had related of himself on 22 August 1878; when a young woman "cleaned out" the idlers in a hotel reading room with her "lacerating" piano rendition of "The Battle of Prague," Clemens alone remained to listen. "I staid," he explained in Notebook 15, "because the exquisitely bad is as satisfying to the soul as the exquisitely good—only the mediocre is unendurable."[8]

By at least 1870 Mark Twain had contrived a name for the literary small game he sought, and the term had associations with his journalism in Nevada and California. In a piece Twain wrote for the November 1870 issue of *Galaxy*, he derided the bathos of an obituary poem, scoffing: "There is something so innocent, so guileless, so complacent, so unearthly serene and self-satisfied about this peerless 'hog-wash,' that the man must be made of stone who can read it without a dulcet ecstasy

creeping along his backbone and quivering in his marrow." He added by way of explanation that "in California, that land of felicitous nomenclature, the literary name of this sort of stuff is 'hogwash.'"[9] Accordingly, in 1876 he scrawled the words "This book belongs to S. L. Clemens's Library of Literary 'Hogwash'" across the flyleaf of his copy of Edward P. Hammond's *Sketches of Palestine*. Hammond, who wrote his impressions of the Holy Land in the form of labored poems, inspired Clemens to jot scornful parodies of these quatrains in their margins. Other volumes in Clemens's personal library bear this "Hogwash" categorization. The unsavory designation of these examples of smelly "hogwash" derived from Twain's Nevada journalism days, and served as a euphemism for language conveying the aroma of unsanitary effluent. By this time Clemens was settling into his new identity as a respectable family man ensconced among the New England literati, and stronger adjectives would have been inadvisable.

Though he inscribed this caustic "Hogwash" invective on the front flyleaves of a number of his victims, just as often he merely made clear their status by vividly insulting their contents. M. M. Ballou's *Under the Southern Cross* (1888) struck Clemens as "a mess of self-complacent twaddle." Daniel F. Beatty's *In Foreign Lands* (1878) had a "pious liar" for an author. S. O. Stedman's problems with syntax, diction, and tone in *Allen Bay* caused Twain to write a brief review of this "idiot novel." In Clemens's opinion Andrew Caster, author of a novel titled *Pearl Island*, should have been flayed and hanged. Clemens found Charles Henry Webb's *Liffith Lank* (1866) to be "enchantingly puerile." James

King Newton's book Clemens ridiculed as "the wild weird whoopjamboreehoo of the embattled jackass." Charles Francis Adams was condemned as someone who writes at "Bret Harte's level." James Milne's *Romance of a Pro-consul* amounted to "cow literature." The writer who employed the pseudonym "Eli Perkins" was a "foetus," a "cur," an "idiot," a "humbug," a "sham," and a "little-minded person." The editor of a guide to Portuguese conversation, Jose da Fonseca, appeared to be "an honest and upright idiot." John Habberton's popular best-seller, *Helen's Babies* (1876), Clemens deemed "the worst and most witless book." David Ker's work amounted to "flatulence." William Mungen's poem "To an Absent One" (1868) was "bosh." A book called *Our Stories* (1888) instead should be titled "Our Thefts." John Alexander Joyce's biography of Edgar Allan Poe drew Clemens's wrath: "If he had an idea he couldn't word it. The most remarkable animal that ever cavorted around a poet's grave." Belton O. Townsend, who wrote *Plantation Lays*, attracted Clemens's special derision because of his dedication page; Clemens wrote indignantly to his friend William Dean Howells, "Think of this literary louse dedicating his garbage to you!" James Buchanan Elmore's *Love Among the Mistletoe* was definitely "hogwash, but not atrocious enough to be first-rate," Clemens concluded.

In books whose historical contents would seem to preclude the usual "Hogwash" epithet, Clemens nevertheless expressed exasperation. Marie Sévigné's tedious *Letters* about life in the French court (1878) were exasperating and "nauseating." The translator of a "revised" edition of *The Works of Tacitus* was so inept that Clemens wondered, "In the name of God what was it like *before* it was 'revised'? Doubtless this translator can read Latin, but he can't write English." Of a clumsy translation of Suetonius's *Lives of the Caesars* (1876) Clemens joked: "Some more pronouns out on a drunk." The charges usually involved the slovenly use of language—a serious crime to Clemens's way of thinking.

Fans who learned of Clemens's appetite for lame exercises of the pen took satisfaction in sending him fresh examples. To one such correspondent, John Horner of Belfast, Ireland, Clemens wrote on 12 January 1906: "Hogwash is a term which was invented by the night foreman of the newspaper whereunto I was attached 40 yrs ago, in the capacity of local reporter, to describe my literary efforts. Many years ago I began to collect Hog-Wash literature & I am glad of the chance to add to it the extraordinary book [Emanda Ros's *Irene Iddesleigh*] which you have sent to me."[10] In an Autobiographical Dictation of 16 December 1908 Clemens recorded that a letter from Howard P. Taylor (written on 1 December 1908) reminded him how Taylor, a Southerner on the staff of the Virginia City *Territorial Enterprise* (he was foreman of the composing room), coined the "word which I have often used in my books when I was talking about poor literary stuff that had a good opinion of itself—when I . . . wanted to compress my disparagement into a single word." Taylor used to wait while Clemens finished scribbling his day's output for the newspaper: "He never had any other name for my literature"—it was always "hog-wash."[11]

Not all of the inferior submissions Clemens received from admirers met his fullest criteria for awfulness. Lewis Elmer Trescott was not a completely legitimate successor to Bloodgood H. Cutter, the "Poet Lariat" whose verses Mark Twain made celebrated in *The Innocents Abroad*; Trescott's poems lacked "idiocy" and "windy emptiness."[12] Cutter, incidentally, appeared to be pleased rather than chastened by Twain's ridicule, flattered to be noticed by such a literary star.[13] However, other obscure writers would hardly have welcomed Clemens's gibes, so it is fortunate that most of his contemptuous remarks were restricted to authors no longer living or were kept within the margins of his books and a close circle of friends and family members. His few published "reviews" were generally directed at prominent and long-deceased writers like James Fenimore Cooper, whose novels from a previous era were overrated, in his estimation.

The vitriol that Twain unleashed against mostly very minor and soon-forgotten literary efforts inevitably raises questions as to why they offended him so greatly, why he bothered to deliberately seek them out, and why he took so much pleasure in demolishing these verbal bumblers who somehow managed to get their banalities into print. After all, beginning in 1869 Twain was an established and increasingly respected writer; these often-pathetic scribblers could hardly be considered competitors of his rank. Why did their productions strike him as being worth his time to debunk them so furiously? Why would he invest those hours in reading them and then stooping to examine their flaws so scathingly? What lay behind this recreation that he found so gratifying?

Several different resentments can be conjectured as having been involved in his

venomous reactions to amateurs' effrontery in displaying their writings to the public. Flowery, ornate diction and hyperbolic figures of speech predictably drew his ire whatever their source, whether in the works of the famous or in the triflings of the neglected. To his mind these false or outmoded effects interfered with the truthful validity of literature. Another habitual trait was his annoyed reaction to instances of grammatical carelessness. As a former printer who had set type for a living and a master stylistic craftsman whose writings have been held up as models of perfection in word choice, sentence structure, and the punctuation of his day, he detested impreciseness in those departments. That preoccupation with stylistic expression would become still more pronounced in the final decade of his life, as attested by the derogatory marginalia in the books he read during that late period. Related to this harsh condemnation of grammatical errors and blunders in expression was Twain's persistent consciousness of his truncated formal education. Lashing out at those who misused words and mechanics conceivably became one of his ways of taking revenge on the fate that had ended his schooling in his early teens. He had pulled himself up from literary obscurity in part by paying close attention to such details in the art of prose composition; why should not these writers, whether novices or not, be held to the same standards that he had met and surpassed?

It could also be argued that this hobby of searching out and condemning inferior literary works betrayed a deep level of insecurity about his own literary credentials, no matter how reassuring the sales figures might be for his latest books. Possibly the same defensiveness about his stature drove him to take outright risks in his speech at the Whittier Birthday Dinner in 1877, a gamble that haunted him to the end of his life. There, of course, he raised a daring question: who in the literary world were the true "imposters"? The privacy afforded by the act of reading offered him much safer opportunities to assert his supremacy. Something in the crushing of upstart authors was essential to his sense of where he himself stood in the literary fraternity. Having ascended to prominence, this celebrated lion not so magnanimously turned around to belittle and demean those who were insufficiently gifted. Twain's invectives rained down on figures who by no stretch of the imagination could be considered his equals or competitors. He found deep fulfillment in showing off to correspondents like William Dean Howells—along with whoever might in the future open the pages of his annotated library copies—how entirely superior were his writerly instincts to the feeble attempts of these incompetent hacks.

Clemens entered the courtroom of critical opinion as though each of these arraigned volumes were on trial and he had been authorized to prosecute a vigorous case against the untalented author. In Clemens's marginalia and unpublished reviews he thus inverted the type of literary criticism practiced by his friend Howells; while Howells passed genial judgments on the upper crust of literature,[14] Clemens rummaged through the bottom shelves of the literary bookcase, finding and ridiculing the "exquisitely bad."

The satiric literary criticism Clemens yearned to write required a healthy dose of animosity, and he found it easy to work himself up to the proper pitch of indignation at the failings of these impostor writers. Why he carried so few of his abortive "reviews" into print is not clear; he may have sensed the unfairness of subjecting these pitiable publications to his mocking scorn, or his interest may have waned after an initial encounter with the book produced his marginalia or a fragmentary manuscript and drained his choler, or perhaps he sensed that he could not adequately educate the public to appreciate the sublimely poor in literature. His effort to make available one example of hogwash literature, "A Cure for the Blues" (1893), which reproduced and mocked Samuel Watson Royston's *The Enemy Conquered* (1845), drew scarcely any public notice. But whatever the considerations that kept nearly all of these sarcasms unpublished, his travesty "reviews" of candidates for his "Library of Literary Hogwash" whetted his critical implements in anticipation of the larger game he chose to carve up either in print or in private correspondence—among them Jane Austen, Oliver Goldsmith, Sir Walter Scott, George Eliot, George Meredith, James Fenimore Cooper, and Bret Harte.

As far as we know Clemens never actually sat down and made a list of the selections for his "Library of Literary Hogwash," but the physical volumes he specifically designated as belonging to it are easily identifiable from his inscriptions and marginalia. A number of additional novels, sketches, and books of poetry qualify as contenders for this dubious distinction on the basis of his caustic comments *about* them. Had he ever set aside a special bookcase for this collection of literary horrors, its shelves presumably would have contained the following sixty-plus titles. (A fuller transcription of his comments about many of them can be found in the Annotated Catalog in *Mark Twain's Literary Resources*, which in the majority of instances provides details about their provenance and location.)

ABBOTT, JOHN STEVENS CABOT (1805–1877). *Daniel Boone, the Pioneer of Kentucky*. Illus. New York: Dodd & Mead, 1872.

Clemens made a note in pencil on a front flyleaf of his copy: "A poor slovenly book; a mess of sappy drivel & bad grammar."[15]

ADAMS, CHARLES FRANCIS, JR. (1835–1915). "Of Some Railroad Accidents," *Atlantic Monthly* 36.217 (November 1875): 571–582.

Upon reading Adams's article, Clemens on 23 November 1875 expressed mock concern that he himself might "jumble words together" and "use three words where one would answer. . . . I shall become as slovenly a writer as Charles Francis Adams if I don't look out." He was jesting, he assured William Dean Howells, since "I never shall drop so far toward his & Bret Harte's level" (*MTHL*, p. 112).

ALLEN, ALEXANDER VIETS GRISWOLD (1841–1908). *Life and Letters of Phillips Brooks*. 2 volumes. New York: E. P. Dutton and Co., 1900. [The edition Clemens read is conjectured; the book was reprinted in 1901 in 3 volumes.]

The Reverend Joseph H. Twichell, a close friend of Clemens, recommended that Clemens read this biography of Phillips Brooks (1835–1893), a prominent American Episcopal bishop. But on 28 August 1901 Clemens wrote to inform Twichell that it was "the very dullest book that has been printed for a century." Brooks had "wearied me; *oh* how he wearied me!" In fact, the work amounted to a "whole basketful of drowsy rubbish."[16]

BALLOU, MATURIN MURRAY (1820–1895). *Under the Southern Cross; or, Travels in Australia, Tasmania, New Zealand, Samoa, and Other Pacific Islands*. Boston: Ticknor and Co., [1888]. [Edition conjectured.]

On 3 September 1895 Clemens reminded himself: "'Under the Southern Cross.' Get this mess of self-complacent twaddle."[17] At the time he was on board a ship sailing from the Hawaiian Islands and approaching the equator.

BEATTY, DANIEL F[ISHER] (1848–1914). *In Foreign Lands, from Original Notes*. Washington, New Jersey: Daniel F. Beatty, Publisher, 1878.

Clemens and an unidentified friend, possibly Joseph H. Twichell, both wrote sarcastic, derogatory comments in the margins of the copy that Beatty inscribed and sent to Clemens on 8 January 1878. Clemens's share of the gibes were mocking: "His English needs interpreting as well as his French"; "The pious liar"; "When this fellow isn't praying he is always lying"; and similar remarks.

BISHOP, LEVI (1815–1881). *The Poetical Works of Levi Bishop*. Third edition. Detroit: E. B. Smith, 1876.

The front flyleaf bears a condemnatory inscription: "This book belongs to/S. L. Clemens's/Library of Hogwash. Hartford, 1876." Clemens underlined sentences in the biographical sketch of Bishop; at its conclusion he characterized Bishop as a useful citizen whose only failing was the delusion that his "jingling twaddle" qualified as poetry. Other marginal notes include the word "Rot" scrawled at the beginning of a poem titled "The Oyster" (p. 490).

BURNEY, FRANCES (FANNY) (1752–1840), later Frances d'Arblay. *Evelina; or, The History of a Young Lady's Entrance into the World*. Collection of British Authors Series. Leipzig: Bernhard Tauchnitz, 1850. [First published in 1778. The title and edition are conjectured; an unidentified edition of this book was in Clemens's library.]

In 1894 Mark Twain noted his intention to review Burney's works and those of other "old-time literary mud idols" (NB 33, TS p. 61).

BURROWS, S[TEPHEN]. M[ONTAGU]. (1856–1935). *The Buried Cities of Ceylon: A Guide Book to Anuradhapura and Polonnarua. With Chapters on Dambulla, Lalawewa, Mihintale, and Sigiri*. Second edition. Colombo [, Ceylon]: A. M. & J. Ferguson, 1894.

"This guide-book is about as mouldy an antiquity as the temples it treats of," wrote Clemens on page 59. On page 62 he objected: "A nobly-padded guide-book. Puts in all the *a & b & c*, with nothing to refer to."

CASTER, ANDREW (d. 1926). *Pearl Island.* Illustrated by Florence Scovel Shinn. New York: Harper & Brothers, 1903.

Clemens penciled markings and sneering comments throughout Pittsburgh stockbroker Caster's novel about two young men shipwrecked in the Indian Ocean. On the front free endpaper Clemens recorded his opinion that "the conversations in this book are incomparably idiotic." At page 57 he comically oversimplified the plot, "Unhappy dog: cast away with idiots on an island." Page 63 especially drew Clemens's scorn: "Son of a bitch, why don't you pray—& *say* you are thankful?" Beside the narrator's hint in the concluding paragraph (p. 267) that further adventures might be related in a forthcoming sequel, Clemens swore, "If you do, you ought to be flayed & then hanged."

CHESEBROUGH, ROBERT AUGUSTUS (1837–1933). *A Reverie and Other Poems.* New York: J. J. Little & Co., 1889.

"I reckon even Cheseborough's [*sic*] poetry failed to kill him," Clemens quipped in a letter to Henry H. Rogers written on 11 November 1894.[18] (Chesebrough, the inventor of Vaseline, ate a spoonful of his petroleum jelly every day, and also used it to cure scrapes, burns, and other bodily ailments). Chesebrough's preface to *A Reverie and Other Poems* promised that "if . . . you like my style, I may assail you again" (p. 4). The tone of his verses ranged from bathetic to morbid. One poem, "My Old Friends," begins, "One by one, silently,/Gone to the tomb;/Following rapidly,/Yet there is room;/Room for the rest of them/Waiting their turn,/After life's history;/Food for the worm" (p. 79).

CLEVELAND, CECILIA PAULINE (b. 1850). *The Story of a Summer; or, Journal Leaves from Chappaqua.* New York: G. W. Carleton & Co., 1874.

On 23 March 1874 Clemens referred to "that unfortunate & sadly ridiculous book of Miss Cleveland's about Chappaqua."[19] He made disparaging marginalia in his copy of the book.

CROSS, ROSETTA OTWELL (1849–1902). *The Suffering Millions* (1890).

Clemens read this book in 1902 while staying with the Sewall family at York Harbor, Maine. He may have grown desperate for reading materials or (more likely) he smelled a possible addition to his imaginary "hogwash" collection. The novel relates the sad family history of the Montrovilles, who have roots in the South but moved to the North. The narrator states that she wishes to convey "the great truth of home influence in the rearing of children." The front pastedown endpaper of the volume records Clemens's verdict: "The trouble about this book is, that it isn't bad enough to be good. Every now & then it drops into something resembling English. SLC".[20]

CURTIS, ELIZABETH ALDEN (b. 1879). *One Hundred Quatrains from the Rubáiyát of Omar Khayyám; A Rendering in English Verse.* Introduction by Richard Burton. No. 227 of 600 copies. Gouverneur, N.Y.: Brothers of the Book, 1899.

Clemens resented this attempt to supersede Edward FitzGerald's translation, writing incredulously from London to the Reverend Joseph H. Twichell on 1 January 1900 to say that Curtis had committed "sacrilege" upon "a noble poem" by endeavoring to recast it line by line. The result, he declared, was as though a Tammany Hall boss should demolish the Taj Mahal and then reconstruct it according to his own concept of what it ought to look like.[21]

CURTIS, LILLIAN E. (fl. 1870s). *Forget-Me-Not. Poems.* Albany, N.Y.: Weed, Parsons and Co., 1872.

Edwin F. Schirely presented this volume by the Chicago poet Curtis to Clemens on 12 July 1889. Clemens read the book thoroughly in search of humorous passages, correcting syntax and rhymes and occasionally making gibes such as the one on page 56 concerning the "Letter to My Cousin, J. W. H., On His Birthday": "Did he have to stand this every year?" On page 58, at the penultimate stanza of the same poem, Clemens urged Curtis to "hit him again next year."[22]

CUTTER, BLOODGOOD HAVILAND (1817–1906). *The Long-Island Farmer's Poems, Lines Written on the "Quaker City" Excursion to Palestine, and Other Poems.* New York: N. Tibbals & Sons, 1886.

Mark Twain preserved this poetaster's place in American letters by calling him the "Poet Lariat" and chuckling over his doggerel verse in *The Innocents Abroad* (1869); thereafter Twain took pleasure in encouraging Cutter's publication of his simplistic and sentimental effusions. Notebooks 8 (1867) and 46 (1903) contain humorous references to Cutter (MTP).

Dagless, Thomas. *The Light in Dends Wood, and Other Stories.* London: Greening & Co., 1903. 116 pp.

Almost certainly someone must have sent Clemens this volume in hopes that he would add it to his burgeoning "Hogwash" library and write back to confirm the fact. Alas, the volume has disappeared from the community library in Redding to which it was donated, so we can only imagine the comments that decorated its pages if Clemens had a pen or pencil at hand. *The Light in Dends Wood, and Other Stories* has been compared to another target of Clemens's derision, Margaret Anne Ross' *Irene Iddesleigh* (1897).One rare book firm advertised the four stories in Dagless's *The Light in Dends Wood* as "bizarre," "sensationalist," "exotic," "weird," and possessing "a ridiculously high body count but almost nothing in the way of narrative" (J and M Books, Limited, Towcester, United Kingdom, 2017).

Deland, Margaret Wade (Campbell) (1857–1945). *John Ward, Preacher* (novel, published in 1888).

Deland's best-selling novel depicts a crisis of religious faith between a Calvinist minister and his wife. "Surely the test of a novel's characters is that you feel a strong interest in them & their affairs—the good to be successful, the bad to suffer failure," reasoned Clemens in February 1889. "Well in John Ward, you feel *no* divided interest, no discriminating interest—you want them all to land in hell together, & right away" (NB 28, *N&J* 3: 446).

Elliott, George W. (1830–1898). "The Dead Canary" and "The Blush Rose" (poems).

Clemens delighted in ridiculing this journalist-poet's efforts when writing to Olivia Langdon. "That creature is oozing his poetical drivel from his system all the time. No subject, however trivial, escapes him. And he dotes upon—he worships—he passionately admires, every sick rhyme his putrid brain throws up in its convulsions of literary nausea." Clemens went on to denounce "this awful bosh, this accumulation of inspired imbecility, this chaos of jibbering idiocy tortured into rhyme. He is the funniest ass that brays in metre this year of our Lord 1869."[23] Elliott was the associate editor of the Fort Plain, New York *Mohawk Valley Register*, in which he published his poetry. Several of his pieces were set to music by others, including "The Banks of the Genessee" (1858).

Elmore, James Buchanan (1857–1942). *Love Among the Mistletoe and Poems*. Alamo, Indiana: Published by the author, 1899.

"Hogwash, but not atrocious enough to be first-rate," Clemens wrote in brown ink on the front pastedown endpaper, which he also signed and dated 1902.[24]

Evans, (Col.) Albert S. (1831–1872). *Our Sister Republic: A Gala Trip Through Tropical Mexico in 1869–70.* Illus. Published by Subscription Only. Hartford, Connecticut: Columbian Book Co., 1870.

Elisha Bliss Jr. decided to publish this book despite Clemens's low opinion of Evans as one of the "fools" who are "so cheap & so plenty." (Clemens had a lingering antagonism toward Evans because of a newspaper feud they had engaged in during the 1860s in California.) Later, on 29 October 1870, Clemens amplified his view of Evans as a "one-horse newspaper reporter," a writer who could never successfully tell a joke, and a man who "would run from a sheep." Clemens asked incredulously, "Who made him a *Colonel*?" He added that "you publishers are pretty hard up for books" if it is the case that "the 'Col.' must be called in to help." Nevertheless, Clemens requested a copy of the book, which he was "suffering" to read.

Upon receiving that volume, Clemens declared as "delicious" Evans's account of haggling with a Mexican vendor over the price of a pair of boots that were already inexpensive, and wrote "coarse" next to the report of an American's effort to breed mules. He commented sarcastically on Evans's insistence on wearing a military uniform because he was in a foreign country. On a front flyleaf Clemens wrote, "Every great personage must be shadowed by a parasite who is infinitely little.—Johnson had

Right: Marginalia written in pencil at the bottom of page 142 in Edward P. Hammond's Sketches of Palestine. *Clemens was unimpressed with Hammond's verse prayer during Hammond's visit to the Garden of Gethsemane.*

Opposite page: Clemens's penciled annotation beside Edward P. Hammond's poetical leave-taking of Palestine on page 153. (Mark Twain Papers, Bancroft Library, University of California, Berkeley; copyright © 2019)

142   LINES.

'Twas in that olive press I felt
  That Thou didst bleed for me ;—
Alas ! how great I saw my guilt
  While in Gethsemane.

I thought of how Thy heart did **throb**,
  While 'all' Thine own did flee,
And left Thee with the cruel **mob**
  In sad Gethsemane.

How earnestly with tears we pled
  For friends across the sea,
That they might cling to Thee who bled
  In lone Gethsemane.

'Twas there I felt my guilt and shame
  In oft forsaking Thee ;
How precious was Thy very name
  In dear Gethsemane.

Should e'er our love to Thee grow **cold**,
  And we forgetful be,
We 'll call to mind Thy love **untold**
  While in Gethsemane.

And now I've thought out all the rot
That rhymes with vowel ε ;
Let not this service be forgot —
Ta-ta, Gethsemane.

his Boswell, Seward [William Henry Seward, U. S. Secretary of State, 1861–1869] his Evans, Victoria her 'John.'"

[**FONSECA, JOSÉ DA** (1792?-1866) **AND PEDRO CAROLINO**]. *The New Guide of the Conversation in Portuguese and English.* Introduction by Mark Twain. Boston: James R. Osgood & Co., 1883.

Mark Twain's introduction to this unauthorized edition mocks its main author (Carolino) as "an honest and upright idiot who believed he knew something of the English language."

GAY, MARY ANN HARRIS (1829–1918). *Prose and Poetry, by a Georgia Lady.* Nashville, Tennessee: Privately printed, 1858.

Hamlin Hill identified Gay's book as the source from which Mark Twain extracted two essays and a poem for graduation elocutions in Chapter 21 of *The Adventures of Tom Sawyer* (1876).[25] In a footnote at the end of the chapter Twain acknowledges that the declamations of Tom's female classmates "are taken without alteration from a volume entitled 'Prose and Poetry, by a Western [*sic*] Lady'—but they are exactly and precisely after the school-girl pattern, and hence are much happier than any mere imitations could be." Eight editions of Gay's book were issued between 1858 and 1873; their titles varied. Sydney J. Krause found the style of Gay's volume to be "Miltonic ornamentation in a country version of the prose of sensibility."[26]

HABBERTON, JOHN (1842–1921). *Helen's Babies. With Some Account of Their Ways, Innocent, Crafty, Angelic, Impish, Witching and Repulsive. Also, a Partial Record of Their Actions During Ten Days of Their Existence. By their Latest Victim.* Boston: Loring, 1876.

Clemens termed *Helen's Babies* a "nauseous & idiotic novel" when writing to Mrs. Fairbanks on 31 October 1877.[27] To another correspondent, Belle C. Greene, Clemens alluded to it as "the very worst & most witless book the great & good God Almighty ever permitted to go to press."[28] He made other slighting comments about the author and the book and remained baffled by their popularity.

HALL, HERBERT BYNG (1805–1883). *The Bric-à-Brac Hunter; or, Chapters on Chinamania.* (First edition published in London in 1875.)

FAREWELL TO PALESTINE. 153

Thou Holy Land, adieu!
    Farewell ye Bible scenes;
Soon thou wilt vanish from our view,
    Thou Land of Palestine.

From thee the Saviour rose
    Victorious o'er the grave,
Thus triumphing o'er all His foes,
    That He the lost might save.

'Twas from thine Olive Mount
    He left the sight of men,
And on that mount His feet shal' stand
    When He shall come again.

We thank our blessed Lord
    That we have seen thy face,
With more of love we'll read His Word,
    And thus its beauty trace.

We've climbed thy rugged hills,
    And scaled thy mountains high;
We've rested by thy sparkling rills,
    But now a long good-bye!

After forty hours of sailing
O'er the classic Mediterranean,
It was on a Lord's-day morning
That they landed in the city
Built by the great Alexander.
    With the help of Captain Layard
They passed thro' the ranks of Arabs,

[Marginalia, in Clemens's hand:] We have said our little say, / We have sham'd our little sham, / We have prayed our little pray— / Yet how few care a damn.

Chapter 20 of *A Tramp Abroad* refers to Hall's "'gushing' over these trifles," showing his "'deep infantile delight' in . . . his 'tupenny collection of beggarly trivialities,'" and prefacing his book with a "picture of himself, seated, in a 'sappy, self-complacent attitude, in the midst of his poor little ridiculous bric-à-brac junk shop.'"

HAMMOND, EDWARD PAYSON (1831–1910). *Sketches of Palestine Descriptive of the Visit of the Rev. Edward Payson Hammond, M.A., to the Holy Land.* Introduction by the Reverend Robert Knox. Boston: Henry Hoyt, n.d. [The Introduction is dated 8 February 1868.]

Hammond wrote these "sketches" in the form of poems. Clemens proclaimed on the recto of the front free endpaper: "This book belongs to S. L. Clemens's Library of Literary 'Hogwash.' Hartford, 1876." Throughout the volume Clemens made prolific and uniformly derisive annotations in pencil. In marginalia on page 142 [Figure 10] he lampooned Hammond's verse prayer about the Garden of Gethsemane, writing: "And now I've thought out all the rot/ That rhymes with vowel E;/Let not this service be forgot—/Ta-ta, Gethsemane." Clemens had similar fun in the margin of page 153 [Figure 11]: "We have said our little say,/We have sham'd our little sham,/We have prayed our little pray—/Yet how few care a damn." Choice passages have been scissored from many pages. Clemens referred to Hammond on page 148 as a "putrid . . . humbug."

On 27 October 1879 Twain notified Albert J. Scott that he had written a review of this "admirable singer."[29] Philip B. Eppard located Twain's anonymously published and highly uncomplimentary essay in the June 1877 issue of the *Atlantic Monthly*.[30]

HOLLAND, JOSIAH GILBERT (1819–1881), pseud. "Timothy Titcomb." *Plain Talks on Familiar Subjects*. New York, 1866. [It is altogether a conjecture that Clemens read this highly popular work.]

Mark Twain informed James Redpath on 18 July 1872 that he was planning a magazine piece that would taunt "Timothy Titcomb." (Holland had recently criticized the prevalence of "buffoons and triflers" on the lecture circuit.) Twain wrote the essay but it was never published. In his response Twain declared that Holland "moves through the lecture field [like] a remorseless intellectual cholera" and only amounts to "a blessed old perambulating sack of chloroform. . . . Dr. Holland's day has gone by. Holland . . . is the very incarnation of the Commonplace."[31]

JAMES, GEORGE PAYNE RAINSFORD (1779–1860). *Heidelberg* (novel, published in 1846).

James set his melodramatic novel in the seventeenth century. Clemens reached a simple judgment: "G P R James's 'Heidelberg' is rot."[32]

JOYCE, JOHN ALEXANDER (1842–1915). *Edgar Allan Poe*. New York: F. Tennyson Neely Co., [cop. 1901].

Clemens made sarcastic notes in pencil throughout the entire volume, scoffing at Joyce's grammar as well as his conclusions. Clemens fixed his view of Joyce at the top of the first page of the text: "If he had an idea he couldn't word it. The most remarkable animal that ever cavorted around a poet's grave." Belittling notes, brief ejaculations ("rot!," "bow-wow!"), and underlinings abound throughout the volume. Clemens compares Joyce's style to that of Mary Baker Eddy before her editors revised her writings (p. xii).

KER, DAVID (1842–1914). "From the Sea to

the Desert," *Cosmopolitan* 6.5 (March 1889): 466–470.

"Pity to put that flatulence between the same leaves with that charming Chinese story [by Wong Chin Foo]," Clemens noted in March 1889.[33]

KIEFER, F. J. *The Legends of the Rhine from Basle to Rotterdam*. Second edition. Translated by L. W. Garnham. Mayence: David Kapp, 1870.

Clemens's annotations in pencil occur throughout the volume. Kiefer's legends were the literary source for some of the stories Mark Twain told in *A Tramp Abroad* (1880). But it was L. W. Garnham's cumbersome translation from the German that tickled Twain immensely. In Chapter one of *A Tramp Abroad* he introduces Garnham's "toothsome" book to his readers, describing the translator's "quaint fashion of building English sentences on the German plan," and quoting a legend called "The Knave of Bergen" as an example. In Chapter 16 he quotes Garnham's sorry attempt to translate the song titled "The Lorelei" into English: "I believe this poet is wholly unknown in America and England; I take peculiar pleasure in bringing him forward because I consider that I discovered him."

KINGSLEY, HENRY (1830–1876). *The Recollections of Geoffry Hamlyn*. Melbourne, Australia: E. W. Cole, n. d. [Edition conjectured. First published in 1859.]

Sailing in the Indian Ocean, Clemens found time on 8 January 1896 to expound on this novel, the first widely read portrait of Australian life: "Henry Kingsley's book, Geoffry Hamlin[,] [*sic*], is a curiosity. In places, & for a little while at a time, it strongly interested me, but the cause lay in the action of the story, not in the story's people. All the people are offensive. Some of them might be well enough if they could be protected from the author's intolerable admiration of them. . . . The reader is lost in wonder that any man can be so piteously bewitched & derationalized by his own creations. The book's grammar is bad, its English poor & slovenly, its art of the crudest. There is one very interesting feature: the author is never able to make the reader believe in the things that happen in the tale. It is not that the things are extraordinary, it is merely that the author lacks the knack of making them look natural. . . . And how misty, vague, unreal, artificial the characters are."[34]

LANDON, MELVILLE DE LANCEY (1839–1910), pseud. "Eli Perkins." *Saratoga in 1901. Fun, Love, Society and Satire.* Illustrated by Arthur Lumley. New York: Sheldon & Co., 1872.

In notes scattered throughout the volume Clemens labeled Landon a "humbug" and a "sham" (p. 104), a "cur" (p. 129), a "little-minded person" (p. 186), and a "foetus" whose book consists of the "Wailings of an Idiot" (p. 152).

LEATHERS, JESSE (1846–1887). "An American Earl" (unpublished autobiography, 1881).

Clemens urged the eccentric Jesse Leathers to submit his autobiography to publisher James R. Osgood, advising Osgood to anticipate "a gassy, extravagant, idiotic book that will be delicious reading, for I've read some of his rot. . . . I believe this ass will write a serious book which would make a cast-iron dog laugh" (*MTLP*, pp 133–134). Leathers insisted that he was the Earl of Durham. His manuscript proved to be unpublishable, but Clemens testified that "The Earl's literary excrement charmed me like Fanny Hill. I just wallowed in it" (*MTLP*, p. 136).

LEWIS, GEORGE EDWARD (1867–1942). *Heart Echoes.* Illustrated by Marie Jewell Clark. Grand Rapids, Michigan: Press of Tradesman Co., [1899].

Clemens annotated the first 103 pages of these poems set in Michigan, correcting the grammar and rewording lines. In some instances his alterations made the verse appear more ridiculous or brought out potential hidden meanings. On page 54 he pointed out that Lewis had used variants of the word "sweet" three times in a three-stanza poem; Clemens wrote "Too much sweet" across the top of the page.

MACDONALD, GEORGE (1824–1905). *Robert Falconer.* [First published in 1868. An American edition was published in 1870.]

Although Clemens became friends with MacDonald and generally admired his writings, he found this novel to be extremely disappointing. To Mrs. Fairbanks, who had recommended the book, he complained on 2 September 1870 that he found nothing praiseworthy after the

middle of the book; in fact he ended up "despising him [Robert] for a self-righteous humbug, devoured with egotism." Clemens culminated this (for him) unusually long literary disquisition by blasting "that tiresome Ericson & his dismal 'poetry'—hogwash, *I* call it." MacDonald gave Robert too many chances "to air some of his piety, & talk like a blessed Sunday-school book with a marbled cover to it." Clemens was sorry that he had "two or three chapters still to read—& that idiot is still hunting for his father. . . . Nothing would do him, clear from juvenile stupidity up to mature imbecility but tag around after that old bummer." In the same letter Olivia inserted dissents to some of her husband's criticisms.[35]

MILLER, GEORGE ERNEST (b. 1855). *Luxilla: A Romance.* [Mobile, Alabama], n.d. [cop. 1885].

According to a notebook Clemens kept during the summer of 1886, he had plans to "review 'Luxilla' that hogwash novel from the South,"[36] but he seems never to have carried through with this intention. Perhaps Miller's melodramatic mishmash was too overdone to support any analysis.

MILLS, S[ALLIE]. M. (b. 1862). *Palm Branches.* Sandusky, Ohio: Register Steam Press, 1878.

This fanciful novel involves a shipwreck, a fortune, and two mysterious children. On the recto of the blank page opposite the copyright notice Clemens speculated that the writer must be about fifteen years old. (He was essentially correct.) He jotted derogatory remarks throughout the volume. On page 65 he penciled his opinion that "puberty will do much for this authoress." He noted on page 120 that when the character named Daisy remained the same "simple, beautiful maiden" despite Mr. Russell's lavishing every luxury upon her (including "pearls and precious gems that a princess might have coveted"), it was "a school-girl's idea of triumph." Clemens made numerous other sarcastic comments.

MILNE, JAMES (1865–1951). *The Romance of a Pro-Consul; Being the Personal Life and Memoirs of the Right Hon. Sir George Grey, K. C. B.* London: Chatto & Windus, 1899.

Clemens used a blank endpaper at the front of the volume to register his scathing opinion:

"The book is affected, artificial, vulgar, airy, trivial, a mess of wandering & aimless twaddle, a literary puke. . . . It is a foolish poor book, & had nothing to say & has accomplished its mission. I have struck out a part of the lavish surplusage; & now & then irrelevancies; also passages which had no discoverable meaning—& no purpose, except to be 'fine.'" Certain sentences he designated as "c.l." ("cow literature") inasmuch as the prose "is intelligible but lumbering & clumsy."

MOORE, JULIA A. (1847–1920). *The Sentimental Song Book*. Grand Rapids, Michigan: C. M. Loomis, 1877. [The edition Clemens read is conjectured; Moore's first edition was published in 1876.]

The "Queen & Empress of the Hogwash Guild" is how Clemens described this poetess to a correspondent in 1906.[37] It is generally agreed that the didactic doggerel of this farmer's wife inspired Emmeline Grangerford's lugubrious elegies in Chapter 17 of *Adventures of Huckleberry Finn* (1885).[38] In *Following the Equator* (1897) Mark Twain returned to *The Sentimental Song Book* ("forgotten by the world in general, but not by me," he declared), and quoted from different poems in Chapters 8 ("Frank Dutton"), 36 ("William Upson"), and 44 ("The Author's Early Life"). Moore, he wrote, had that ineffable and "subtle touch" necessary for genuine hogwash— "the touch that makes an intentionally humorous episode pathetic and an intentionally pathetic one funny" (Ch. 36).

MUNGEN, WILLIAM (1821–1887). "To an Absent One" (poem, published in 1868).

Clemens condemned this poem by an Ohio Congressman as "bosh" and "Mungenical poetry."[39]

MUNICH. PINAKOTHEK, ALTE. *Catalogue of the Paintings in the Old Pinakothek, Munich*. Introduction by Franz von Reber. Translation by Joseph Thacher Clarke [d. 1920]. "Unabridged Official Edition." Illus. Munich: Verlagsanstalt für Kunst und Wissenschaft, n.d.

In Chapter 16 of *A Tramp Abroad* (1880) Mark Twain joked that the "peculiar kind of English" in art historian Clarke's translation of this catalogue qualified him as a rival of L. W. Garnham, whose "quaint fashion of building

English sentences on the German plan" as a translator made F. J. Kiefer's *The Legends of the Rhine* such "toothsome" reading.

NEWTON, JAMES KING (d. 1892). "Obligations of the United States to Initiate a Revision of Treaties Between the Western Powers and Japan," *Bibliotheca Sacra* 44 (January 1887): 46. Also published as a separate pamphlet in Oberlin, Ohio in 1887.

In an essay published in 1888, "American Authors and British Pirates," Mark Twain sneered that "this queer work is made up of rags and scraps of sense and nonsense, sham and sincerity, theft and butter-mouthed piousness, modesty and egotism, facts and lies, knowledge and ignorance . . . mingled with the wild weird whoopjamboreehoo of the embattled jackass."

Our Stories, by the School Children of the State of New Jersey, Fifteen Years of Age and Under. Written for the George W. Altemus Jr. gold prizes. Portraits of the child authors. Philadelphia, 1888.

Clemens complained in his marginalia: "The title should have been Literary Thefts." In another note he railed: "There doesn't seem to be an unstolen page in the book." Subsequently he altered the word "Thefts" to read "Imitations" and changed "unstolen" to "unborrowed" instead. He finally let the writers off the hook by reminding himself, "All things (except the phrasing) in ALL books are borrowed, May, 1908."

PRESCOTT, WILLIAM HICKLIN (1796–1859). *History of the Conquest of Peru, with a Preliminary View of the Civilization of the Incas* (first published in 1847).

In 1891 or 1892 Clemens wrote to Olivia during a sea voyage about "reading the *Conquest of Peru*. "It is interesting—hideously interesting—and the diction is smooth, flowing, graceful, happy—but!! Mr. Prescott's English is not exact enough—it is devilish inexact in lots of places. Sometimes his grammar is bad; and now and then he reels you off a sentence that makes you think of Ben Hur Wallace, it is so slovenly and obscure."[40]

ROBERTS, WILLIAM CULVER, JR. ("BOBS ROBERTS"). *The Boy's Account of It: A Chronicle of Foreign Travel by an Eight-Year-Old. Translated by a Patient Printer from the Manuscript of "Bobs"*

Roberts (William Culver Roberts Jr.). Illustrated with photographs. New York: Waterloo Press, 1909.

By 1909 Clemens was no longer much in the mood to turn his guns on amateur publications. When the "friend of the big writer/Bobs Roberts" sent a presentation copy of *The Boy's Account of It*, Clemens merely wrote below the flattering inscription on the endpaper: "It is the handwriting of a boy of 15, & <so is> the literature is as old."

ROSE, GEORGE (1817–1888), pseud. "Arthur Sketchley." *Mrs. Brown Series.*

Throughout the 1860s, 1870s, and 1880s, Rose produced more than two dozen humorous volumes chronicling the British adventures of the irrepressible Mrs. Brown, including *Mrs. Brown on the Battle of Dorking, Mrs. Brown on the Tichborne Case, Mrs. Brown at Margate*, and *Mrs. Brown in the Highlands.* Clemens had only one word for Mrs Brown: "(rot)."[41]

ROSS, MARGARET ANNE (1860–1939), pseud. Emanda M'Kittrick Ros. *Delina Delaney.* Belfast, Ireland: R. Aickin, n.d. (novel, published in 1898).

Clemens signed and dated a copy of *Delina Delaney* that John Horner, encouraged by Clemens's pleasure in *Irene Iddesleigh*, sent him from Belfast, Ireland on 21 April 1906.[42] A grateful Clemens made notes and markings in the volume, with pages 51, 170, 178, and 179 showing evidence of close and critical reading.

_____. *Irene Iddesleigh.* Belfast, Ireland: W. & G. Baird, 1897.

John Horner of Belfast, Ireland sent this volume to Clemens on 15 December 1905, and Clemens made annotations in it up to page 55. In a letter to the book's sender dictated on 12 January 1906, Clemens expressed his immense delight in the "enchanting" volume, and speculated that Julia A. Moore's reign as undisputed Empress of the Hogwash Guild might finally be at an end.[43] Ross's fiction had already been disparaged by reviewer Barry Pain in *Black and White* (a copy of which Horner enclosed), and prominent critics and writers over the years would be equally fascinated and repulsed by her bathos, hyperbole, and relentless alliteration.

ROYSTON, SAMUEL WATSON (d. 1855). *The Enemy Conquered; or, Love Triumphant.* New Haven, Connecticut: T. H. Pease, 1845.

Professor Francis Bacon of Yale College loaned a copy of this absurd novelette to George Washington Cable, and Cable then introduced Clemens to the tale of Indian fighter Major Elfonzo's courtship of Ambulinia Valeer, a Southern belle.[44] On 29 January 1884 Clemens requested Charles L. Webster to procure him a copy, instructing Webster to "pay two or three dollars if necessary."[45] But eventually it was Cable who, in 1889, came through with copies of the book for which Clemens hungered; on the blue envelope in which he kept these copies Clemens wrote, "Cable's precious pamphlet/ Ambulinia, written by a jackass." Clemens annotated and cut sections from both copies. He made a note to remind himself to return "one of those old New Haven pamphlet novels" to Cable in 1889, and in 1891 he again referred to "Cable's New Haven Idiot's Romance."[46] Eventually Mark Twain reprinted the entire novelette, with a satiric introduction, as "A Cure for the Blues" in *The £1.000,000 Bank-Note* (1893). His mocking analysis of a forgotten work drew barely any public attention. Guy A. Cardwell treated Twain's obsession with this pathetic romance in an insightful article that accounts for his motives behind the writing of "A Cure" and his disappointing efforts to make Royston seem funny.[47]

SELMER, LOUIS. *Boer War Lyrics.* New York: Abbey Press, [1903].

Selmer inscribed a copy of *Boer War Lyrics* to Clemens. On a letter from Selmer laid in the volume Clemens scribbled: "Preserve this rhymed slush & also this ass's letter. S. L. C."

SÉVIGNÉ, MARIE DE RABUTIN-CHANTAL, MARQUISE DE (1626–1696). *The Letters of Madame De Sévigné to Her Daughter and Friends.* Edited by Mrs. Sarah Josepha (Buell) Hale (1788–1879). Revised edition. Boston: Roberts Brothers, 1878.

Clemens generally enjoyed reading scandalous literature that placed the French in a bad light, but he found this book disappointing in both organization and content. "The idea of arranging these letters by massing those to each *person*, instead of massing them by *date*, was certainly the inspiration of an idiot," he observed at the top of page 368. On page 352 he had noted, "What this book mainly lacks, is notes which convey information which we lack." As for the correspondence itself, "Madame de Sevigne is even more nauseating here than when she is adoring her daughter," he wrote on page 276. "She is a pretty offensive old cat, in all, or nearly all, her aspects." After reading Sévigné's last letter to her daughter, Clemens lamented on page 296: "Being hungry, I drank this barrel of feeble soup in the hope of getting the bean in the bottom, but there was no bean."

STEDMAN, S[AMUEL]. O[LIVER]. *Allen Bay, A Story.* Philadelphia: J. B. Lippincott, 1876. 152 pp.

On 23 November 1877 William Dean Howells asked Clemens, "Didn't you once read me some passages out of an idiot novel called Allen Bay?"[48] Clemens undoubtedly had singled out certain parts for Howells's amusement, but the copy of *Allen Bay* from which he had read was then no longer in existence; he had torn many pages from the volume in the course of writing a thirty-nine-page unpublished manuscript, "Burlesque Review of Allen Bay."[49] He used purple ink and Crystal Lake Mills ruled paper in writing the undated manuscript, a paper-and-ink combination that mainly occurred during 1876 and 1877. It is one of Mark Twain's fullest book reviews, inspired in this case by his abhorrence of Stedman's style. Twain claims to have reread the Virginia author's book seven times after a first reading, and launches into a stylistic analysis of its mixed metaphors, marrings of tone, poor transitions, faulty diction, and other flaws. Gradually it dawns upon the reader that Twain is producing a burlesque review, spoofing the vocabulary and clichés of book reviewers as well as the reprehensible tastes of the readers and writers of such sentimental trash. Moreover, in many instances Twain's purple-ink revisions of the extracts he removed from the book distort the original wording and punctuation to heighten Stedman's already-woeful problems in syntax, diction, image, and sense. Twain tore out pages 143–150 to demonstrate the fatuity of Stedman's

highflown bathos, and plundered other pages for shorter extracts. The narrative—about a misanthropic hermit who adopts a baby girl, Judith, only to watch her (as a teenager) die of grief over her boyfriend's drowning in a millpond—is undeniably atrocious, but Mark Twain's revisions emphasize its ludicrous qualities by compressing, italicizing, and isolating them.

SUETONIUS, TRANQUILLUS C. (fl. second century CE). *The Lives of the Twelve Caesars.* Translated in 1796 by Alexander Thomson (1763–1803). Revised and corrected by T[homas]. Forester. Bohn's Classical Library Series. London: George Bell and Sons, 1876.

Clemens reveled in Suetonius's history; indeed it was one of his favorite books. The sloppy translation of this version, however, inflamed his wrath. On the verso of the half-title page he characterized the dismal result: "Translated into Cowboy English." "Drunk again!" he noted on page 150. On page 341 he observed, "Some more pronouns out on a drunk." He summed up his objections on page 480: "This book is one mass of chuckle-headed construction & idiotic grammar."

TACITUS, CORNELIUS (55?-after 117 CE). *The Works of Tacitus. The Oxford Translation, Revised. With Notes.* Harper's New Classical Library Series. 2 vols. New York: American Book Co., n.d.

Clemens signed this volume in 1905. He relished Tacitus's work, but was horrified by the wretched translation. On its title page Clemens twice underscored the word "Revised" and wrote beneath it: "What, the English of it? If so, in the name of God what was it like *before* it was 'revised'?" He made numerous annotations in both volumes objecting to shortcomings in the translation. "Execrable English," he noted on page 122 of the first volume. "Doubtless this translator can read Latin, but he can't write English" (p. 202). Page 205 drew the remark "'pidgin' English." Again, "What does this ass mean by that?" (p. 242). On page 219 of Volume 2 Clemens declared, "This book's English is the rottenest that was ever puked upon paper." (The title page does not disclose the identity of the translator reviled by Clemens.)

TOWNSEND, BELTON O'NEALL (1855–1891).

Plantation Lays and Other Poems. Columbia, South Carolina: C. A. Calvo Jr., Printer, 1884.

Clemens labeled his copy of *Plantation Lays* emphatically: "A volume of unspeakable rot." In a letter of William Dean Howells on 24 May 1884, Clemens referred to the planter-attorney Townsend as an "idiot" who "deserves hanging any-way & in any & all cases—no, boiling, gutting, brazing in a mortar—no, no, there is no death that can meet his case. Now think of this literary louse dedicating his garbage to you. . . Let us hope there is a hell, for this poet[']s sake, who carries his bowels in his skull, & when they operate works the discharge into rhyme & prints it."[50]

TRESCOTT, LEWIS ELMER (1883–1910).

The twenty-three-year-old Trescott submitted samples of his own verse when a humor columnist in the Brooklyn *Daily Eagle* conducted a semi-serious contest in November 1906 to name a successor to the recently deceased Long Island poet Bloodgood H. Cutter, whom Mark Twain had jokingly designated as the "Poet Lariat" in *The Innocents Abroad* (1869). In February 1907 it was announced that Trescott, who claimed to have known Cutter, had won the title of the new "Poet Lariat" based on his florid verse. Informed of this news afterward, Clemens pointed out that, however wretched Trescott's poetry might be, it was inadequate in a few areas: "incoherency," "idiocy," "windy emptiness," and "putrid & insistent bastard godliness."

VAN ZANDT, GEORGE HARRISON (1832–1889). *Poems of George Harrison Van Zandt.* Philadelphia: Jay & Co., 1886. [Edition conjectured.]

In 1887, while Clemens was managing the business affairs of Charles L. Webster & Company, the Philadelphia lawyer Van Zandt approached the publishing firm with a proposal to write a historical romance. In an undated letter to Charles L. Webster, Clemens recommended that Webster consult with Van Zandt about the project.[51] At the top of a letter of 21 June 1887 from Van Zandt, however, Clemens advised his representative at Charles L. Webster & Company, Fred J. Hall, not to dispel Van Zandt's delusion that he could write another *Ben Hur*, but neither to encourage his proposals.

"His volume of alleged 'poems,'" Clemens assured Hall, "is mere hogwash."[52]

VICTOR, METTA VICTORIA (FULLER) (1831–1886). *A Bad Boy's Diary.* New York: J. S. Ogilvie & Co., 1880. [Edition conjectured.]

"I would not be the author of that witless stuff (Bad Boy's Diary) for a million dollars," Clemens wrote to Charles L. Webster on 19 September 1882.[53]

WALLACE, LEWIS (1827–1905). *The First Christmas, from "Ben-Hur."* Illustrated by William Martin Johnson and by photographs. New York: Harper & Brothers, 1902.

Clemens signed a copy of this book in York Harbor, Maine in October 1902. On page vii of the preface Clemens scoffed: "Ah—the finger of God in it. How nice." At the end of the preface Clemens wrote: "In this fairy tale we have a curiously grotesque situation: God, ambushed in a Pullman sleeper, surreptitiously & unfairly <employing> betraying an unsuspecting good & honest infidel [the prominent agnostic Robert G. Ingersoll] into converting Lew Wallace. To what trivial uses may we come at last."

_____. *Lew Wallace: An Autobiography.* 2 vols. Illus. New York: Harper & Brothers, 1906.

Clemens inscribed Volume One with a critical appraisal: "S. L. Clemens/The English of this book is incorrect & slovenly, & its diction, as a rule, barren of distinction. I wonder what 'Ben Hur' is like."

WARDER, GEORGE WOODWARD (1848–1907). *The Cities of the Sun.* New York: G. W. Dillingham, 1901.

Mark Twain made approximately two hundred words of marginal notations in his copy of this book. Most of these comments and underlinings occur in Chapter 12. Warder's philosophy reminded Twain of Mary Baker Eddy's. Twain planned to publish a derogatory review—"About Cities in the Sun"—that survives in the Mark Twain Papers at Berkeley (DV357) and reveals his amusement with the book. Although he went so far as to jot notes to an editor in the margins of this manuscript, it never appeared in print. Mainly he pokes fun in the review at his fellow Missourian for taking St. John's vision of the New Jerusalem as located literally in the sun

(Book of Revelation. 21: 1–27). Twain especially ridicules Warder's efforts to construct a precise picture of the heavenly city. He also derides Senator Chauncey M. Depew for endorsing "this turbulent philosopher." Warder's cosmology theory led him to write other books with titles such as *The Stairway to the Stars* (1902) and *The Universe a Vast Electric Organism* (1903).

WEBB, CHARLES HENRY (1834–1905), pseud. "John Paul." *Parodies. Prose and Verse.* New York: G. W. Carleton & Co., 1876. [This is one of Webb's books that Clemens might have seen.]

In 1905 Clemens announced: "I hate both the name and memory of Charles Henry Webb, liar and thief."[54] A few months later Clemens added: "His prose was enchantingly puerile, his poetry was not any better; yet he kept on grinding out his commonplaces at intervals until he died, two years ago, of over-cerebration."[55]

WEBSTER, DANIEL (1782–1852). *The Private Correspondence of Daniel Webster.* Edited by Fletcher Webster. 2 vols. Boston: Little, Brown and Co., 1875. [This edition is conjectured as the one Clemens read. The book was first published in 1857.]

Clemens wrote to his friend the Reverend Joseph H. Twichell from Elmira, New York on 29 August 1880: "Been reading Daniel Webster's Private Correspondence. Have read a hundred of his diffuse, conceited, 'eloquent,' bathotic (or bathostic) letters written in that dim (no, vanished) Past when he was a student. . . . The only *real* thing about the whole shadowy business is the sense of the lagging dull & hoary lapse of time that has drifted by since then."[56]

WILDMAN, EDWIN (1867–1932). *Aguinaldo: A Narrative of Filipino Ambitions.* Boston: Lothrop Publishing Co., [1901].

Wildman sent Clemens an inscribed copy dated September 7, 1901. In the margins of the book Clemens expressed his mounting distaste for Wildman's viewpoint, writing on page 92: "This is a disastrous friend: he always defends us [the United States] by making us out idiots. It is a comical book. The govt ought to gag the author or drown him. Still, it is the very book that is needed—it tells the dismal truth without intending to." At the top of

page 105 Clemens noted: "He never quotes an authority—his own [is] quite sufficient for his purposes." Clemens made numerous other disparaging notes. The Mark Twain Papers at Berkeley contains a lengthy book review of *Aguinaldo* favorable to the rebel leader (and condemnatory of Wildman) that Twain never completed or published.

YONGE, CHARLES DUKE (1812–1891). *The Life of Marie Antoinette, Queen of France.* New York: Harper & Brothers, 1876. [Edition conjectured.]

Clemens wrote to Mrs. Fairbanks about reading "Mr. Yonge's recent 'Life of Marie Antoinette,' which is without exception the <worst> blindest & slovenliest piece of literary construction I ever saw, & is astounding in another way; it starts out to make you a pitying & lamenting friend of Marie, but only succeeds in making you loathe her all the way through & swing your hat with unappeasable joy when they finally behead her."[57]

NOTES

1   *Mark Twain as Critic* (Baltimore: Johns Hopkins Press, 1967), p. 1.

2   *Mark Twain: Man and Legend* (Indianapolis: Bobbs-Merrill, 1943), pp. 207–208.

3   *Mark Twain and John Bull: The British Connection* (Bloomington: Indiana University Press, 1970), p. 296.

4   Clemens's notations on its pages initially disparage the characters and dialogue, then reveal a grudging admiration for certain aspects of the novel, and finally become openly complimentary.

5   *The Literary Apprenticeship of Mark Twain* (Urbana: University of Illinois Press, 1950), p. 139.

6   "Three Thousand Years Among the Microbes," published in Mark Twain's *Which Was the Dream? And Other Symbolic Writings of the Later Years*, ed. John S. Tuckey (Berkeley: University of California Press, 1967), p. 460. This is, of course, a variation of Twain's more famous adage in a letter written in 1888 about "the difference between the almost-right word & the right word" amounting to the contrast "between the lightning-bug & the lightning" (*Mark Twain: His Words, Wit, and Wisdom*, ed. R. Kent Rasmussen (New York: Gramercy Books, 1997), p. 300.

7   The Willard S. Morse Collection, Yale Collection

of American Literature, Beinecke Library, Yale University.

8   *Mark Twain's Notebooks & Journals*, Volume II (1877–1883), ed. Frederick Anderson, Lin Salamo, and Bernard L. Stein (Berkeley: University of California Press, 1975), p. 142—hereafter referred to as *N&J*. Mark Twain added a few variations in telling about this incident in Chapter 32 of *A Tramp Abroad* (1880).

9   "Hogwash," *Galaxy* 9 (June 1870): 862; "Favors from Correspondents," *Galaxy* 10 (November 1870): 735. Twain also denounced such funereal "hogwash" in "A Western Obituary" in "The Contributors' Club" in the November 1881 issue of *Atlantic Monthly*.

10   Quoted from a dictation copy kept by Isabel V. Lyon, Clemens's secretary (MTP).

11   *Autobiography of Mark Twain*, Volume 3, ed. Benjamin Griffin and Harriet Elinor Smith (Berkeley: University of California Press, 2015), p. 288—hereafter cited as *AutoMT*.

12   Clemens to Ossian Herbert Lang, 21 August 1907, Mark Twain Papers, Bancroft Library, University of California at Berkeley—hereafter cited as MTP.

13   See Miller Hageman, "Bloodgood Cutter's Home!," *Mark Twain Journal* 47.1–2 (Spring/Fall 2009): 101.

14   For the most part Clemens let Howells and other established critics take care of what he once—in 1887—called "high & fine literature" (*Mark Twain-Howells Letters*, ed. Henry Nash Smith and William M. Gibson [Cambridge: Harvard U Press, 1960], p. 587—hereafter cited as *MTHL*). Though he was grateful to Howells for introducing him to such arrivals of talent as William Allen White's *In Our Town* (*MTHL*, pp. 808, 814–815), Clemens's most fervent praise tended to be lavished on minor authors whom he had the advantage of "discovering" himself: writers who published magazine short stories, out-of-the-way guidebooks, unnoticed novels, or overlooked poems. Phoebe Brown's autobiography, for instance, never published and still in manuscript, kept him up far into the night with its quaint charm (*MTHL*, p. 381). The issuance of E. W. Howe's *The Story of a Country Town* seemed to him an unheralded event that deserved congratulations (see C. E. Schorer, "Mark Twain's Criticism of *The Story of a Country Town*," *American Literature* 27.1 [March 1955]:109–112).

15   "A Record of the Small Foolishnesses of Susie

& 'Bay' Clemens (Infants)," MS p. 101, CWB; *A Family Sketch and Other Private Writings,* ed. Benjamin Griffin (Oakland, California: University of California Press, 2014), p. 88.

16   *The Letters of Mark Twain and Joseph Hopkins Twichell,* ed. Harold K. Bush, Steve Courtney, and Peter Messent (Athens: University of Georgia Press, 2017), p. 284– hereafter cited as *LMTJHT.*

17   NB 35, TS p. 41, MTP.

18   *Mark Twain's Correspondence with Henry Huttleston Rogers,* 1893–1909, ed. Lewis Leary (Berkeley: University of California Press, 1969), p. 94.

19   *Mark Twain's Letters,* Volume 6, ed. Michael B. Frank and Harriet E. Smith (Berkeley: University of California Press, 2002), 6: 86)—hereafter referred to as *MTLet.*

20   See Peter Salwen, "Be Sure to Save the Gentians!," *Mark Twain Journal* 48.1–2 (Spring/Fall 2010): 116.

21   ALS in MTP; *LMTJHT*, p. 255.

22   Mark Twain Archive, Gannett-Tripp Learning Center, Elmira College, Elmira, New York.

23   6 September 1869, *MTLet* 3: 336.

24   Mark Twain Archive, Elmira College.

25   "The Composition and the Structure of *Tom Sawyer,*" *American Literature* 32.4 (January 1961): 379–392.

26   *Mark Twain as Critic*, pp. 114–117.

27   *Mark Twain to Mrs. Fairbanks,* ed. Dixon Wecter (San Marino, California: Huntington Library, 1949), p. 211—hereafter cited as *MTMF.*

28   ALS, MTP.

29   Newberry Library, Chicago.

30   "Mark Twain Dissects an Overrated Book," *American Literature* 49.3 (November 1977): 430–440.

31   *MTLet* 5: 123 n. 5.

32   NB 15, *N&J* 2: 126.

33   NB 28, *N&J* 3: 457.

34   Notebook 37, TS pp. 3–4, MTP.

35   *MTLet* 4: 188–189.

36   Notebook 26, *N&J* 3: 240.

37   Clemens to John Horner, 12 January 1906, dictation copy by Clemens's secretary, Isabel V. Lyon (MTP); quoted in Walter Blair's *Mark Twain & Huck Finn* (Berkeley: University of California Press, 1960), p. 212.

38   See, for example, Walter Blair, *Mark Twain & Huck Finn,* pp. 209–213, 406 n. 13; *Huckleberry Finn: Text, Sources, and Criticisms,* ed. Kenneth

S. Lynn (New York: Harcourt, Brace & World, 1961), pp. 156–160; *The Art of Huckleberry Finn: Text, Sources, Criticisms*, ed. Hamlin Hill and Walter Blair (San Francisco: Chandler, 1962), pp. 445–451; and *Adventures of Huckleberry Finn: An Annotated Text, Backgrounds, and Sources*, ed. Sculley Bradley, Richmond Croom Beatty, and E. Hudson Long (New York: W. W. Norton & Co., 1962), pp. 253–254.

39   *Washington in 1868*, ed. Cyril Clemens (Webster Groves, Missouri: International Mark Twain Society, 1943), pp. 11–14.

40   Clara Clemens, *My Father, Mark Twain* (New York: Harper & Brothers, 1931), p. 99.

41   Notebook 19, *N&J* 1: 363.

42   ALS, MTP.

43   ALS, MTP.

44   According to the preface in *A Cure for the Blues*, ed. Charles V. S. Borst (Rutland, Vermont: Charles E. Tuttle, 1964), pp. vii-viii, which appears mistaken in dating the incident as occurring in February 1884. Borst reports that the Reverend Joseph H. Twichell subsequently obtained six copies of *The Enemy Conquered in New Haven* for Clemens's private amusement, but that Clemens somehow misplaced these and appealed to Cable for another copy in 1889. "I have searched everywhere and cannot find a vestige of that pamphlet," Clemens wrote to Cable. "I possess not a single book which I would not sooner have parted with."

45   *Mark Twain, Business Man*, ed. Samuel C. Webster (Boston: Little, Brown, 1946), p. 233—hereafter cited as *MTBus*.

46   Notebook 29, *N&J* 3: 490; Notebook 31, TS p. 17, MTP.

47   "Mark Twain's Failures in Comedy and *The Enemy Conquered*," *Georgia Review* 13. 4 (Winter 1959): 424–436.

48   *MTHL*, p. 209.

49   MS in MTP (Paine 59).

50   *MTHL*, p. 488.

51   ALS, Berg Collection, New York Public Library.

52   Quoted from Philip C. Duschnes Catalog No. 49, item 125.

53   *MTBus*, p. 197.

54   Albert and Shirley Small Special Collections Library, University of Virginia, Charlottesville, PH in MTP.

55   Autobiographical Dictation, 23 May 1906; *MTE*, p. 151; *AutoMT* 2: 50.

56   *MTB*, p. 683; *MTL*, p. 384; *LMTJHT*, p. 102.

57   6 August 1877; *MTMF*, p. 207.

An earlier version of this chapter appeared in American Literary Realism *9.1 (Winter 1976): 64–76.*

10

Susy Clemens's Shakespeare

Certain books have the capacity to conjure up dramatic incidents in the lives of their owners. Wallace Stegner in *Wolf Willow* muses about the symbolism of three volumes of Shakespeare that his nomadic parents bought from a peddler, took with them as they moved from city to city, loaned to a neighbor, recovered from a house fire, and ultimately discarded. Finding these books once again, Stegner reflects on the vicissitudes of his family's existence as signified by those stained volumes. The simple words "Olivia S. Clemens/Oct 1st 1890/Radnor Hall/Mamma"—an inscription written in a set of Shakespeare plays acquired in 1981 by the Harry Ransom Center at the University of Texas at Austin—tell a comparable tale about the household of Samuel L. Clemens and register a fateful juncture in the life of the author's oldest (and quite possibly favorite) daughter, Olivia Susan ("Susy"), when she temporarily parted from her protective, adoring father and tried to achieve an independent adult identity. Her venture would falter, but by that very token these books possess a special poignancy.

Previously unknown volumes once owned by any member of the Clemens household are now extremely rare in the book trade, and inscribed and annotated ones are even more scarce. Thus the abrupt appearance of this twenty-eight-volume set of Shakespeare on the book market in 1981 was cause for excitement in the field of Mark Twain studies. A few of the volumes bear indications that Clemens himself read and annotated them, and the availability to him of another edition of Shakespeare in the Clemens family library is important to our knowledge of his literary resources. Apparently Clara Clemens Samossoud, Susy's sister, was fond enough of these mementos that she held back the Shakespeare set from the amateurishly conducted auction of her private library in Hollywood in 1951.[1] Clara's death in 1962 came four years before that of her second husband, Jacques Samossoud, who bequeathed these books, along with an inscribed and autographed Hillcrest edition of Mark Twain's works and other miscellaneous items, to Henry and Mary Shisler.[2] The Shislers had possession of these materials from 1968 until 1981, when almost all except the Shakespeare volumes were purchased by a prominent rare book dealer in Santa Barbara, California. Because of the books' significance for literary scholarship, the Shislers chose to sell the Shakespeare set to the Harry Ransom Center.

One basis for the academic interest in these volumes is the fact that, in the late phase of his writing career, Mark Twain joined the company of skeptics who were questioning the authorship of the plays and poems attributed to William Shakespeare; indeed, Twain's long essay titled *Is Shakespeare Dead?* (1909) derided Shakespeare's credentials so energetically that some people have erroneously inferred that Twain scorned Shakespeare's writings. But just the obverse was true; Twain stood in such awe of Shakespeare's literary genius that he could not imagine an unschooled, little-known actor as being the author of those plays. This argument that no writer of Shakespeare's stature could have emerged from the backwater village of Stratford-on-Avon seems a curious line of reasoning for someone like Twain, who himself had slight formal education while growing up in the small town of Hannibal, Missouri. In Chapter 13 of *Is Shakespeare Dead?* Twain was troubled by the thought that the bard "was never famous during his lifetime, [and] he was utterly obscure in Stratford," since "if he had been a person of any note at all, aged villagers would have had much to tell about him many and many a year after his death, instead of being unable to furnish inquirers a single fact connected with him."[3] It was simply incredible to Twain that "you can find out *nothing*" about this "most colossal prodigy" of English literature.

Despite these misgivings about Shakespeare's authorship (a most appropriate riddle to infatuate the American writer who was fond of nom de plumes, disguises, and literary themes of twin identities and impersonations), Twain's own writings display a detailed familiarity with the plays and poems we attribute to Shakespeare. Certainly these allusions and quotations are more prolific and pervasive than we might expect to encounter in the fiction and sketches of a great American realist. To take just a few examples, in Twain's travel narrative *The Innocents Abroad* (1869), the phrase "so lame and impotent a conclusion" occurs in Chapter 4 (cf. *Othello*, 2.1.162); another, "speak by the card," in Chapter 22 (cf. *Hamlet*, 5.1.148); and still another, "golden opinions," in Chapter 26 (cf. *Macbeth*, 1.7.33).[4] In a book that formerly belonged to Twain's personal library—*The First Christmas, from "Ben Hur"* (1902), now in the Harry Ransom Center—Twain paraphrased a Hamlet speech in the margin of a page wherein popular novelist Lew Wallace recounts his Christian conversion after hearing some casual talk by agnostic Robert G. Ingersoll. In a derogatory comment, Twain quipped, "To what trivial uses may we come at last" (cf. *Hamlet*, 5.1 .223).[5] Twain's best-known, if facetious, use of Shakespearean lines occurs in Chapter 21 of *Adventures of Huckleberry Finn* (1885), where the charlatan Duke delivers a ridiculous pastiche of lines from *Hamlet*, *Macbeth*, and *Richard III*.

Twain's burlesque in *Huckleberry Finn* indicated veneration, however, and not any measure of disrespect. We know that he read Shakespeare avidly, often soliloquizing aloud for the entertainment of his wife, daughters, and friends. One testament to Twain's admiration for the English playwright involved the typesetting machine in which Twain disastrously invested so much of his capital, and whose ingenious inventor, James W. Paige, Twain called "the Shakespeare of mechanical invention."[6] At a point when things looked propitious for mass-marketing the temperamental machine, Mark Twain paused to record a historic moment: "*Monday, Jan. 7* [1889]—4:45 p.m. The first proper name ever set by this new keyboard was *William Shakspeare* [*sic*]. I set it, at the above hour," Twain noted for posterity.[7]

One of the texts Twain favored was *The Works of Shakespeare* (1871) in six volumes, edited by Professor Henry N. Hudson.[8] In May or early June 1885, Twain made note of the "Ginn, Heath &Co/New York/(Expurgated Shakspeare [*sic*]"[9]; he must have meant Professor Hudson's *Plays of Shakespeare, Selected and Prepared for Schools, Clubs, Classes and Families*, published in 1880 by Ginn, Heath & Company of Boston. Twain later jotted down a related memorandum, "Get Susy a Shakspre [*sic*],"[10] another step toward the eventual purchase of the volumes acquired by the Harry Ransom Center. The HRC's edition was prepared by the same Professor Henry N. Hudson (1814–1886), an American Shakespearean scholar, professor at Boston University, and ordained priest of the Protestant Episcopal Church, who issued Shakespeare's works in a variety of formats and series during the 1870s and 1880s. The Clemens set, a reprint edition, has twenty-two titles that survive, lacking such plays as *The Comedy of Errors, Love's Labor's Lost, Measure for Measure, All's Well That Ends Well, The Merry Wives of Windsor, The Taming of the Shrew*, and *Troilus and Cressida*. Tragedies

and history plays are better represented than comedies among the extant volumes, and no poems are included. (Mrs. Clemens owned additional copies of *History of King John* and *King Richard the Second*, which are also part of the set at HRC.) There is no series title on the title page or the spines; each unnumbered volume merely carries a designation resembling this one: *Shakespeare's As You Like It. With Introduction, and Notes Explanatory and Critical. For Use in Schools and Families.* According to the dates on the individual title pages, the publisher, Ginn & Company of Boston, brought out this uniform but untitled series between 1884 and 1890.

Although this particular set of Shakespeare volumes was not purchased for Samuel Clemens, he made his characteristic penciled brackets and underlinings in its copies of *King Richard the Third* (at Richmond's lines that "True hope is swift, and flies with swallow's wings/Kings it makes gods, and meaner creatures kings"); in *Romeo and Juliet* (notations on the front pastedown endpaper, and "The more I give to thee,/The more I have" [Juliet] underlined on page 74); in *King Henry the Eighth* (underlining "my hopes in Heaven do dwell," page 133); and also in other plays. Six of the books—three volumes of *History of King John* (one title page dated 1884, the others 1885) and three volumes of *King Richard the Second* (one title page again dated 1884, the others 1885)—were acquired earlier than the twenty-two volumes and were signed by Olivia Langdon Clemens, Samuel Clemens's wife and Susy's mother. Olivia used black ink to write in these copies "Olivia L. Clemens/ Hartford/June 1886." They were purchased from the Hartford bookstore of Brown &

Gross (a predecessor of Israel Witkower's illustrious firm); Brown & Gross bookstickers appear on the rear pastedown endpapers of four of these six books.

The remaining twenty-two volumes were acquired especially for Susy Clemens. They were a logical gift: Shakespeare had been the most important author in her family's evening programs of oral readings, scenes from plays, and parlor games such as charades. At thirteen Susy had learned part of *The Merry Wives of Windsor* to act with her sister Clara, and at fourteen Susy's favorite game, invented by herself, was that of declaiming lines from Shakespeare while another girl stood behind the speaker and made (usually inappropriate) gestures. In her eighteenth year, Susy took part in theatrical entertainments at the Onteora Park Club near Tannersville, New York, a resort in the Catskill Mountains, where she played Hamlet to Clara's Ophelia. In the summer of 1890, however, Susy had a French tutor and was intent on matters other than acting out Shakespeare: her family was proud that she had passed the Bryn Mawr entrance examinations in six subjects—arithmetic, algebra, English, physical geography, German and Latin composition, and Virgil—but knew that upon enrolling in college she would be required to pass further examinations in French grammar and plane geometry."[11]

Just prior to taking Susy to the Bryn Mawr campus in September 1890, Clemens and his wife spent a week-long vacation with Susy at the Murray Hill Hotel in New York City. During that shopping and sightseeing trip they most probably obtained Susy's college set of Shakespeare, a set with green, pebble-grained buckram covers and gold-stamped spines. From New York, they proceeded directly to Bryn Mawr, staying at the Summit Grove Inn. Evidently Olivia delayed the task of inscribing the new books until Susy had received her dormitory assignment and then, either in the small woman's residence hall named Radnor, or else in Olivia's room at the Summit Grove Inn, she sat down at a writing desk on Wednesday, 1 October, and painstakingly inscribed each volume in black ink that has now faded to brown: "Olivia S. Clemens/ Oct 1st 1890/Radnor Hall/Mamma." Only in the copy of Shakespeare's *Twelfth Night* did she vary the wording, writing (out of habit) "From O L C" instead of "Mamma." The pride of a mother shines through the precise inscriptions. Her entire family was meticulous about signing their books, but for Olivia to inscribe this many volumes at a sitting was exceptionally industrious. It must have been Olivia's way of saying a fond farewell to her daughter, and of ensuring that other girls in the residence hall would not borrow the freshly purchased volumes without asking permission. The numerous markings the volumes received suggest that Susy made frequent use of this set of books; aside from the extra copies of *History of King John* and *King Richard the Second*, all of the volumes bear penciled brackets, underlinings, and study notes. The copies of *Julius Caesar* and *Othello, the Moor of Venice* contain the most extensive annotations, but other volumes are also marked with thoroughness.

Justin Kaplan, a discerning Mark Twain biographer, observed that one of Susy's burdens was a relationship with her father "compounded of hectoring and worship."

Clemens left her at Bryn Mawr with great regret and was halfway pleased "to hear she was almost too homesick to stay at college." As Clemens remembered their leave-taking, "our train was moving away, and she was drifting collegeward afoot, her figure blurred and dim in the rain and fog, and she was crying."[12] On 20 October 1890, the eighteen-year-old Susy wrote:

> I am glad of course that I am in Bryn Mawr as I was working all last year to get in and now that I am here there is a great deal that I enjoy most thoroughly. The work is delightful and the people are lovely and altogether Bryn Mawr is an ideal place, but oh! it *does* not, *can* not compare with home![13]

Gradually Susy's loneliness abated, and she eagerly performed the part of Phyllis in a production of Gilbert and Sullivan's *Iolanthe* after returning to college from a Hartford Christmas. Her father visited Bryn Mawr on Monday, 23 March 1891, and delivered a program of readings; on that afternoon he embarrassed her by telling a ghost folktale, "The Golden Arm," which she had specifically asked him to omit, thinking it less than genteel and unbefitting for her father to relate in such a setting. (In the tale, a man intends to dig up his wife's corpse to retrieve her golden arm.)

At Bryn Mawr, Susy enrolled in three Latin courses, French, and the required physical education course. Whether it was the mandatory physical education course that sapped her strength, or merely the severe winter spent away from her family's care, Susy's health, fragile like that of all the Clemens children

and their mother, declined noticeably as the spring term ended. When Olivia brought Susy home in April 1891, the damage had been done, in Clemens's opinion. He later asserted that "Bryn Mawr began it. It was there that her health was undermined."[14] But disturbing signs of Susy's vulnerability were apparent even before her abortive struggle to lead a normal existence away from the spotlight of being "Mark Twain's daughter." Whatever their cause, Susy's illnesses became more frequent and more serious after her first and only college year; in fact, she never enjoyed truly good health again.

Susy's days at Radnor Hall came in a period of increasingly unhappy times for her entire family, and this shift was suggested by their departure, at the end of Susy's first year at college, from the Hartford residence where the three daughters had enjoyed halcyon days. In June 1891, two months after Susy came home from Bryn Mawr, the Clemenses left Hartford—they hoped for only one or two years—to travel and reside in European cities and health resorts. Before going, the girls walked disconsolately about the library, the many bedrooms, the little conservatory that had held fragrant plants. They shut up the house, little realizing that it would never be reopened for the same family again. The Clemenses left the United States partly to find a treatment for Olivia, who was displaying early symptoms of the heart disease that would debilitate her by degrees until her death in 1904; more than that, however, they were intent upon reducing their household expenses. Twain's publishing firm no longer showed its reassuring profits, and his investments in the typesetting machine had cascaded into the ruinous trend that would eventually bankrupt him.

In Europe, Susy was delighted to find some of the sites mentioned in Shakespeare's plays, writing excitedly from Venice in 1893 after visiting "the house of my beloved Othello and his statue."[15] Her father recalled, "I cannot remember when she first began to carry around a vast Shakespeare. She was never without it. It was a trouble in traveling, but she had to have it."[16] There may have been a single-volume work, now lost, that Twain was describing, but the worn and annotated condition of the Shakespeare set in the Harry Ransom Center makes it probable that these twenty-eight volumes constituted this "vast Shakespeare" Susy insisted on toting around Europe.

During the family's vagabond life on the Continent, Twain continued to manifest the interfering, patriarchal attitude that seems to have prevented his daughters from enjoying an ordinary routine of boyfriends and serious suitors. (Only Clara, at an advanced age, would fight her way into the state of marriage, to pianist-conductor Ossip Gabrilowitsch, in 1909.) At last, following her father's financial failure, Susy returned to her aunt's Quarry Farm in Elmira, New York, to wait for her father, mother, and sister Clara, who undertook a voyage around the world that would enable Twain to recoup, from the proceeds of lectures and a book about the tour, his floundering fortunes. The Clemenses felt that Susy's health might benefit from the salubrious outdoor atmosphere of unhurried farm life. Her youngest sister, Jean, also stayed in Elmira. But after returning to Hartford to prepare for a voyage that would have reunited the family members in England, Susy became ill; growing worse daily, she was taken to the temporarily reopened Hartford house, where she wrote and walked about the rooms as her fever raged. Susy died there of spinal meningitis on 18 August 1896, at the age of twenty-four.

As it turned out, then, the inscriptions made in her Shakespeare books in 1890 marked a final period of relative health and unalloyed pleasure for Susy, and now they lastingly evoke a crucial, personal instant, glimpsed momentarily across the abyss of many years. This Shakespeare set bears mute testimony to a strong bond among the members of a famous family; once on the shelves of a dormitory room at a fashionable women's college, it likewise represents Susy Clemens's brave but brief Bryn Mawr experiment. The volumes also testify to an adulation of Shakespeare's works that went beyond the conventional taste of the 1890s and signified the fresh awakening of American appreciation for Renaissance drama and poetry that was enriching the nation's culture. Susy's relish for amateur theatricals (which resembled her father's appetite for home and neighborhood performances) is betokened here as well. These volumes further suggest Twain's affection for Shakespeare's writings and the integration of allusions and quotations throughout his own literary productions. A well-used set of Shakespeare volumes, viewed from these manifold perspectives, opens to us vivid scenes of hope and regret, ambition and futility, domestic bliss and frustration. More than mere artifacts of literary history, these books symbolize the keenness of Samuel Clemens's aspirations for his favorite daughter, and the anguish of his blighted hopes for her and his family.

Notes

1   Alan Gribben, "The Dispersal of Samuel L. Clemens's Library Books," *Resources for American Literary Study* 5.2 (Autumn 1975): 147–65. (A revised version of this essay appears as a chapter in the present volume.)

2   Included among these materials were more than 100 volumes from Clara's personal (post-1910) library collection. Many of these items entered the extensive Mark Twain collection of Nick Karanovich of Fort Wayne, Indiana. These volumes were subsequently acquired by Kevin Mac Donnell of Austin, Texas. He donated many of them to the Mark Twain Archive at Elmira College in Elmira, New York. The majority of these volumes were religious works, inspirational writings, and self-help guides. Email, Mac Donnell to Gribben, 20 January 2019.

3   Mark Twain, "Is Shakespeare Dead?" in *What Is Man?*, Vol. 12, *The Complete Works of Mark Twain*, Authorized Edition (New York: Harper & Brothers, 1917), pp. 372–76.

4   L.G. Crossman, Professor Emeritus at the University of Regina, provided these examples and augmented scores of allusions listed in the Annotated Catalog. The numbering of acts, scenes, and lines-follows that of the *Cambridge Shakespeare*, often cited as the Globe edition.

5   The volume is described more fully in my "Mark Twain's Library Books in the Humanities Research Center," *The Library Chronicle* 11 (1979): 11–26.

6   *Autobiography of Mark Twain, Volume 1,* ed. Harriet Elinor Smith (Berkeley: University of California Press, 2010), 1: 102. Mark Twain made the comparison around 1890.

7   Notebook 28, included in *Mark Twain's Notebooks & Journals, Volume 3,* ed. Frederick Anderson *et al.* (Berkeley: University of California Press, 1979), 3: 443—hereafter cited as *N&J*.

8   These volumes, originally owned by Clemens's brother-in-law, Theodore Crane, are now in the Mark Twain Archive, Gannett-Tripp Learning Center, Elmira College, Elmira, New York.

9   Notebook 24, *N&J* 3: 159.

10 Notebook 25, *N&J* 3: 212.

11 These and other facts pertaining to Susy Clemens's activities derive from *Susy and Mark Twain: Family Dialogues,* ed. Edith Colgate Salsbury (New York: Harper & Row, 1965), pp. 277–83 especially.

12 Justin Kaplan, *Mr. Clemens and Mark Twain: A Biography* (New York: Simon and Schuster, 1966), pp. 308–09.

13 Salsbury, *Susy and Mark Twain,* p. 283.

14 Salsbury, *Susy and Mark Twain,* p. 289.

15 Salsbury, *Susy and Mark Twain,* p. 328.

16 Notebook 39 (1897), TS p. 48, Mark Twain Papers, Bancroft Library, University of California at Berkeley.

An earlier version of this chapter appeared in The Library Chronicle *[University of Texas at Austin] New Series 27 (1984): 95–103.*

11

'It Is Unsatisfactory to Read to One's Self'
Mark Twain's Informal Readings

A year before Samuel Clemens would marry Olivia Langdon, he sketched for his fiancée his notion of "how pleasant it would be to sit, just us two, long winter evenings, & study together, & read favorite authors aloud & comment on them & so imprint them upon our memories. It is so unsatisfactory to read a noble passage & have no one you love, at hand to share the happiness with you. And it is unsatisfactory to read to one's self, *anyhow*—for the uttered voice so heightens the expression. I think you & I would never tire of reading together."[1] Nearly two months later, he wrote again to her about the literary atmosphere he desired: "And so *you* have been having visions of our future home, too, Livy? I have such visions every day of my life, now. . . . You & I . . . reading & studying together when the day's duties are done—in our own castle, by our own fireside, blessed in each other's unwavering love & confidence."[2]

Within five years of their wedding Clemens built in Hartford the "castle" he had promised Olivia, and they were often able, as he had hoped, to conclude the day sitting by the fireside, "reading & studying together." The realization of this dream prompted a custom that was to have an impact on his conception of literature: he came to think of reading as ideally an oral pastime. From his new home, Clemens wrote on 23 November 1875 to tell William Dean Howells of plans to read his friend's new novel in the *Atlantic Monthly*: "Company interfered last night, & so 'Private Theatricals' goes over till this evening, to be read aloud. . . . This is going to be a splendid winter night for fireside reading, anyway."[3]

As Clemens's children grew older they joined the family circle for this entertainment; each read silently and then shared passages by giving them to Papa to read to the group. In a Munich hotel room, Clemens informed Howells on 17 November 1878, he and his family, with a friend and a servant also present, "gathered around the lamp, after supper, with our beer & my pipe, & in a condition of grateful snugness tackled the new magazines. I read your new story [*The Lady of the Aroostook*] aloud, amid thunders of applause."[4] In fact

Clemens's hearthside renditions of Howells's fiction became a regular ritual in the Clemens household.

The outcome of this practice was predictable: Clemens gradually raised informal literary readings from the level of a favorite recreation to that of an oral art. Family reading sessions evolved into impromptu performances. Clemens's nephew Jervis Langdon recalled that "one of the pleasantest neighborhood customs that grew up in the Hartford home was the gathering, of an evening, around the library fire while Mr. Clemens read aloud. He liked stirring poetry, which he read admirably, sometimes rousing his little audience to excitement and cheers." Langdon particularly remembered hearing Clemens read from the writings of Shakespeare and Robert Browning. "The listeners invariably demanded at the end three favorites, 'How they brought the Good News from Ghent to Aix,' 'Up at a Villa, Down in the City,' and, for climax, [Macaulay's] 'The Battle of Naseby,' which he delivered with supreme eloquence and emotion."[5]

Women's "study groups" for appreciating English authors were in vogue during the 1880s. If it gratified Clemens to share with Olivia a particularly delicious passage from Browning, how much more pleasurable to address an entire roomful of her women friends. Clemens's authorized biographer, Albert Bigelow Paine (along with other subsequent commentators)[6] expressed mystification at Clemens's attraction to Browning and his conducting Wednesday morning Browning classes throughout 1886 and 1887. "In his early life," mused Paine, "he had cared very little for poetry, but along in the middle eighties he somehow acquired a taste for Browning and became absorbed in it."[7] This matter seems less strange if one recalls that Browning refined the dramatic monologue as a poetic form; his characters relate miniature stories that supply setting, background, and plot. Clemens reveled in certain of Browning's poems because they were essentially dramatic speeches suitable for reading to audiences.[8] When Mary Bushnell Cheney heard Clemens read Browning to one of his study groups, initially she was simply curious as to what Clemens would do about his drawl,[9] "but for the most part it simply disappeared." Cheney considered the diminishment of the reader's conspicuous presence to have been Clemens's most impressive accomplishment.[10]

His copies of Browning's works bear testimony to his painstaking preparation for the readings. In *Men and Women*,[11] for instance, he annotated most of the poems—especially "Old Pictures in Florence"—for reading aloud, indicating syllabic stresses, connecting certain stanzas, and glossing difficult words or phrases. Almost all of the poems in *Parleyings with Certain People of Importance in Their Day*[12] exhibit heavy pencil marginalia, and "With Daniel Bartoli" (pp. 39–53) is surrounded by numerous speculations about possible interpretations—some cancelled as new meanings emerged and were substituted. Clemens's markings underscore lines, add stress marks to denote pronunciations, and furnish explanatory notes. He devised this system of penciled notations, he wrote in his copy of *Dramatis Personae*, "in order to give the eye instant help in placing & shading emphases—a very necessary precaution when one reads Browning."[13] Probably he first tried these interpretations between meetings of the class; in any event Clara Clemens remembered that "at one time he was inclined to read Browning aloud at the table, but Mother objected, declaring she would not be able to understand a single word amid the clatter."[14]

Clemens did not confine his many informal readings to Browning. William Dean Howells recollected that his friend favored certain poems by John Hay and others. A powerful persona and an intensely emotional appeal seemed to draw his attention. One such dramatic situation, narrated by the type of frank, brusque persona whom Clemens favored, prevails in a poem that Howells recalled Clemens "liked to read to you, and he read, of course, splendidly." Howells "remembered how he fiercely revelled in the vengefulness of William Morris's *Sir Guy of the Dolorous Blast*, and how he especially exulted in the lines which tell of the speaker's joy in slaying the murderer of his brother."[15] Howells was alluding to one of the villains in Morris's "Shameful Death," a poem collected in *The Defence of Guenevere, and Other Poems* (1858). Sir Guy of the Dolorous Blast and Sir John the Knight of the Fen ambushed and hanged the newly married Lord Hugh; the poem's speaker, Lord Hugh's brother, tells of his revenge on the cowardly murderers:

> I am threescore and ten,
> And my hair is all turn'd grey,
> But I met Sir John of the Fen
> Long ago on a summer day,
> And am glad to think of the moment when
> I took his life away.

In the next, penultimate stanza, the narrator iterates:

> I am threescore and ten,
> And my strength is mostly pass'd,
> But long ago I and my men
> When the sky was overcast,
> And the smoke roll'd over the reeds
> of the fen,
> Slew Guy of the Dolorous Blast.

Clemens found pleasure in lighter fare as well, including stories from Joel Chandler Harris's *Uncle Remus: His Songs and His Sayings* (1880)—particularly the one titled "Brer Rabbit, Brer Fox, and the Tar Baby." Susy and Clara Clemens "knew his book by heart through my nightly declamation of its tales to them," Clemens once remarked.[16] On 5 November 1892 Clemens wrote to Clara from Florence to describe his recent literary readings at Villa Viviani; after laying aside Browning ("too somber & difficult") and Tennyson ("too tame & effeminate"), he and his circle of acquaintances were "bracing up on Uncle Remus, evenings, for a change."[17]

As one consequence of these encouraging responses, Clemens adopted oral reading as his main criterion for critical interpretation and judgment. A concern for the aural quality is evident in his opinion of Mary August Ward's immensely popular novel, *Robert Elsmere* (1888), as he informed Rudyard Kipling in 1889: "I read it, of course, for the workmanship. . . . The effect on me was exactly as though a singer of street ballads were to hear excellent music from a church organ. . . . I listened and I liked what I heard. I am speaking of the grace and beauty of the style."[18] By 1906, when Clemens was dictating his autobiography to a stenographer in order to capture the sonorous rhythm of spoken monologue, he routinely evaluated literary works submitted to him in a manner that suggested oral auditions. In a letter of 24 June 1906 praising William Allen White's *In Our Town* Clemens alluded to that "most exacting of tests" he had applied to White's book—"the reading aloud."[19] When Mark Twain cited selections from William Dean Howells's writings (in the July 1906 *Harper's Monthly*) to demonstrate Howells's accomplishments in prose style, he again stressed this point. "And, of course," he cautioned, "read it aloud. I may be wrong, still it is my conviction that one cannot get out of finely wrought literature all that is in it by reading it mutely."[20]

In the summer of 1906 Clemens wrote modestly to Charlotte Teller from Dublin, New Hampshire: "I read aloud, nights—poetry—which is hardly in my line."[21] By then his patient auditor Olivia was gone, but he recruited others willing to listen: his daughters Clara and Jean, a few close friends, and especially Isabel V. Lyon, the secretary whom his wife had employed in 1902 and who remained as his social secretary and factotum. Her private journals teem with enraptured accounts of Clemens's discovering and then reading good passages to her. She noted on 17 May 1906, for example: "Mr. Clemens reads poetry to Jean and me every evening. Such reading it is. There never was anyone to read so beautifully before and to charm you so and hurt you so."[22] On 9 October 1906 she recorded what was evidently a regular occurrence: "Tonight after dinner he wanted Shakespeare. I took him the 4 volumes I had

Sketch of Clemens in his library in 1891 (Mark Twain House and Museum, Hartford, Connecticut)

brought up here [to Dublin] and he selected 'Julius Caesar' and read to us for an hour and a half. It was fine. The King [her affectionate name for Clemens] acts the characters with modified gestures and inflections of voice."[23] After Charlotte Teller sent her "Mirabeau" play[24] to Clemens in Dublin, he explained to her on 16 June 1906 what transpired: "I tried reading the play to myself, knowing I should arrive nowhere by that process—& that is where I arrived. I must read it aloud, if I would arrive somewhere. . . . Then I . . . shut off Miss Lyon's afternoon walk, yesterday, & required her to act as audience, which she was properly glad to do. For a first-night, I doubt if any performance ever went off with a more intemperate & sustained enthusiasm."[25] Isabel Lyon recorded in her journal how Clemens read straight through all five acts, resting now and then. "Mr. Clemens read it beautifully. He has to read anything like a play aloud to get at its values," she noted.[26]

Lyon also chronicled Clemens's steadily increasing admiration for Kipling's stories and poems during this period. In May and June 1906 Clemens often read to his household from Kipling's Mowgli tales in *The Jungle Books* before retiring in the evenings.[27] On the evening of 11 June 1906 Clemens "read aloud" the short story "Red Dog" and praised Kipling's diction in picturing the python, Kaa ("the light seemed to go out of his eyes and leave them like stale opals" was Kipling's phrase). "'Stale opals'—such a good description, he said. I wish Kipling could hear him read those masterpieces," Lyon wrote.[28]

During Clemens's sojourn in Bermuda in 1908 he repeatedly read aloud from Kipling's poetry to groups of vacationing Americans.

"These people had never, never heard anything of the real Kipling before," Lyon commented in her journal. Following a reading on March 27th she heard one of the fifteen people present, a Mr. Chamberlain, declare that "there isn't anyone else in the world who could read between the lines as the King can."[29] When Clemens read on the night of February 29th, Henry H. Rogers, the millionaire Standard Oil executive who had helped him salvage his financial affairs, was in attendance. "We went from shouting joys to tears over the beauties, the perfections," Lyon recorded.[30] Clemens read again for Rogers and the others on March 26th, and "he was never in better spirit—never in a completer understanding." His rendition of "Soldier an' Sailor Too," Lyon averred, was "a thing never again to be repeated."[31]

Another account of these Kipling readings—one that offers clues to Clemens's oral techniques—appears in Elizabeth Wallace's valuable memoir.[32] Wallace, the dean of women at the University of Chicago, heard Clemens entertain Rogers and other friends in his hotel room in Hamilton, Bermuda on several occasions in March and April 1908. She remembered that Clemens held his pipe in one hand and gesticulated with it during highly dramatic passages—especially when reading "M'Andrew's Hymn." Rogers urged his friend Clemens not to read "too slowly." Even the hard-boiled Rogers, however, "blinked hard" to suppress tears when Clemens read the most successful poem, "The *Mary Gloster*." The group "laughed delightedly" at "The Ballad of the *Bolivar*." Clemens also read "Soldier an' Sailor Too," "Mandalay," "Chant-Pagan," and "Tomlinson."[33]

Those private performances allowed

Clemens to give rein to the acting abilities about which his contemporaries often remarked. In reading these works the material became his as well as the author's; he shared in the listeners' approbation. Judicious gesture and intonation conveyed meaning; in a sense he participated in the creative process. And so his reading sessions whenever he was alone became a search for appropriate material with which to entertain a small audience. To Clara, who sent him one of her own literary compositions, he wrote on 3 August 1906 from Dublin: "I first read it to myself—merely to get the hang of it, for nothing is to be found out about a piece of literature by a mute reading of it. Next day I read it aloud to Lyon, and then the light broke out all over it & we saw that it was fine & strong & deep & moving." He assured Clara that "if others fail to see the piece's merits it will be only because they will read it mutely—people always do that stupid thing."[34]

He often inveighed against the obtuseness of readers who settled for "mute" readings, and his own oral renditions were so impressive that his audiences readily agreed that such techniques were vastly superior to reading to oneself. When he left them to their own devices, however, he found to his despair that they inevitably returned to their old habits. Not everyone had Mark Twain's trained ear for nuances of speech, nor his willingness to perform publicly.

Clemens's dismissal of Isabel V. Lyon in 1909[35] deprived him of his most faithful listener. Clara frequently lived away from Redding, Jean struggled with illness until she died at the end of 1909, and Paine was preoccupied with writing Clemens's biography. In desperation Clemens sometimes turned for an audience to his "Angelfish Club," but these young girls did not always prove to be satisfactory auditors. He complained about fifteen-year-old Helen Allen in 1910 while staying in Bermuda; she listens to excellent books "for a long stretch of ten minutes—great & choice passages—and look[s] wooden & atrophied; & when you are through, will thank you for your trouble with—perfectly ghastly silence!"[36] At the end of his life Clemens finally found himself—for the first time in forty years—lacking an appreciative audience.

Nothing else known about Clemens's reading habits seems as significant as his preference for oral readings before other people, a practice that surely helped develop the flexible narrative voice he strove to reproduce in his fiction. He read his daily output of prose to his family and friends as regularly as he introduced them to excerpts from his daily reading. When he discovered material that elicited favorable audience responses under varied conditions, he stuck with it gratefully.

Throughout much of his life Mark Twain read professionally in public for both the income and the gratification it provided.[37] Most of his selections for formal readings were taken from his own works (often before publication), but he occasionally read from the Uncle Remus sketches or the poems of Browning and Kipling. He never mastered stage acting beyond amateur theatricals (which he enjoyed hugely),[38] yet from all accounts his public and private readings were superlative. It seems unfortunate that his life ended shortly before phonographic recording devices came widely into use, for Clemens developed his oral techniques so keenly and edited the passages he read sufficiently to give them a now irrecoverable imprint of his own literary genius.

NOTES

1   2 January 1869, *Mark Twain's Letters, Volume 3, 1869*, ed. Victor Fischer and Michael B. Frank (Berkeley: University of California Press, 1992), 3: 4—hereafter cited as *MTLet*.

2   27 January 1869, *MTLet* 3: 116–117.

3   *Mark Twain-Howells Letters*, ed. Henry Nash Smith and William M. Gibson (Cambridge, Massachusetts: Belknap Press of Harvard University Press 1960), p. 113.

4   *Mark Twain-Howells Letters*, p. 240.

5   *Samuel Langhorne Clemens: Some Reminiscences* (Privately printed, 1938), pp. 14–15.

6   Edward Wagenknecht wrote: "The great surprise is Browning. One would have expected Mark Twain to hate him, as he hated James and Meredith. With the perversity so characteristic of him, he decided instead to love him" (*Mark Twain: The Man and His Work*, 3rd ed. [Norman: University of Oklahoma Press, 1967], p. 35). Arthur L. Scott—*On the Poetry of Mark Twain* (Urbana: University of Illinois Press, 1966), p. 22—thought it "surprising that Browning appealed to him so strongly. Their personal acquaintanceship may have helped; also the robust vigor of certain poems." Walter Blair perceptively recognized that Clemens "appreciated . . . the monologue revealing character" and points to Simon Wheeler's monologue in Mark Twain's "Celebrated Jumping Frog" (*Native American Humor, 1800–1900* [1937; rpt. San Francisco: Chandler, 1960], p. 157).

7   *Mark Twain's Letters*, ed. Albert Bigelow Paine (New York: Harper & Brothers, 1917), 2: 490—hereafter referred to as *MTL*.

8   Browning's "overheard" monologues such as "Soliloquy of the Spanish Cloister" and his self-justifying speaker in "My Last Duchess" seem germane to Mark Twain's "King Leopold's Soliloquy" and "The Czar's Soliloquy" (1905). Twain tried to emulate Browning's methods of allowing his narrators to condemn themselves by introducing evidence of their own hypocrisy and cruelty, but Twain's efforts are different because his moral indignation at their crimes shows through so noticeably.

9   This feature of Clemens's conversational speech was usually one of the first characteristics people noticed when they met him for the first time. The descriptions of Clemens set down in 1876 by Mrs. James T. Fields (*Memories of a Hostess*, ed. M. A. DeWolfe Howe [Boston: Atlantic Monthly Press, 1922], p. 250) and in 1887 by Grace King (Robert Bush, "Grace King and Mark Twain," *American Literature* 44.1 [March 1972]: 32), for example, both allude to his prominent and peculiar drawl.

10 Robert Underwood Johnson of *Century Magazine* likewise stated that Clemens "was the most perfect reader I have ever known. His voice was peculiarly musical and had its own attraction, while his clear renderings of meanings in the most involved versification was sometimes like the opening of a closed door" (quoted by Edward Wagenknecht, *Mark Twain*, p. 46).

11 This volume is part of the Mark Twain Papers, Bancroft Library, University of California, Berkeley—hereafter cited as MTP.

12 Formerly in the Estelle Doheny Collection, Edward Laurence Doheny Memorial Library, St. John's Seminary, Camarillo, California. Sold at auction in 1989 .

13 Quoted by Robert Dawson Wallace, "An Analytical-Historical Study of the Factors Contributing to the Success of Mark Twain as an Oral Interpreter," Doctoral dissertation, University of Southern California 1962, p. 291. Wallace studied Mark Twain's use of published writings in his professional platform appearances. In Chapters 4 and 5 Wallace expertly investigated Mark Twain's speech patterns, lecture revisions, and stage techniques. On pages 291–346 Wallace transcribed and discussed Clemens's notes and markings in seven volumes of Robert Browning's poetry that were sold at auction in Hollywood in 1951.

14 *My Father, Mark Twain* (New York: Harper & Brothers, 1931), p. 57.

15 *My Mark Twain: Reminiscences and Criticisms*, ed. Marilyn Austin Baldwin (1910; rpt. Baton Rouge: Louisiana State University Press, 1967), p. 16. See also William Dean Howells's *Literary Friends and Acquaintances*, ed. David F. Hiatt and Edwin H. Cady (Bloomington: Indiana University Press, 1968), pp. 265, 332.

16 Autobiographical dictation of 16 October 1906, *Autobiography of Mark Twain, Volume 2*, ed. Benjamin Griffin and Harriet Elinor Smith (Berkeley: University of California Press, 2013), 2: 260.

17 ALS in MTP.

18 *From Sea to Sea: Letters of Travel* (New York: Doubleday and McClure, 1899), 2: 180.

19 *MTL*, p. 797.

20 "William Dean Howells," reprinted in *The Writings of Mark Twain, Definitive Edition* (New York: Gabriel Wells, 1922), 26: 230.

21 Undated ALS in the Henry W. and Albert A. Berg Collection, New York Public Library, Astor, Lenox and Tilden Foundations.

22 Isabel V. Lyon Journals, TS p. 159, Mark Twain Papers, University of California, Berkeley—hereafter cited as IVL Journals, MTP.

23 IVL Journals, TS p. 193, MTP.

24 For the writing of which Clemens had loaned Teller some books about the French Revolution, according to her preface for a privately printed pamphlet, "S. L. C. to C. T." (New York, 1925), TS in the Henry W. and Albert A. Berg Collection, New York Public Library.

25 ALS in the Henry W. and Albert A. Berg Collection, New York Public Library, Astor, Lenox and Tilden Foundations.

26 IVL Journals, TS p. 166, MTP.

27 IVL Journals, TS pp. 161, 163, MTP.

28 IVL Journals, TS p. 164, MTP.

29 IVL Journals, TS p. 313, MTP.

30 IVL Journals, TS p. 306, MTP.

31 IVL Journals, TS p. 313, MTP.

32 *Mark Twain and the Happy Island* (Chicago: A. C. McClury & Co., 1913), pp. 93–100.

33 Kipling was hardly a new-found author for Clemens. In February 1891 he replaced the Browning poem in his program for a reading at Bryn Mawr with Kipling's "Gunga Din," and listed "Danny Deever" and "To Thomas Atkins" as tentative additions (Notebook 30, *Mark Twain's Notebooks & Journals*, Volume 3, ed. Robert Pack Browning, Michael B. Frank, and Lin Salamo [Berkeley: University of California Press, 1979], p. 605). In a newspaper interview in 1895 Mark Twain singled out "Mandalay" as a "poem of mingled pathos and humour [which] had the aroma of the Orient, the sound of the sea on the sand and the breezes among the palms in it" ("Mark Twain Put to the Question," 14 October 1895 issue of the Adelaide *South Australian Register*; *Mark Twain: The Complete Interviews*, ed. Gary Scharnhorst [Tuscaloosa: University of Alabama Press, 2006],

p. 236). Clemens liked Kipling's "The Bell Buoy" so much that he once wrote: "Some day I hope to hear the poem chanted or sung—with the bell-buoy breaking in, out of the distance" (Clemens to F. N. Doubleday, 12 October 1903, *MTL*, p. 746). Howard G. Baetzhold—*Mark Twain & John Bull* (Bloomington: Indiana University Press, 1970), pp. 187–195—reviewed the entire Clemens-Kipling relationship.

34 TS in MTP.

35 Hamlin Hill traced Clemens's growing dependence on Lyon and his abrupt severance of their relationship in *Mark Twain: God's Fool* (New York: Harper & Row, 1973).

36 Manuscript notes that were in the collection of Bigelow Paine Cushman in 1976.

37 Stanley Donner called attention to Mark Twain's platform artistry in "Mark Twain as a Reader," *Quarterly Journal of Speech* 33 (1947) 308–311; later Fred W. Lorch—*The Trouble Begins at Eight: Mark Twain's Lecture Tours* (Ames: Iowa State University Press, 1968), pp. 152–160—treated this aspect of Mark Twain's career.

38 In 1876 Clemens played the role of Peter Spyk in a Hartford production of James Robinson Planché's *The Loan of a Lover* (first performed in 1834). Clemens enlivened the silly romantic plot by injecting off-the-cuff remarks into the script. His ad-libbing was hilarious to the audience, but the other members of the dramatic club, lacking Clemens's ease before the footlights, found his additions nerve-wracking as they tried to remember lines and cues (William W. Ellsworth, *A Golden Age of Authors: A Publisher's Recollection* [Boston: Houghton Mifflin, 1919], p. 223). Clemens declined a proposal to perform the one-act play in New York. "By re-writing Peter Spyk, I managed to change the language & the character to a degree that enabled me to talk the one & represent the other after a fashion—but I am not equal to the Metropolitan boards yet," Clemens wrote to Augustin Daly on 4 May 1876 (Joseph Francis Daly, *The Life of Augustin Daly* [New York: Macmillan, 1917], p. 146).

An earlier version of this chapter appeared in Quarterly Journal of Speech *62.1 (February 1976): 49–56.*

12

'A Splendor of Stars & Suns'

Mark Twain as a Reader of Browning's Poems

Samuel Clemens's infatuation with the poetry of Robert Browning during and after the 1880s demonstrated the subtle dimensions in Browning's verse that a gifted oral interpreter can disclose. Whatever first attracted Clemens to the Browning canon, however, it was not the poetry of Elizabeth Barrett Browning. When Clemens began courting Olivia Langdon she was already a partisan of Mrs. Browning's works, and the couple had several good-natured exchanges about the intelligibility of her poems. In a letter of 17 May 1869 Clemens jocularly alluded to "some dark & bloody mystery out of the Widow Browning"; on another occasion he turned to Olivia for an explanation of obscurities in *Aurora Leigh*.[1] In the second week of Olivia Clemens's marriage she appended a teasing note to a letter Clemens was writing to Mary Mason Fairbanks, vowing that she, along with Clemens's sister and niece, "will make Mr Clemens read aloud to us in Mrs Browning—Felicity to us—but what to him?"[2] On 2 February 1873 Clemens declared, in a letter written to Olivia, "If they were to set *me* to review Mrs. Browning, it would be like asking you to deliver judgment upon the merits of a box of cigars."[3] This minor disagreement was another manifestation of the differences that rapidly became apparent in the Clemenses' literary tastes. Olivia adored George Eliot's novels, for instance, whereas Clemens "dragged through three chapters" of *Daniel Deronda*, "& then was honest enough to quit, & confess to myself that I haven't *any* romance-literature appetite."[4] After reading *Middlemarch*, Clemens claimed that he "nearly died from over-work. I wouldn't read another of those books for a farm."[5] Olivia Clemens's favorite novels were not always highbrow, of course; she enjoyed many bestsellers that her friends recommended. But the pattern of literary discussions within Clemens's marriage generally remained the same (unless Clemens himself introduced a book into the household): Olivia would purchase or borrow a book, then praise its merits; soon thereafter her husband would peruse the book, dislike it heartily, and berate the work to Olivia, their daughters, and whomever he might be corresponding with at the time. He never attacked Olivia's literary standards directly; rather, he castigated the characters and plot in the novel or the obscurity of theme and the inadequacies of rhyme and meter in the poem, invariably concluding his diatribes by emphasizing his own lack of literary sophistication and education. Thus he would first demolish the fiction or poetry in question and then add humbly, but who am I to criticize a work I probably can't even properly appreciate?

In a way this habit was one variation of the comic formula discernible in his travel narratives—assail a detested object, mention the persona's lack of critical credentials, then ridicule the hated object still more. In Notebook 15 Clemens denounced the famous painting by J. M. Turner: "What a rag is to a bull, Turner's 'Slave Ship' is to me. Mr. [John] Ruskin is educated in art up to a point where that picture throws him into as mad an ecstasy of pleasure as it throws me into one of rage. His cultivation enables him to see water in that yellow mud; his cultivation reconciles the floating of unfloatable things to him—chains &c. . . . A Boston critic said the Slave Ship reminded him of a cat having a fit in a platter of tomatoes. That went home to my noncultivation."[6] Twain developed these protests even further in Chapter 24 of *A Tramp Abroad* (1880), where he execrated *The Slave Ship* at length.

It is possible to see in his suspicions about high-toned art more than mere indications that he was uneasy about his powers of critical appreciation; in fact, one may view them as part of Clemens's lifelong insecurity about his own literary writings and the cultural status

of his audience. In the instance of his family's reading tastes, he was at odds with the fairly conventional tastes of his wife—and his daughters, too, who tended to follow their mother's inclinations in the matter of literature. (Susy Clemens reported from Bryn Mawr in 1890: "I am reading 'Daniel Deronda' and enjoying it, endlessly; much more than I did Adam Bede.")[7] The history of the Clemenses' divergence over Mrs. Browning's poetry makes more significant and more symbolic Clemens's eventual liking for the verse of Mrs. Browning's husband. It may partly explain why he publicized his discovery of Robert Browning's poems so ardently, and why the poet meant so much to him. For in Clemens's fondness for Browning's works lay one of his few convergences with the opinions of established literary critics concerning literature written during his lifetime. He agreed about the virtues of his friend William Dean Howells's fiction and criticism, to be sure. But though he admired such classics as Malory's *Morte D'Arthur*, Cervantes's *Don Quixote*, Defoe's *Robinson Crusoe*, and Swift's *Gulliver's Travels*, not to mention Shakespeare, whom he venerated greatly, he was baffled by literary critics who extravagantly praised Austen, Goldsmith, Fielding, Smollett, Lamb, Thackeray, Scott, Meredith, Ruskin, Cooper, Hawthorne, James, and other "classic" authors.

Robert Browning called on Clemens in London in the summer of 1873,[8] yet the manner of Clemens's introduction to Browning's verse remains a matter for speculation. Olivia Clemens very possibly was responsible; when she wed Clemens her personal book collection already included a copy of *Men and Women*

Clemens's library in his Hartford house, where he conducted weekly readings of Robert Browning's verse in 1886–87 (Mark Twain House and Museum, Hartford, Connecticut)

(Boston: Ticknor and Fields, 1856), the flyleaf of which she signed "Livie L. Langdon/1864/New York."[9] Clemens himself marked most of its contents in preparation for reading aloud, indicating stresses, connecting stanzas, glossing terms. He also penciled a number of marginal notes; those surrounding "Old Pictures in Florence" are the most extensive. In any event, Clemens's longtime literary adviser, Howells, declined to take credit for acquainting his friend with Browning's poetry, explaining, "I was away at the time of his great Browning passion, and I know of it chiefly from hearsay."[10] The earliest date for this "passion" exists as an inscription on the flyleaf of the first volume in *The Poetical Works of Robert Browning*, 2 vols. (Leipzig: Bernhard Tauchnitz, 1872): "To Susie Clemens,/These volumes, (in place of a promised mud turtle,) are presented, with the love of Papa./May 25, 1882/N. B. The turtle was to have been brought from New Orleans, but I gave up the idea because it seemed cruel. S.L.C."[11] Clemens had returned to Hartford on 24 May 1882 following a month-long trip to New Orleans and tour of the Mississippi River during which he gathered material for *Life on the Mississippi*.

However Clemens first encountered Browning's poems, by 1886 Howells's reference to his "passion" accurately suggested his enthusiasm. "Think of it!" he wrote to Mrs. Fairbanks on 16 November 1886. "I've been elected Reader to a Browning class. . . . Mind you, I'm on the ABC only—his *easy* poems."[12] Details about the initial organization and composition of this study group are now somewhat blurred, but apparently the students were mostly Olivia's women friends. Guest auditors sometimes attended out of curiosity about Clemens's reading abilities. Clemens conducted the meetings, which took place on Wednesday mornings in the Clemenses' oak-paneled library room on the first floor of their Hartford home. He lavished considerable labor on his readings in advance of the meetings. "I am pretty proud of my Browning class," he informed Mrs. Fairbanks on 22 March 1887. "I study & prepare 30 or 40 pages of new matter for each sitting."[13] The best evidence of his success is the fact that the classes continued for forty-two weeks.[14]

Clemens had delivered lectures and readings on the public platform for two decades, deriving a considerable amount of his income from these professional appearances. As a result his chief talent lay in performing rather than analyzing, and eventually he eschewed explication during the Browning sessions. "They say the poetry never gets obscure till I begin to explain it," he wrote to Mary Hallock Foote on 2 December 1887. "So I've stopped being expounder, and thrown my heft on the reading." Teachers might profit from this "moral," he felt: "Don't explain your author, read him right and he explains himself." Ample preparation and native ability combined in his case. "Put me in the right condition and give me room according to

my strength," he vowed (echoing one of his bragging raftsmen in *Life on the Mississippi*), "and I can read Browning so Browning himself can understand it. It sounds like stretching, but it's the cold truth."[15]

His listeners agreed with his opinion if not his idiomatic expression. Mary Bushnell Cheney, daughter of the prominent Hartford clergyman Horace Bushnell, recorded her impressions of a study group meeting she attended one morning in Clemens's library. She was there by invitation, joining a "small circle of women" seated near "the flowers and filtered sunshine" of an adjoining conservatory. She "perceived that the place was in itself a sort of revelation of poetic meanings." By her own admission, she was then a "doubter of his [Browning's] comprehensibility, even to the point of wondering whether Browning himself knew or cared very much what he meant." That morning Cheney heard Clemens read from *The Ring and the Book*, *Strafford*, and *Sordello*. Once he entered "the flowing tide" of *The Ring and the Book*, "all else was forgotten in its strong thoughts and brilliant sentences." As Clemens progressed, he succeeded in diminishing his listeners' awareness of a speaker physically present. "The reading was not oratorical and aimed at no effects of cadence. Free from self-consciousness, attempting only to let those sentences speak for themselves as the author meant them, mastering in the easiest way the parenthetical style so habitual with Browning, sentence within sentence conveying the thought, Mr. Clemens . . . let him interpret himself with no intrusion of his own personality." Cheney had observed how "other men have tried to read Browning in a dramatic way with swelling voice and tragic emphasis, and their ornamentation served merely to confuse the meaning," whereas with Clemens's technique "the thought was the thread he followed and which he was usually able to keep clear and free from entanglements."[16] New Orleans author Grace King, who visited the Clemenses during the summer of 1887 when Clemens was reading *The Ring and the Book* to a study group, testified that "to him there were no obscure passages to be argued over, no guesses at meaning. His slow deliberate speech and full voice gave each sentence its quota of sound, and sense followed naturally and easily. He understood Browning as did no one else I ever knew."[17] She also heard Clemens read aloud from Browning to the guests of artist Frederick E. Church at his "Olana" estate near the Hudson River in June 1887.[18]

For informal gatherings of friends and relatives, Clemens usually drew more upon poetry than prose for his reading texts.[19] Robert Underwood Johnson of the *Century Magazine* staff heard a rendition of Browning's poetry by Clemens in 1892 that Johnson termed "remarkable" for its "sympathetic interpretation."[20] Lecture agent Carlyle Smythe reported in 1898 that "the one poet whose works afford him [Clemens] any pleasure is Browning, whom he reads aloud with a rare understanding of the spirit of the verse."[21] Clemens's daughter Clara corroborated this assessment. "The only poetry Father wholly enjoyed was that of Robert Browning," she recalled.[22]

Various commentators have puzzled over Clemens's lasting affinity for Browning, whose poems strike them as an odd choice for an American realist writer who stressed the paramount importance of clarity and straightforwardness in style, and whose second-favorite poet for oral interpretations was Rudyard Kipling. Clemens's designated biographer, Albert Bigelow Paine, remarked, "It is one of the puzzling phases of Mark Twain's character that, notwithstanding his passion for direct and lucid expression, he should have found pleasure in the poems of Robert Browning."[23] Edward Wagenknecht concurred: "The great surprise is Browning. One would have expected Mark Twain to hate him, as he hated James and Meredith. With the perversity so characteristic of him, he decided instead to love him."[24] Another scholar-critic, Arthur L. Scott, thought it "surprising that Browning appealed to him so strongly. Their personal acquaintanceship may have helped; also the robust vigor of certain poems."[25]

An investigation of which Browning poems Clemens preferred, however, allows one to see that Clemens's affection for the poetry was neither puzzling, perverse, nor even surprising. He came to the Browning canon, after all, in search of material suitable for reading aloud to sizable audiences; he was scarcely interested in the effect the verse produced in what he disparagingly called "mute readings." The Browning poems he read aloud repeatedly were those in which a speaking voice dominates, often a male persona who ironically reveals more of his characteristics and motivations than he presumably intends to. Browning's affectionate but humorous depiction of a lowbrow Philistine in "Up at a Villa—Down in the City," for example, entertained Clemens's classes "a couple of dozen times."[26] The Reverend Joseph H. Twichell of Hartford declared in 1896 that "whoever may have had the good fortune to hear his rendering of anything from Browning—for instance, 'Up at a Villa—Down in the City,' which is one of his favorites—will not be likely to forget the pleasure of it."[27] Unfortunately Clemens's copy of *Dramatic Lyrics* has not resurfaced since his daughter Clara sold it (for $2.25!), along with hundreds of other books from her father's library, at a public auction held in 1911. But we can safely suppose that numerous poems in that volume, especially "My Last Duchess" and "Soliloquy of the Spanish Cloister," bear Clemens's annotations. *Dramatic Lyrics* formed the second volume in a set owned by Clemens, *The Poetic and Dramatic Works of Robert Browning*, 6 vols. (Boston: Houghton, Mifflin, 1887). The first volume of the same set can be seen in the Mark Twain Library at Redding, Connecticut; it exhibits profuse markings in pencil: marginal comments refer to Clemens's progress in reading orally during March, April, and May 1889 (for instance, "Finished here March 20/89. I *declare!* What *time* it is!" [p. 81]); other notes edit lines for reading aloud, adding marks for word emphasis, syllable stress, and thematic comprehension. It seems evident from these marginalia that Clemens viewed Browning as an able collaborator in their joint effort to achieve dramatic effects.

The verse Clemens selected did not need to be entirely ironic, however. When he read at Smith College on 21 January 1889 he included "Andrea del Sarto," the revealing monologue spoken by the Florentine painter to his wife Lucrezia. Clemens's notes for that reading indicate that he also planned to read the poem titled "Muléykeh" (in which

Hóseyn races against a thief riding Hóseyn's horse, Muléykeh the Pearl).[28] It's sufficient to imagine the pounding rhythm that a skillful reader like Clemens could create in the poem he referred to as the "horse-race." Here and elsewhere we are reminded that Clemens enjoyed performing in amateur theatricals in Hartford. When he chose verse for oral renditions, he favored emotional narratives that contained either action or character, and preferably both elements. Browning's poems typically supplied background details, physical settings, and plot developments as well; to a student of his nuances, they were miniature short stories in poetic form. During the last two decades of Clemens's life, when he tended to read aloud more and more works by Rudyard Kipling, he chose these poems too for their dramatic potential and their psychological character—pieces like "Soldier an' Sailor Too," "Tomlinson," "Gunga Din," "Mandalay," "M'Andrew's Hymn," and "The *Mary Gloster*."

Clemens's most revered poem, however, was one he seldom if ever read in public. In an Autobiographical Dictation of 7 October 1907 he said of FitzGerald's translation of Omar Khayyám's *Rubáiyát*: "No poem had ever given me so much pleasure before, and none has given me so much pleasure since."[29] Considering his affection for the *Rubáiyát*, it seems significant that Clemens listed "Rabbi Ben Ezra," commonly viewed as Browning's reply to the FitzGerald version of the Persian poem, among the pieces he had read to his study group "a couple of dozen times."[30] As late as three years before Clemens's death, he was still reading this Browning poem to interested listeners. Isabel V. Lyon, Clemens's secretary-factotum, noted that after a luncheon on 8 March 1907 "Mrs. [Franklin] Whitmore asked him to read Rabbi Ben Ezra to us—which he did."[31] Clemens presumably took up his volume of *Dramatis Personae* and began, "Grow old along with me!/The best is yet to be. . .!" and concluded with Browning's analogy of the potter's wheel:

> So, take and use Thy work:
> Amend what flaws may lurk,
> . . . Perfect the cup as planned!
> Let age approve of youth, and death
> complete the same!

Another poem "called for the oftenest" in his Browning classes was the dramatic monologue by a German musician, "Abt Vogler." Apparently Clemens's audience found particular gratification in Vogler's assurance that "There shall never be one lost good! What was, shall live as before;/. . . On the earth the broken arcs; in the heaven, a perfect round" (ll. 69–72).

Clemens's library books (at least the volumes that have reappeared since the two auctions of his book collection in 1911 and 1951) provide additional indications of the relative popularity of Browning's poems. He must have read frequently from his copy of *Parleyings with Certain People of Importance in Their Day* (Boston: Houghton, Mifflin, 1887).[32] He marked most poems in this volume with pencil. (Only two pieces are entirely ignored—"With Gerard de Lairesse" and "Fust and His Friends: An Epilogue.") He made extremely profuse markings in "With Bernard de Mandeville." The poem entitled "With Daniel Bartoli" contains numerous

speculations about possible interpretations; some were canceled as he recognized new meanings and recorded these. At the bottom of page 49, for example, Clemens wondered (as other readers probably have): "(Is this to say our girl found a lion (a King) about to <destroy> diminish a dukedom, using the duke's love for *her* as a means, & she nobly checkmated his little game by renouncing her big chance & backing out from the marriage?)" He noted at the top of page 51: "How mistake so long that the present love was not *love* at all—the *real* moon was *behind* this cloud, all the time.)" And on page 84, the last page of "With George Bubb Dodington," he wrote: "Let him speak sincerely from his heart, & this is what he would have to confess. When the people recognized that he was telling the bold clear *truth*, they would fall down, overawed by the splendid sincerity." In "With Francis Furini" he noted at the bottom of page 88, "Tries to be a poet," and on page 89, "Gives him a slam for trying to be a poet?" Penciled markings in these and other poems in *Parleyings with Certain People* underscore lines, add stress marks to denote intonations, and offer explanatory notes.

Clemens frequently annotated his library volumes,[33] but these notations were unusually thorough for him. Obviously it was the illusion of *talk* that attracted Clemens to these poems, the sense of casual conversations addressed to famous personages. ("With Gerard de Lairesse" opens with the words "Ah, but"; "With Christopher Smart" begins "It seems as if. . . or did. . . .") Browning's facility at compressing language so that philosophical ideas and historical incidents take the form of monologues would naturally have impressed

Clemens, who after 1906 resorted to dictating daily sections of his autobiography to a stenographer in an effort to reproduce in print the desirable sound of a human voice talking casually. Browning masterfully captured the pauses, ellipses, and digressions that characterize intimate conversation.

Clemens also acquired a seven-volume set of Browning's works (Boston: Houghton Mifflin, 1883–85).[34] Clemens inscribed each volume: "Livy L. Clemens/1886." On a flyleaf of the heavily marked *Dramatis Personae, Dramatic Romances and Lyrics* (1884), he noted: "The pencilings in this book are inexplicable, except by this explanation, which is the true one: they were made in order to give the eye instant help in placing & shading emphases—a very necessary precaution when one reads Browning aloud." (In another set of *Dramatis Personae* Clemens likened certain of Browning's lines to the "vague dim flash of splendid humming-birds through a fog."[35])

Olivia Clemens owned (and signed in 1887) a copy of *Ferishtah's Fancies* (Boston: Houghton, Mifflin, 1886).[36] Clara Clemens entered the title of this work in her commonplace book around 1888.[37] Clemens may have purchased a publication by the Browning Society of London, *Illustrations to Browning's Poems* (London: Trübner, 1882, 1883), since he jotted the title and publisher's name on the flyleaf of his copy of Edgar Watson Howe's *The Story of a Country Town*, inscribed to Clemens by Howe in 1884.[38] Robert Browning's daughter-in-law evidently gave Clemens a copy of *Asolando: Fancies and Facts*, Eighth edition (London: Smith, Elder, 1890), which she inscribed "For Mr. Clemens/with Mrs. Browning['s]/affectionate regards/Venice

1892." This volume is in the Mark Twain Library in Redding, Connecticut.

Were there any discernible results in Clemens's intellectual development, public performances, or published writings as a consequence of his infatuation with Browning's poetry? One can never be certain, but he could have been affected by the images of European historical personages, the Middle Ages, and the Roman Catholic church that populated Browning's verse. It is also conceivable that certain of Browning's poems may have been initially responsible for Clemens's interest in, and affection for, the countryside of Italy and the city of Florence. He would visit Italy several times, would reside at the Villa Viviani near Florence in 1892 and 1893, when he wrote most of *Joan of Arc* and declared that "carefree life at a Florentine villa is an ideal existence," and would take Olivia Clemens back to Florence during her final illness in 1903–1904 for a sad sojourn in the Villa di Quarto. After Olivia's death he built in Redding, Connecticut in 1908 a large villa-style mansion with terraces and grounds that resembled those he had seen and visited in Italy.[39]

Frequent oral readings of Browning's works surely helped Clemens refine his delivery techniques for the public platform. His daughter Clara, for instance, recalled his renditions of Browning's companion pieces about a fatal duel, "Before" and "After": "Never shall I forget," she wrote, "the ring of awe in his voice as he read the last words . . . , 'Cover the face.'"[40] Clemens's public association with an eminent English poet very likely gained him invitations to take part in events where a humorist of the American vernacular might otherwise have seemed an inappropriate figure. Designated to speak at a Shelley-Keats memorial program on 14 February 1907, for example, Clemens elected to read Browning's "Memorabilia," which begins, "Ah, did you once see Shelley plain"—thus paying tribute to Browning as well as to the earlier Romantic poet.

In the last decade of Clemens's life he attempted to emulate the monologues of Browning in "King Leopold's Soliloquy" and "The Czar's Soliloquy," two polemical fictions that appeared in 1905. Like their models, Twain's narrators inadvertently disclose more than they suppose—namely, their heinous actions in the Belgian Congo and in Russia—but the topics infuriated Twain, and there is an understandable lack of subtlety in their speeches. The dated topical nature of these monologues discourages many modern readers. Twain's caricatured figure of Leopold rages against exposures of his imperialist policies to the world: "Miscreants—they are telling *everything!*" Of his butcheries, he rationalizes that "business is business, and I've got to live, haven't I, even if it does cause inconvenience to somebody here and there?" As he leafs through unfavorable press clippings, he bemoans the invention of "the incorruptible *kodak*" that now can record his soldiers' atrocities.[41] "The Czar's Soliloquy" is a better effort. Examining himself in the mirror, the Russian ruler muses: "Without my clothes I should be as destitute of authority as any other naked person." (He credits Carlyle's *Sartor Resartus* for first recognizing this clothes-philosophy.) "We have done as we pleased for centuries," he reflects. "Our common trade has been crime, our common pastime murder, our common beverage

blood—the blood of the nation." Such admissions scarcely reflect the oblique ironies of Browning's "overheard" monologues. There are some effective passages, however. The Czar, too, like Leopold inspects a collection of "depressing newspaper-clippings" and then confronts his naked likeness: "To think that this thing in the mirror—this vegetable—is an accepted deity to a mighty nation, an innumerable host, and nobody laughs."[42] The reader today should acknowledge the arduous task that Clemens set himself in these political satires.

If the beneficial literary effects of Browning are difficult to discern in Clemens's writings, the aesthetic gratification and intellectual challenge that the poetry afforded him are manifestly apparent. On 23 February 1887 Clemens entered on the flyleaf of his copy of *Dramatis Personae* his most memorable appraisal of Browning's artistry: "One's glimpses & confusions, as one reads Browning, remind me of looking through a telescope (the small sort which you must move with your hand, not clockwork). You toil across dark spaces which are (to *your* lens) empty; but every now & then a splendor of stars & suns bursts upon you and fills the whole field with flame."[43] The American realist writer who expressed this humble-sounding assessment also acquired (and annotated) an extensive collection of Browning's works. Here is a side of Clemens's private literary tastes and public oral performances that Hal Holbrook's impersonations could never suggest—Clemens the inquisitive, perfectionist oral interpreter of poetry, the professional platform reader who invested countless hours in preparing a poet's texts prior to informal performances for friends, relatives, and Browning devotees. Clemens's endorsement of Browning—and his inclusion of certain poems in his programs at professional appearances—represented one of his few attitudes toward celebrated contemporary authors that he could share with his wife and various literary critics; therefore he must have found special satisfaction in reading passages from Browning to Olivia Clemens's friends and acquaintances in the sanctity of their home library. As one examines Clemens's meticulous notations in his numerous volumes of Browning, the transience of his efforts in that pre-electronics period seems nothing short of deplorable. What an experience it might be to hear that vibrant, expertly modulated voice undertake once again the challenge of reading a poem "so Browning himself can understand it."

NOTES

1   *Mark Twain's Letters, Volume 3, 1869*, ed. Victor Fisher and Michael B. Frank (Berkeley: University of California Press, 1992), 3: 241, 26—hereafter cited as *MTLet.*

2   *MTLet* 4: 72.

3   Quoted in Clara Clemens's *My Father, Mark Twain* (New York: Harper, 1931), p. 47—hereafter cited in the text as *MFMT.*

4   Clemens to William Dean Howells, 12 July 1885, *Mark Twain-Howells Letters*, ed. Henry Nash Smith and William M. Gibson (Cambridge: Harvard University Press, Belknap Press, 1960), p. 533—subsequently referred to as *MTHL.*

5   *MTHL*, pp. 533–534.

6   *Mark Twain's Notebooks and Journals, Volume II*, ed. Frederick Anderson, Lin Salamo, and Bernard L. Stein (Berkeley: University of California Press, 1975), 2: 139—hereafter cited as *N&J.*

7   Quoted by Edith Colgate Salsbury, *Susy and Mark Twain* (New York: Harper & Row, 1965), p. 279.

8   *Mark Twain's Letters*, ed. Albert Bigelow Paine (New York: Harper, 1917), p. 207. See also *MTLet5*: 397n.1.

9   This volume is part of the Mark Twain Papers, Bancroft Library, University of California, Berkeley—hereafter designated as MTP.

10 *My Mark Twain: Reminiscences and Criticisms,* ed. Marilyn Austin Baldwin (Baton Rouge: Louisiana State University Press, 1967), p. 16.

11 Collection of Kevin Mac Donnell, Austin, Texas. Clemens merely signed the second volume "To Susie Clemens from Papa."

12 *Mark Twain to Mrs. Fairbanks*, ed. Dixon Wecter (San Marino, California: Huntington Library, 1949), pp. 258–259—hereafter cited in the text as *MTMF.*

13 *MTMF,* pp. 260–61.

14 Clemens to Mrs. Mary Hallock Foote, 2 December 1887, published as *When Huck Finn Went Highbrow*, ed. Benjamin de Casseres, Limited edition of 125 copies (New York: Thomas F. Madigan, 1934), p. 7.

15 *When Huck Finn Went Highbrow*, p. 7.

16 "Mark Twain as a Reader," *Harper's Weekly* 55 (7 January 1911): 6.

17 *Memories of a Southern Woman of Letters* (New York: Macmillan, 1932), p. 84.

18 King to Nina Ansley King, 10 June 1887, quoted by Robert Bush, "Grace King and Mark Twain," *American Literature* 44.1 (March 1972): 35.

19 See my essay, "'It Is Unsatisfactory to Read to One's Self': Mark Twain's Informal Readings," *Quarterly Journal of Speech* 62.1 (February 1976): 49–56. (A revised version of this essay appears as a chapter in this present volume.)

20 *Remembered Yesterdays* (Boston: Little, Brown 1923), p. 321.

21 "The Real 'Mark Twain,'" *"Pall Mall Magazine* 16 (September 1898): 30–31.

22 *MFMT*, p. 66.

23 *Mark Twain's Letters*, p. 490.

24 *Mark Twain: The Man and His Work*, 3rd ed. (Norman: University of Oklahoma Press, 1967), p. 35.

25 *On the Poetry of Mark Twain* (Urbana: University of Illinois Press, 1966), p. 22.

26 Clemens to Mary Mason Fairbanks, 22 March 1887, published in *MTMF*, pp. 260–61.

27 "Mark Twain," *Harper's Magazine* 92.552 (May 1896): 822.

28 *N&J* 3: 435.

29 *Autobiography of Mark Twain, Volume 3*, ed.

Benjamin Griffin and Harriet Elinor Smith (Berkeley: University of California Press, 2015) 3: 159.

30 *MTMF*, pp. 260–261.

31 Isabel V. Lyon Journals, TS p. 229, MTP.

32 The volume was formerly in the Carrie Estelle Doheny Collection at St. John's Seminary, Camarillo, California.

33 As described in my essay, "'Good Books & a Sleepy Conscience': Mark Twain's Reading Habits," *American Literary Realism* 9.4 (Autumn 1976): 299–303. (A revised version of this essay appears as a chapter in this present volume.)

34 Now in the Mark Twain Papers in the Bancroft Library at the University of California, Berkeley. Portions of its marginalia are quoted by Robert Dawson Wallace, "An Analytical-Historical Study of the Factors Contributing to the Success of Mark Twain as an Oral Interpreter" (Doctoral dissertation, University of Southern California, 1962), pp. 291–346.

35 Quoted by Albert Bigelow Paine in *Mark Twain: A Biography*, 2 vols. (New York: Harper & Brothers, 1912), p. 847—hereafter *MTB*.

36 The volume belongs to the Mark Twain Library, Redding, Connecticut.

37 Paine 150, MTP.

38 Reported in *The Twainian* 27 (March-April 1968): 1.

39 The home burned in 1925, after which a similar but smaller version of Clemens's "Stormfield" went up in its place.

40 *MFMT,* p. 66.

41 Reprinted in *Mark Twain: Life as I Find It*, ed. Charles Neider (Garden City, New York: Hanover House, 1961), pp. 275–295.

42 *Mark Twain: Life as I Find It*, pp. 267–272.

43 *MTB*, p. 847.

An earlier version of this chapter appeared in Browning Institute Studies *6 (1978): 87–103.*

13

How Tom Sawyer Played
Robin Hood 'By the Book'

Smarting from Becky Thatcher's rebuff, Tom climbs Cardiff Hill in Chapter 8 of *The Adventures of Tom Sawyer* (1876) to sulk in the solitude of its woods. There his playmate Joe Harper challenges him to a duel with lath swords. In this make-believe combat the two boys pretend to be Robin Hood and Guy of Guisborne; afterwards they play-act four other scenes from the Robin Hood legend of outlawry.

For a hundred years no subsequent editors of the novel noticed that Mark Twain relied on a specific literary source for the Robin Hood episodes Tom and Joe enact. Several clues pointed toward this fact. The narrator himself observes that the boys prompted each other like stage actors and "talked 'by the book,' from memory." At the climax of their swordplay, moreover, Tom is obliged to quote from the script to remind the overzealous Joe:

> "*I* can't fall; that ain't the way it is in the book. The book says '*Then with one back-handed stroke he slew poor Guy of Guisborne.*'

You're to turn around and let me hit you in the back."

There was no getting around the authorities, so Joe turned, received the whack, and fell.[1]

Wherever he appears in Mark Twain's fiction, Tom Sawyer intimidates his opposition by flaunting his extensive reading in adventurous romances—but only someone as credulous as Joe Harper or Huckleberry Finn would trust Tom's interpretation of his beloved "authorities." In this instance Tom misconstrues the term "back-handed" but properly quotes his source, a children's book by Joseph Cundall entitled *Robin Hood and His Merry Foresters* (1841). Cundall's description of Robin Hood's combat with the king's ranger ends with virtually the same sentence that Tom cited:

> Robin Hood . . . fought skilfully with his fiery and more athletic antagonist, who poured down an incessant shower of strokes upon him. Once the bold outlaw fell; but

recovering himself sufficiently to place a foot upon the earth, he thrust his sword at the ranger, and as he drew back to avoid it, Robin Hood sprung up, *and with one sudden back-handed stroke slew poor Guy of Gisborne upon the spot.*[2]

The other episodes that Tom schedules for performance are also included in Cundall's book—Friar Tuck's quarterstaff bout with Robin Hood (pp. 73–80), the archery match of Much the Miller's Son (pp. 70–71), the death of the Sheriff of Nottingham (p. 150), and Robin Hood's death (pp. 157–158). The latter event concluded the histrionics on Cardiff Hill:

Then Tom became Robin Hood again,

and was allowed by the treacherous nun to bleed his strength away through his neglected wound. And at last Joe, representing a whole tribe of weeping outlaws, dragged him sadly forth, gave his bow into his feeble hands, and Tom said, "Where this arrow falls, there bury poor Robin Hood under the green-wood tree."[3] Then he shot the arrow and fell back and would have died but he lit on a nettle and sprang up too gaily for a corpse. (*TS*, p. 91)

Cundall's account of the same scene incorporates four lines from a folk ballad. Wounded by an arrow, Robin Hood was

taken to Kirkleys Nunnery, where he was treacherously suffered to bleed to death by the prioress. As he found his end approaching he

THE GREATEST AND BEST.

Left, "The Death of Robin Hood," page 83, and right, drawing of Robin Hood in Chapter 26, The Adventures of Tom Sawyer *(Hartford, Connecticut: American Publishing Company, 1876)*

called Little John to him. "Carry me into the woods, I entreat thee," he said to him; "And give me my bent bow in my hand, And a broad arrow I'll let flee; And where this arrow is taken up There shall my grave digged be." The outlaw shot his last bow. His shaft flew feebly to a short distance, and fell beneath an oak. He leaned back into the arms of his faithful attendant—and died. (pp. 157–158)

Tom also plays Robin Hood in Chapter 26 of *Tom Sawyer*, while he and Huck Finn mark time on Cardiff Hill until they can search the haunted house for buried treasure. Huck, a virtual *tabula rasa* concerning historical personages, listens with interest to Tom's depiction of Robin Hood as "one of the greatest men that was ever in England—and the best. He was a robber"; when Tom explains that this outlaw "loved" poor people and waylaid "only sheriffs and bishops and rich people and kings, and such like," Huck expresses complete approval: "Well, he must 'a' been a brick" (p. 200). Tom then easily persuades Huck to try a game of Sherwood Forest: "It's noble fun. I'll learn you."[4]

Since Mark Twain strove to invest his novel with historical authenticity, Cundall's book was an appropriate source for language and details. The events recounted in *Tom Sawyer* are to be imagined as taking place "thirty or forty years ago"—that is, between 1836 and 1846. *Robin Hood and His Merry Foresters* was first published in London by Tilt & Bogue in 1841; the next year it was issued by J. & H. G. Langley in New York and by Munroe & Francis in Boston. The book soon established itself as a staple for American publishers of children's literature, and during three decades

ROBIN HOOD.

Front cover illustration for **Robin Hood and His Merry Foresters** *(London: Tilt and Bogue, 1841).*

in the mid-nineteenth century it held a near monopoly on the Robin Hood myth for junior readers. At the time Mark Twain wrote *Tom Sawyer* this perennial favorite was still available as a one-dollar volume from James Miller of New York or as a cheap paperback in "Munro's Ten-Cent Novels" series (New York: G. Munro & Co., [1867]). Between 1842 and 1876 it received at least ten American reprintings.

Possibly Sam Clemens memorized portions of this book while growing up in Hannibal; he was six years old when the first American edition came out. In a letter written to his boyhood chum Will Bowen on 6 February 1870, Clemens recalled former days when "we used to undress & play Robin

Hood in our shirt-tails, with lath swords, in the woods on Holliday's Hill on those long summer days."[5] Their play-acting doubtless was modeled on Cundall's chronicle of Robin Hood's exploits.

Cundall's narrator is a grownup who rehearses the tales he once related to schoolyard companions after reading a volume of old ballads. He calls himself "Stephen Percy," the pseudonym Cundall had employed previously in writing *Tales of the Kings of England* (1840) for a juvenile audience. The British author and photographer had a more ambitious career in adult publications: under his real name, Joseph Cundall (1818–1895) edited numerous illustrated collections of decorative art, paintings, manuscripts, poetry, and biographies of artists' lives; he also produced histories of bookbinding, photography, and wood engraving. Despite Cundall's learned pursuits, "Stephen Percy" tells simple stories about Robin Hood, embellishing the tales with formulaic archaisms and peopling them with bold highwaymen, wickedly wealthy churchmen, chaste maidens, powerful feudal lords, cowed villagers, and a cunning sheriff.

Mark Twain gently—almost affectionately—burlesques the grandiloquent speech and lofty deportment of Cundall's characters. Though the modern reader can no longer recognize Cundall's forgotten volume as his target, the burlesque techniques still generate humor from incongruities of situation, language, and action. Tom's romance reading leads him to honor a mythicized highwayman as "the noblest man that ever was," though he perceives a disparity in contemporary society.

"They ain't any such men now, I can tell you," he sadly informs Huck. Identification of this literary source enables us to appreciate how Mark Twain drew upon Cundall's earnest stories to create two wryly humorous passages in *Tom Sawyer*.

NOTES

1 *The Adventures of Tom Sawyer, Tom Sawyer Abroad, Tom Sawyer, Detective*, ed. John C. Gerber, Paul Baender, and Terry Firkins (Berkeley: University of California Press, 1980), p. 90—hereafter cited as *TS*. The second italics are added.

2 *Robin Hood and His Merry Foresters.* By Stephen Percy [pseud.] (New York: Henry G. Langley, 1844), p. 52. Italics added. Mark Twain curiously inserts a *u* in spelling "Guisborne," unlike Cundall or the ballad in Bishop Percy's *Reliques*—"Robin Hood and Guy of Gisborne"—upon which Cundall based his story. Twain's misspelling suggests that he might have paraphrased Cundall's book at least partly from memory. However, True Williams's sketch of Robin Hood on page 200 of Twain's novel is clearly based on the cover illustration for *Robin Hood and His Merry Foresters,* so Twain had evidently obtained a copy of Cundall's book.

3 This phrase occurs near the beginning of Cundall's first tale: "Robin Hood . . . lived in the forests under the green-wood trees" (*Robin Hood and His Merry Foresters*, p. 13). Mark Twain planned to utilize the episode depicting Robin Hood's demise in a dramatization of *Tom Sawyer*, according to working notes he made in 1884: "Sits down on a nettle after shooting his last arrow—close RH with that" (*Mark Twain's Hannibal, Huck and Tom*, ed. Walter Blair [Berkeley: University of California Press, 1969], p. 389). The scene was not included in the script for "Tom Sawyer: A Play," however.

4 *TS*, pp. 181–182.

5 *Mark Twain's Letters, Volume 4, 1870–1871*, ed. Victor Fisher and Michael B. Frank (Berkeley: University of California Press, 1995), 4: 50.

An earlier version of this chapter appeared in English Language Notes *13.3 (March 1976): 201–204.*

14

Mark Twain, Phrenology, and the 'Temperaments'

A Study of Pseudoscientific Influence

The independent scholar, biographer, and prominent rare bookseller Madeline Stern (1912–2007) noticed in 1969 that Mark Twain's curiosity about phrenological character analysis prompted him to consult a practicing phrenologist several times during his adult life.[1] She drew her evidence mainly from the columns of the *American Phrenological Journal*, whose editors boasted that they had twice examined Mark Twain's skull and recorded its salient features. The following essay amplifies Stern's findings by demonstrating that his fascination with this pseudoscience had begun by the time he was nineteen years old; that he made use of its terminology and tenets in a persistent manner in his literature; that while he scorned its practitioners, he displayed a lifelong uncertainty about the soundness of its theories; and that one of the fundamental doctrines he absorbed from his early study of phrenology—the notion of "temperaments"—not only shaped his self-concept but also influenced his choice

of language in expressions of his later deterministic philosophy.

The first tangible indication of his acquaintance with phrenological propositions is contained in Clemens's 1855 notebook, his earliest extant journal.[2] Samuel C. Webster published extracts from this document in his biographical work,[3] and he reported that a large proportion of entries in the small memorandum book were devoted to phrenology. In researching the contents of that notebook I discovered the book from which Clemens copied these phrenological passages: the Reverend George Sumner Weaver's *Lectures on Mental Science According to the Philosophy of Phrenology* (New York: Fowlers & Wells, 1852).[4]

THE TEMPERAMENTS

Most of what Clemens transcribed is not concerned with phrenology as such, but with the principles of an auxiliary theory, the division of mankind into four basic types of "temperaments." This particular doctrine was giving renewed currency to an older word pertaining to differences in emotional dispositions. For Clemens and Weaver and their contemporaries the term "temperament" still possessed a connotation of *physicality*, of correspondence between mind and body, that has since been largely erased.[5] This shift in meaning graphically points up the ascendancy of modern psychology over the once-popular theories of constitutional typology. Midway through the nineteenth century, however, the idea that human intellect and character gave external signs in the face and body was generally conceded. The original developers of phrenology, ever schematic, had united this belief with the outlines of the ancient physiological theory of cardinal humors and produced a hybrid system classifying the varieties of human appearance. By 1847 the *American Phrenological Journal*, undisputed serial authority on every subject within its field, was routinely defining "the doctrine of temperaments" as "the physiology and general form of body and face, as indicating character."[6]

The custom of using the four temperaments to supplement phrenological assumptions concerning the human cranium was first introduced by Johann Gaspar Spurzheim (1776–1832), the German physician who traveled to America and promulgated the theories and research findings of Franz Joseph Gall (1758–1828). Spurzheim declared that a determination of the predominating temperament, or "bodily constitution of the individual subject," should routinely precede the phrenologist's examination of the skull.[7] He and his successors assumed that the physiological makeup of the bodily systems affects the brain, and must therefore be taken into account in interpreting character. Few people today are aware that the conformation of the skull by itself was considered insufficient for complete phrenological knowledge of a person, and that the temperaments were an indispensable component of the discipline worked out by Spurzheim.

The publications of Spurzheim were widely influential, and George Combe (1788–1858), a Scottish disciple of Spurzheim, further encouraged in his own writings the acceptance of his mentor's fourfold typology of temperaments. Combe explained that the temperaments were organized around the main systems of the body: the lungs, heart, and blood vessels caused the "sanguine temperament"; the muscles, bones and fibers originated the "bilious temperament"; the brain and nerves produced the "nervous temperament"; and the glands and digestive organs were responsible for the "lymphatic temperament."[8] The most obvious thing about this arrangement is its indebtedness to the ancient and medieval theory of personality types based on the predominance of one of four fluids, or "humors," of the body—yellow bile (choler), black bile (melancholy), blood, and phlegm.[9] Combe and later phrenologists, again following the example set by Spurzheim, were in agreement that they usually encountered mixtures of the temperaments in the people they examined, generally in combinations of sanguine-lymphatic, nervous-lymphatic, and nervous-bilious.

This suggestion that the physical appearance of the body could provide clues to one's psychological disposition was of

No. 6—Bilious. No. 7—Lymphatic. No. 8—Sanguine. No. 9—Nervous.

Illustrations that accompanied the description of "temperaments" in Weaver's Lectures on Mental Science *(1852). The Fowler & Wells firm was careless about acknowledging sources; these are slightly redrawn versions of illustrations that appeared previously in George Combe's* Elements of Phrenology.

vital importance to the practicing American phrenologists, compelled by their vocation to render hundreds of character judgments annually. American writers on the subject adopted the four divisions directly from the works of Spurzheim or Combe (who himself cited Spurzheim as the principal source for his views). In *Mental Science* George Sumner Weaver acknowledges that he is describing "the divisions of temperament made by the most eminent phrenologists."[10] Although his classifications are identical with those of his more illustrious predecessors, many of the copious details were of Weaver's own devising; the descriptions offered by Spurzheim and Combe were considerably more general and condensed. Clemens copied the lengthy passages on three of the four temperaments almost verbatim from Weaver's book, but to the description of the "sanguine" person he added several attributes to modify and extend certain points in order that they might apply more manifestly to himself. Furthermore, he placed the discussion of the sanguine temperament

first in his notebook—presumably because it was to him the most important. Weaver listed this temperament third in order, and stated that the sanguine is "the warming temperament. . . . the burning, flaming, flashing temperament. Hence it hangs out its signs of fire in its red, blazing hair and countenance, its florid or sandy skin. It has blue eyes; round, full features; pliable, yielding muscles; full, ample chest; generally, a thick, stout build; sometimes chestnut hair."[11] Clemens was not entirely satisfied with these explicit details. Thus, to Weaver's statement that persons in whom the sanguine temperament predominates generally have blue eyes, he added, "or gray." He likewise qualified Weaver's assertion that sanguine temperaments are fond of "out-of-door jollity" with the laconic comment, "(*not always*)." In addition, he composed two sentences that he inserted into the body of the description; aside from what they reveal about his self-image, they demonstrate his early ability to imitate an established prose style without difficulty. Clemens inserted: "It is very sensitive and is first deeply hurt at a slight, the next emotion is violent rage, and in a few moments the cause and the result are both forgotten for the time being. It often forgives, but never entirely forgets an injury."

Clemens also compiled a set of "notes" that follow and summarize the chief identifying characteristics of the four temperaments; Weaver has no such synopses in his book. In his digest following the sanguine temperament Clemens repeated his previous assertion that such persons can have "light gray" as well as blue eyes, and adds that these eyes "flash and glitter under excitement" and are usually accompanied by "sandy hair."[12] But he left the color of the hair tentative: it could also be "light or red hair" or "sometimes chestnut hair." Clemens was more positive about the mental character of this type of person: "Quick action, quick speech & quick decision; when under no compulsion, is restless, & will not sit long in one place; constantly casts his eye from one place to another," he wrote.

According to Weaver, people dominated by this temperament generally display "great elasticity and buoyancy of spirit; readiness, and even fondness for change; suddenness and intensity to the feelings; impulsiveness and hastiness of character; great warmth of both anger and love." This temperament, declared Weaver, "loves excitement, noise, bluster, fun, frolic, high times, great days, mass meetings, camp meetings, big crowds. . . . It is always predominant in those active, stirring, noisy characters that are found in every community."

A letter Clemens wrote to his mother and sister from Carson City in 1862 dispels any doubts that he definitely identified with this temperament or that he had familiarized himself with rudimentary phrenological terminology. In the letter Clemens glowingly predicted bonanza success for a mine in which he owned shares. But he urged Pamela not to take his enthusiastic forecasts too seriously:

Don't you know that I have only *talked*, as yet, but proved nothing? Don't you know that I have expended money in this country but have made none myself? Don't you know that I have never held in my hands a gold or silver bar that belonged to me? . . . Don't you know that people who always feel jolly, no matter where they are or what happens to them—who have the organ of Hope preposterously developed—who are endowed with an uncongealable sanguine temperament— who never feel concerned about the price of corn—and who cannot, by any possibility, discover any but the *bright* side of a picture— are *very* apt to go to extremes, and exaggerate, with 40-horse microscopic power? Of course I never tried to raise these suspicions in your mind, but then your knowledge of the fact that some people's poor frail human nature is a sort of crazy institution anyhow, ought to have suggested them to you.[13]

If he was sanguine by nature, his brother Orion occurred to him as the nearest example of the "nervous temperament," the fourth temperament described in *Mental Science*. Orion's name is inserted parenthetically on the notebook page beside the title of the description. This is the temperament, Weaver wrote, which "seeks mental pursuits, rather than physical; thinks, loves, aspires, with great ardency and devotion. . . . It is the poetic temperament, and fills the mind with the flames of poetic fire. . . . It is the temperament which makes geniuses, precocious children, people of purely intellectual habits and tastes."[14]

Clemens also copied, in reverse image, a line drawing of a human head that illustrated the "mental groups" of conventional phrenological faculties within the skull. He concluded his studies with a transcription of Weaver's passage (p. 95) explaining how a "loving power" motivates each organ. According to Weaver, every faculty feels affection for its particular object—thus, "Benevolence loves an object of need"; "Comparison loves analogies"; "Acquisitiveness loves money"; and "Constructiveness loves mechanics." Clemens's entry ends with Weaver's statement that therefore "man's whole active nature is expressed by the word *love*." These phrenological excerpts interrupt and replace French language exercises the young journeyman printer had been dutifully setting down for memorization on page after page. But even though French lessons gave way to phrenology (and chess game strategies) the notebook remained largely a record of exercises in self-education. Judging from the memorandums on other pages, Clemens probably made most of these entries in St. Louis in the spring and early summer of 1855.

GEORGE SUMNER WEAVER

There is no way to know precisely how Sam Clemens was introduced to Weaver's book, but its author was close at hand. George

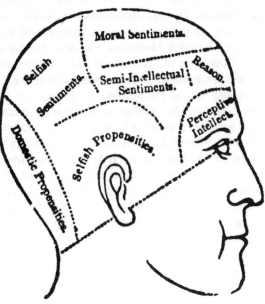

MENTAL GROUPS.

GROUPS OF ORGANS.

Diagram of "Mental Groups" that Clemens copied from Weaver's Lectures on Mental Science *in 1855. He later employed the rearward position of the Selfish organs in a projected attack on Whitelaw Reid.*

Sumner Weaver (1818–1908) was listed in the St. Louis city directory for 1854–55 as the pastor of the Universalist Church. He had been ordained as a Universalist minister in 1847, and had moved to St. Louis from Marietta, Ohio, in 1852. The series of lectures that made up his book had been delivered at the Western Liberal Institute in Marietta, a denominational academy of 125 students over which Weaver's brother-in-law presided, assisted by Weaver's sister. Weaver himself completed the faculty, although he had no college education; he taught classes in "mental and moral science."[15] (Even thirty-one years later the cultural and literary critic Brander Matthews [1852–1929] was complaining about the "pretentious sham" of this type of "freshwater college, with its full faculty of five Professors and its President who is also a clergyman as well as Lecturer on Mental and Moral Philosophy.")[16] Instead of an author's royalty Weaver received from his publishers a half-price discount on his own books, which he sold at a profit wherever he was invited to lecture in the St. Louis vicinity.[17] Hannibal, Missouri was among the towns in which he spoke. On June 30, 1853 the Hannibal *Missouri Courier* reported: "Rev. G. S. Weaver, of St. Louis, will address the Temple of Honor and Social Degree at Collins' Grove, in the vicinity of Hannibal, on next Monday, the 4th. And also Mrs. Weaver will address the Social Degree at their hall in the evening." Sam Clemens may have departed from Hannibal for St. Louis before the Fourth of July in 1853, but this announcement at least indicates the prestige that Weaver already possessed in the region. Disturbed by the growing turmoil over slavery, Weaver left St. Louis in 1860 and became a pastor in Lawrence, Massachusetts.

The Strong Appeal of Phrenology

The alliance of Universalism and phrenology in Weaver's career is less incongruous than it might appear. In the years before the Civil War phrenology was one of a variety of optimistic systems that promised to ameliorate the lives of the American masses by means of instructive handbooks. Carl Bode[18] observed that the vogue for self-improvement manuals was closely related to the trend toward liberal religious dogmas. By the 1850s the practitioners of phrenology held that the self-knowledge it afforded could result in the diminution (or at least the control) of undesirable human tendencies and the expansion of praiseworthy personality traits. The germs of this encouraging thesis had been implicit in Spurzheim's work, but it was left to the practicing phrenologists, especially the Fowler brothers in America, to develop and fully exploit this incentive. Early theoretical textbooks (before 1835) generally had been restricted to descriptions for neophytes of the configuration of specimen skulls. After this initial phase, however, American phrenologists sought procedures to build up and maintain large followings of lay believers in what promised to become a lucrative movement; they had become convinced that "cultivation" or "training" of individual organs could favorably affect one's character. And the Fowlers and their house authors were foremost in publicizing this aspect of their phrenological endeavor. In the opinion of Weaver and the Fowlers, no individual was inherently sinful, depraved or corrupted: he was merely ignorant of the guidelines requisite for achieving phrenological balance. In *Mental Science* Weaver starts from the confident premise that

the *exercise* of each, of any organ, causes it to expand, and become both more strong and active. Any portion of the brain that is rigidly and strongly put to labor will acquire an increase in size and strength by that labor. The general law holds good here which is applicable to the muscles, the nerves, the glands, or any other portion of the body. The blacksmith's arm acquires its huge dimensions and giant strength by the repeated strokes which day after day, and year after year it is called to give. The farmer's hand is made large and powerful from a similar cause. . . . If any portion of the brain is too small, it can be whipped into the traces, and put vigorously at work till it acquires both the strength and activity of the other portions. . . .

By a critical self-examination, which every one should daily make, we can discover our weaker organs, and apply the only remedy. . . . When harmony is attained, when a balance of mind is secured, when all the organs are of equal strength and activity, then with us the millennium has come, the day when the gates of joy and usefulness will be thrown wide open, for us to enter the kingdom of righteousness and peace.[19]

In addition to teaching its students about remedying faults within themselves, phrenology also was applicable to friends, acquaintances, and strangers. Weaver is frank about this potentiality: "It . . . enables us to read character, to study both ourselves and our fellows, to go in, as it were, into the sanctuary of their souls, and sit in meditation there when they know not what we are doing, to examine the actions and states of their minds, and make ourselves acquainted with them as they really are."[20] The key to this opportunity is a competent knowledge of the temperaments, "for the student very soon accustoms himself to associate with any given temperament, the peculiar mental states which it confers or predisposes to; and thus he comes into almost immediate contact with mind. . . . He forms all his alliances, friendships, relations with mind; lives and dwells perpetually with mind, so that all his conceptions of men are

elevated, spiritualized."[21] Twenty-five or thirty years earlier these same inducements had won over the adolescent Weaver when he lived on a farm near Rockingham, Vermont. Weaver would recall phrenology's early appeal for him in his *Autobiography*, written late in his life: "Here was an attempt to get near the mysteries of mind, to find and explain the laws of its action, to interpret human life by a rational method, to give reasons for differences of character and conduct—in a word, to understand men. . . . I began to study it as I found it in the heads and bodies of my associates."[22]

Yet if the attraction of these doctrines is accountable, it is less easy to explain why Samuel Clemens chose to copy from this particular book—*Mental Science*. Even by the modest stylistic standards of contemporary phrenological treatises Weaver's prose is sententious, inflated, and monotonous.[23] Nor was he in any respect an original theorist in the field; by 1852 the period of laboratory research was well past, and phrenology was making progress solely in the production of persuasive rhetoric. Weaver simply enveloped the already-simplified schemata of the Fowlers in language supposedly suitable for instructing impressionable youth—exhortative pulpit oratory abounding in moral didacticism and facile generalizations. It is a noteworthy example of the pompous Sunday school prose against which Mark Twain later would react, for Weaver draws grandly from Biblical figures, European royalty, American heroes, and state politicians alike in illustrating exemplary character traits. Above all he is intent upon stressing the infinite goodness available in each faculty of the brain, especially regarding

Amativeness, the organ of sexual love in the rear of the skull that was often abused "because of its wonderful charms."

In spite of these defects the book probably had wide circulation, since its publisher was Fowler & Wells,[24] a firm that proliferated inexpensive manuals on the subjects of phrenology, water cure, temperance, health diets, mesmerism, matrimony, child-rearing,[25] phonetic shorthand, and a variety of other topics. The house published handbooks extolling the advantages of phrenology from every conceivable viewpoint; Weaver's bombastic treatise was supposed to illustrate its applicability to lessons about Christian virtue and piety. In an Autobiographical Dictation on December 26, 1906 Mark Twain testified to the extreme popularity of these publications: "In America, forty or fifty years ago, Fowler and Wells stood at the head of the phrenological industry, and the firm's name was familiar in all ears. Their publications had a wide currency, and were read and studied and discussed by truth-seekers and by converts all over the land."[26] One indication of the pervasiveness of their sales distribution was the advertisement that appeared in Orion Clemens's Hannibal *Daily Journal*, May 19, 1853, in which Dr. B. H. Washington proudly announced himself as the agent for all publications of Messrs. Fowlers & Wells, "orders respectfully solicited." Keith & Woods sold their books in St. Louis.[27]

LITERARY APPLICATIONS

By 1855 Samuel Clemens was himself a convert to phrenology, and it was not long before he incorporated his new-found knowledge into a literary effort. The vehicle for this experiment was a somewhat callous character

sketch entitled "Jul'us Caesar."[28] In this essay Clemens lampoons with unexplained malice a young acquaintance who, he claims, was known as "Jul'us Caesar" because of his habit of invoking that emphatic phrase upon every possible occasion. The narrator states that he knew this person in a Philadelphia boarding-house, but however accurate that may be, Jul'us Caesar bears a striking resemblance to Clemens's later descriptions of Pet McMurray, the journeyman printer in Ament's Hannibal shop when Clemens worked there as an apprentice.[29] Clemens describes his subject explicitly in phrenological terms, first analyzing his temperament and then speculating upon the faculties indicated by the configuration of his skull:

> Our Caesar stood about five feet eight inches in his stockings (or somebody else's, for, according to his regular weekly complaint, his washerwoman *never did* bring back the same clothes she took away with her,); very thick heavy build; long, fiery red hair, and large, round, coarse face, which looked like the full moon in the last stage of small pox. . . . "Jul'us Caesar" was a phrenological curiosity: his head was one vast lump of Approbativeness; and though he was as ignorant and as void of intellect as a Hottentot, yet the great leveller and equalizer, Self-Conceit[,] made him believe himself fully as talented, learned and handsome as it is possible for a human being to be.

Clemens provides still other characteristics, such as Caesar's quotidian unwillingness to get up in the morning, to mark him clearly as one dominated by the lymphatic temperament, what Weaver called "the slip-shod-and-go-easy temperament, the eating and sleeping temperament. . . . It makes good-natured, easy, quiet, harmless people. . . . They go to bed early, sleep soundly, and rise reluctantly to a late breakfast, which to such good feeders is the strongest temptation to seduce them from their slumbers. Their mental perceptions are generally dull and cloudy, and their actions all sluggish."[30]

In its unmodified, direct forms, of course, phrenology was ill-suited to employment in literature. Furthermore, popular acceptance of its doctrines began to wane noticeably after the Civil War, and its terminology thereafter was meaningful to a steadily diminishing portion of readers. Mark Twain must have sensed this, or learned it very quickly. Once he attained recognition as an author, overt references to phrenology or its special vocabulary seldom turned up in his writings. It is useful to keep in mind the possibility of their isolated occurrence, however, to appreciate fully his comic intention in certain passages.[31] One example of this can be supplied from *The Innocents Abroad* (1869). Apologizing in Chapter 23 for his irreverent comments about the paintings of Christian martyrs in Venice, the narrator reflects with mock sorrow upon an erstwhile pledge to his ship companions that he would desist from expressing his "uncouth sentiments."

But alas! I never could keep a promise. I do not blame myself for this weakness, because the fault must lie in my physical organization. It is likely that such a very liberal amount of space was given to the organ which enables me to *make* promises, that the organ which

should enable me to keep them was crowded out. But I grieve not. I like no half-way things. I had rather have one faculty nobly developed than two faculties of mere ordinary capacity.[32]

The narrator's facetious excuse denotes that an excessively developed organ of Hope has taken over the contiguous cranial position of his Conscientiousness. George Combe stated that people in whom Hope is magnified "promise largely, but rarely perform"; likewise, those in whom Conscientiousness is deficient suffer a loss of "the sentiment of obligation, duty, incumbency, right and wrong."[33]

This penchant for phrenological diction is also discernible in Twain's well- known "Lost in a Snowstorm" story in *Roughing It* (1872). After realizing that they have been following their own circling tracks for two hours, the narrator, Ollendorff, and Ballou are relieved at sighting the Overland stage bound for Carson City; their faith in the unknown stage driver affords them a temporary sense of security. "We hesitated no longer, now, but took up our march in its wake, and trotted merrily along, for we had good confidence in the driver's bump of locality" (Chapter 31). George Sumner Weaver had described this organ (located in the forehead above each eye) as "the pilot-general of the traveler. It always gives directions about the *way*, keeps watch for the right road, knows the points of the compass, which way is home, and which way is the destined place. It is the faculty that never gets lost."[34]

But ten years afterward, when Mark Twain wrote the concluding chapters for *Life on the Mississippi* in 1882, he displayed apprehension about relying on phrenological jargon in a similar instance. Describing the dishabille of Henry Clay Dean, a gifted but eccentric orator who possessed extraordinary powers of memory, he mentions that Dean's unkempt costume included a "small, stiff-brimmed soldier-cap hung on a corner of the bump of—whichever bump it was" (Chapter 57). By shrinking here from technical terminology Twain partly continues the comic tone of belittlement with which he has introduced the rustic Dean (thus setting the stage for an account of Dean's masterful speech to an Iowa audience in 1861), but this expedient also blurs the location of Dean's most prominent organ—his memory-giving faculty of Eventuality in the center of his forehead. To hang Dean's cap on this memory "bump" would seem preposterous, and so the lackadaisical narrator drops the subject rather than confront the difficulty of determining another appropriate "bump." This circumlocution underscores the clumsiness of the phrenological apparatus for literary purposes, and by his impatient gesture Mark Twain expresses dissatisfaction with its superannuated skull diagrams.

Rather than dispense with phrenological notions altogether, he occasionally sought to submerge them in his prose, deprived of their telltale nomenclature. A somewhat esoteric example of this occurs in Chapter 21 of *A Connecticut Yankee* (1889), where Hank Morgan, who has joined a procession of Christian pilgrims, witnesses and grimly relates the flogging of a young slave woman about to be sold away from her husband. The Yankee is appalled by the lack of compassion revealed by his fellow travelers as they comment nonchalantly on the cruel spectacle;

not only do they fail to sympathize at all with the girl's piteous cries, but they are moved by admiration to praise the expert application of the whip. Morgan remarks with disgust: "This was what slavery could do, in the way of ossifying what one may call the superior lobe of human feeling; for these pilgrims were kindhearted people, and they would not have allowed that man to treat a horse like that." While the Yankee's opinion is comprehensible on the surface, it gains an additional dimension if we are aware that the phrase "what one may call the superior lobe of human feeling" depends for part of its effect upon the specific phrenological reference to the ennobling organ of Benevolence, appropriately located by phrenologists at the top and front of the head. This faculty was thought to produce compassion and a desire for the happiness of others.

Gradually these increasingly self-conscious allusions to phrenological concepts diminish in Mark Twain's writings, and eventually they disappear altogether. Throughout his career, however, he occasionally treats its professional practitioners in a straightforward way that requires no special knowledge from the reader; in these cases his aim is always to discredit those who were profiting by commercial exploitation of the field.[35] In Chapter 12 of *The Adventures of Tom Sawyer*, for instance, the narrator documents Aunt Polly's earnest gullibility by describing her as "a subscriber for all the 'Health' periodicals and phrenological frauds" that contain "rot," among other things, about "what frame of mind to keep one's self in." At one point, advised by "quack periodicals," she determinedly subjects Tom to a rigorous regimen of water cure treatment when he becomes inexplicably mopish. The author quite probably had in mind the publications of Fowler & Wells, for this firm published the monthly *Water Cure Journal* as well as its impressive list of books on health and phrenology. In the same novel the narrator associates the touring phrenologist with the circus and the mesmerizer, entertainers whose only redeeming function was to enliven for village boys the tedium of the school year (Chapter 22).

Nor did Mark Twain relent in this depreciatory view when he was writing *Adventures of Huckleberry Finn*. Even in his early notes for the novel[36] he had already decided that the King and the Duke would have phrenology as one of their stock-in-trade schemes for raising money fraudulently: "The two printers deliver temp. lectures, teach dancing, elocution, feel heads, distribute tracts, preach, fiddle, doctor (quack)." In the completed novel, accordingly, the Duke describes himself as a "Jour printer, by trade; do a little in patent medicines; theatre-actor—tragedy, you know; take a turn at mesmerism and phrenology when there's a chance . . . most anything that comes handy, so it ain't work."[37] Further on, the Duke shows the King some of his equipment for the last-named swindle:

> The duke went down into his carpet-bag and fetched up a lot of little printed bills, and read them out loud. One bill said "the celebrated Dr. Armand de Montalban, of Paris," would "lecture on the science of phrenology" at such-and-such a place, on the blank day of blank, at ten cents admission, and "furnish charts of character at twenty-five cents apiece." The duke said that was *him*.[38]

James Cox observed that despite a prevailing impression to the contrary, "a major part of Mark Twain's career is a long display of innocent poses against parties and ideas relatively safe to ridicule." Cox reminded us that in regard to most of the cultural subjects Twain chose to satirize, "he was not with the minority but with the majority; he had not chosen the unpopular but invariably the popular cause. This was, as he came increasingly and hostilely to know, one of the costs of being a humorist."[39] In this case, too, he was hardly focusing criticism upon a sacrosanct topic. By the last quarter of the nineteenth century phrenology had lost much of its credibility even for unlearned laymen, and an almost unanimous hostility to its ideas prevailed in scientific circles.[40]

Phrenology once occurred to Clemens as a possible literary weapon— a device to inflict stinging derision—and in this instance his supercilious attitude toward the pseudoscience is altogether absent. In 1882, during a period when Clemens imagined that Whitelaw Reid, editor of the New York *Tribune*, was engaged in an unprovoked campaign against his reputation, Clemens filled the pages of his personal notebook with inspirations for a vicious biography of Reid that he planned to write in retaliation. The book as he envisioned it would feature a phrenological diagram of Reid's skull, with the "selfish organs" drawn so as to comprise fully half of his faculties, "so heavy they weigh down back of head & tilt his face upward."[41] An accompanying sketch in Clemens's 1882 notebook illustrates the rearward placement of the "Selfish Sentiments." Was he reminded of the similar drawing he had copied from Weaver's treatise in 1855?

Weaver had stated that the organs in this group "are ever consulting the dignity, importance, and nobility of this wonderful child of God I."[42] Clemens also made notes for Reid's "phrenology" character-chart to indicate that "CAUTION" would have dominated all propensities, "Constructiveness" would only have manifested itself in Reid's "lying & slander," and the portion of Reid's character influenced by "Personal Honor" would have been rendered "too small to read."

These invectives probably were suggested to Clemens by his reading George Combe's *Notes on the United States of North America During a Phrenological Visit in 1838–39–40*, a travel narrative he consulted preparatory to writing *Life on the Mississippi*.[43] Combe's book is heavily infused with the doctrines of phrenology, and his "Introduction" includes a brief account of the various organs, their effects, and their locations. In the first volume (which Clemens owned and annotated), Combe also discusses the temperaments, and throughout both volumes he devotes nearly as much space to phrenology as he does to the details of his tour. But whether or not Clemens derived his insults from perusing Combe's *Notes*, he fortunately never brought this libelous scheme into print. He belatedly discovered, upon searching the pages of the *Tribune*, that the reports of Reid's supposed attacks had been enormously exaggerated, and so he dropped his plans with some private embarrassment.

At the time that he changed his mind about attacking Reid, Clemens wrote to William Dean Howells about his decision, lamenting that "my three weeks' hard work have got to go into the ignominious pigeonhole."[44]

Later that same year, after his Mississippi River trip, he devised a way to salvage the phrenological portion from his abandoned project of retribution: he bestowed the affliction of enlarged organs upon a fictional steamboat captain described in *Life on the Mississippi*, relying on a tall-tale flavor of exaggeration to integrate it into the monologue of a yarn-spinning pilot, Rob Styles. Quite possibly Mark Twain himself still associated phrenology with the Mississippi Valley, and thus was striving to introduce additional local color into the narrative of his recent journey down the river.[45] Rob Styles, recognizing Mark Twain in the pilot house, improvises a series of absurd assertions about river piloting, including a monstrous lie about "alligator water," and concludes by characterizing Captain Tom Ballou as "the most immortal liar that ever I struck." Styles declares that "he had more selfish organs than any seven men in the world—all packed in the stern-sheets of his skull, of course, where they belonged. They weighed down the back of his head so that it made his nose tilt up in the air. People thought it was vanity, but it wasn't, it was malice."[46]

Testing Phrenology's Claims

At no point during the evolution of this joke about selfish organs did Clemens evince any disdain for the system of belief which he was employing. And despite his deprecatory assignment of phrenology to the carpetbags of frauds and charlatans in his fiction, we know that Clemens privately experimented with its procedure of examination again and again. Still another instance signifying his interest if not credence can be set beside the three and possibly four character readings adduced by

Madeleine Stern. In 1885, at about the time that *Huckleberry Finn* was being published, Mark Twain visited Cincinnati, Ohio during a lecture tour with George Washington Cable. Ozias Pond, the brother of lecture agent James B. Pond, reported in his diary that in that city on January 3, 1885 Clemens submitted to the extravagance of an analysis by a phrenologist.[47] The examiner was Dr. Edgar Charles Beall (b. 1853), editor of *The Phrenological Journal* and a prolific author whose *The Brain and the Bible; or, The Conflict Between Mental Science and Theology* (1881) had contained a preface by the prominent agnostic Robert G. Ingersoll. Beall would become recognized as the leading authority in his field and his *The Life Sexual: A Study of the Philosophy, Physiology, Science, Art, and Hygiene of Love* (1905) would cause a national stir. Dr. Beall lost no time in reporting his famous client's attributes; the next day the Cincinnati *Commercial Gazette* carried an article titled "Mark Twain's Head Analyzed." Beall had found that Twain's head "measures 22 ½ inches, which is half an inch less than the average intellectual giant. . . . He has very ardent affections, strong love of approbation, sense of justice, firmness, kindness and ability to read character; with small self-esteem, love of gain, or inclination to the supernatural." (That finding of "small self-esteem" might have been a relief to Clemens.) The phrenologist also detected that he was "excellent in wit, but super-excellent in humor. Secretiveness is very marked in . . . the nearly closed eyes, compressed lips, slow, guarded manner of speech, etc." He praised "the temperament of our great humorist, which is . . . the spare, angular mental, or mental-motive, which is favorable to hard

sense, logic, general intelligence and insight into human nature."[48]

Moreover, at the time of Clemens's death he possessed a copy of Orson S. and Lorenzo N. Fowler's *New Illustrated Self-Instructor in Phrenology and Physiology* in his personal library. Marks had been placed in the chart of faculties at the front of the book before "Self-Esteem," "Veneration" and "Calculation," and the volume contained his signature, "Clemens, 1901."[49] This date corresponds with his appointment with Jessie Allen Fowler for a character reading on March 7, 1901; he most likely was given the book when he underwent this analysis in New York City.[50] One wonders whether he was not disappointed that her observations, published in the *American Phrenological Journal* and quoted by Madeleine Stern in her article, interpreted his disposition as one which did *not* belong to the sanguine temperament: "From his father he received his rugged, wiry organization; his large Vitativeness giving him his hold on life, his *motive-mental temperament*, his executive spirit, and his great determination of mind."[51] In the new classification of temperaments, the "motive" was equivalent to the previous "bilious," and "mental" referred to the earlier "nervous." Fowler's analysis does not once mention the "vital" temperament, which combined the former categories of "sanguine" and "lymphatic," a fact that illustrates the difficulty of applying labels derived from caricature models to the heads and bodies of real people.

For literary purposes, at any rate, Mark Twain recalled his previous visits to Jessie Fowler's father much more vividly. In his Autobiographical Dictation on the topic of phrenology (26 December 1906) he derides the abilities of a phrenologist named Fowler whom he consulted in London in 1872 or 1873.[52] He went to Fowler, he says, with the intention of "personally testing" the man's professional acumen. On his first appraisal Fowler purportedly found a cavity where Mark Twain's bump of humor ought to have been. When Mark Twain returned three months later under his celebrated pen name (he had used a fictitious name the first time), the phrenologist thereupon discovered "a Mount Everest . . . the loftiest bump of humor he had ever encountered in his life-long experience! I went from his presence prejudiced against phrenology."[53] Mark Twain is referring to Lorenzo Niles Fowler (1811–1896), who settled in London after his retirement from the Fowler & Wells firm in 1863. Fowler resided in England until 1896.

There is no need to remind the reader that Mark Twain's efforts at writing truthful autobiography frequently fell into the comic patterns of his fiction. He rarely could resist the temptation to provide his audience with a satisfying "nub" for a promising anecdote. In this case the unreliability of Lorenzo Fowler's calipers had already furnished Mark Twain with materials for fiction as well as reminiscence. Four or five years earlier he had produced an elaborate burlesque of these same visits to the former Fowler & Wells partner in Book II (Chapter 2) of a travesty of history textbooks, "The Secret History of Eddypus, the World-Empire," written in 1901 and 1902. In this garbled reconstruction of nineteenth-century American culture as recovered from the surviving books of "Bishop" Mark Twain, the narrator quotes

from an account of the "Bishop's" two visits to "BRIGGS AND POLLARD, AMERICAN PHRENOLOGISTS." The Bishop, writing many centuries before his historical narratives were discovered and venerated, explains that he consulted these specialists simply for an assessment of a large swelling on his head induced by a prodigious compliment. "I knew what my mental calibre had been before the change, and I also knew what my disposition and character had been,"[54] the Father of History writes. He wishes to know whether this new protuberance indicates that a massive alteration is taking place in his personality. (Presumably his organ of Self-Esteem has been swollen by praise.)

To avoid influencing the diagnosis he disguises his name and occupation on the first visit. His depiction of the examining team, their methods and their office (filled with bald-headed busts, "checkered off like township maps") probably would be more humorous to a generation familiar with the Fowler brothers. The phrenologists—both of whom are quite intoxicated—measure, massage and thump his skull, and then deliver a series of insulting opinions about its contents. One of the men, says the Bishop, "drifted into what sounded like a lecture; not something fresh, I thought, but a flux of flatulent phrases staled by use and age." This "lecture," reproduced in "Eddypus," actually consists of a slightly condensed rendering of the Fowler & Wells explanation for their scale of numerical sizes for organs (ranging from 7, "very large," to 1, "very small"), together with corresponding adjectives. Mark Twain lifted words, phrases and entire clauses from the description of this comparative system published in the preface

(p. viii) of the Fowler brothers' *Self-Instructor in Phrenology and Physiology*, which he had acquired from Jessie Allen Fowler in 1901.

The narrator of "Eddypus" explains that, as a result of this unflattering reading, the Bishop "had come to believe that the phrenologists were merely guessers, nothing more, and that they could rightly guess a man only when they knew his history." The Bishop tests this theory by returning for another examination under his proper, well-known name. Receiving then a fawning, adulatory diagnosis, he concludes that "Phrenology is the 'science' which extracts character from clothes." These words convey the impression of representing Mark Twain's final, unequivocal views on the matter after repeated experiments, yet it seems likely that his attitude toward the pseudoscience never crystallized into firm disbelief. He concludes even his gibes against Lorenzo Fowler in his *Autobiography* with the acknowledgment that "it may be . . . that I ought to have conferred the prejudice upon Fowler, and not upon the art which he was exploiting."[55]

OTHER LITERARY DETRACTORS

It should be added that in lampooning the pretensions of the Fowler brothers Mark Twain was in fact working within an established tradition of American humor. For instance, John Phoenix (George H. Derby) had parodied them by visiting "Flatbroke B. Dodge, Professor of Phrenology" in a pre-Civil War sketch, "A New System of English Grammar." Mark Twain selected this piece to appear in *Mark Twain's Library of Humor* (pp. 498–505), the anthology he edited in collaboration with Howells and Charles H. Clark and whose publication by Charles L.

Webster & Company he supervised in 1888. Phoenix's phrenologist drank brandy and water, chewed tobacco, and as a sideline sold bottles of "hair invigorator" to his clients. Professor Dodge was also an advocate of the Fowlerian numerical scale of organ sizes, and Phoenix proposed in his sketch that similar numbers be substituted for adjectives in the English language so that "we become at once an exact, precise, mathematical, truth-telling people" (*Library of Humor*, p. 503)—a suggestion Mark Twain much later implemented when describing the Taj Mahal in Chapter 59 of *Following the Equator* (1897).

George Ade had written a more recent example of this type: he scoffed at phrenologists in "The Fable of the Visitor Who Got a Lot for Three Dollars," the opening sketch in his *Fables in Slang* (1899). Mark Twain may have read this twitting depiction of an invariably complimentary phrenologist whose office was adorned with plaster of paris heads and comparative charts. For three dollars Ade's phrenologist would examine a truck driver's head resembling "a Rocky Ford Cantaloupe" and pronounce it worthy of the presidency of a theological seminary. Ade drew a characteristic moral: "A good Jolly is worth Whatever you Pay for it."[56] Virtually all of the phrenological elements in Twain's "Eddypus" and *Autobiography* episodes had been exploited previously by these and other American humorists who recognized the comic potentiality inherent in mass examinations of the nation's skulls.

TWAIN RETURNED TO THOSE TEMPERAMENTS

In addition to these recurrent manifestations of his interest in phrenology, it can also be shown that the lessons Clemens diligently learned as a youth about the temperaments proved equally ineradicable. Over the years this essentially Spurzheimean concept of innate temperaments was assimilated with Clemens's later reading about human heredity and morals, and resulted in the view of mankind that dominated his last period of writing. In 1898 he constructed much of the dialogue in *What Is Man?* around the term "temperament," which he defines there as "the disposition you were born with." This piece of phrenological phraseology would cling to his thought and expression to the end of his life. In *What Is Man?* the Old Man, a proponent of a seemingly irrefutable mechanistic logic, declares that "*You can't eradicate your disposition nor any rag of it*—you can only put a pressure on it and keep it down and quiet." He adds that "beliefs are *acquirements*, temperaments are *born*; beliefs are subject to change, nothing whatever can change temperament. . . . Where the temperament is two-thirds happy, or two-thirds unhappy, no political or religious beliefs can change the proportions."[57]

Such an opinion about the causal forces behind man's behavior was radically at variance with the phrenological premises of the Fowlers. While early phrenological theorists had been noncommital about the prospect of changing the predetermined bodily constitution, the Fowlers (and Weaver) announced that the ideal character, such as George Washington's, displayed all the temperaments in equal proportions. Therefore in their *Self-Instructor* (pp. 37–38) the Fowlers suggested that by taking certain prescribed measures one might hope to emulate the Washington standard by "restraining" predominant temperaments and "exercising" deficient ones. Mark Twain broke completely with their basic assumptions about the possibility of "cultivating" one's moral attributes (which for them as for Clemens merged with the temperaments) toward perfection. The view Twain stated in *What Is Man?* and "A Defence of General Funston" (1902) [58]—that our innate dispositions can only be temporarily braced, trussed and repressed, but never altered appreciably or permanently—repudiates the entire "self-improvement" thesis which had supported the latter phases of phrenology. In contradicting the optimistic system of thought that he had long before espoused, perhaps he was deliberately invoking one of its central terms in his rebuttal, seeking to turn the very vocabulary of the doctrine back upon it.

Many readers may recall that Mark Twain reiterated this view in Letter VIII of "Letters from the Earth," which he wrote in the autumn of 1909. "God gives to each man his temperament, his disposition, at birth," Satan reports. "Man cannot by any process change this temperament, but must remain always under its dominion."[59] That same year, on Dec. 27, 1909, a few days after the death of his daughter Jean, Twain added a paragraph of philosophic reflections to his autobiographical dictations. The sorrowing father posed the question:

> Shall I ever be cheerful again, happy again? Yes. And soon. For I know my temperament. And I know that the temperament is *master of the man*, and that he is its fettered and helpless slave and must in all things do as it commands. A man's temperament is

born in him, and no circumstances can ever change it.

My temperament has never allowed my spirits to remain depressed long at a time. That was a feature of Jean's temperament, too. She inherited it from me.[60]

Shortly thereafter Mark Twain repeated this self-analysis of his sanguine temperament in an article entitled "The Turning Point of My Life," published in the February 1910 issue of *Harper's Bazar*. Recalling the circumstance that provided him with the money to leave Keokuk, Iowa in 1856 for a proposed expedition to South America, he again stressed the paramount importance of temperament. The word as he adapted it now meant something slightly different from what Weaver intended, but if we read closely we can recognize a cluster of mental associations (including the disputed blue/gray eye coloration) that had their inception in the notes he copied 55 years earlier about his impulsive sanguine temperament:

[The partner of Circumstance] is man's *temperament*—his natural disposition. His temperament is not his invention, it is *born* in him, and he has no authority over it, neither is he responsible for its acts. He cannot change it, nothing can change it, nothing can modify it,—except temporarily. But it won't stay modified. It is permanent, like the color of the man's eyes and the shape of his ears. Blue eyes are gray in certain unusual lights; but they resume their natural color when that stress is removed.

A Circumstance that will coerce one man, will have no effect upon a man of a different

temperament. If Circumstance had thrown the banknote in [Julius] Caesar's way, his temperament would not have made him start for the Amazon. His temperament would have compelled him to do something with the money, but not that. . . .

By temperament I was the kind of person that *does* things. Does them, and reflects afterward. So I started for the Amazon, without reflecting, and without asking any questions. That was more than fifty years ago. In all that time my temperament has not changed, by even a shade.[61]

Clemens' ununiform appraisals of phrenology and the temperaments suggest that, as in many other areas of his thought, his intellectual position on this topic was unsystematic, variable, even contradictory. However, several overlapping patterns of attitude can be distinguished. By the time he was nineteen years old Clemens clearly had embraced the system of phrenology and the temperaments as a method of predicting character traits. His straightforward employment of phrenological locutions, never frequent or prominent in his writings after he became a professional author, decreased through the years, apparently ceasing altogether around 1890. In *The Adventures of Tom Sawyer* (1876) he began introducing phrenologists explicitly into his literature, always in a derogatory manner, and he commented unfavorably on them in *Adventures of Huckleberry Finn* (1885), "Eddypus" (1901?), and an autobiographical dictation of 1906. But these unsympathetic treatments of the subject, since they merely exposed the exploitations of a gullible public by charlatans, left open by implication the possibility of scientific validity for the discipline as a whole.

At the same time, moreover, Clemens was continuing to investigate its claims, discreetly and privately, as though still uncertain whether to add or withhold his name from the dwindling lists of its adherents. His final conclusion on the matter is unclear, and was perhaps merely a sense of uncomfortable ambivalence. It is apparent that he earnestly wished to believe in the existence of an infallible means of character detection and psychological remedy. Furthermore, as he grew older he prided himself on his deviance from popular tastes and enthusiasms; thus the increasing disenchantment with phrenology would not necessarily have affected his opinion of its ultimate soundness—indeed, in the unorthodox mood of his late years its public neglect must surely have been for him an enticement rather than a dissuasion.

Finally, one important part of his vocabulary in his deterministic thesis—man's inherent "temperament"—appears to derive from his previous reading in phrenology. But the passage of time has obscured for Americans the specific meanings of words prominent in a pseudoscience that has now been thoroughly debunked. In fact, its doctrines have been so effectually disparaged that we occasionally need to remind ourselves that phrenology gained its supporters primarily because it sought to utilize the emerging conclusions of European researchers about the locations and varieties of the brain's functions. To the dismay of its enthusiasts this particular attempt to link the configuration of the exterior skull (and the general physical appearance of the body) with mental capacity and specific character traits eventually proved to be an unsustainable theory. Yet during one period of the mid-nineteenth century the system had its assortment of eminent men and women who at least experimented with if they did not totally endorse the fad. Now we know that Mark Twain joins Poe, Simms, Holmes, Stowe, Melville and Whitman among American authors who gave it a more or less serious treatment in their literary works.[62] For someone like Clemens—who avidly collected the opinions of palmists, who rejoiced at each new experience of mental telepathy (which he sometimes termed "phrenography"),[63] and who maintained a skeptical but lifelong interest in spiritualism—phrenology and the temperaments quite understandably had an irresistible, recurring appeal.

NOTES

1   "Mark Twain Had His Head Examined," *American Literature* 41.1 (May 1969): 207–218.

2   Notebook 1, *Mark Twain's Notebooks & Journals, Volume 1*, ed. Frederick Anderson, Michael B. Frank, and Kenneth M. Sanderson (Berkeley: University of California Press, 1975), 1: 21–35.

3   *Mark Twain, Business Man* (Boston: Little, Brown, 1946), pp. 20–28.

4   Page citations throughout the text of my essay refer to this edition—hereafter cited as *Mental Science*. Weaver's book was apparently reissued a number of times. I have seen an identical 1854 edition, and the firm continued to advertise the title during the 1850s. It is worth noting that this book is one of Clemens's earliest reading experiences which can be conclusively documented.

5   William Herbert Sheldon (1898–1977) made a well-known attempt to re-establish the relations between physique and temperament; he propounded a classification of temperament by variations in body build—endomorphy, mesomorphy and ectomorphy—and identified three primary clusters of traits. See Sheldon's *The Varieties of Human Physique: An Introduction to Constitutional Psychology* (1940) and *The Varieties of Temperament:*

A Psychology of Constitutional Differences (1942).

6   "Signs of Character," *American Phrenological Journal* 9 (1847): 377.

7   Spurzheim, *Phrenology, in Connexion with the Study of Physiognomy* (Boston: Marsh, Capen & Lyon, 1833), pp. 30–31.

8   Combe, *Elements of Phrenology*, 4th ed. (Edinburgh: Maclachlan & Stewart, 1836), pp. 20–21.

9   Spurzheim disapproved of the older and broader implications of phrenological temperaments. In *Outlines of Phrenology* (London: Treuttel, Wurtz & Richter, 1829), pp. 4–5, he referred to the "ancient doctrine" of the temperaments, which (erroneously) "has long been and is still often considered sufficient to explain the great differences of the mental dispositions of man." Phrenology, he explained, corrects this mistaken concept by restricting the function of the temperaments to mere determination of "more or less activity to the fundamental [mental] faculties."

10 Weaver, *Mental Science*, p. 74. The four temperaments ultimately were telescoped into three divisions: the newer *Motive* temperament corresponded to the bilious; the *Vital* temperament combined the sanguine and the lymphatic; and the *Mental* temperament was formerly called the nervous. The reduction would be noted in an article entitled "Temperaments" in the *American Phrenological Journal* 27 (February 1858): 19–20. Weaver acknowledged the tripartite classifications in *Mental Science*, but professed to prefer the system of four categories "as much more purely scientific, and more readily comprehended by the tyro in the science" (p. 81).

11 Weaver, *Mental Science*, p. 78.

12 In his biographical study of the Hannibal years— *Sam Clemens of Hannibal* (Boston: Houghton Mifflin, 1952), p. 124—Dixon Wecter concluded that young Clemens possessed "sandy curls" and "blue-gray eyes."

13 Clemens to Jane Clemens and Pamela Moffett, 8 February 1862, *Mark Twain's Letters, Volume 1, 1853–1866*, ed. Edgar Marquess Branch, Michael B. Frank, and Kenneth M. Sanderson (Berkeley: University of California Press, 1988), 1: 156–157—hereafter cited as *MTLet*.

14 Weaver, *Mental Science*, p. 80. For a valuable account of the degree to which Edgar Allan Poe came to epitomize the "nervous" or "mental" temperament, see Madeleine B. Stern, "Poe: 'The Mental Temperament' for Phrenologists,"

American Literature 40.2 (May 1968): 155–163.

15 *Autobiography of George Sumner Weaver, D. D.: A Sketch of a Busy Life, 1914*, Privately printed, edition limited to 125 copies (Albany, New York: Argus-Greenwood, 1965), pp. 39–40.

16 Matthews, "The Future Literary Capital of the United States," *Lippincott's Monthly Magazine* 37 (January 1886): 105.

17 Weaver, *Autobiography*, pp. 40–41, 51. One of Weaver's associates in St. Louis was the Reverend Erasmus Manford (1815–84), a Universalist minister who is also mentioned in Clemens's first notebook. During the mid-1850s Weaver assisted Manford in editing *The Golden Era*, a denominational journal published in St. Louis.

18 *The Anatomy of American Popular Culture 1840–1861* (Berkeley: University of California Press, 1959), p. 128.

19 Weaver, *Mental Science*, pp. 59–60.

20 Weaver, *Mental Science*, p. 54.

21 Weaver, *Mental Science*, pp. 81–82.

22 Weaver, *Autobiography*, p. 15.

23 Despite such shortcomings, *Mental Science* was only one of more than a dozen books Weaver published, including *Hopes and Helps for the Young of Both Sexes* (1853), *Aims and Aids for Girls* (1854), *The Ways of Life* (1855), *The Christian Household* (1855), *The Open Way* (1873), *Lives and Graves of Our Presidents* (1884), and *Looking Forward, for Young Men* (1891).

24 Sometimes Fowlers & Wells on the title page; because of personnel changes the Fowler name in the firm title varied from plural to singular over the years. Madeleine B. Stern completed a study of this enterprising family and its activities—*Heads & Headlines: The Phrenological Fowlers* (Norman, Oklahoma: University of Oklahoma Press, 1971).

25 A copy of Orson Squire Fowler's *Love and Parentage, Applied to the Improvement of Offspring*, 40th ed. (New York: Fowler & Wells [c. 1844]) is extant that reportedly belonged to Orion Clemens. In 1972 it was in the possession of Ralph Gregory (1909–2015), Marthasville, Missouri.

26 Published in *The Autobiography of Mark Twain*, ed. Charles Neider (New York: Harper & Brothers, 1959), p. 64—hereafter cited as *Autobiography*— and in *Autobiography of Mark Twain, Volume 2*, ed. Benjamin Griffin and Harriet Elinor Smith (Berkeley: University of California Press, 2013), 2: 335 (the latter hereafter referred to as *AutoMT*).

27 Advertising notice in *American Phrenological Journal* 28 (October 1858): 61.

28 *Early Tales & Sketches, Volume 1, 1851–1864*, ed. Edgar Marquess Branch and Robert H. Hirst (Berkeley: University of California Press, 1979), pp. 111–112.

29 See, for instance, the letter from Clemens to Olivia Clemens, January 23, 1885, in *The Love Letters of Mark Twain*, ed. Dixon Wecter (New York: Harper & Brothers, 1949), p. 233.

30 Weaver, *Mental Science*, pp. 77–78.

31 Of course in each instance it is necessary to distinguish between truly phrenological locutions and those which simply reflect the "faculty psychology" vocabulary prevalent in discussions about mental processes in the nineteenth century. Phrenology itself was partly a spinoff of the respectable Scottish School of faculty psychology (see Edwin G. Boring, *A History of Experimental Psychology*, 2nd ed. [New York: Appleton, 1957], pp. 53, 205–208).

32 *The Innocents Abroad* (Hartford, Connecticut: American Publishing, 1869), p. 239.

33 Combe, *Elements of Phrenology*, pp. 88,85.

34 Weaver, *Mental Science*, p. 191.

35 But Clemens also defended phrenologists who impressed him as disinterested and scholarly, judging from an undated marginal comment in his copy of *Thackeray's Lectures: The English Humorists* (New York: Harper & Brothers, 1868), p. 9, where Thackeray noted that when Jonathan Swift's skull was unearthed in 1835, "phrenologists had a low opinion of his intellect, from the observations they took." Clemens rejoined: "Possibly it was some poor parish idiot's skull they got instead—'medics' are seldom very authentic. Think of these learned, spectacled Doctors of Phrenology gravely getting up an 'opinion' of Swift's intellect by examining another man's skull!" (Mark Twain Library, Redding, Connecticut; quoted in *Mark Twain's Margins on Thackeray's "Swift,"* ed. Coley B. Taylor [New York: Gotham House, 1935], p. 33).

36 First published by Bernard DeVoto in *Mark Twain at Work* (Cambridge: Harvard University Press, 1942), p. 66.

37 *Adventures of Huckleberry Finn*, ed. Victor Fischer and Lin Salamo (Berkeley: University of California Press, 2003), pp. 160–161 (Chapter 19).

38 *Adventures of Huckleberry Finn*, p. 168 (Chapter 20).

39 *Mark Twain: The Fate of Humor* (Princeton: Princeton University Press, 1966), p. 196.

40 See John D. Davies's authoritative account of the decline of the movement in *Phrenology: Fad and Science* (New Haven: Yale University Press, 1955), pp. 172–173.

41 Notebook 20, *Mark Twain's Notebooks & Journals, Volume II*, ed. Frederick Anderson, Lin Salamo, and Bernard L. Stein (Berkeley: University of California Press, 1975), 2: 441.

42 Weaver, *Mental Science*, p. 89.

43 In manuscript passages deleted from the first edition of *Life on the Mississippi* Mark Twain mentions and praises *Notes on the United States of North America*, 2 vols. (Philadelphia: Carey & Hart, 1841); see the appendix to the Limited Editions Club text of *Life on the Mississippi*, ed. Willis Wagner (New York: Heritage Press, 1944), pp. 402, 405. Clemens's copy of Combe's *Notes* (Volume 1 only) is now in the Mark Twain Papers, Bancroft Library, University of California, Berkeley—hereafter referred to as MTP. The whereabouts of Volume 2 of Combe's *Notes* has never been recorded.

44 *Mark Twain-Howells Letters*, ed., Henry Nash Smith and William M. Gibson (Cambridge: Harvard University Press, 1960), p. 389.

45 It may be significant that the team of Fowler & Wells had offered several courses of phrenological lectures and examinations in New Orleans during the years when Clemens was a river pilot. Their second visit was advertised in the New Orleans *Daily Picayune*, February 27–28, 1858.

46 *Life on the Mississippi* (Boston: James R. Osgood, 1883), pp. 270–271 (Chapter 24). This image was recurrent: Mark Twain had similarly described himself as a cub pilot, "brim full of self-conceit and carrying my nose as high as a giraffe's," in "Old Times on the Mississippi," *Atlantic Monthly* 35.211 (May 1875): 573.

47 "Extracts from the Diary of Ozias W. Pond," TS copy in the Cable Collection, Tulane University, New Orleans; cited by Guy A. Cardwell in *Twins of Genius* (East Lansing: Michigan State College Press, 1953), p. 33.

48 Cincinnati, Ohio *Commercial Gazette*, 4 January 1885, p. 8, column 5. I am grateful to Victor Fischer and Robert H. Hirst for drawing my attention to this newspaper item.

49 *Anderson Auction Company Catalogue No. 892* (New York, 1911), p. 57. The *Self-Instructor* was first issued in 1849. A revised edition (which was the one Clemens possessed) was copyrighted in

1859; it was republished in 1869, 1877, 1890 and possibly in other years as well.

50 Madeleine Stern appears to have been mistaken in her logical surmise that the examiner in 1901 was Edgar C. Beall, a business partner in the firm of Fowler & Wells ("Mark Twain Had His Head Examined," pp. 212–13). Clemens's notebook for 1901 contains an entry reminding him of an appointment with Jessie A. Fowler at 10:30 on March 7, 1901 (Notebook 34, TS, p. 7, MTP). Jessie Allen Fowler (1856–1932) was the daughter of Lorenzo Niles Fowler (1811–1896), one of the founders of the firm; she was herself a practicing phrenologist as well as a writer and lecturer on the subject. Since 1897 she had been editor in chief of the *American Phrenological Journal*, so in all likelihood she wrote the 1901 article analyzing Clemens's character in that publication.

51 Quoted by Madeleine Stern in "Mark Twain Had His Head Examined," p. 216; italics added.

52 Mark Twain's account of Fowler's contradictory diagnoses exists in two versions; the shorter one, written as a letter, was published in the London *Daily Graphic* without his approval (see Stern, "Mark Twain, Had His Head Examined," pp. 216–17). He included both versions in his 26 December 1906 Autobiographical Dictation (published in Charles Neider's *Autobiography*, pp. 63–66 and in *AutoMT* 2: 335–336).

53 Neider, *Autobiography* p. 66 and *AutoMT* 2: 335–336. We ought to note in assessing the truthfulness of this anecdote that its elements resemble Clemens's scheme to expose Madame Caprell, a New Orleans fortune-teller, in 1861: "*Ergo*, I would disguise myself and go again, one of these days, when other amusements failed" (*MTLet* 1: 111).

54 "The Secret History of Eddypus, the World-Empire," *Mark Twain's Fables of Man*, ed. John S. Tuckey (Berkeley: University of California Press, 1972), pp. 349–350. Mark Twain may have been thinking here of Weaver's assertion that "in cases where the organ is large, and has been subject to great intensity of action, the outward prominence is distinct and sharp" (*Mental Science*, p. 49).

55 Dictated on 26 December 1906; published in Neider's *Autobiography*, p. 66 and in *AutoMT* 2: 336.

56 *Fables in Slang* (Chicago: Herbert S. Stone, 1900), p. 7. Oliver Wendell Holmes had produced the classic lampoon of phrenologists in *The Professor at the Breakfast-Table* (1860).

57 *What Is Man? and Other Philosophical Writings*, ed. Paul Baender (Berkeley: University of California Press, 1973), pp. 168, 212–213.

58 "A Defence of General Funston," *North American Review* 174.546 (May 1902): 613–624. It is revealing that Mark Twain compares Funston to George Washington throughout this caustic essay, thereby using the Fowlers' favorite specimen of the "well-balanced temperament." In his 1906 autobiographical dictation Twain again would refer to the revered "Washington standard" of phrenology (Neider, p. 65 and *AutoMT* 2: 335).

59 *Letters from the Earth*, ed. Bernard DeVoto (New York: Harper & Row, 1962), p. 37.

60 Quoted by Albert Bigelow Paine in *Mark Twain: A Biography* (New York: Harper & Brothers, 1912), p. 1552. See *AutoMT* 3: 613, which explains that this addition to the autobiography has not been located among the manuscripts. George Sumner Weaver had stated that the sanguine temperament "feels grief and sorrow most bitterly, but soon becomes calm and forgets it all" (*Mental Science*, pp. 78–79).

61 Collected in *What Is Man? and Other Philosophical Writings*, pp. 460–461.

62 Tom Quirk—*Mark Twain and Human Nature* (Columbia: University of Missouri Press, 2007), pp. 24–30—discussed Twain's connection with phrenology and added helpful perspectives. Much earlier, James D. Wilson looked at phrenology among Twain's various enthusiasms in "'The Monumental Sarcasm of the Ages': Science and Pseudoscience in the Thought of Mark Twain," *South Atlantic Bulletin* 40.2 (May 1975): 72–82.

63 Clemens described "phrenography" in a letter dated October 28–31, 1881, TS in MTP. He also used the word as the title for a talk before the Monday Evening Club on November 21, 1881 (*The List of Members of the Monday Evening Club Together with the Record of Papers Read at Their Meetings 1869–1954*, ed. Howell Cheney [Hartford, Connecticut, 1954], p. 36). In an essay titled "Mental Telegraphy" Twain predicted the invention of a "phrenophone," a method of mind communicating with mind (*The £1,000,000 Bank-Note and Other New Stories* [New York: Charles L. Webster & Co., 1893], p. 65).

An earlier version of this chapter appeared in American Quarterly *24.1 (March 1972): 45–68.*

15

Tom Sawyer, Tom Canty, and Huckleberry Finn

The Boy Book and Mark Twain

Few scholars like to think of Mark Twain as having written within certain literary trends of his day, sensing perhaps that this fact might seem to detract from his much-lauded originality. Nonetheless, off and on for several decades I have followed the lead of Walter Blair and others in studying Twain's particular relationship to the nineteenth-century "Boy Book," a curious stepchild of American fiction that drew its first breath with Thomas Bailey Aldrich's *The Story of a Bad Boy* (1869) and (some would say) expired in Booth Tarkington's droll *Penrod* (1914)—whose sketches occasionally stray into racial stereotypes—and its Penrod sequels.[1] The most psychologically compelling of the narratives about boy-life produced within this half-century tradition were Harold Frederic's poignant "My Aunt Susan" and "The Eve of the Fourth," which were collected in his *Marsena and Other Stories of the Wartime* (1894), and Stephen Crane's Whilomville tales, such as "His New Mittens" (1898) and "The Fight" (1900). Authors as diverse as Charles Dudley Warner (*Being a Boy*, 1878), William Dean Howells (*A Boy's Town*, 1890), Hamlin Garland (*Boy Life on the Prairie*, 1899), and William Allen White (*The Court of Boyville*, 1899) made memorable contributions. It should be a comfort to those perhaps bothered by Twain's participation in this American Boy Book parade to reflect that his *The Adventures of Tom Sawyer* (1876) was only the second in the sequence of their publication, and that its scenes of fence-painting, schoolroom antics, Sunday School competitions, church service boredom, puppy love, pirate camp, murder trial, and cave exploring have long been acclaimed as the high point of Boy Book achievements.

It can be established that Samuel Clemens was familiar with a number of these memoirs and novels about men's childhoods. We know that Clemens had read Aldrich's *The Story of a Bad Boy* at least by December 1869 and perhaps even earlier, though his personal copy of the book has never surfaced. A copy of Warner's *Being a Boy* (1878) was among the Clemens family's library books. Clemens called William Dean Howells's *A Boy's Town* (1890) "perfect as the perfectest photograph the sun ever made." He owned at least eight of Hamlin Garland's books, so he might have possessed a no-longer-extant copy of *Boy Life on the Prairie* (1899). A 1904 edition of William Allen White's *The Court of Boyville* was part of his personal library. He also acquired a copy of Stephen Crane's *The Monster and Other Stories* (1899), which contained the horrific story about Jimmie Trescott's survival and his African American savior's disfigurement as well as a poignant short story about another boy's misery, "His New Mittens." Clemens stated that he admired Harold Frederic, but apparently left behind no copies of his books. Booth Tarkington did not begin writing his Penrod stories until 1914. Henry James, of course, did not get around to writing about his boyhood years until his (largely intellectual) recollections, *A Small Boy and Others* (1913) and *Notes of a Son and Brother* (1914), which appeared a few years after Clemens's death and shortly before James passed away in 1916.

In my first study,[2] I examined in detail the indebtedness of Mark Twain to Aldrich's *Story of a Bad Boy*, a book Twain dismissed but which I see as the text he both emulated and reacted against in writing *Tom Sawyer*. My essay presented numerous parallels and analogues between the two books, and even gave credit to Aldrich for Tom Sawyer's first name. The boy in Aldrich's story admires the same romances esteemed by Tom Sawyer, I pointed out, and plays an immense prank on the entire town. I also sought there to defend the role Tom Sawyer plays in *Adventures of*

Huckleberry Finn (1885), even in the much-maligned final chapters of that novel.

A second essay was briefer but more ambitious.[3] It showed that the term "Boy Book" is so imprecise as to embrace a heterogeneous assortment of sentimental autobiography, juvenile romance, sociological documentary, comic slapstick, and literary burlesque. Twain's *Tom Sawyer* seems superior to the other entries in the genre largely because its author, unlike Aldrich, elected to rely as much on literary invention as on nostalgic recollections from his actual boyhood; it was the first true novel to be written in the United States in this vein. Moreover, I identified Thomas Hughes' *Tom Brown's School Days* (1857), a popular Victorian novel about a youth's life in Berks county, England and at Rugby, as the most likely inspiration for Aldrich's ground-breaking *Story of a Bad Boy*. (Aldrich's book even refers to Hughes' work as "one of the best books ever written for boys.") Clemens owned copies of Hughes' *Tom Brown's School Days* and its sequel, *Tom Brown at Oxford*, and had access to additional copies of these autobiographical novels whenever he visited Quarry Farm in Elmira, New York. In this second essay I went on to classify Twain's masterful *Adventures of Huckleberry Finn* as a Boy Book, or at least as a novel whose title as well as opening and closing chapters are designed to mislead nineteenth-century readers into expecting, and purchasing, another Boy Book. To quote my article, "The probability is that Twain wanted to exploit the increasingly popular Boy Book trend while experimenting with some new artistic possibilities that occurred to him."[4] I then summarized some of the features that the Boy Books had in common as a literary tradition: a magnified scale of appearances and events, a yearning for the abandoned "savagery" of Native Americans, the illness of a boy character (including Tom Sawyer's several feverish swoons), the disappearance or death of a parent (usually the father), boy-gang shenanigans, democratic acceptance of social inferiors, schoolboy crushes on girls, fights with schoolyard bullies, a climactic test of courage (almost invariably on a lake, in a river, or on the sea), protective parental figures who reassert their control at the conclusion, and a concluding departure for college or work or (symbolically) manhood. "But if Mark Twain initially planned to abide by prevailing conventions of the autobiographical Boy Book," I observed, "his decision to allow this boy to narrate his own story *without first growing up* blocked those intentions, obliging (or rather enabling) Twain to ignore, and ultimately elude, the limitations of a predictable form."[5]

A third essay combined and condensed the contents of my previous two articles, added some new material, and defended Twain's creation of Tom Sawyer as a valuable literary character.[6] "It is too constraining," I argued, "to surmise, as many modern readers do, that Tom Sawyer serves no purpose by appearing in *Huckleberry Finn*. . . . When the book opens, Tom's presence provides one of the main points of continuity between the earlier book and its successor. . . . And Huck would never be so appealing or seem so authentic if the officious Tom were not there as an increasingly ludicrous foil."[7]

At this point it would be relevant to look at a larger issue that has seldom been confronted: the question as to *why*, other than Thomas

Hughes' example twelve years earlier, Thomas Bailey Aldrich came to write *The Story of a Bad Boy* and the majority of distinguished male authors of the day then proceeded to emulate his example by producing boyhood chronicles of their own. The standard answer to this conundrum was probably the one supplied by Tony Tanner in 1965: that these writers "had spent their childhood in the Eden of pre-Civil War America," and their subsequent "dismay with the harsh reality of post-war corruption and spoliation of the continent thrust them back to the psychic reality of their youth," so that "youth, for those who had spent it before the war, took on a paradisiacal, mythical glow."[8] This is a powerful bit of theorizing, and I really do not wish to displace it at all; one thinks of the big city political bosses, the graft of President Grant's administration, the often-unpopular Reconstruction policies, the labor strife and harsh factory conditions, the influx of impoverished European immigrants, the financial depressions, the rise in anonymous crimes, the gradual awareness of environmental pollution—and the appeal of the lost era before 1861 becomes entirely comprehensible, indeed predictable. So I shall let Tanner's explanation stand, and simply place three other notions on beside it. (Tanner was working toward a treatment of Mark Twain's obsession with youth as a lifelong literary theme and personal fetish, and here again he seems quite discerning.)

On the one hand, those familiar with nineteenth-century American literature will recall that a typical pattern for the post-Civil War authors, including Twain and William Dean Howells, was migration from birthplaces on rural farms or in small towns, often in the Midwest, to large metropolitan cities, generally in the Northeast. Aldrich himself was living in Boston when he conjured up his boyhood memories of charming Portsmouth, New Hampshire. (To be entirely accurate, I should note that Aldrich still visited Portsmouth in the summers and in fact said that he began writing his book there.) Harold Frederic had been residing in London since 1884, far from the Mohawk Valley that his Civil War stories evoked. Stephen Crane's Whilomville stories are nonspecific in their locales, but they hardly reflect his bohemian existence in New York City or his foreign travels. Howells had moved to New York City by the time he sketched the river village in Ohio where he grew up. Twain and Charles Dudley Warner were residents of bustling Hartford, Connecticut when they set down their sketches of boyhood life in Hannibal, Missouri and rural Massachusetts, respectively (though Twain retired in the summers to the bucolic hillside of Quarry Farm). Hamlin Garland's story of deprivation on the prairies of Wisconsin and Iowa found expression during his Chicago period, following almost a decade spent in Boston. Therefore in a highly significant way the Boy Books that these men created were evocations of the farm and the small town by city-bound sophisticates as much as they were tributes to an earlier time. They paid homage to the simplicity and values of farm families and village characters because, for these respected writers, there was no going back except in their imaginations. Not the war, not the corruption and greed of the Gilded Age, but a commitment to urban life and its cosmopolitan advantages intervened between them and their (belatedly) cherished

memories. These are the sentimental laments of men who had long ago turned their back on primitive rural or restrictive village life and its limiting disadvantages for those ambitious to become recognized as authors. Like fond letters mailed back to the home folk, these books repressed all traces of the challenge and pain of leaving one way of life for another. (James L. Machor made some relevant observations about this phenomenon in his book about urban pastoralism.)[9]

How much if any of the appeal of the American Boy Book for some authors lay in the security of their very *maleness*—that is, in the absolute inability of women writers to compete in this genre—is impossible to determine. Hawthorne's fretful remark about the commercial success of domestic and sentimental novels by those "scribbling women" turned out to be merely the first expression of a long if often-friendly rivalry. Certainly there must have been a sense of relief, during the decades that saw Harriet Beecher Stowe, Sarah Orne Jewett, Mary Wilkins Freeman, and other women authors progress to the point of dominating the realm of regional Local Color fiction in the literary monthlies, that here at least gender formed a prohibitive barrier. What woman could write with authority of boy-gangs, swimming-holes, fishing expeditions, schoolyard taunts and fights, the pleasures of hooky, the dangers of night-time expeditions? While it is surely more than an incredible coincidence that Louisa May Alcott's *Little Women* (1868–69) preceded Aldrich's book by only a few months, still the domestic flavor of the story of the four March sisters—Meg, Jo, Beth, and Amy—places it in a different category entirely. If anything, perhaps the immense popularity of this novel prompted Aldrich and Twain to ransack their memories for the far more mischievous, daring, even shocking misdeeds of their youth. Clearly the Boy Book would be set off by this streak of bloodthirsty roguery—so much so that it is often aptly called the "Bad Boy Book" and Tom Sawyer is seen as an adolescent pathologically deluded by desires to act out his romantic fantasies. The cultural tensions reflected in this brother-sister conflict among American authors is promising territory for feminist critics.

Another line of thinking might be even more suggestive, however—the sort of realization that probably could only occur during an era such as ours, when we are still within half a century of the bitter aftermath of the unpopular Vietnam War, not to mention the more recent and costly conflicts in the Mid-East. It is an often-noted fact that the three greatest male authors of the literary era known as American Realism—Twain, Howells, and James—did not participate (at least not more than a few weeks, in Twain's case) in the military events of the American Civil War. Twain initially tried to join a Confederate volunteer unit in Missouri, but soon left that region to wait out the conflict in Nevada and California; Howells received an opportune consular appointment in Venice as the reward for preparing a political campaign biography; and James, complaining of an injury, found someone else to take his place in the military draft. What is not so well-known, perhaps, is that many other prominent male authors, especially those who would write Boy Book tales, likewise had other activities to occupy them during the years that the Civil War

raged across so many states and took a toll of 625,000 men's lives. John DeForest and Ambrose Bierce are notable for their military records and the fiction that reflected their battle experiences, but they were exceptions in this regard. Walt Whitman, of course, made his unofficial volunteer service in the Washington military hospitals a central feature of his *Memoranda During the War* (1875) and *Specimen Days and Collect* (1882), though he certainly had no intention of entering the hostilities himself. In other cases, contact with the brutality of combat was even more remote, or at least fleeting. Thomas Bailey Aldrich was briefly a war correspondent in 1861 for the New York *Tribune*, but after a few months he gave up this assignment and returned to New Hampshire before moving to New York City to commence his literary career. Harold Frederic only experienced the Civil War as it affected the home front; he had been born in 1856. Hamlin Garland was born one year before the war's beginning, and Stephen Crane and William Allen White after its conclusion. Charles Dudley Warner started editing the Hartford *Courant* in 1861; the war reports carried in that newspaper were his closest contact with the battlefront.

For someone like Twain, who wrote several versions of "The Private History of a Campaign That Failed" (1885), a serio-comic effort to rationalize his decision to avoid serving in the war, his rising fame during the 1870s and 1880s brought an increased sensitivity to the fact that he had deliberately missed out on the major historical event of American history in his century. During his return trip down the Mississippi River in 1882, he finally came to terms with the enormity of the military operations in the Mississippi Valley, and he visited a military cemetery and talked with the survivors of the Vicksburg siege. Perhaps his fervent admiration for Colonel Robert G. Ingersoll's oration at the reunion of federal troops in 1879, like his devout worship of General Ulysses S. Grant, betokened the guilty sense that he had not fully played his part in the national ordeal. In an age when men were routinely introduced by the military rank such as "Colonel" that they had held in the late war (including Twain's lecture agent *Major* James B. Pond, who had survived an ambush by William Quantrill's guerilla unit at Baxter Springs, Kansas), *Mr.* Samuel L. Clemens, whatever his literary fame, was surely self-conscious about his suspect war record. Casual conversations in our own age—as men (and, increasingly, women) mention with pride if not exactly satisfaction their service in the Vietnam War or the Mid-East conflicts, while those who elected (or were able, by education deferment or luck in the lottery in the Vietnam War) to avoid enlistment now sometimes feel uncomfortable as those wars gain glory through the mythologizing haze of books, films, and television series—can help us discern the unease that someone attuned to popular opinion like Twain might have felt.

If this scenario is plausible—that literary men who had led safe civilian lives during the years that their fellow males slogged through the mud in Pennsylvania, charged into blinding smoke in Tennessee, and bivouacked tiredly in Georgia later became sensitized to the implications of their exemption from risk and sacrifice—then perhaps it is possible to guess why, in 1869 and thereafter, books about antebellum boyhoods became appealing for

them to write. Since they had little in common with millions of American males where the war years were concerned, how attractive it must have seemed to concentrate instead on the male bonding of an earlier period, of the years *before* the war madness, back when they were all boyhood comrades of equal rank. And so, one after another, the non-combatant male authors sat down to picture their youthful years, asking in each case, "Don't you remember, brothers and friends?" A nation thoroughly weary of war and tiring of stories involving soldiers turned gratefully to this fresh change of subject, and an unconscious aim was achieved: these authors were welcomed back into the male fraternity by book reviewers who recognized a common background in the boy-life portrayed. What a therapeutic effect it must have been for Aldrich, Warner, Twain, and the rest to find that they were in fact forgiven for their non-service by male readers who recognized, as they had hoped, that they shared an older, deeper bond: they had all been boys together, and the code of that secret society overlooks all subsequent misdeeds and omissions. "The reader remembers," Twain writes assuredly in the first chapter of *Tom Sawyer*, that special moment when a new way of whistling was discovered, "if he has ever been a boy." Across the continent, generations of war-worn men nodded and wished to be boys again—with Aldrich and Twain and Warner and the rest. A new rite of authorship was established; the non-military man could make amends by producing this obligatory homage to pre-Civil War boyhood play. And Twain, whose burden of insecurity about his Southern heritage and abandoned battlefield service would weigh more heavily than those others who could identify with the victorious side in the conflict, created the greatest literary characters in this tradition and stayed with the Boy Book vogue longer than anyone else.

It is easy to forget that Twain actually left behind a *third* Boy Book besides *Tom Sawyer* and the Boy Book that far excelled its genre, *Huckleberry Finn*. Intervening between these publications, and composed during the same period when Twain was, by turns, also completing *Huckleberry Finn*, was a novel hardly ever taught today, *The Prince and the Pauper* (1881). It opens with a head note emphasizing the bonding effect of male lineage: "I will set down a tale as it was told to me by one who had it of his father, which latter had it of *his* father, this last having in like manner had it of *his* father—and so on, back and still back, three hundred years and more, the fathers transmitting it to the sons and so preserving it."[10] Nowadays we mainly recall that Twain's contemporary friends and reviewers were more ecstatic about this historical romance than much of his fiction that we currently value far more highly. Virtually overlooked is the fact that Twain's contemporaries received this tale as another "Boy Book" by the author of *Tom Sawyer* ingeniously moved backward in time to demonstrate the truism that boys are the same in every age, and that the code of loyalty and democracy is inbred in all lads of all cultures from the 1830s or 1840s to sixteenth-century England. In this retreat into distant history, prefiguring the time-travel of *A Connecticut Yankee in King Arthur's Court* (1889) and *The Mysterious Stranger* manuscripts, Twain escapes the after-effects of the American Civil War and sets the action in an era when England still had no awareness of its own coming civil war and Puritan reconstruction.

The sequence of Mark Twain's composition of three successive Boy Books is worth noting briefly. He completed *The Adventures of Tom Sawyer* in the summer of 1875. Initially he made good headway on a sequel to be related by Tom's companion, writing to William Dean Howells in the summer of 1876 that he had begun "another boy's book . . . It is Huck Finn's Autobiography."[11] After a fair amount of progress, however, he laid it aside and resolved instead to set his next Boy Book in Victorian England; then artistic problems with that initial intention obliged him to undertake historical research to find a suitable reign of a British monarch in which to locate a tale of switched identities of two boys. One resulting spin-off from this extensive reading program was a bawdy little vignette about Queen Elizabeth's court, "1601, or Conversation As It Was By the Social Fireside, in the Time of the Tudors," written in 1876. Finally settling on the coronation of Edward Tudor as the proper subject, he wrote portions of *The Prince and the Pauper* between November 1877 and February 1878, then added further chapters in 1880, and revised the work extensively in 1880 and the first month of 1881. The novel appeared in December 1881 to generally flattering reviews. Thereafter, having revisited the Mississippi River region in 1882 to obtain materials for a travel narrative, *Life on the Mississippi* (1883), Twain resumed his labors on *Huckleberry Finn* in the summer of 1883, revising the manuscript between September 1883 and April 1884. It would issue in the United States early in 1885.

As Hugh H. Davis has astutely pointed out, from the beginning there were clear similarities between the latter two of Twain's Boy Books, the chapters of which he alternated in writing during the summer of 1880.[12] Twain stipulated that the artist for his illustrated edition of *The Prince and the Pauper* should "always picture the Prince & Tom Canty as lads of 13 or 14 years old,"[13] the approximate age most commentators assign to Huckleberry Finn. John D. Stahl, who perceptively examined family relationships in the two novels in 1986, argued that in each work "Twain's orphaned sons seek to accomplish the impossible: to recover their lost fathers; and in the process they invent themselves."[14] Twain's description of Tom Canty to Howells on 11 March 1880 is analogous to the famous tribute he would later pay to Huckleberry Finn on the lecture circuit when alluding to him as a boy with "a sound heart and a deformed conscience"; his new tale, he informed Howells, concerns "the prince of Wales & a pauper boy of the same age & countenance (& half as much learning & still more genius & imagination)."[15] Thomas Bailey Aldrich seemingly appreciated the Boy Book features of the novel, writing to Twain within a few weeks of its publication to extol it as "a charming conception and charmingly worked out."[16]

In Twain's story, as everyone remembers, a young Tudor prince, seized by a whim, exchanges clothes with a street urchin who resembles him, Tom Canty of Offal Court. Before the boys can regain their identities, the Prince is summarily thrown into the mob outside Westminster Palace and the pauper Tom Canty is swept up into the political intrigues of the court. The narrative follows the boys' adventures along parallel lines; the false prince is indulged and manipulated, the protesting genuine prince is beaten and inducted into a gang of robbers. When King Henry dies and the coronation of his heir approaches, an ex-soldier named Miles Hendon assists the rightful prince in his travels to London to claim the throne. A Tom Sawyer-like scene of spectacle and resolution concludes the tale, as the boys interrupt the pageantry to re-exchange their identities before an awestruck assemblage. Miles and Tom are then rewarded with royal favors for their services to Edward during his travails, which have chastened and educated him. The narrative abounds in puns and connotations of doublings: "Tudor" (*two doors* reminding us of the palace chamber door through which the Prince hastily exits, and then is not permitted to re-enter), "Canty" (for both the discouraging *can't* and the smug uses of courtly *cant*), "Offal Court" (literally *awful* partly as the result of royal waste). The Prince Edward character, tricked out in the finery of his father's court and confined by customs and ceremonies dictated by his royal birth, is a more elaborate version of the authority-ridden Tom Sawyer, who was already (by 1881) the hero of his own book and of the opening three chapters of Huck Finn's in-progress narrative. More importantly, the comeuppance that the deposed young prince receives in the form of scoffs and blows and general ill-usage, from the highborn to the beggars, was perhaps sufficient enough punishment for this Tom Sawyer twin so that Twain could feel disposed, in 1883, to reintroduce the Prince's unrepentant doppelganger Tom Sawyer in Chapter 33 of *Adventures of Huckleberry Finn*. An atonement-by-surrogate idea is actually suggested within the text of *The Prince and the Pauper* itself, which describes an official whipping-boy, someone whose task is to endure the punishment Edward earns. The lad explains to an astonished Tom Canty that "none may visit the sacred person of the Prince of Wales with blows; wherefore when he faulteth, 'tis I that take them; and meet it is and right, for that it is mine office and my livelihood." Taken aback, "Tom stared at the tranquil boy, observing to himself, 'Lo, it is a wonderful thing,—a most strange and curious trade; I marvel they have not hired a boy to take my combings and my dressings for me—would heaven they would!'"[17] One might say that the hapless displaced prince, just then being mocked and cuffed, served as a sort of whipping-boy for Tom Sawyer, absorbing the blows Tom possibly seemed (to Twain and many subsequent commentators) to deserve but never receive.[18] Twain's fascination with twins and duplicates has long and routinely been documented, but comparatively little attention (aside from Hugh H. Davis's recent essays) has been paid to this crucial pairing of boys who, like the Siamese twins in *Pudd'nhead Wilson*, are almost inseparable from the finer and more authentic work that Twain was still dedicated to finishing.

If Tom Sawyer's devotion to European romances and haughty demeanors link him to the young Prince who is inadvertently cast out of the court, Tom Canty of Offal Court, a street urchin driven to petty crime by a vicious father, afforded Twain a feasible way to try out certain inspirations that would find their ultimate expression in a gestating first-person novel. But in the cases of both Edward Tudor and Tom Canty, whoever is wearing the royal costume and enjoying the privileges of a ruler loses his Huck-like view of practicalities and his instinctive sympathies with the downtrodden. One might say that during the exchange of identities, the desperate little king gradually becomes more like Huckleberry Finn (though less resourceful) and Tom Canty begins to resemble Tom Sawyer, drinking in the pomp and luxuries of the royal palace and learning how to benefit from his servants and his role. Tom Canty finds that "he came to enjoy being conducted to bed in state, at night, and dressed with intricate and solemn ceremony in the morning. It came to be a proud pleasure to march to dinner attended by a glittering procession of officers of state and Gentlemen-at-Arms—insomuch, indeed, that he doubled his guard of Gentlemen-at-Arms, and made them a hundred. He like[d] to hear the bugles sounding, down the long corridors, and the distant voices responding, 'Way for the king!'"[19] Whoever inherits the royal mantle appears to put on Tom Sawyer's illusions and imitate his grandstanding. As Huckleberry Finn remarks of the Dauphin in Chapter 23 of the subsequent book, "All I say is, kings is kings, and you got to make allowances. Take them all around, they're a mighty ornery lot. It's the way they're raised." Edward "easily concluded that the pauper lad, Tom Canty, had deliberately taken advantage of his stupendous opportunity and become a usurper."[20] Nevertheless, Edward's ensuing record is, on balance, commendable; when he finally retrieves his status, awakened and transformed by his recent ordeal, he becomes a mild and generous potentate whose decrees possess integrity and good sense. The public acclamation that greeted *The Prince and the Pauper* in the year following its appearance in December 1881, approbation encouraged by the sanitizing distance of historical perspective, was somehow liberating—nearly as instrumental, indeed, as Twain's return trip down the Mississippi River in 1882—in unleashing Twain's sudden ability to complete and publish *Huckleberry Finn*.

The parallels between Tom Canty and Huckleberry Finn, and their connections with Samuel Clemens' biographical experiences in Hannibal, are numerous. For example, a passage describing the forsaken monarch's miserable journey in Chapter 18 strikingly evokes Huck Finn's eerie reveries:

> All his sensations and experiences, as he moved through the solemn gloom and the empty vastness of the night, were new and strange to him. At intervals he heard voices approach, pass by, and fade into silence; and as he saw nothing more of the bodies they belonged to than a sort of formless drifting blur, there was something spectral and uncanny about it all that made him shudder. Occasionally he caught the twinkle of a light—always far away, apparently—almost in another world; if he heard the tinkle of a sheep's bell, it was vague, distant, indistinct; the muffled lowing of the herds floated to him on the night wind in vanishing cadence, a mournful sound; now and then came the complaining howl of a dog over viewless expanses of field and forest; all sounds were remote; they made the little king feel that all life and activity were far removed from him, and that he stood solitary, companionless, in the centre of a measureless solitude.[21]

It is generally accepted that a Hannibal boy whom Clemens knew in his childhood, Tom Blankenship, served as one prototype for Huck Finn. Walter Blair states that Tom Blankenship "was a member of the gang to which Sam Clemens belonged, although several boys were forbidden to play with him."[22] This Tom coincidentally had a twin (a girl, named Martha). In manuscript notes Twain made in 1897, he recalled that Tom Blankenship's parents were "paupers and drunkards" and characterized Tom as a "kindly young heathen" who was "never sent to school or church."[23] In Chapter 3 of *The Prince and the Pauper* Tom Canty mentions that he has twin sisters.

So complete is the role-reversal of the two boys, Edward Tudor and Tom Canty, that Tom Canty appears to anticipate his future mistaken identity. In Chapter 2, for instance, the narrator notes that owing to the books of romance Tom Canty had absorbed at a priest's house he began to emulate courtly behavior until "daily the mock prince was received with elaborate ceremonials borrowed by Tom from his romantic readings." Apart from begging in the street, "he put in a good deal of his time listening to good Father Andrew's charming old tales and legends about giants and fairies, dwarfs and genii, and enchanted castles, and gorgeous kings and princes. His head grew to be full of these wonderful things, and many a night as he lay in the dark . . . he unleashed his imagination and soon forgot his aches and pains in delicious picturings to himself of the charmed life of a petted prince in a regal palace."[24] As a consequence, "by and by Tom's reading and dreaming about princely life wrought such a strong effect upon him that he began to act the prince, unconsciously. His speech and manners became curiously ceremonious and courtly, to the vast admiration and amusement of his intimates. . . . In time he came to be looked up to, by them, with a sort of wondering awe, as a superior being."[25]

Like *Adventures of Huckleberry Finn*, it should be noted, *The Prince and the Pauper* is very much about the potent powers of literacy; the kindly priest teaches Tom Canty "a little Latin, and how to read and write,"[26] and this opens up to his ken the world of kings and princes and ultimately leads to his visiting Westminster Palace. Tom Canty's recitation of the inexpensive joys of London boyhood (privileges the pampered prince has never tasted)—puppet shows, monkeys, stage plays, cudgel-fights, races, swimming, may-poles, sand-piles, mud-pies—lure the Prince into insisting upon the momentous change of clothes. "'Twould be worth my father's kingdom but to enjoy it once!" the Prince says with unintentional irony.

This swapping of raiment, accomplished merely to gratify each boy's curiosity, is one of

"SHE WAS AT HIS SIDE."

A re-issue of Mark Twain's **The Prince and the Pauper, A Tale**
(New York: Charles L. Webster and Co., 1887)

the few actions that takes place in the novel without force or the threat of physical punishment as a motivation. Tom's father and grandmother abuse him regularly, the captain of the palace guards mistreats him (and also strikes the Prince, without recognizing him), Miles Hendon's wife is threatened by Sir Hugh, and so on. A doggedly loyal Miles Hendon, bereft of his legal possessions, takes the place here of the slave Jim figure, and in this situation knows more about London life than his young ward, though he is also ignorant of the largest fact—that he really is protecting the king. Indeed, secrets are rife in *The Prince and the Pauper*, such as the murderously insane hermit's insistent "secret" in Chapter 20 that he is actually an archangel. In that novel as in *Huckleberry Finn*, a misnamed boy bears a crucial secret (his true commoner identity here, and Jim's runaway status in Twain's book-in-progress). Twice Huckleberry Finn will feel pangs of conscience (in Chapters 16 and 31) about helping Jim escape; in a parallel manner Tom Canty wrestles with his conscience in Chapter 30: "His first royal days and nights were pretty well sprinkled with painful thoughts about the lost prince . . . but as time wore on . . . he was become an unwelcome spectre, for he made Tom feel guilty and ashamed."[27] Likewise in Chapter 31, when his mother recognizes him but is shoved back into the crowd of the poor, "a shame fell upon him which consumed his pride to ashes and withered his stolen royalty. . . . Royalty had lost its grace and sweetness, its pomps were become a reproach; remorse was eating his heart out."[28] Huckleberry Finn has the advantage of possessing white skin in a Southern society that still practiced human slavery; Edward Tudor, by similar good fortune, is entitled to the crown by birth in an England that worships royalty. Both Tom Canty and Huck Finn agonize over a moral decision that lies within their power to put into effect, and in each instance it involves a truth that could reveal how they have been playing a false role and have committed a major criminal offense.

With this clever intermediate tale, Mark Twain extended Tom Sawyer's romps, postponed the plot difficulties with his other Boy Book, and rehearsed the case of mistaken identities that would complicate Huckleberry Finn's arrival at the Phelps farm in the final chapters of the in-progress work, where Huck is mistaken for Tom Sawyer and Tom Sawyer poses as his brother Sid. Twain drew on the simple pleasures of boyhood in writing both books, and relied on similar elements—abusive fathers (as Andrew Levy noted),[29] fraudulent claimants to thrones (the King purports to be heir to the French crown in *Huckleberry Finn*), sympathetic but marginalized surrogate father-figures (Miles and Jim), an eventful journey in the company of con men and thieves, a neat restoration of identities and social stations at the end—the earlier book climaxing with "a wonderful floating pageant on the Thames" and a grandiose "recognition-procession" (p. 299) that would have thrilled Tom Sawyer, and the latter novel revealing the boys' true names and uncovering Jim's freedom after their abortive attempt to escape on the Mississippi River. The showy processions and grand coronation scene hark back more to the staged spectacles of *The Adventures of Tom*

Sawyer than to the modest goals preferred by Huck, but overall *The Prince and the Pauper* constitutes an impressive piece of writing that is midway, artistically and thematically, between Twain's first and third examples of the Boy Book. If we grasp these affinities, we can recover and enjoy certain features of the middle book that are otherwise puzzling, and we can also trace the imminent arrival of Huckleberry Finn, heralded by his usurper twin from the alleyways of London.

NOTES

1   See, among other studies, Walter Blair, "On the Structure of *Tom Sawyer*," *Modern Philology* 37.1 (August 1939): 75–88; John Hinz, "Huck and Pluck: 'Bad' Boys in American Fiction," *South Atlantic Quarterly* 51 (January 1952): 120–129; Albert E. Stone Jr., *The Innocent Eye: Childhood in Mark Twain's Imagination* (New Haven: Yale University Press, 1961), pp. 62–72; Jim Hunter, "Mark Twain and the Boy-Book in 19th-Century America," *College English* 24.6 (March 1963): 430–438; Anne Trensky, "The Bad Boy in Nineteenth-Century American Literature," *Georgia Review* 27.4 (Winter 1973): 503–517; Judith Fetterley, "Disenchantment: Tom Sawyer in *Huckleberry Finn*," *PMLA* 87.1 (January 1972): 69–74; Glenn Hendler, "Tom Sawyer's Masculinity," *Arizona Quarterly* 49.4 (Winter 1993): 35–59; and Marcia Jacobson, *Being a Boy Again: Autobiography and the American Boy Book* (Tuscaloosa: University of Alabama Press, 1994).

2   Gribben, "'I Did Wish Tom Sawyer Was There': Boy-Book Elements in *Tom Sawyer* and *Huckleberry Finn*," *One Hundred Years of "Huckleberry Finn": The Boy, His Book, and American Culture*, ed. Robert Sattelmeyer and J. Donald Crowley (Columbia: University of Missouri Press, 1985), pp. 149–170.

3   Gribben, "Manipulating a Genre: *Huckleberry Finn* as a Boy Book," *South Central Review* 5.4 (Winter 1988): 15–21. (A revised version of this essay appears as a chapter in this present volume.)

4   "Manipulating a Genre, p. 16.

5   "Manipulating a Genre," pp. 20–21.

6   Gribben, "Boy Books, Bad Boy Books, and *The*

Adventures of Tom Sawyer," *The Adventures of Tom Sawyer*, ed. Beverly Lyon Clark. Norton Critical Edition Series. New York: W. W. Norton, 2007), pp. 290–306.

7   Gribben, "Boy Books, Bad Boy Books," pp. 305–306.

8   Tanner, *The Reign of Wonder: Naivety and Reality in American Literature* (Cambridge: Cambridge University Press, 1965), p. 97.

9   Machor, *Pastoral Cities: Urban Ideals and the Symbolic Landscape of America* (Madison: University of Wisconsin Press, 1994).

10   *The Prince and the Pauper*, ed. Victor Fischer and Lin Salamo (Berkeley: University of California Press, 1979), p. 45—hereafter cited as *P&P*.

11   9 August 1876, *Mark Twain-Howells Letters*, ed. Henry Nash Smith and William M. Gibson (Cambridge, Massachusetts: Belknap Press, Harvard University Press, 1960), p. 144—hereafter cited as *MTHL*.

12   "*The Prince and the Pauper*," *Mark Twain and Youth: Studies in His Life and Writings*, ed. Kevin MacDonnell and R. Kent Rasmussen (London: Bloomsbury Academic, 2016), pp. 169–175; with some added remarks in "'It's *Tom Sawyer!*' (No it ain't . . . it's Huck Finn!)," *Critical Insights: Adventures of Huckleberry Finn*, ed. R. Kent Rasmussen (Ipswich, Massachusetts: Salem Press, 2017), pp. 235–237. Davis's cogent analysis anticipated several points in my present essay that was then in progress, and I have tried to dovetail my findings around his shrewd discussions of the novel. Also of interest: *Readings on "The Prince and the Pauper*," ed. Jann Einfeld. Literary Companion to American Literature Series (San Diego: Greenhaven Press, 2001), a collection of previously published commentaries.

13   Clemens to A. V. S. Anthony, 9 March 1881; quoted by Beverly R. David, *Mark Twain and His Illustrators, Volume II (1875–1883)* (Albany, New York: Whitston Publishing Co., 2001), p. 210.

14   John Daniel Stahl, "American Myth in European Disguise: Fathers and Sons in *The Prince and the Pauper*," *American Literature* 58.2 [May 1986]: 207.

15   *MTHL*, p. 291.

16   Aldrich to Clemens, 11 January 1882, Mark Twain Papers, Bancroft Library, University of California at Berkeley; quoted in *P&P*, p. 13.

17   *P&P*, p. 164.

18   For example, see Jeffrey Steinbrink, "Who Shot

Tom Sawyer?," *American Literary Realism* 35.1 (Fall 2002): 29–38.

19 *P&P*, pp. 295–296.

20 *P&P*, p. 121.

21 *P&P*, p. 209.

22 *Mark Twain's Hannibal, Huck & Tom*, ed. Walter Blair (Berkeley: University of California Press, 1969), p. 345—hereafter cited as *HH&T*.

23 *HH&T*, p. 31.

24 *P&P*, pp. 51–52.

25 *P&P*, p. 54.

26 *P&P*, pp. 50–51.

27 *P&P*, pp. 297–298.

28 *P&P*, p. 305.

29 *Huck Finn's America: Mark Twain and the Era That Shaped His Masterpiece* (New York: Simon & Schuster, 2015), p. 83.

An earlier version of this chapter appeared in the Mark Twain Journal: The Author and His Era *55.1–2 (2017): 127–144.*

CLIMBING THE FIR-TREE AFTER THE KESTREL'S NEST. P. 263.

Illustration from an American edition of Tom Brown's School Days,
by an Old Boy, *this one published by Macmillan and Co. in 1884*

16

Manipulating a Genre:
Huckleberry Finn as Boy Book

Scholars routinely classify Mark Twain's *The Adventures of Tom Sawyer* (1876) among the designated "Boy Books" of nineteenth-century American literature, that series of works extolling American boyhood which burst forth in emulation of Thomas Bailey Aldrich's *The Story of a Bad Boy* (1869). However, Twain's *Adventures of Huckleberry Finn* (1885) is much less frequently assigned to this category at least in part because *Huckleberry Finn* seems so manifestly superior to any label. For that matter, it might be observed that the American Boy Book itself is one of the most casually accepted notions in literary history and criticism. The curious assortment of what we loosely define as "Boy Books" (or sometimes "Bad Boy Books") embraces an amazingly heterogeneous collection of writings—sentimental autobiography, juvenile romance, quasi-sociological documentary, comic slapstick, literary burlesque—that mainly have in common a reverence for boyhood, an autobiographical flavor, a setting in the past, and a code of behavior alien to most adults.

Thomas Hughes probably sired this particular type of Victorian nostalgia with his *Tom Brown's School Days* (1857); the shenanigans of Tom Brown in his native Berks county village and his hazing at the hands of Flashman at Rugby set the tone and established many of the incidents of the successful Boy Book. Charles Dickens's novels depicting boyhood deprivations, including *Oliver Twist* (1838), *David Copperfield* (1850), and *Great Expectations* (1861), rehearsed the pangs of childhood disappointments and terrors, but cannot be said to have produced the nearly complete formula that Thomas Hughes offered to Thomas Bailey Aldrich. (In Chapter 10 of *The Story of a Bad Boy*, Aldrich significantly refers to *Tom Brown's School Days* as "one of the best books ever written for boys.") Since Twain neither began nor ended the Boy Book, it helps to appreciate his achievements if we read forward and backward in the tradition of the Boy Book, especially in Charles Dudley Warner's sentimental recollections of Massachusetts farm-life, *Being a Boy* (1878); William Dean Howells's wistful and occasionally chilling chronicle of small-town life in Ohio, *A Boy's Town* (1890); Hamlin Garland's *Boy Life on the Prairie* (1899), a record of sensory privilege and cultural martyrdom for a boy transported by ox-cart to the Iowa prairie, there to grow into manhood; and Stephen Crane's tales about boyhood in a small town in New York state (many of them collected in *Whilomville Stories* [1900]), so evocative of the victories and humiliations of childhood.[1]

What literary critics nowadays dislike most about Twain's greatest fictional work are actually the vestigial parts of the conventions within which it originated. As Edwin Cady astutely pointed out, *Huckleberry Finn* "consists of a long central narration, picaresque in form and substance and framed on either end by boy-book narratives"; consequently it "returns upon itself to end as it began in boy-life."[2] Our contemporary readers, barely familiar with Aldrich's Tom Bailey or Warner's farmboy John, find fully satisfying only the chapters in which Huck outwits his degenerate father, links up with a fleeing slave, and surveys the sparsely settled banks of a river from the vantage point of a raft. The rest they dismiss as just an artistic mistake on Twain's part, owing (depending on the critic's point of view) to Twain's absurd affection for Tom Sawyer, his penchant for literary burlesque, his inability to understand his true strengths as an author, the inhibiting effect of his friends and family, or the lamentable tastes of the New England literary and publishing scene.

Very likely the publishing world *was* responsible for the inconsistencies in mood and theme that many readers abhor in *Huckleberry Finn*, but not for the reasons ordinarily given. The probability is that Twain wanted to exploit the increasingly popular Boy Book trend while experimenting with some new artistic possibilities that occurred to him. Those resulting internal shifts are one reason the novel could never possibly be duplicated by imitators, as Aldrich's book repeatedly was; there are built-in defects of structure and mood that incalculably contribute to its qualities of originality and its impression of spontaneity.[3]

Taking the fictional and the purely autobiographical works together, what *did* these diverse books by Aldrich, Warner, Twain, Howells, Garland, and others have in common as a literary tradition? To begin with an obvious feature, one can perceive that in every Boy Book the normal adult sense of scale, of perspective, is tremendously magnified. Since these are books about children, an Ohio or Missouri or New Hampshire village becomes equivalent in dimensions and cultural activity to a metropolis as important as London. Predictably, then, the basic order of the town—its legal, political, and social codes—can never be fundamentally challenged, as Judith Fetterley pointed out.[4] The wintertime snowball wars recounted in Warner's *Being a Boy* pay tribute to the random raid of American Indians, not the wholesale upheaval of revolutionaries. All the same, the boys in these books often make fools of the townspeople and farmers, causing communities to form into anxious, mindless mobs (as in the cannon-firing episode of *The Story of a Bad Boy* or the abolitionist-scare conclusion to *Huckleberry Finn*). A preponderance of the Boy Books, including Howells's study of his Ohio childhood, also insist that to most of their boys the few surviving bands of unregenerate Native American Indians exemplified an ideal state of existence—packs of unruly outsiders able to merge at will with the shadowy forest surrounding orderly villages.[5]

Abandoned barbarity, however, is what the boys merely long for during a few hours of the day, when they seek to escape the rigors of school or the discipline of family life. The family unit may be the victim of their bloody fantasies, but it is simultaneously a solace and refuge for besieged warriors. Stephen Crane's "His New Mittens" and "The Fight" effectively convey this anomaly, as do Howells's sensitive recollections. Indeed, in virtually every Boy Book or short story, well-intentioned parents or guardians resume control of the situation at the end, as in Aldrich's and Twain's narratives, removing the boy from the environment of his adventures (the endings of Aldrich's and Howells's books do this, for example, and Huckleberry Finn himself is about to be returned to St. Petersburg at the end of his narrative).

Of course, there was only so much that could be portrayed by the dedicated chronicler of boyhood; the possible experiences of a nineteenth-century boy, after all, were inherently limited—his education, siblings, church, chores, gangs, games, pranks, and a few other subjects defined the extent of a boy's permitted activities and illicit aspirations. Again, the cue for potential subject matter often came from Thomas Hughes's account of *Tom Brown's School Days*. In Part II of Hughes's novel, Tom's close friend, George Arthur, lies ill at Rugby with a contagious "fever" for many days, until Tom is finally summoned to his bedside. "Tom remembered a German picture of an angel which he knew; often had he thought how transparent and golden and spirit-like it was; and he shuddered to think how like it Arthur looked" (305). Arthur survives, but another lad, Thompson, sickens and dies at Tom's school, and illnesses would thereafter confine and chasten many American boy-outlaws, who must be nursed by solicitous relatives and visited by anxious chums. Mark Twain traced this convention to the Sunday School books for children, but Hughes's book probably had a large influence in making serious illness a fixture of juvenile literature. Certainly Thomas Bailey Aldrich's boy-character Tom Bailey sets a fine example for his Boy Book brethren-to-be, reacting to a playmate's drowning death with an alarming collapse: "I was in a forlorn state, physically and mentally. Captain Nutter put me to bed between hot blankets, and sent Kitty Collins for the doctor. I was wandering in my mind, and fancied myself still on Sandpeep Island . . . and, in my delirium, I laughed aloud and shouted to my comrades. . . . Towards evening a high fever set in, and it was many days before my grandfather deemed it prudent to tell me that the Dolphin had been found, floating keel upwards" (170–171). This is to say, in other words, that Tom Sawyer's feverish swoons that conclude both *The Adventures of Tom Sawyer* and *Adventures of Huckleberry Finn* actually became a staple of Boy Books, usually prolonging the illness of the boy-hero or his good friend to the point of near-death. The modern reader should therefore not be skeptical when encountering the passage in which Tom, being transported on a mattress in Chapter 42 of *Huckleberry Finn*, "turned his head a little, and muttered something or other, which showed he warn't in his right mind" (351).

Other story patterns also indicate the common heritage of American Boy Books.[6] Perhaps Dickens's novels about children were responsible for the high mortality rate among boys' parents. Frequently, though not always, the primary character is, or becomes, an orphan. Tom Sawyer suffers this fate, of course, and Huck Finn unknowingly joins him (when Jim discovers Pap Finn's body) partway through Huck's novel. Tom Bailey loses his father to cholera at the end of *The Story of a Bad Boy*, and Tom's days as a Centipedes gang member are ended by his grieving mother's arrival in town and his own decision to leave school. The death of Doctor Arnold at the conclusion of *Tom Brown's School Days* affects Tom Brown so profoundly that Arnold's role as a father-figure is apparent: "If he could only have seen the Doctor again for one five minutes; have told him all that was in his heart, what he owed to him, how he loved and reverenced him, and would by God's help follow his steps in life and death. . . ." (374).

Huck Finn joins a boy-gang at the beginning of his book, another way in which he resembles the typical Boy Book protagonist. Also, Huck's peers do not discriminate against him, in spite of his outcast status in St. Petersburg, and this basic egalitarianism of boy-comrades is a tendency emphasized in virtually every Boy Book. Thomas Hughes writes, "Squire Brown held . . . that it didn't matter a straw whether his son associated with lord's sons, or ploughmen's sons, provided they were brave and honest. He himself had played football and gone birds'-nesting

with the farmers whom he met at vestry and the labourers who tilled their fields, and so had his father and grandfather with their progenitors. So he encouraged Tom in his intimacy with the boys of the village" (53). William Dean Howells remembered that in childhood "his closest friend was a boy who was probably never willingly at school in his life. . . . Socially, he was as low as the ground under foot, but morally he was as good as any boy in the Boy's Town, and he had no bad impulses" (191). In *Huckleberry Finn*, as in most Boy Books, there is no rank except what one earns in the neighborhood; adult-assigned economic hierarchies and social distinctions count for next to nothing.

Yet the differences that set *Adventures of Huckleberry Finn* apart from its rivals are the more fascinating aspects of Twain's achievement. For example, the schoolboy "crush" quickly became a standard bit of comedy in the American Boy Book—Tom Bailey moons over the unattainable Miss Nelly Glentworth: "I wonder if girls from fifteen to twenty are aware of the glamour they cast over the straggling awkward boys whom they regard and treat as mere children," sighs the narrator (231). Warner's boy named John stammers out his admiration for Cynthia Rudd and walks her home under the stars from a party. Tom Sawyer's antics for the purpose of catching Becky Thatcher's attention are legendary. However, Huck Finn is truly helpful to Mary Jane Wilks, and his shy affection for her seems practically noble because it gives him the courage to save her from embarrassment and financial ruin; his reward is her gratitude when, "laying her silky hand on mine in that kind of a way that I said I would die first," she says, "You tell me what to do, and whatever you say, I'll do it" (240).

Huck does not face and vanquish a school bully, as plucky Tom Brown must outwit and outfight the swaggering Flashman and Aldrich's Tom Bailey must thrash Conway, who "never failed to brush against me, or pull my cap over my eyes. . . . I felt it was ordained ages before our birth that we should meet on this planet and fight" (65). Tom Sawyer opens his novel by "licking" a newcomer to St. Petersburg, whereas in Stephen Crane's splendid boy-tale "The Fight" (1900), Johnnie Hedge, forced to win a place for himself in the Whilomville school yard, bloodily defeats both Jimmie Trescott and his leader, Willie Dalzel. Huck Finn, on the contrary, finds a friend rather than an enemy in Buck Grangerford, and Huck's only antagonists are scheming adults.

Then, too, Huck is not the addict of romance-reading that Tom Bailey, Tom Sawyer, and others prove to be; even Warner's farmboy John conceals a worn copy of the *Arabian Nights* in the barn, imagining that he "had but to rub the ring and summon a genius [*sic*], who would feed the calves and pick up chips and bring in wood in a minute" (70). Aldrich's juvenile hero finds a trunk in the garret of his grandfather's house that contains a "collection of novels and romances, embracing the adventures of Baron Trenck, Jack Sheppard, Don Quixote, Gil Blas, and Charlotte Temple—all of which I fed upon like a bookworm"; he also keeps copies of *Robinson Crusoe* and the *Arabian Nights* near his bed (40–41). But Huck Finn, less deluded, periodically rejects Tom Sawyer's appeals to published "authorities"—"I couldn't see

no profit in it," says Huck, resigning after a month of membership in Tom's robber gang; "we hadn't killed any people, but only just pretended" (14).

In most Boy Books the climactic test of courage involves a large, dangerous body of water, a sudden, thunderous storm, and a boatload of foolhardy boys. The expedition in Hamlin Garland's *Boy Life on the Prairie* occurs on Clear Lake, where a storm almost upends the boys' sailboat. Little Binnie Wallace is not so lucky in Aldrich's *Story of a Bad Boy*; Binnie drowns in a storm after the boys take their small boat, the *Dolphin,* out in the bay to Sandpeep Island. Tom Sawyer, of course, commands a watery expedition midway through his novel: Tom, Huck, and Joe Harper establish a pirate-camp on Jackson's Island that is besieged by a "furious blast," "one blinding flash after another," and "peal on peal of deafening thunder," and then they return to town, chastened yet triumphant, to witness their own funeral services.

Adventures of Huckleberry Finn turns this element of the ritual "expedition" across water into a full-scale journey rather than a single episode—a panoramic view of islands, steamboats, small towns, and the South in general. In other words, Twain's second attempt at a Boy Book about Tom and Huck was not limited to one locale, as Aldrich's had been, or even to one point of view (since *Adventures of Huckleberry Finn* presents both Tom's and Huck's in tandem). When Twain forwent the privilege of commenting directly and explicitly on his own childhood, instead delegating the narrative to a boy not even old enough or sophisticated enough to know whether he was writing an epistolary novel, a truthful letter, or an autobiography, this decision ultimately led to the structural feature that chiefly distinguishes *Huckleberry Finn* from its Boy Book companions. After Pap Finn abducts and transports his son outside the St. Petersburg environs, Huck is drawn by circumstances into a slow drift down the massive Mississippi River. The journey format moved the novel closer in the direction of Le Sage's *Histoire de Gil Blas de Santillane* (1735) than toward *The Story of a Bad Boy*, yet Twain still enjoyed the commercial advantage of having produced a volume that could be marketed as another American Boy Book. And by casting the work in fiction rather than in a purely autobiographical mode, he was able (as he had been previously with *Tom Sawyer*) to put the emphasis on the "Adventures" promised in his book title, making the other entries in the Boy Book field seem tame by comparison. If the first three and the last eleven chapters of *Huckleberry Finn* were to be considered together as an integral unit, the volume would recognizably resemble another humorous (if brief) conventional Bad Boy Book about Tom Sawyer.

At the end of Huck's book, there is no actual departure for college or the business world or another region (and ultimately, for manhood), as in the books by Dickens, Hughes, Aldrich, Garland, and others. Huck Finn ends his novel in the present tense, an immensely daring decision on Twain's part; Huck does not grow up and look back wishfully at his boyhood, like Garland's Lincoln Stewart. In one sense, Huck's narrative, so vastly dissimilar from Garland's idealized, softened adult view of his "days of cattle-herding, berrying, hazel-nutting, and all the other now vanished

pleasures of boy life on the prairies" (423), is absolutely the best Boy Book of them all. Huck's "expedition" has mythic dimensions, and his random brushes with death can be taken as the real thing, unlike Tom Sawyer's gleeful, make-believe demises in Twain's earlier book. Huck, presumed dead by his fellow villagers, gloomily views himself as already departed from earthly society, and thus is capable of risking damnation to save a fearful slave. To put it another way, *Huckleberry Finn* manages to overcome most restrictions of the Boy Book.

Certain recognizable features do link *Adventures of Huckleberry Finn* with *The Adventures of Tom Sawyer* and other Boy Books; at its beginning and in its conclusion, the boys fear and defy adult authorities, adulate brave deeds, experiment with various identities, are controlled by parental decisions, plot rebellions against injustice, and play cruel pranks. But if Mark Twain initially planned to abide by prevailing conventions of the autobiographical Boy Book, his decision to allow this boy to narrate his own story *without first growing up* blocked those intentions, obliging (or rather enabling) him to ignore, and ultimately elude, the limitations of a predictable form. The principal determinant in this outcome was his protagonist: Huck simply existed too far beyond the pale of family and propriety to be capable of the speech, viewpoint, and action of typical boy characters. It might be said that in *Adventures of Huckleberry Finn*, Twain set out to write another conventional Boy Book but his experiences and reading—and above all, his literary imagination—got the better of him, and the book veered away from generic formulas to become something even more vital and inspiring—a combination of voice and place and event that has moved and challenged writers and readers ever since.

NOTES

1   In preparing this study I have consulted the following editions: Thomas Hughes, *Tom Brown's School Days* (New York: Macmillan, 1884); Thomas Bailey Aldrich, *The Story of a Bad Boy* (Boston: Houghton Mifflin, 1914); Mark Twain, *The Adventures of Tom Sawyer, Tom Sawyer Abroad, Tom Sawyer, Detective*, ed. John C. Gerber, Paul Baender, and Terry Firkins (Berkeley: University of California Press, 1980); Charles Dudley Warner, *Being a Boy* (Boston: James K. Osgood, 1878); *Adventures of Huckleberry Finn*, ed. Victor Fischer and Lin Salamo (Berkeley: University of California Press, 2003); William Dean Howells, *A Boy's Town, Described for "Harper's Young People"* (New York: Harper & Brothers, 1890); Hamlin Garland, *Boy Life on the Prairie*, intro. by B. R. McElderry Jr. (Lincoln: University of Nebraska Press, 1961); Stephen Crane, *The Complete Short Stories & Sketches of Stephen Crane* (Garden City, New York: Doubleday, 1963). All quotations derive from these volumes. To focus and condense my discussion, I am omitting other examples of this subgenre, including, most notably, Harold Frederic's poignant "My Aunt Susan," "The Eve of the Fourth," and "The War Widow" (written in 1892), William Allen White's *Court of Boyville* (1899), and Booth Tarkington's *Penrod* (1914). For treatments of this branch of literary realism, see John W. Crowley's perceptive "*Little Women* and the Boy Book," *New England Quarterly* 58.3 (September 1985): 384–399 as well as Crowley's "Polymorphously Perverse? Childhood Sexuality in the American Boy Book," *American Literary Realism* 19.2 (Winter 1987): 2–15 and Marcia Jacobson's *Being a Boy: Autobiography and the American Boy Book* (Tuscaloosa: University of Alabama Press, 1994).

2   Edwin H. Cady, *The Light of Common Day: Realism in American Fiction* (Bloomington: Indiana University Press, 1971), pp. 101, 118.

3   I previously investigated in detail the relationship of Aldrich's *Story of a Bad Boy* to Twain's most esteemed works of juvenile fiction; see "'I Did Wish Tom Sawyer Was There': Boy-Book Elements in *Tom Sawyer* and *Huckleberry Finn*," in *One Hundred Years of* Huckleberry Finn: *The Boy, His Book, and American Culture*, eds. Robert Sattelmeyer and J. Donald Crowley (Columbia: University of Missouri Press, 1985), pp. 149–170. However, in consulting this article one should bear in mind the fact that the composition of Twain's "A Boy's Manuscript" only began to be dated as 1868 or early 1869—rather than 1870—subsequent to when my essay appeared in 1985.

4   Judith Fetterley, "The Sanctioned Rebel," *Studies in the Novel* 3.3 (Fall 1971): 293–304.

5   See especially Alfred Habegger's incisive study of Howells's *A Boy's Town* in *Gender, Fantasy, and Realism in American Literature* (New York Columbia University Press, 1982), pp. 139, 215, though in Howells's book the Native American and his wilderness are portrayed as vanishing sights, lost causes, a doomed order of natural harmony.

6   Like many other scholars, I am indebted to John G. Cawelti's example in studying the impact of a *literary formula*, even though he originally employed that term as an aid in understanding the relationships between American culture and stories about detectives, gangsters, science-fiction, Westerns, and social melodramas. It is tempting to apply Cawelti's general ideas about conventional story patterns to the Boy Book, which was, when Twain wrote his contributions, a nascent formula establishing its traditions very rapidly in the Realist period of American literature, and if the Boy Book did not flourish with the long-term-commercial success of Cawelti's examples of adventure, romance, and mystery, it nevertheless exhibited traits that are suggestive along the same lines. See John G. Cawelti, *Adventure, Mystery, and Romance: Formula Stories as Art and Popular Culture* (Chicago: University of Chicago Press, 1976).

An earlier version of this chapter appeared in South Central Review *5.4 (Winter 1988): 15–21.*

17

If I'd a Knowed What a Trouble
It Was to Quote a Book

Literary Knowledge in Mark Twain's *Adventures of Huckleberry Finn*

Despite Huck Finn's evident amateurishness as a writer, virtually anyone will acknowledge that his narrative routinely incorporates belletristic devices that would do credit to a sophisticated author. One of his (and his inventor's) most effective practices, employed so casually as nearly to escape notice, consists of the dozens of literary allusions and echoes that chart Mark Twain's variegated reading around the time the novel was composed. Scholarly sleuthing by Walter Blair, culminating in his pioneering *Mark Twain & Huck Finn*, revealed extensive layers of literary referents underlying the book. Blair's meticulous studies uncovered manifold "debts . . . to humorists of the prewar period, . . . to local-color writers[, and] to specific writers."[1] Although Twain repeatedly denied much literary acumen ("personally I never care for fiction or story-books," he testified typically, in 1889),[2] Blair's breakthroughs encouraged others to follow his lead in reevaluating Twain's artistry in terms of his absorption and integration of literary texts produced by others. Dale Billingsley illustrated in 1979 how literary motifs link various episodes.[3] Victor A. Doyno's deductions, notably, first pointed out the novel's pervasive emphasis on a central but overlooked facet: "Numerous explicit references to literacy, to the act of reading or of writing, constitute, I would suggest, a complex motif within the novel."[4] Along the same line Anthony J. Berret, in an excellent evaluation of Twain's sources, remarked that "references to books, reading, and writing reinforce the distinctness of Huck's narrative. They help make the narrative say, 'I am a book, and only a book.'"[5] The impeccably specific documentations assembled in the Mark Twain Project's edition of *Adventures of Huckleberry Finn* gave ample evidence of the bookish foundations of many passages in the novel.[6]

This is not to say that the reading record Twain could bring to Huck's tale was anything like the deliberately programmatic campaigns

Twain had undertaken to prepare for previous books. In particular Twain's travel writings had shown an unabashed dependence on the guidebooks produced by writers who preceded him. Likewise his preparations for the historical romance *The Prince and the Pauper* (1881) involved years of preliminary explorations of published information; during this inquiry Twain immersed himself in historical works relating to the Tudor period, compiling fifty-five pages of study notes. That his voluminous reading on behalf of a rather contrived story about the English court fed into, and enriched, his forthcoming book with another child-hero and a Mississippi River setting cannot be disputed. Likewise contributing to the latter novel was his voluminous research while composing *Life on the Mississippi* (1883), a significant portion of which, he confided to William Dean Howells, had been "mainly stolen from books, tho' credit given."[7]

All of this earnest erudition—along with reading experiences he had enjoyed in the lavish surroundings of his large personal library in Hartford and in the Cranes' collection at Quarry Farm—was available to Twain when he sat down to write a manuscript whose very first sentence referred the reader to another, earlier text, "a book by the name of 'The Adventures of Tom Sawyer.'" Huck ambiguously assured readers that Twain's prequel "is mostly a true book." Many types of Twain's recreational library browsing wound up in Huck's extension. For example, among the references were (predictably) several tied to *The Arabian Nights*, which Twain had been rereading yet again in 1883, when he wrote an affectionate burlesque of that classic. Indeed,

his lifelong fascination with *The Arabian Nights* qualifies that work, along with the Bible, *The Rubáiyát*, Malory's *Morte d'Arthur*, Shakespeare's plays, *Don Quixote, Robinson Crusoe, Gulliver's Travels*, Jules Verne's novels, Oliver Wendell Holmes' poems and witticisms, William Dean Howells's fiction and essays, Joel Chandler Harris's tales, James Whitcomb Riley's verse, and the poetry of Tennyson, Browning, and Kipling, to appear in any short list of Twain's favorite literary works. (Twain's ambivalent and changeable feelings about Charles Dickens's stories and novels, many of whose passages he initially admired and knew by heart, appear to place that writer in a separate category.) Chapter 55 in *Life on the Mississippi* (1883) had alluded to Aladdin's lamp, so it seems logical that Tom Sawyer's raid on the Sunday-school picnickers in Chapter 3 of *Huckleberry Finn* draws quite obviously upon *The Arabian Nights* (along with *Don Quixote*) for inspiration. In Chapter 23 Huck provides a mistaken summary of *The Arabian Nights* ("he made every one of them tell him a tale every night; and he kept that up till he had hogged a thousand and one tales that way, and then he put them all in a book"), and more absurdly misidentifies Scheherazade's tyrannical husband as King Henry VIII rather than Shahryar.[8] Thus the pattern of garbled allusion is established as basically identical to the ones Twain had employed in *Tom Sawyer*. According to the formula Twain had established there, literary references, whether classical or popular, were to serve as foils for Tom's and Huck's half-literate misreadings and faulty memorizations.

These allusions to familiar literary characters and episodes had begun earlier, in

Chapter 1, with Huck's sudden disenchantment with "Moses and the bulrushers" upon his learning that the Biblical figure was already dead. Shortly thereafter Tom Sawyer borrows from Robert Montgomery Bird's *Nick of the Woods* (1837) to intimidate his boy-gang in Chapter 2, and then in Chapter 3 relies on "a boy to run about town with a blazing stick" as Walter Scott had depicted. Later, cataloguing the Grangerford's family library in Chapter 17, Huck stumbles over the "tough" statements in John Bunyan's allegorical tale of another kind of journey than Huck's, *Pilgrim's Progress*.

Twain's master stroke with this sort of drollery takes the form of mixed-up literary quotations uttered, not by Huck or Tom, but by two ne'er-do-well adults. Superior to any of Tom's misconstrued interpretations of his beloved "authorities" is the scrambled mishmash the Duke makes in Chapter 21 of lines from *Hamlet*, *Macbeth*, and *Richard III*. Huck commits the whole travesty to memory while the king is learning his dramatic part. This piece of hilarity worked—and still strikes most readers as amusing; yet when Twain tried to repeat the same technique by parodying in the eleven concluding chapters of *Huckleberry Finn* various examples of "dungeon" fiction that were relatively well-known in 1885, the results are far less successful with modern-day audiences. Whereas the previous Shakespeare bit was being rehearsed by adult scoundrels, the idea of young boys imitating "prison escape" episodes drawn from Casanova, Baron Trenck, Dumas, and Cellini—augmented by William Harrison Ainsworth's once-popular romance *The Tower of London*, Thomas Carlyle's *French*

Revolution, Jules Michelet's *Historical View of the French Revolution*, and Joseph Xavier Boniface Saintine's now-forgotten *Picciola* (which depicts a prisoner painstakingly rescuing and tending a plant)—goes over the line into sheer ludicrousness. Orders for a rope ladder, a bloody journal, a homemade pen, a grindstone, trained rats and snakes, smuggled tools, and a mullen stalk or an onion (Tom has trouble deciding) prolong the burlesque to the point of utter silliness. More importantly, the entire episode requires of our contemporary readers a familiarity with certain books that, except possibly for Dumas's *The Man in the Iron Mask* and *The Count of Monte Cristo*, no longer belong to most people's fund of literary knowledge. The fact that Chapters 34 and 35 of *Huckleberry Finn*—in which Jim is kept locked up in a cabin—disappoint the majority of readers as a set-up for the novel's conclusion can be partially explained by the rare error Twain made in guessing whether future readers would be likely to find his spoof of prison escape narratives amusing if his literary models were no longer remembered.

In more serious tributes to his literary predecessors, Twain shapes Pap Finn's diatribe in Chapter 5 so that one part of it resembles a speech in Charles Dickens's *Our Mutual Friend*. Huck's startling discovery of "ashes of a camp fire that was still smoking" on Jackson's Island in Chapter 8 is a nod to the famous footprint scene in Defoe's *Robinson Crusoe* that produced repeated vibrations in Twain's writings. The ferry boat owner in Chapter 13 identifies a wrecked steamboat as "the Walter Scott," another jab at Twain's frequent target. Twain may have had in mind

Horace W. Fuller's account of imposters to the title of Louis XVII (from Fuller's *Noted French Trials* [1882]) when the king spins his yarn about being the lost French Dauphin in Chapter 19. Mary Boewe[9] and other commentators have detected the influence of W. E. H. Lecky's *History of European Morals from Augustus to Charlemagne* (1874) among the underpinnings of Twain's novel, as in Huck's conclusions in Chapter 16 about the importance of a person's getting "started right when he's little." Lecky's detailed history was a work that Twain read and reread repeatedly in multiple copies—arguing with some passages, agreeing with many others—during his halcyon summers at Quarry Farm as well as amid the bustle of his home in Hartford. It was among the half-dozen non-fiction books in Twain's library that made a lifetime impression on his thought and literature. One scholar has detected in the "evasion" sequence the discernible beginnings of Twain's "determinism, a philosophy based on what he had read in Paine, Holmes, Darwin, and Taine about the laws, processes, and mechanics that ruled behavior."[10]

There were various other instances of intertextuality in *Huckleberry Finn*, of course. Biblical allusions occur with effective frequency. Twain relied on Francis Grose's *Classical Dictionary of the Vulgar Tongue* as a source for certain phrases such as "burning shame." Scholars have pointed out potential prototypes for a clutch of colorful incidents—like the acrobatic circus act that awes an unsuspecting Huck in Chapter 22—in the writings of William Tappan Thompson, Joseph G. Baldwin, Richard M. Johnston, Johnson J. Hooper, George Washington Harris, and other humorists of the Southern frontier. Anthony J. Berret counted explicit references to more than twenty books in Huckleberry Finn, and he estimated that there must be "allusions or influences from at least twenty more," as well as "many general images of books, reading, and writing."[11] A complete listing of journal articles that have speculated about Twain's literary indebtednesses in this novel would be lengthy.

What is worth remembering, above all, is that Huck Finn, who, like Mark Twain, managed to affect a highly "unliterary" pose in telling a story based mainly on river lore and childhood memories, subtly reflected a strong acquaintance with the literary culture of England and America. Occasionally Huck disparages his ability to read as being merely hard, unrewarding work—and in Chapter 3 his father crudely admonishes him for demonstrating his newfound literacy by reading "something about General Washington and the wars"—but more often than not Huck seems to enjoy the pastime. When he discovers "a lot of books" in a skiff tied to the wrecked steamboat *Walter Scott*, he subsequently (in Chapter 14) reads "considerable" from them to Jim about the doings of European royalty and nobility. This capacity of Huck, Tom, the Duke, the King, and other characters (and their creator) to read widely and to make unexpected uses of their literacy amounts to another potent element to be taken into account in explaining the abiding appeal of Huck and Jim's intrepid voyage down that river.

NOTES

1   Blair, *Mark Twain & Huck Finn* (Berkeley: University of California Press, 1960), p. 117. Also valuable is Blair's "The French Revolution and Huckleberry Finn," *Modern Philology* 55.1 (August 1957): 21–35.

2   Rudyard Kipling, "An Interview with Mark Twain," *Sea to Sea: Letters of Travels.* 2 vols. New York: Doubleday and McClure, 1899. 2: 180.

3   Billingsley, "'Standard Authors' in *Huckleberry Finn*," *Journal of Narrative Technique* 9.2 (Spring 1979): 126–131.

4   Doyno, *Writing Huck Finn: Mark Twain's Creative Process* (Philadelphia: University of Pennsylvania Press, 1991), p. 177.

5   Berret, "Huck Finn's Library: Reading, Writing, and Intertextuality," *Making Mark Twain Work in the Classroom.* Ed. James S. Leonard (Durham: Duke University Press, 1999), p. 202. See also Berret's "The Influence of *Hamlet* on *Huckleberry Finn*," *American Literary Realism* 18.1–2 (Spring/ Autumn 1985): 196–207.

6   *Adventures of Huckleberry Finn.* Ed. Victor Fischer and Lin Salamo (Berkeley: University of California Press, 2003).

7   Gribben, "'Stolen from Books, Tho' Credit Given': Mark Twain's Use of Literary Sources," *Mosaic: A Journal for the Comparative Study of Literature and Ideas* 12.4 (Summer 1979): 151. (A revised version of this essay appears as a chapter in this present volume.)

8   Twain's novels were not the only Boy Books that celebrated *The Arabian Nights* and other favorites of Tom Sawyer; see my "Manipulating a Genre: Huckleberry Finn as Boy Book," *South Central Review* 5.4 (Winter 1988): 15–21. (A revised version of this essay appears as a chapter in this present novel.)

9   Boewe, "Twain on Lecky: Some Marginalia at Quarry Farm," *Mark Twain Society Bulletin* 8 (January 1985): 1–6.

10 Sherwood Cummings, *Mark Twain and Science: Adventures of a Mind* (Baton Rouge: Louisiana State University, 1988), p. 156.

11 Berret, "Huck Finn's Library," p. 200.

An earlier version of this chapter appeared in Huck Finn: The Complete Buffalo & Erie County Public Library Manuscript— Teaching and Research Digital Edition. *Buffalo, New York: Buffalo & Erie County Public Library, 2002.*

18

Mark Twain Reads Longstreet's
Georgia Scenes

Mark Twain's indebtedness to ante-bellum Southern humorists is well accepted, but little can be established about his familiarity with specific stories. Origin, overlapping, and borrowing among tales are, in fact, virtually impossible to identify in this genre. Publications were generally issued in ephemeral format, and even the facilities of the best research libraries do not provide the comprehensive collections and adequate indexes necessary to recognize the true nature of the humorists' interchanges. Yet the work of such writers as A. B. Longstreet, George W. Harris, Joseph M. Field, William Tappan Thompson, Johnson J. Hooper, Joseph G. Baldwin, Thomas B. Thorpe, and Richard Malcolm Johnston was unquestionably present in Twain's fund of memories. One may read the conjectures of Bernard DeVoto[1] and Walter Blair[2] with profit, but even these authorities remain cautious about assigning direct "influence." Blair simply concludes that "whether his indebtedness was specific in any particular instance or not, there is no denying that in many passages of his works the subject matter

and the attitudes of Mark Twain are definitely in the tradition of Southwestern Humor."[3]

The problem of gauging Mark Twain's knowledge of these humorists is further complicated by that lack of documentary materials. Many of the tales originally appeared in newspapers and magazines; even if Twain read and remembered these pieces, he would not have retained perishable clippings. He might have acquired books that reprinted these sketches, but during his early adulthood Clemens's nomadic existence precluded his owning much of a personal library.[4] Consequently we have no books that record his interest in this influential group of authors during the first four decades of his life. But after Clemens and his wife moved into their new home in Hartford late in 1874, they had the income and leisure to stock their new library shelves; a large proportion of their extant books bear inscriptions dated 1875, 1876, and 1877. Among these is a copy of A. B. Longstreet's *Georgia Scenes*. During the 1880s this Longstreet volume and others by Southern frontier humorists figured in a program of systematic reading that surely had ramifications for Mark Twain's subsequent writings. The immediate purpose of his reading was the compilation of a large one-volume collection of sketches representing the foremost native humorists in American literary history. Under the arrangement agreed upon early in 1882, Twain read selections submitted to him by Charles H. Clark and William Dean Howells. Though Twain's notebooks register his industry on the project as early as 1880, the volume would not be issued until 1888, when it appeared as *Mark Twain's Library of Humor* without credit to the co-editors. In the early 1880s, however, Twain read avidly in hopes of bringing out the book straightaway. "I am at work upon Bret Harte," he informed Howells on 23 March 1882, "but am not enjoying it. . . . The things which you and Clark have marked, are plenty good enough in their way, but to my jaundiced eye, they do seem to be lamentably barren of humor."[5] Two Bret Harte volumes that he was reading are now in the Mark Twain Papers in the Bancroft Library at the University of California at Berkeley, replete with caustic marginalia that detail his reasons for rejecting certain of Harte's stories.

Mark Twain intended to complete his share of the editing during his summer sojourn in Elmira. On 27 March 1882 he insisted to Howells that he could evaluate additional material while simultaneously writing the manuscript that would become *Life on the Mississippi*: "I think there is no reasonable doubt that I can read all summer without any inconvenience. I can read all

THE HORSE-SWAP.   25

and hip bones had not disclosed the fact, *he* never would have done it; for he was in all respects as cheerful and happy as if he commanded all the corn-cribs and fodder-stacks in Georgia. His height was about twelve hands; but as his shape partook somewhat of that of the giraffe, his haunches stood much lower. They were short, strait, peaked, and concave. Bullet's tail, however, made amends for all his defects. All that the artist could do to beautify it had been done; and all that horse could do to compliment the artist, Bullet did. His tail was nicked in superior style, and exhibited the line of beauty in so many directions, that it could not fail to hit the most fastidious taste in some of them. From the root it dropped into a graceful festoon; then rose in a handsome curve; then resumed its first direction; and then mounted suddenly upward like a cypress knee to a perpendicular of about two and a half inches. The whole had a careless and bewitching inclination to the right. Bullet obviously knew where his beauty lay, and took all occasions to display it to the best advantage. If a stick cracked, or if any one moved suddenly about him, or coughed, ~~or hawked,~~ or spoke a little louder than common, up went Bullet's tail like lightning; and if the *going up* did not please, the *coming down* must of necessity, for it was as different from the other movement as was its direction. The first was a bold and rapid flight upward, usually to an angle of forty-five degrees. In this position he kept his interesting appendage until he satisfied himself that nothing in particular was to be done; when he commenced dropping it by half inches, in second beats, then in triple time, then faster and shorter, and faster and shorter still, until it finally died away imperceptibly into its natural position. If I might compare sights to sounds, I should say its *settling* was more like the note of a locust than anything else in nature.

Either from native sprightliness of disposition, from uncontrollable activity, or from an unconquerable habit of removing flies by the stamping of the feet, Bullet

C

Page 25 of Clemens's copy of Georgia Scenes, *from which he removed an indelicate expression (Henry W. and Albert A. Berg Collection, New York Public Library, Astor, Lenox and Tilden Foundation)*

the Saturdays and Sundays and also an hour each evening."[6] Though the anthology soon fell behind his optimistic schedule, Twain's notebooks record his enthusiastic search for suitable material until 1888.

The books of humor consulted during this editorial stint would likely contain clues to what Mark Twain valued in early Southern humor, if they survived. But apparently they did not. The very preference Twain showed in choosing from their contents also doomed them as documents of literary history. At Twain's behest, the printers of his anthology tore apart the volumes he selected and used the loose pages as typesetting copy. Originally Twain also planned to employ engravings from these volumes as illustrations for his book; however, E. W. Kemble was commissioned to draw most of the pictures that ultimately decorated the text. Presumably this explains why no copies of George W. Harris's *Sut Lovingood: Yarns*, Johnson J. Hooper's *Adventures of Captain Simon Suggs*, Richard Malcolm Johnston's *Dukesborough Tales*, or William Tappan Thompson's *Major Jones's Courtship* were included in the auction lists of Mark Twain's library. Selections from these works appeared in Twain's anthology of American humor. They were apparently cannibalized and then discarded. His copies of the Bret Harte volumes in the Mark Twain Papers at Berkeley only exist today because he found them insufficiently amusing (aside from the pages containing "A Jersey Centenarian," which he tore out of *Tales of the Argonauts, and Other Sketches*), and instead chose several pieces from Harte's other books.

One surviving exception illustrates the types of annotation that Twain very likely made in the margins of the vanished books. The Henry W. and Albert A. Berg Collection in the New York Public Library contains Clemens's copy of *Georgia Scenes, Characters, Incidents, &c., in the First Half Century of the Republic. By a Native Georgian*. Second edition. Illustrated (New York: Harper & Brothers, 1845), a reimpression from the 1840 plates of the second edition. Augustus Baldwin Longstreet (1790–1870) first published these collected sketches in 1835. This volume was listed in the catalog of books sold from Clemens's library in 1911.[7] The recto of its front free endpaper is signed "James W. Hunt"; below this signature Clemens added his own in pencil: "S. L. Clemens Hartford, 1876." A 1911 auction label and the bookplate of W. T. H. Howe are affixed to the front pastedown endpaper. Laid in the book is a note dated 26 August 1938 to Howe from Isabel V. Lyon, Clemens's one-time secretary, that authenticates Clemens's ownership of the volume.

Clemens's marginalia mainly transform two passages into printer's copy. He made blue ink marks on pages 9 and 11 of "Georgia Theatrics" and on pages 23 and 31 of the story titled "The Horse-Swap." In the same ink he also jotted a few instructions: concerning the illustration that depicts a youth's imaginary fight (opposite page 10), he wrote, "Reproduce & use this picture. SLC"; on pages 23 and 24 of "The Horse-Swap" he changed several italicized words to "Rom." (i.e., roman type) in the margins; near the illustration of a horseback rider opposite page 24 he directed, "Make fac-simile of this picture & use it. SLC"; and on page 25 he deleted the words "or hawked" in the sentence reading "If a stick cracked, or if any one moved suddenly about him, or coughed, or hawked, or spoke a little louder than common, up went Bullet's tail like lightning." Evidently Clemens felt the emendation of that latter coarse expression was necessary for a subscription book directed toward a family audience.

A notebook that Clemens kept during 1880 and 1881 confirms that he intended to employ portions of *Georgia Scenes* in his projected anthology of humor. The title of Longstreet's book appears in a list of humorists and their works that Mark Twain began in 1880.[8] Shortly thereafter he wrote the words "Hall (Georgia Scenes [)],"[9] alluding to one of the pseudonyms Longstreet assigned to his sketches in *Georgia Scenes*. The title page of Longstreet's book does not name the author, and Longstreet alternates between "Hall" and "Baldwin" in crediting most of his tales. In 1881 Twain reminded himself of "Georgia Sketches,"[10] more likely a reference to Longstreet's work than to Richard Malcolm Johnston's *Georgia Sketches* (1864), which Johnston had republished in 1871 as *Dukesborough Tales*.

The two stories Mark Twain annotated in his copy of *Georgia Scenes* were both ascribed by Longstreet to "Hall." One of them, "Georgia Theatrics," is the first sketch in Longstreet's collection (on pages 9–11); it describes a ploughboy's pretended thrashing of an absent but detested opponent. Walter Blair remarked on the similarities between this bloodless battle and Tom Sawyer's struggle with an imaginary foe in Chapter 18 of *The Adventures of Tom Sawyer*.[11] The other tale, "The Horse-Swap" (pages 23–31), relates how a boastful fellow nicknamed Yellow Blossom

("I'm a *leetle*, jist a *leetle*, of the best man at a horse-swap that ever trod shoe-leather") trades an ornery swayback called Bullet for the gentle sorrel Kit, owned by a farmer named Peter Ketch. "I'm for short talk in a horseswap," declares the seemingly gullible Ketch, so the inequitable exchange takes place hurriedly. Afterward the wily Yellow Blossom assures Peter Ketch, "I'm for no rues and after-claps," and Ketch agrees: "I never goes to law to mend my bargains" (page 29). In addition to Bullet's obvious flaws, Ketch soon discovers that the horse has a huge sore on his back—Blossom had deviously hidden the infirmity under a blanket and saddle. The townspeople laugh at Peter Ketch's disappointment, but moments later Yellow Blossom learns that he has acquired an animal both blind and deaf. "Come, Neddy, my son," Ketch says to his boy, "let's be moving; the stranger seems to be getting snappish" (page 31).

Longstreet's stories were worthy of inclusion in Mark Twain's anthology, and Twain's marginal notes signal his desire to use the illustrations as well; still, for some reason Longstreet's work was omitted from the final version of *Mark Twain's Library of Humor*. Possibly Charles L. Webster & Company, Twain's publishing firm, encountered difficulties in copyright and royalty negotiations with Harper & Brothers, which had reprinted *Georgia Scenes* as recently as 1884. Perhaps suggestive of this explanation is the fact that not a single author on the house list of Harper & Brothers is represented in *Mark Twain's Library of Humor*. Whatever the obstacle, it preserved for us the only volume of ante-bellum Southern humor known to have belonged to Twain. His reading program of humorous works during the 1880s—along with the probable destruction without replacement of nearly all his copies of works by these Southern frontier humorists—should be taken into account by anyone studying the traditions of Mark Twain's comic devices.

NOTES

1   *Mark Twain's America* (Boston: Little, Brown, and Co., 1932), pp. 252–257.

2   *Native American Humor, 1800–1900* (New York: American Publishing Co., 1937; repr. San Francisco: Chandler Publishing Co., 1960), pp. 147–162.

3   *Native American Humor,* pp. 155–156.

4   See my article, "The Formation of Samuel L. Clemens's Library," *Studies in American Humor* 2.3 (January 1976):171–182. (A revised version of this essay appears as a chapter in this present volume.)

5   *Mark Twain-Howells Letters*, ed. Henry Nash Smith and William M. Gibson (Cambridge: Harvard University Press, 1960), p. 396; hereafter cited as *MTHL.*

6   *MTHL*, p. 398.

7   "The Library and Manuscripts of Samuel L. Clemens," Anderson Auction Company, Catalogue No. 892, 7–8 February 1911, lot #298. This catalog quotes Clemens's marginalia, which I have corrected against the book in the Berg Collection.

8   *Mark Twain's Notebooks & Journals, Volume II*, ed. Frederick Anderson, Lin Salamo, and Bernard L. Stein (Berkeley: University of California Press), 2: 362—hereafter cited as *N&J* 2.

9   *N&J* 2: 363.

10 *N&J* 2: 429.

11 *Native American Humor*, pp. 153, 287–289; also discussed in Blair's *Mark Twain & Huck Finn* (Berkeley: University of California Press. 1960), p. 62.

An earlier version of this chapter appeared in Gyascutus: Studies in Antebellum Southern Humorous and Sporting Writing, *New Series 5–6 (1978): 101–111.*

19

'That Pair of Spiritual Derelicts'

The Poe-Twain Relationship

Many decades ago, V. S. Pritchett astutely proclaimed that "everything really American, really non-English, comes out of that pair of spiritual derelicts, those two scarecrow figures with their half-lynched minds," Edgar Allan Poe and Mark Twain.[1] Since then a small procession of scholars and critics has tried to link these seminal authors more firmly, pointing out similarities in their works and suggesting Twain's indebtedness to Poe's writings. Several dozen scholarly books and articles speculate, at least tangentially, about Poe's place among Twain's literary models. My purpose here is to examine Twain's knowledge and recorded opinions of Poe, survey briefly the studies on the relationship of these two writers, note some additional parallels, and suggest unexplored lines of inquiry for future critical work, especially with reference to Twain's and Poe's dark or comic/satiric modes, doubles, and detective stories.

TWAIN'S FAMILIARITY WITH POE'S WRITINGS

Relatively few scholars have ventured direct Twain-Poe comparisons, principally because the record of Twain's contact with Poe's writings is one of the odder vacuums in our knowledge about Samuel Clemens's private library and reading tastes. Partly, one supposes, the problem is that Poe died in 1849 when Clemens was in his mid-teens, two years before he would attempt his first paragraph in his brother's Missouri newspaper and three years prior to his first national publication in the Boston *Carpet-Bag*. Only a few of the titles in Clemens's personal library from this time have survived. But in view of the fact that he eventually owned more than three thousand volumes in his adulthood, it seems singularly strange that not a single Poe volume can be definitely ascribed to Clemens's ownership. (A few other authors and titles obviously crucial to his literary heritage and artistic development—Swift's *Gulliver's Travels* and LeSage's *Gil Blas*, for example—are likewise missing from surviving collections of his personal library books.) At least we can locate his copy of John A. Joyce's biography of *Edgar Allan Poe*, published in 1901, in which Twain made sarcastic notes about Joyce's grammar and opinions. "It is a shame that this sentimental hyena should be allowed to disinter Poe's remains & paw them over," Twain wrote on page x; on the overleaf he called the biography "an impertinence—an affront," with "old tenth-rate thoughts, triumphs of commonplace—hashed up & warmed over" (p. xi). "If he *had* an idea he couldn't word it," Twain noted on the first page of Joyce's biography, the "most remarkable animal that ever cavorted around a poet's grave" (p. 1)[2]

Twain did allude explicitly to Poe's literary status a number of times. He observed in 1896, "What a curious thing a 'detective' story is. And was there ever one that the author needn't be ashamed of, except 'The Murders in the Rue Morgue'?"[3] But another remark, this one in 1909, shows Twain's ambivalence; Twain compared Poe's prose to that of his detested symbol of genteel English fiction, Jane Austen, alleging that "to me his [Poe's] prose is unreadable."[4] Given the currency of this pronouncement in modern critical studies and the lack of controverting evidence, Twain's statement needs some explaining. The context is especially significant; he is writing privately to William Dean Howells, rebelling, as he often did, against the "classic" writers whom Howells and the literary critic Brander Matthews commended—Austen, Eliot, Meredith, James—because their literary style was too "high" for his own critical standards. Twain's basic critical tenet for every evaluation by that decade in his life was "phrasing," and he increasingly tested this feature in his last years by reading literature aloud to someone. "Phrasing is everything, almost," he declared."[5] Applying this principle

in 1909, the author who had helped shape the movement known as American Realism clearly found Poe's richly suggestive, exotic, often ironic diction and his teasing syntax to be unsatisfactory. But in rejecting the prose style that linked Poe to an earlier age, Twain was not necessarily denying the writer's literary stature.

In 1864 or 1865, Twain, like many humorists before and after him, wrote a bad parody of Poe's "The Raven" (1845); Twain's was titled "The Mysterious Chinaman."[6] Although we cannot be certain that Twain had read the damaging allegations in the 1850 "Memoir" that Rufus W. Griswold included in an edition of Poe's works, in 1866 Twain perhaps revealed a knowledge of Griswold's charges against Poe's character when he jokingly defined "geniuses" as "people who dash off weird, wild, incomprehensible poems with astonishing facility, & then go get booming drunk & sleep in the gutter." In the same document, Twain's Notebook 7, he added another possible allusion to Poe: a man who "wears out the affection & the patience of his friends & then complains in sickly rhymes of his hard lot, & finally . . . persists in going up some back alley & dying in rags & dirt, he is beyond all question a genius."[7] Most of the contextual evidence, then, frustrates the effort to establish a single definition of Twain's view of Poe and leaves open the question of the extent of his knowledge of and regard for Poe's writings. However, a similar pattern of early admiration, later professed scorn, relatively few surviving association copies, but indisputable literary parallels has long been accepted concerning Twain's knowledge of Charles Dickens. And even though Twain's final library lacked certain volumes of Austen, Scott, and Cooper, irrefutable proof exists that he once owned and read most of their books. (Moreover, the Clemenses' daughters owned and read these same authors whom he professedly viewed as passé.)

In assessing Twain's view of Poe, it is especially germane to observe that many comic passages in Twain's travel narratives and novels poke fun at potentially harmful "illusions" encouraged by the "romances" that boys once imbibed. With a degree of seriousness, Twain went so far as to blame Walter Scott for stifling progress in the American South, and he held James Fenimore Cooper responsible for the literati's overly sentimental view of the Native American Indian. Because Clemens associated Poe with his own early reading in romances—the residents of Keokuk, Iowa, recalled that Clemens carried around "the tales of Edgar Allan Poe" in 1856 or 1857[8]—he conceivably reacted against Poe, along with other romantic authors, as representing a stage of indebtedness he consciously wished to outgrow. "Those were pleasant days," he once recalled of his Hannibal years. "None since have been so pleasant, none so well worth living over again. For the romance of life is the only part of it that is overwhelmingly valuable, & romance dies with youth."[9] As the antics of Tom Sawyer make clear, the books of boyhood, often untruthful and frequently misconstrued, are a component of this "romance of life" that must be left behind with one's lamented, foolish immaturity. While it seems incredible that a major writer should resent his earliest reading experiences, this may be the most likely explanation for those otherwise-inexplicable gaps in Twain's private library and in recollections of reading that obviously influenced his own art.

INTRIGUING PARALLELS

Studies up to the 1980s that connected Twain and Poe can be rapidly summarized. Several scholars asserted that the digging for Murrell's buried treasure in *The Adventures of Tom Sawyer* is related to "The Gold-Bug"; others noted that the dual personalities in "William Wilson" parallel Twain's struggle with his conscience in "The Facts Concerning the Recent Carnival of Crime in Connecticut"; and Twain's parody of "A Descent into the Maelstrom" in his "The Invalid's Story" was remarked upon.[10] Additional studies that advance arguments about Twain's borrowing from Poe will be noted in the following discussion or are listed in the Annotated Catalog. All point to clear-cut congruencies of theme, symbol, and pattern that link these geniuses of two different eras in American literature.

One foundation for these convergences may be the striking correspondences in the biographies of these two artists. Both men were Southerners by breeding, deprived early of father figures, and fond of idealizing women. Both were fascinated by such public enthusiasms as mesmerism, phrenology, and the occult (especially palmistry, in Twain's case, reincarnation and demonology in Poe's). Both were active in the literary quarrels and political debates of their day. And both admired *Robinson Crusoe* and relished literary parodies and burlesques, detective tales of ratiocination, and accounts of premature burials and nightmares.

In any survey of the similarities in these writers' works, the importance to Twain of

Poe's *Narrative of Arthur Gordon Pym* (1838) merits exploration. The Poesque metaphor of drifting, storm-battered sea vessels would become an obsessive image in Twain's letters and notebooks after his financial disasters in 1894; these becalmed derelicts, so reminiscent of the helpless vessels hauntingly described in Poe's "MS. Found in a Bottle" (1833) and at key points throughout *Pym*, might have taken an early and lasting hold on Twain's imagination. His late manuscripts, for example, are filled with sea voyages, mutinies, murders, death wishes and dream existences that recall Poe's long narrative. More particularly, the Coleridgean ghost brig that passes Pym's hulk in Chapter 10—its passengers scattered about in the "most loathsome state of putrefaction" while Pym and his desperate companions stand "shouting to the dead for help"—has its counterparts in the graveyard of ships that Twain named "the Everlasting Sunday"[11] and in the corpse-carrying balloons the narrator floats among in a manuscript version of *Life on the Mississippi* (an episode eventually discarded before publication because of its ghoulishness).[12]

In *Adventures of Huckleberry Finn* (1885), Huck's claustrophobic experience "up in the upper berth, cornered" in a stateroom on the doomed steamboat *Walter Scott*—he listens breathlessly as two desperadoes plot to kill their confederate—has congruences with Pym's fearful wait below deck in the *Grampus* while Dirk Peters and the crew seize control of the ship. Judith L. Sutherland's shrewd analysis of Poe's longest story, though not explicitly comparing it to Twain's novel, nevertheless evokes resemblances in her examination of the Pym-Augustus relationship, whose terms

suggest aspects of the Huck Finn-Tom Sawyer friendship.[13] Finally, Kenneth S. Lynn[14] and James C. Wilson[15] have investigated the many equivalences between *Arthur Gordon Pym* and Twain's uncompleted tale, "The Great Dark," written in 1898. Wilson concludes that Twain's "Henry Edwards, like Pym and Ahab, finds himself on a derelict ship, adrift in the Great Dark" (p. 241). Twain's working notes suggest that, had he continued "The Great Dark," Edwards, white-haired from terror, ultimately would have found a Great White Glare and mummified corpses—as Wilson writes, "the utter absence of meaning: nihilism" (p. 241).

Poe's comic/satiric stories often feature devices having analogues in Twain's humorous work. One can hardly read Poe's "Some Words with a Mummy" (1845) without thinking of such Twain sketches as "The Petrified Man" (1870), "A Curious Dream" (1870), and "A Ghost Story" (1870). The absurd interrogations of Poe's reanimated Egyptian corpse also bring to mind the non sequiturs in Twain's "Encounter with an Interviewer" (1875). The Mummy's revelations about the unreliability of "un-re-written" history books make the point that Twain would reiterate with Hank Morgan's "authentic" account of *A Connecticut Yankee in King Arthur's Court* (1889) as well as "Bishop" Mark Twain's version of events in "The Secret History of Eddypus, the World-Empire" (1972). Moreover, the narrator's faux pas (and rebukes by other members of the examining group) suggest the effrontery that Mark Twain's fictional companion "Mr. Brown" would brashly achieve (and the embarrassment he would cause) in their wide travels during the 1860s. Twain's half-finished stories such as "A Medieval Romance" (1870) and "A Story Without an End" (*Following the Equator*, 1897) have their equivalents in Poe's "The Premature Burial" (1844), "The Sphinx" (1846), and other hoaxes that lead the reader into unforeseen explanations and entrapping jokes. In "Never Bet the Devil Your Head" (1841), Toby Dammit thumbs his nose just as Twain's prehistoric figure does in "The Petrified Man." Moreover, Poe's story opens with an admonition against seeking "a moral" (that is, interpreting hidden intentions) in every fictional work, just as Twain warns against moral-hunting at the beginning of *Huckleberry Finn*.

Finally, Twain's stories often display the kind of dark irony for which Poe is well known. Chapter thirty-one of *Life on the Mississippi* (1883) competes with "The Cask of Amontillado" (1846) in the matter of savoring the torture of one's enemy: Karl Ritter gloatingly watches his wife's murderer suffer in a Bavarian mortuary, observing, "yes, he had a long, hard death of it." The shroud-wrapped Franz Adler, assumed to be dead, had rung one of the bell-wires attached to the hands of each corpse (Poe's narrator in "The Premature Burial" [1844] wishes to have this same precaution taken at his death), then waited for succor, "suffering unimaginable terrors." Twain's "The Californian's Tale" (1893) and "Which Was the Dream?" (1968) portray insane delusions that recall Poe's examinations of a diseased human mind. Twain was similarly interested in practical jokes that go awry with tragic consequences, as in the insanity that afflicts Conrad von Geisberg in *A Tramp Abroad* (1880) after Catherina and his friends fool him with disguises and

a fabricated story. In a "strange and tragic" anecdote in *Life on the Mississippi* that recalls "The Black Cat" (1843), a man attempts to save his wife from a sinking steamboat but inadvertently slays her with a stroke of the axe he uses to break through her cabin ceiling. The character's name, "Captain Poe," may not be coincidental.

DOUBLES, DETECTIVES, AND DEATHS

Several other parallels link the psychological patterns of Poe and Twain even more closely. As Patrick F. Quinn pointed out many years ago, "the phenomenon of the *Doppelgänger* is perhaps the most characteristic and persistent of Poe's obsessive fantasies," so much so that, "in a real sense, Poe's heroes are all doubles, one of another."[16] Unquestionably Poe's "William Wilson" (1839), "The Fall of the House of Usher" (1839), "The Man of the Crowd" (1840), "Ligeia" (1845), and other tales with double motifs would have appealed to Twain, a tireless chronicler of twins, disguises, exchanged roles, and contrasting but linked personalities. The mistakenly switched Edward Tudor and Tom Canty in *The Prince and the Pauper* (1881), Huckleberry Finn and Tom Sawyer in *Huckleberry Finn*, Hank Morgan and the King (sold as slaves) in *A Connecticut Yankee*, and Thomas à Beckett Driscoll and Valet de Chambre in *Pudd'nhead Wilson* (1894) represent only the best known of Twain's many explorations of alter ego variations. Several of Twain's modern biographers, like Poe's, have discovered a divided, tormented personality—in Twain's case, partly suggested by his adoption of a nom de plume and his affection for pseudonyms (in 1882, for instance, returning to the Mississippi River to gather literary material, he registered at hotels as "Mr. C. L. Samuels"). Mysterious subterfuges involving names and identities had tremendous allure for the imaginations of both writers.

Another affinity meriting further investigation is apparent in their stories of crime detection and puzzle solving. If Twain never matched the complexity of detail or level of suspense in Poe's "The Murders in the Rue Morgue" (1841), "The Mystery of Marie Rogêt" (1842), "The Gold-Bug" (1843), "The Oblong Box" (1844), and "The Purloined Letter" (1844), he nonetheless followed Poe's lead in many respects. Unfortunately for Twain, the requirements of the evolving detective-story genre seldom seemed in accord with his preferred settings of small towns and rural farms. *Tom Sawyer, Detective* (1896) suggests Twain's resoluteness about essaying this type of narrative and illustrates the sporadic, incongruous humor he introduced, but also embodies the cumbersome plot that ultimately defeats the story as a reading experience. Similar shortcomings beset "Simon Wheeler, Detective" (written 1877–98) and "Tom Sawyer's Conspiracy" (written 1897–1900). Twain did successfully spoof the infallible sagacity of literary detectives in "The Stolen White Elephant" (1882), presumably having in mind Allan Pinkerton's exploits, but sadly botched a Sherlock Holmes parody, "A Double-Barrelled Detective Story" (1902). The clues and sleuthing techniques in Twain's most notable murder mystery, *Pudd'nhead Wilson*, bear the greatest resemblance to elements in Poe's tales. Indeed, the melodramatic denouement of Twain's novel, staged in a crowded courtroom and eliciting

a prompt confession, appears to be directly connected with the ingenious narrator's feat in Poe's "Thou Art the Man" (1844). Twain's novel depends upon the new science of fingerprinting to expose the true character of some principal citizens in Dawson's Landing; Poe's storyteller employs a box labeled Château Margaux wine, delivered to "a very large and highly respectable company at Mr. Goodfellow's house," to frighten a confession from a villain whom the citizens of Rattleborough had respected.

In all of these instances, it is less essential to know whether Twain was imitating a particular Poe work—it seems evident that he often was—than it is to grasp the more significant fact that two American authors with vastly divergent literary reputations and public images actually have many curious intersections of situation, mood, theme, symbol, and phrase. In recent decades much of Twain's fiction has been seen as more somber, brooding, even eerie, than it was formerly understood to be. A commentator on *Huckleberry Finn* wrote almost casually that "death or its threat is the climax of virtually every major or minor sequence in the novel," and that the book "is a comedy that totters on the edge of tragedy."[17] Other scholars have noted that "horror is very real in *Tom Sawyer*," that St. Petersburg in this novel is "a phantom town inhabited largely by ghostly presences," and that "an ominous air of violence hangs over the entire tale."[18] G. R. Thompson, meanwhile, raised the problem of interpreting "a Gothic humorist" like Poe, calling for "a new way of reading Poe—a way just as informed as the new readings of Mark Twain and Herman Melville which have in the last few decades saved their works from consignment to the adolescent's bookshelf." In order to appreciate the comic and satiric sides of Poe, Thompson declared, we must relinquish "the traditional Gothicist view of Poe" as either "mad genius of the macabre tale" or "dreamy poet of the 'ideal' world of supernal Beauty."[19] Proceeding with studies of the manifold resemblances in Poe's and Twain's fiction could ultimately help to correct prevailing biases about these two comic ironists who animated their national literature.

Notes

1   V. S. Pritchett, "Books in General," *New States-man and Nation* (London) 22 (August 3, 1941): 113, as quoted by Hamlin Hill in "Huck Finn's Humor Today," *One Hundred Years of "Huckleberry Finn": The Boy, His Book, and American Culture*, ed. Robert Sattelmeyer and J. Donald Crowley (Columbia: University of Missouri Press, 1985), p. 304.

2   See the Annotated Catalog in this study.

3   Notebook 38, TS p. 32, Mark Twain Papers, Bancroft Library, University of California, Berkeley.

4   *Mark Twain-Howells Letters*, ed. Henry Nash Smith and William M. Gibson (Cambridge: Harvard University Press, Belknap Press, 1960), 2: 841.

5   "Three Thousand Years among the Microbes," in *Mark Twain's Which Was the Dream? and Other Symbolic Writings of the Later Years*, ed. John S. Tuckey (Berkeley: University of California Press, 1968), p. 460.

6   Reprinted in Arthur L. Scott's *On the Poetry of Mark Twain, with Selections from His Verse* [Urbana: University of Illinois Press, 1966], p. 53).

7   *Mark Twain's Notebooks & Journals*, ed. Frederick Anderson *et al.* (Berkeley: University of California Press, 1975), 1: 250–251.

8   Albert Bigelow Paine, *Mark Twain: A Biography* (New York: Harper & Brothers, 1912), p. 106.

9   *Mark Twain's Letters to Will Bowen*, ed. Theodore Hornberger (Austin: University of Texas Press, 1941), p. 27.

10   See, for instance, Minnie M. Brashear, *Mark Twain: Son of Missouri* (Chapel Hill: University of North Carolina Press, 1934), p. 213, n. 39; Walter Blair, *Mark Twain & Huck Finn* (Berkeley: University of California Press, 1960), pp. 61, 319–320; *Hannibal, Huck & Tom*, ed. Walter Blair (Berkeley: University of California Press, 1969), p. 159, n. 15; Pascal Covici Jr., *Mark Twain's Humor: The Images of the World* (Dallas: Southern Methodist University Press, 1962), pp. 148–156; Jack Scherting, "Poe's 'The Cask of Amontillado': A Source for Twain's 'The Man That Corrupted Hadleyburg,'" *Mark Twain Journal* 16.2 (Summer 1972): 18–19; J. R. Hammond, *An Edgar Allan Poe Companion* (London: Macmillan Press, 1981), p. 194, n. 16; Steven E. Kemper, "Poe, Twain, and Limburger Cheese," *Mark Twain Journal* 21.1 (Winter 1981–1982): 13–14; Millicent Bell, "*Huckleberry Finn* and the Sleights of the Imagination," in *One Hundred Years of "Huckleberry Finn"* (1985), p. 129; Robert C. Comeau, "Reading Poe on Salary: Mark Twain's Use of 'The Raven,' 'Hop Frog,' and 'William Wilson' in 'The Facts Concerning the Recent Carnival of Crime in Connecticut,'" *Southern Literary Journal* 29.1 (Fall 1996): 26–34; and Dennis W. Eddings, "Sam Clemens Reads Edgar Poe," *Mark Twain Journal: The Author and His Era* 56.2 (Fall 2018): pp. 124–133. For other articles, see the Annotated Catalog entry for Poe's "William Wilson."

11   In "The Enchanted Sea-Wilderness" (written in 1896), *Mark Twain's Which Was the Dream?*, pp. 77–86.

12   I have described these and related images of the painful, the ghastly, and the grotesque in "Those Other Thematic Patterns in Mark Twain's Writings," *Studies in American Fiction* 13 (Autumn 1985): 185–200. (A revised version of this essay appears as a chapter in the present volume.)

13   Judith L. Sutherland, *The Problematic Fictions of Poe, James, and Hawthorne* (Columbia: University of Missouri Press, 1984), p. 33.

14   Kenneth S. Lynn, *Mark Twain and Southwestern Humor* (Boston: Little, Brown, 1960), pp. 274–276, discussing "Poe-like" parallels in the "weird symbolism and psychological atmosphere" of Twain's projected novel, "The Great Dark," the fragmentary manuscript published in *Mark Twain's Which Was the Dream?*, pp. 99–150.

15   James C. Wilson, "'The Great Dark': Invisible Spheres, Formed in Fright," *Midwest Quarterly* 23.2 (Winter 1982): 229–243.

16   Patrick F. Quinn, *The French Face of Edgar Poe*

(Carbondale: Southern Illinois University Press, 1957), pp. 197, 226.

17   Michael Egan, *Mark Twain's "Huckleberry Finn": Race, Class and Society*. Text and Context Series (Sussex: Sussex University Press, 1977), pp. 128, 133.

18   Tom H. Towers, "'I Never Thought We Might Want to Come Back': Strategies of Transcendence in *Tom Sawyer*," *Modern Fiction Studies* 21.4 (Winter 1975–76): 510; Cynthia Griffin Wolff, "*The Adventures of Tom Sawyer*: A Nightmare Vision of American Boyhood," *Massachusetts Review* 21.4 (Winter 1980): 638, 644.

19   G. R. Thompson, *Poe's Fiction: Romantic Irony in the Gothic Tales* (Madison: University of Wisconsin Press, 1973), p. 8.

An earlier version of this chapter appeared in Poe Studies *18.2 (December 1985): 17–21.*

Poe Studies *masthead, 1985*

20

Those Other Thematic Patterns
in Mark Twain's Writings

One singular facet of Mark Twain's mind has not been explored in any systematic fashion: the series of obsessive themes, expressed in recurrent patterns of imagery in his fiction, letters, and notebooks, revealing his fascination with the painful, the ghastly, the grotesque. Partly this habit could be attributable to his acquaintance with the earthy backwoods characters introduced by writers such as George Washington Harris and Johnson Jones Hooper, uninhibited Southern frontier humorists who enjoyed a liberating license to mention the unmentionable. Twain's family members, audiences, and literary critics have not generally shared his taste in these matters. As an early biographer phrased it, "Olivia [Clemens] . . . was revolted by the macabre and the gruesome. . . . Most readers would agree with her. A fruit of Mark Twain's frontier life was a tendency to treat death and decay as funny. . . . The secrets of the charnel house are not funny to readers with sensitive minds and viscera."[1] Nonetheless, these "macabre and gruesome" passages suffuse Twain's published and unpublished writings, including even his light-spirited boy-books. If *The Adventures of Tom Sawyer* (1876) is a "hymn" to boyhood, as Twain once alleged, its hymn-like qualities can be said to evoke fear and anguish as well as joyous elation. That ostensibly sunny landscape of *Tom Sawyer* is illusionary; the decisive struggles take place in the graveyard, in a deserted and "haunted" house, at the Widow's lonely residence on the hill, and in the gloomy cave, scenes that belie the innocent reputation of this work. "Horror is very real in *Tom Sawyer*," one commentator contended, "and it is horror and Tom's reactions to it that . . . connect it to the dark unity of Twain's later works."[2] Twain shared this trait with another nineteenth-century novelist capable of creating memorably humorous characters and situations, Charles Dickens. R. G. Collins observed that Dickens demonstrates "the seriousness of concern of a comic writer in the close correlation that he draws between the extravagant emotion that produces joy and that which produces terror." Collins pointed out how Dickens "uses shock as a special device, the humor of exaggeration as a control, to convey a serious truth, doing it in the same fashion, say, as Kafka was to, in the early twentieth century."[3]

Whether the majority of the grim details and incidents in Mark Twain's writings represented deliberate authorial stances and effects or were reflections of Justin Kaplan's thesis and James M. Cox's argument that Twain was to some degree an internally divided man whose tensions became apparent in his fiction, his pervasive images of discomfort and anxiety can be grouped into three thematic categories that could be called *The Eternal Solitude, The Waiting Grave,* and *The Transcendental Deliverance.* In nearly every case, his disquieting depictions had literary antecedents. Most readers assume that Twain's ghoulish images are simply aberrations from his genuine style (presumably concessions to the sensation-seeking publishers of subscription books, who knew their readers' fondness for the horrific)[4] or quirky flashes of his latent, impending bitterness. Such interpretations miss the indications of Twain's enduring vision of human joy and human woe, mellow mirth and chilling terror, all hopelessly interlocked, and overlook how adeptly Twain was gratifying his readers' need for comedy while catering to their concomitant, less wholesome appetites. Among American authors, only Edgar Allan Poe's admixture of wryness and grotesquerie compares with this artistic feat of Twain's, but even Poe could barely maintain the impression of comedy in the balance, and his tales are often taken more seriously than he probably expected them to be.

THE ETERNAL SOLITUDE

The themes highlighted in this study are less recognizable than Twain's much-noted interests in pseudonyms, twins, alter egos, exchanged roles, contrasting personalities, and mysterious strangers, yet these and other better-understood patterns merge with those not usually discussed. Twain's early absorption with the idea of doubleness, for instance, had its counterpart in the freakish monstrosities evoked in "The Siamese Twins" (1872) and "Some Learned Fables for Good Old Boys and Girls" (1875).[5] Never reticent about referring to gruesome incidents like the dismemberment calmly introduced in "Aurelia's Unfortunate Young Man" (1864), Twain's casual morbidity had prompt origins and an unrelenting development. Its superficial innocuousness is a prominent feature of the first thematic category, *The Eternal Solitude,* which takes various forms. One version involves crafts that float on water or in air, and it could be labeled *vessels adrift.* Twain was a seasoned passenger on ships traversing the Atlantic Ocean, so it was almost predictable that during his long, anxious press for additional funding for the Paige typesetting machine he persistently linked that monetary goal with the image of a secure harbor. He often promised his wife Olivia that their "ship" would soon dock safely, much as the fictional Foster family believes their own optimism in "The $30,000 Bequest" (1904), and when the investment ordeal seemed nearly over in 1894, Clemens pledged that "when the anchor is down, then I shall say: 'Farewell—a long farewell—to *business!*'"[6] Subsequently, in the aftermath of the collapse of his publishing and typesetting enterprises, the image of that same storm-driven vessel, now a "derelict" ship, haunted his thoughts. "Behold us in this shabby Life adrift!" Twain wrote in his burlesque of Omar Khayyám's *Rubáiyát*, and he described, farther on in this poem, an elderly man as "that poor Life, a Wreck forlorn,/Dismantled driving toward the Unknown Lands."[7] To William Dean Howells he commented: "We *are* a pair of old derelicts drifting around, now, with some of our passengers gone & the sunniness [*sic*] of the others in eclipse."[8]

Conceivably Twain was remembering in these metaphors the excruciatingly becalmed ship on which he and the other travelers stirred restlessly for twenty-five days in 1866 during a prolonged voyage home to San Francisco from the Sandwich Islands. Although he wrote to his mother and sister in a reassuring mood ("I enjoy it"), the same letter reported that "we do not move an inch," that "sometimes the ocean is as dead level as the Mississippi River, & glitters glassily like it was polished," that we "drift, drift, drift," and that another ship was abreast of theirs, "both of us in a dead calm."[9] When he employed these experiences in *Roughing It* (1872), he stressed that "the calm was absolutely breathless," called it a "lonely voyage," and averred that "we were at sea five Sundays; and . . . all the other days were Sundays too."[10] Specifying this source for Twain's "vessels adrift" motif necessarily involves taking issue with Susan K. Harris, whose otherwise illuminating study of patterns and images in Twain's literature treated the *Smyrniote* becalming under the heading of "The Imagery of Contentment"; in her schemata, it was part of "an effort to transcend human time through the creation of an eternal present" whenever Twain used that image.[11] Yet in most cases Twain's becalmed vessels signify despair, violence, and

death rather than some beatific ideal. In fact, several sea tales by W. Clark Russell evidently interested Twain because they reminded him of his earlier ordeal. Twain's "Burlesque Sea Story"[12] appears to follow the plot of Russell's *The Wreck of the "Grosvenor"* (1877), but it owes still more to Russell's *The Death Ship: A Strange Story* (1888), a weird combination of motifs from Coleridge's *The Rime of the Ancient Mariner* and the legend of *The Flying Dutchman*. In *The Death Ship*, a youthful Englishman, adrift in the sea, is pulled aboard an eerie vessel manned by a crew who resemble the walking dead. He falls in love with a young girl who shares his horrid fate, but she is killed during their escape in one of the boats. The miserable man drifts with her body for weeks until he is finally rescued, and he then seeks to tell his woeful tale to any soul who will listen. This sensation of suspended, eternal stasis—and the hideous loneliness it produces—had an abiding pull upon Twain's imagination. For instance, in "The Enchanted Sea-Wilderness," written in 1896, Twain depicts a ship carried southward into a part of the Antarctic known as "The Everlasting Sunday," a graveyard of derelict ships, drifting hopelessly in a dead calm.[13] The parallels of this and other sea tales of Twain's last decades with Poe's *Narrative of Arthur Gordon Pym* (1838) are unmistakable.[14]

Actually, Twain's engrossment with drifting vessels stretches back still earlier in his writing career. There were gas-filled balloons hovering perpetually in *Life on the Mississippi* (1883), one of them carrying, "to all eternity" and in utter "lonesomeness," the "everlasting" mummified corpses of a bridal party, "a pathetic ending to a pretty dream!" (this bizarre chapter, now in the Pierpont Morgan Library, was eventually discarded before publication). Unpiloted balloons figure in several notebook entries and in *Tom Sawyer Abroad* (1894), in which a murderous professor plunges to his death from a balloon gondola, a dangling car that then "got lonesomer and lonesomer," according to Huckleberry Finn.[15] The feeling of suspension and helplessness under fearful circumstances belongs to that category best termed "The Eternal Solitude," inasmuch as the victims of this condition are trapped in excruciating situations—like the narrator of Poe's "A Descent into the Maelström" (1841)—seemingly unable to alter their predicaments and incapable of escaping.

But other manifestations of a similar sensation of stasis also deserve to be classified in the same order. Certain ubiquitous passages can be called *Sabbath stillness*, after a phrase occurring in *Roughing It*: "All was solitude and a Sabbath stillness. As I turned the corner, around a frame house, there was a great rattle and jar." In most of its variations, this pattern is associated with a disengagement from human society and is followed promptly by a calamitous development (in *Roughing It*, for example, by Twain's description of a major earthquake he witnessed in San Francisco). It also has connections with Twain's visit in 1866 to the Sandwich Islands, "that peaceful land, that beautiful land, that far-off home of profound repose, and soft indolence, and dreamy solitude, where life is one long slumberous Sabbath."[16] The phrase "Sabbath stillness" also appears in "My Platonic Sweetheart" (a sexual fantasy, written in 1898, about an ever-changing, ever-elusive young girl), *Following the Equator* (1897),

and other letters and manuscripts. "In the colonies, Sunday is Sunday," Clemens noted in December 1895 in Australia, "as strictly & Puritanically so as is the case in Canada. Not only is there no Sunday paper here but no rolls for breakfast."[17] On May 23, 1896, Clemens wrote to his wife from Pretoria, South Africa, mentioning "these wide deserted streets, this deep Sunday stillness, this mysterious & impressive absence of life and movement. This is the Puritan Sabbath of two centuries ago come back to the earth again."[18]

Generally in fiction he links the scene with didactic religious instruction, mournful sounds, absence of human fellowship, and impending crisis. At least fifty passages in his writings refer explicitly to Sunday and evoke this ominous mood. The most famous, of course, is Huck Finn's admission of deep dread as he approaches the Phelpses' farmhouse in Chapter 32 of *Adventures of Huckleberry Finn* (1885):

> When I got there it was all still and Sunday-like, and hot and sunshiny . . . and there was them kind of faint dronings of bugs and flies in the air that makes it seem so lonesome and like everybody's dead and gone. . . . I heard the dim hum of a spinning wheel wailing along up and sinking along down again: and then I knowed for certain I wished I was dead—for that *is* the lonesomest sound in the whole world.[19]

Henry Nash Smith assigned Huckleberry Finn's "deep depression" to "the emotional coloring of the author's recollections" of "the farm of his Uncle John A. Quarles where he spent summers as a boy" and to "a strong and not easily explicable feeling of guilt."[20] George C. Carrington Jr. pointed out "the feeling of sadness," "the thought of death," "the experience of horror [in] the use of Twain's obsessive image, the wailing sound of the spinning wheel," and Huck's immediate "destruction of his own identity" that the atmosphere induces.[21] Forrest G. Robinson, exploring Huck's attacks of conscience and depression and their association with "loneliness, fear, and awe," emphasized the connections of death with "running away" and "dreamy forgetfulness" to explain "Huck's enigmatic behavior."[22] These implications assume greater magnitude upon the recognition that Twain compulsively rehearsed essentially this same effect in work after work.

The Eternal Solitude takes other forms, one of which can be categorized as *processions of the dead*. Around Twain's axis of frozen motion revolved inexorable, constant processionals—the parade of skeletons in "A Curious Dream" (1870), the historical pageants in Chapters 9 and 31 of *The Prince and the Pauper* (1881), the slave-train that Twain injected into Malory's *Morte d'Arthur* in *A Connecticut Yankee in King Arthur's Court* (1889), the symbols of the history of London in "Queen Victoria's Jubilee" (1897), the dishonored national floats in "The Stupendous Procession" (written 1901), the "forlorn wrecks from all the world and from all the epochs and ages" in "No. 44, The Mysterious Stranger" (written 1902–1908), the culminating celestial "torchlight procession" of angels in "Extract from Captain Stormfield's Visit to Heaven" (1909), and other visual images suggesting the purposeless cycle of humankind's impenitent behavior.

Sometimes the sense of entrapment is mental rather than spatial and temporal, as in the case of *suffering married couples*. Twain's accounts of married life are seldom pleasant: they include peephole glimpses of the McWilliamses, whose tribulations Mr. McWilliams stoically relates in a series of three tales told to strangers about lightning, membranous croup, and burglar alarms; the Richardses, cursed by their outward propriety and inward hypocrisy in "The Man That Corrupted Hadleyburg" (1899); and the Fosters, sexually and financially maladjusted by a promised inheritance in "The $30,000 Bequest" (1904). And if the couples *are* contented, their honeymoons are usually of brief duration. The idyll of Hank Morgan and Alisande de Carteloise is torn asunder by roaring centuries in *A Connecticut Yankee*. Twain knew Milton's *Paradise Lost* and wrote several versions of the Garden of Eden story from the Book of Genesis. In "Extracts from Adam's Diary" (1893) and "Eve's Diary" (1905), the main figures—prototypes for succeeding generations of husbands and wives—exist in a blissful if uncomprehending state, but the calamity of their expulsion from Paradise beclouds their relationship.

The *refuge of insanity* can offer another type of "The Eternal Solitude" for Twain's characters. The haven of unreason shelters a middle-aged prospector from grief in "The Californian's Tale" (1893) and bewilders Tom Sedgewick in "Which Was the Dream?" (1966), among various stories involving madness or amnesia. Typically the victim relives a protracted moment of anguish that shattered his domestic relationships.

Twain was also fascinated with the morbid

theme of the *practical joke with tragic consequences*, a trick played on an unsuspecting friend or relative that goes awry in a terrible way. The version of this sequence told in *A Tramp Abroad* (1880), titled "The Legend of Dilsberg Castle," recounts how Conrad von Geisberg is fooled by his beloved Catharina into believing he has slept like Washington Irving's Rip Van Winkle for fifty years; when the pranksters doff their disguises and reveal the jape, they discover to their horror that von Geisberg is still possessed by the delusion they playfully manufactured: he has lost his sanity. He and the remorseful Catharina suffer, die, and are buried together, according to the raft captain who relates this tale. There are similar tragic aftermaths in "Doughface" (written in 1897?), in *Life on the Mississippi* (where a sudden confrontation with a friend wearing a shroud and false face provokes the insanity), "The Mysterious Chamber," and "Indian-town," among other instances of this awful penalty. "In those extremely youthful days," Twain once said of his years in Hannibal, "I was not aware that practical joking was a thing which, aside from being as a rule witless, is a base pastime and disreputable."[23] Whatever his sense of guilt, his fiction contained recurrent exercises in expiation.

Karl Ritter torments his wife's murderer, sipping brandy and reading newspapers while the man gradually weakens and succumbs in Chapter 31 of *Life on the Mississippi*. Ritter's victim is among several individuals who suffer *slow torture* in Twain's writings. One of Clemens' favorite fantasies in the 1890s was the thought of capturing James W. Paige, whose typesetting machine had cost Clemens nearly two hundred thousand dollars, and

placing him in a steel cage so Clemens could "shut out all human succor and watch that trap till he died."[24]

Twain's fiction also depicts *stricken narrators*, people whose will to live has been broken but who are nevertheless compelled, like Coleridge's Ancient Mariner, to relate their tale to relieve a burden. Comically if tastelessly, Twain sketches a narrator in "The Invalid's Story" (1882) whose "health was permanently shattered" by events he must narrate. Karl Ritter of *Life on the Mississippi* was another such person: his "face was wasted and colorless" and he "lay silent, abstracted, and absorbed." The Connecticut Yankee, encountered by Mark Twain in a hotel near Warwick Castle, "lay on his back . . . talking brokenly but with spirit," his appearance made spectral by "his glassy eyes and his ashy face."

In a few instances, Twain's characters suffer the fate that Edgar Allan Poe's short stories often recounted: *premature burial*. A young man's entrapment (in his mother's tomb, on the evening before his scheduled wedding) is touched upon briefly in "Villagers of 1840–3" (written in 1897) and a variant of this situation is more fully developed in "The Mysterious Chamber." In the latter manuscript, Carol de Piacenza is trapped for twenty years (in his wedding costume) in an unfrequented room within his fiancée's castle; his plight recalls Twain's familiarity with Thomas Bayly's "The Mistletoe Bough," a poem about the same theme of entrapment (and death, in that case) on the eve of the victim's marriage.

Nightmares constitute a final category of The Eternal Solitude theme. As in Anatole France's more playful *Le Crime de Sylvestre Bonnard* (1881), narrators are sometimes catapulted into unearthly dream existences in which anything seems possible, even their becoming particles in the bloodstream of huge creatures. "Which Was It?," "Which Was the Dream?," "Three Thousand Years among the Microbes," "The Great Dark," and sections of "No. 44, The Mysterious Stranger" rely on these fantastic dreams.

THE WAITING GRAVE

A second major division of Twain's thematic patterns, *The Waiting Grave*, compels readers to confront the fact of the sudden, violent interruption of death (or, sometimes, merely its looming imminence). These examples take a variety of forms—the first one, duels, being an obvious situation. Leland Krauth skillfully documented the fact that dueling was "one of Mark Twain's obsessive themes. He returned to it in one form or another in *Roughing It*, *A Tramp Abroad*, *Life on the Mississippi*, the unfinished *Simon Wheeler, Detective*, and *Pudd'nhead Wilson*, as well as in minor short stories and essays. His recurrent interest is a manifestation of unresolved conflicting emotions."[25] To Krauth's listing might be added Twain's essay titled "Dueling" (1923), comparing the rituals in France and in Austria, and "Randall's Jew Story" and "Newhouse's Jew Story" (both first published in 1972), which recount shrewd, brave actions of Jewish gentlemen in using the dueling code to defeat lecherous gamblers. In the majority of these tales, the possibility of instant death is a tangible hairbreadth away for the intervening "outsider" with whom readers are encouraged to sympathize.

It is instructive to look at how many times Twain referred to thunderstorms. The word "lightning" occurs more frequently than the name of any other natural phenomenon. In *Life on the Mississippi*, Horace Bixby is a "lightning pilot," and Twain vividly recounts the atmospheric pyrotechnics that caused the *City of Baton Rouge* to tie up to the river bank and wait out a thunderstorm. But Twain's fascination with the natural force of *lightning* goes far beyond visual and aural descriptions. In a generally disappointing manuscript, "The International Lightning Trust" (1972), a character named Jasper Hackett schemes to make a fortune by selling lightning-insurance policies. As Jasper confides to his friend Stephen Spaulding, people are hardly ever hit by lightning bolts, yet everyone is deathly afraid of the prospect. Whenever an inquest rules that death occurred by lightning, the International Lightning Trust pays the policyholder's estate a large sum. (Only twenty-eight people were actually killed in the United States annually by this means, as Hackett knows.) The firm's seal shows a blacksmith, their first victim-beneficiary, cracked by lightning, accompanied by the motto "In Providence We Trust." A comical, melodramatic plot ultimately rewards the young schemers with wealth as well as the women they want to marry. But the point here is the motto: Twain invariably associates the lightning stroke and its attendant thunderclap with the Mississippi River (and usually with his hometown of Hannibal) and with a divine Providence that angrily exacts an awesome vengeance for petty human misconduct. At the conclusion of "The International Lightning Trust," for instance, Jasper is drawn to Arkansas Flats on the Mississippi, where he witnesses two men being killed by lightning after breaking the Sabbath by fishing. This odd, almost childish linking of lightning with deserved punishment, specifically retaliation for religious lapses, and with the Mississippi, somehow signified more for Twain's psyche than he could ever state fully on the printed page. But he kept on trying.

In *The Adventures of Tom Sawyer*, Tom Sawyer and Joe Harper are afraid to desist from saying their evening prayers "lest they might call down a sudden and special thunderbolt from Heaven." Farther on in that boy-book, the frolics of Tom Sawyer's pirate-gang are interrupted by a tumultuous thunderstorm with lightning flashes that "lit up the forest. . . . A furious blast roared through the trees, making everything sing as it went. One blinding flash after another came, and peal on peal of deafening thunder" (p. 136). Storms with thunder and lightning occur at crucial points in *Huckleberry Finn*—in Chapter 9, when Jim and Huck are hiding in the cavern on the island, there is "one of these regular summer storms," its lightning "as bright as glory, and you'd have a little glimpse of tree-tops a-plunging about, away off yonder"; in Chapter 12, below St. Louis, "we had a big storm after midnight, with a power of thunder and lighting," enabling Huck and Jim to spot the wrecked steamboat *Walter Scott* ("the lightning showed her very distinct"); and in Chapter 29 a storm rages while the Arkansas villagers dig up Peter Wilks' grave ("all of a sudden the lightning let go a perfect sluice of white glare, and somebody sings out: 'By the living jingo, here's the bag of gold on his breast!'"). At the Phelps farm, it might be added, in Chapter 40 Huckleberry Finn escapes from confinement the way he and Tom have often left the house: "I was up stairs in a

second, and down the lightning rod in another one, and shinning through the dark for the lean-to."[26] In *Tom Sawyer Abroad* (1894), Tom grapples with the crazed professor-balloonist in the dark, and the aghast Huck Finn can only glimpse the scene in intermittent frames lit by lightning bolts: "Then it was awful still, and I reckon a person could a counted four hundred thousand before the next flash come. . . . But when the next flash come I was watching, and down there I see somebody a-swinging in the wind on that ladder, and it was Tom!"[27]

Often the effect of a lightning bolt is initially comical but then is associated with instant isolation; in Chapter 5 of *Roughing It*, when the coyote decides to part company with the town-dog, "there is a rushing sound, and the sudden splitting of a long crack through the atmosphere, and behold that dog is solitary and alone in the midst of a vast solitude!" Sometimes the humor is even more far-fetched; in "The Stolen White Elephant" (1882), the rampaging beast kills a lightning-rod agent. But generally the emphasis is on the utter grandeur and electric potential of the bolts. In Chapter 37 of *Following the Equator* (1897), Twain pauses to pay tribute in the Ceylon tropics to "that sudden invasion of purple gloom fissured with lightnings,—then the tumult of crashing thunder and the downpour— and presently all sunny and smiling again."

Clemens's personal calamities reminded him of the glare and concussion of the lightning-bolt. In 1886 he shakenly informed William Dean Howells that "yesterday a thunder-stroke fell upon me out of the most unsuspected of skies. . . . I found that all their lives my children have been afraid of me!"[28]

Recalling how he learned about his daughter Susy's death when someone handed him a cablegram in 1896, Clemens said that "it is one of the mysteries of our nature that a man, all unprepared, can receive a thunder-stroke like that and live."[29] Lightning was the metaphor that occurred to Clemens in 1904 in one of his first accounts of Olivia's death: "It is a thunder-stroke," he wrote to Henry H. Rogers.[30] Intermittent flashes of blinding power, of deadly force, of instant potential annihilation of man and his trivial purposes and ambitions: this image illuminated for Clemens the landscape of his life, with its losses and his fears of further losses. Quite likely it was Clemens's long nighttime shifts in pilothouses on the Mississippi River that made him the unqualified literary master of the awe-inspiring electrical charges that stretch from sky to earth.

Twice in *Life on the Mississippi* Mark Twain links the drowning of a playmate—especially in the case of "Dutchy," whose corpse-wrist the narrator touched in a creek that emptied into the Mississippi—with the Sabbath ("one Sunday he made himself the envy of all the youth . . . by reciting three thousand verses of Scripture without missing a word: then he went off the very next day and got drowned," he writes of Dutchy), with heedless juvenile amusements, with night-time thunderstorms, and with fearful, restless sleep and intentions to reform. This same quaternion of images connects events in *Tom Sawyer,* where the three boys, believed to have drowned in the river, reappear in their church on Sunday morning after they had been chastened from their games by a lightning-storm on the island and then had slept restlessly. *Drowning,*

a silent, swift death, is usually the "fault" of someone: of the boys who egged Dutchy into staying underwater and then hid laughing on the creek bank; or in another instance, of Tom Sawyer, who arranged the pirates' expedition and indirectly convinced the townspeople they had drowned. (One recalls the drowning death of little Binny Wallace off Sandpeep Island while his three friends watch in distress in Thomas Bailey Aldrich's early boy book, *The Story of a Bad Boy.*)[31]

The most excruciating for the victim (and for the reader to contemplate) of all violent deaths in Twain's writings is probably the *burning alive* of figures like the tramp in *Life on the Mississippi*. In this particular incident, Mark Twain again sets the scene in his boyhood town and depicts an ostensible kindness—his procuring the drunken tramp a match for a smoke—as the cause for the ghastly incident. But people burn to death (or are threatened with this ordeal) in numerous of Twain's stories. A bumbling Sherlock Holmes is to be burned at the stake in "The Double-Barrelled Detective Story" (1902). Of course the historical figure Joan of Arc dies by fire in Twain's *Personal Recollections of Joan of Arc* (1896); Twain had read accounts of her horrible suffering in preparing to write his work. The Indian custom of *suttee* is examined in detail, as are the cremation boats of the Ganges River, in *Following the Equator*. Frau Brinker is set afire in "No. 44, The Mysterious Stranger" (written in 1902–08), burned as a witch. Clemens's library contained several volumes treating witchcraft and the methods for disposing of witches. Galileo's relative is put to the flame in "Eddypus" (written in 1901–1902). It scarcely seems surprising that the author should have discussed cremation in detail in *Life on the Mississippi* and have approved (but later removed) a graphic illustration for the book showing himself in flames. The preparations for burning Hank Morgan are elaborate and nearly efficacious in *A Connecticut Yankee.* ("The stillness was so profound," says the Yankee, "that if I had been blindfolded I should have supposed I was in a solitude. . . . The fagots were carefully and tediously piled about my ankles, my knees, my thighs, my body.")[32]

A few things can be concluded for certain: Twain associated deadly flames with the naiveté of the victims and the guilt of the torch-bearers, with (particularly if one accepts Louis D. Rubin Jr.'s contention that medieval England represented the South for Twain's imagination[33]) the Mississippi River Valley, with the persecution of eccentric people who were superior to their times, with (in the case of the cremation of corpses) the ultimate sanitation-procedure, and with, in most instances, commendable fidelity to a cause.

One cannot help but recall that it was Sam Clemens who arranged for his brother Henry to be employed as a clerk on the steamboat *Pennsylvania*, which exploded and burned in 1858 with great loss of life, and that Clemens sat for days by Henry's bedside in Memphis as the youth lay dying of scalding burns. Could the guilt of those agonizing days later have translated itself into these retellings of deaths by burning? (He depicts this scene of futile nursing in *Life on the Mississippi*.) It seems worth noting that in *Life on the Mississippi* Mark Twain claims that one night he awoke "my younger brother" and asked his opinion regarding the degree of guilt he

should feel about the drunken tramp who burned himself to death with the matches Clemens gave him. Does this fraternal bond have some relationship with Twain's stories of fiery death, especially those in which the death resulted from the actions of a person who intended to do a favor? Seen from this perspective, Twain's tale of the tramp who died in the Hannibal jail ("he seemed like a black object set against a sun, so white and intense was the light at his back") could have served as an analogue for his brother Henry's agony and Clemens's haunting sense of responsibility.[34] *Life on the Mississippi* contains another story of tragically mistaken suppositions: Captain Poe, his steamboat sinking, uses an ax to smash through the ceiling of his wife's cabin to free her from a watery coffin but finds to his grief that one of his ax strokes has accidentally slain the woman, who had been sleeping in the upper berth. This story of a man named Poe who accidentally killed his wife in the course of trying to save her suggests a larger pattern in Twain's thought, the ironic notion that tragedies can result from well-intentioned deeds by *would-be rescuers*. (We cannot help but notice the coincidental naming of this horrified river captain— "Poe.") A young angel named Satan would confirm the essential truth of such reflections about good deeds in Twain's "The Chronicle of Young Satan" (1969).

An accomplished author must of course deal with the blunt facts of mortal existence, but the frequency of Twain's depiction of death in its violent forms seems as much compulsion as artistry. In his recreational reading Samuel Clemens relished the gory anecdotes in Tacitus and Suetonius about the Roman emperors' excesses, tortures, executions, and assassinations. We should not be surprised that virtually every section of *Huckleberry Finn* includes brushes with death, sometimes Huck's own (his staged murder, the steamboat-raft collision), sometimes others' (Pap Finn, the feuding Grangerfords and Shepherdsons, Boggs). The Connecticut Yankee expects to be "waked only just in time to keep from being hanged or drowned or burned, or something." And there is no question that Twain abhorred and thoroughly feared the normal path to The Waiting Grave, the aging process itself. As a consequence, in his personal life he elevated the language of boyhood and the appearance of youthfulness to the status of a private cult.[35]

THE TRANSCENDENTAL DELIVERANCE

Perhaps for these reasons Twain managed to create a variety of situations that enabled his characters to overcome the fates of premature burial or outright death that he feared and that Poe had projected in a series of terrifying tales. These escapes can be grouped within a third category it is possible to term *The Transcendental Deliverance*. In the sphere of Twain's fiction it became possible for him to deny—however arbitrarily, illogically, and ludicrously—the very finality of death. In defiance of the churchyard elegy tradition of Thomas Gray and other poets, in several of his works the non-living return to life. To be sure, the treatment is often slapstick or zany rather than occult in tone, and admittedly such improbable situations were part of Twain's "vulgar" heritage from the yarns of the Mississippi pilot-house and the gab

of the Far West mining camp, as well as the ghost tales of the plantation South. But morbidness is present along with humor in the stories of *reanimated corpses* that arise and converse (however nonsensically) in "A Curious Dream," "A Ghost Story," "An Encounter with an Interviewer," "A Strange Dream," and other tales. Even "Jim Blaine's Ram Story" in *Roughing It* contains references to a corpse that sits up and talks. Sometimes these undead take the opportunity to criticize their own funeral and burial arrangements. "At the funeral he bursted off the lid and riz up in his shroud . . . becuz he could *not* stand such a coffin as that," relates Jim Blaine in the tale of how old Robbins outsmarted the undertaker. Speech capabilities of the living dead were present in many of Clemens's probable reading experiences, beginning with Charles Dickens's ghost of Marley in "A Christmas Carol" (1843). The mute departed can be equally scary in Twain's telling. In a passage deleted from the final manuscript of *Adventures of Huckleberry Finn*, the runaway slave Jim recounts a horrendous night he spent in the dissecting room of a medical college; one of the cadavers opens his eyes, moves his legs and toes, and tumbles to the floor.[36] But the corpses do stay passively deceased in "The Undertaker's Tale," "The Invalid's Story," and "Buck Fanshaw's Funeral."

It is impossible, in contemplating the reawakened dead in Twain's writings, to avoid thinking of the corpse that young Sam Clemens supposedly stumbled upon in his father's law office, a body being kept for an inquest. Then, too, there were his vividly recalled memories of standing, as a boy, before his older brother Benjamin's open coffin; later, in front of his father's casket in 1847; and next, in 1858, facing his brother Henry's coffin (after having received a dream precognition of this scene, replete with the flowers that would be placed on his brother's chest). Some biographers have also speculated that Clemens may have glimpsed the postmortem autopsy performed on the body of his father, John Marshall Clemens. But it is hardly necessary to trace the exact biographical origin of this fantasy; the point is that Twain had a sporadic desire to repeal the inexorable rule of the grave. Several of his whimsical story titles themselves suggest this audacious mood: "Is He Dead?," "Is He Living or Is He Dead?," and "Is Shakespeare Dead?," for example. There are other variations on this theme of The Transcendental Deliverance besides these unburiable corpses. The grave-robbing scene in *Tom Sawyer* can incidentally be seen as a resurrection of sorts for poor Hoss Williams, viewed in this light. (We know that Twain was familiar with Dickens's *A Tale of Two Cities* [1859] with its body-snatcher character Jerry Cruncher.) In Twain's favorite ghost story, "The Golden Arm," a man sets out to unearth his wife's corpse, determined to retrieve her golden limb, but is deterred by her spectral voice.[37] Captain Stormfield's celestial flight in "Extracts from Captain Stormfield's Visit to Heaven" (1907–08) is another instance of a physical victory over the grave.

Susan K. Harris investigated Mark Twain's desire to discover a release from the limiting conditions of the human plight, particularly Twain's wish to find transcendence in a *dream-life*.[38] However, there were other means of escape that occurred to Twain. The *immortal fame* of historical and literary figures—Thomas

Malory, King Arthur, Lancelot, Joan of Arc, Christopher Columbus, Shakespeare, George Washington, Alfred Lord Tennyson, Henry M. Stanley, Ulysses S. Grant, perhaps even Mark Twain—seemed to ensure their "survival," by reputation at least. Insanity, horrid in certain respects, might still be an escape from an awareness of oppressive circumstances (though also a type of protracted death and interment). The gamble for instant and immense wealth appealed to Twain partly because it afforded the chance for the lucky investor to rise above all vulnerability, all susceptibility to ordinary cares.[39] Possibly for this reason (and because his father-in-law, Jervis Langdon, had installed him in a splendid house in Buffalo and had wiped away all of his financial worries in 1870 and the years immediately following), Twain's fiction contains numerous eccentric benefactors whose wealth resolves (or appears to resolve) every problem of their fortunate beneficiaries: "The £1,000,000 Bank-Note," "The $30,000 Bequest," *Following the Equator* (including the story of a Memphis wharfboat clerk whom Commodore Vanderbilt lifts to high estate), "You've Been a Dam Fool, Mary," and other pieces. In his own life, Clemens attempted to confer comparably liberating favors—financial, moral, and social—on a series of deserving people, including sculptor Karl Gerhardt, inventor James W. Paige, private secretary Isabel V. Lyon (until their estrangement), and biographer Albert Bigelow Paine. His responses to Henry H. Rogers's effort to untangle Clemens's hopeless investments and debts reveal an urgent wish for the arrival of a financial savior who would bail out this embarrassed literary celebrity. For Clemens, at least in certain of his moods, the promise of virtually *inexhaustible money* seemed tantamount to deliverance from the anxieties and images that haunted his dreams and his fictions.

There are in Twain's writings scores of nightmarish images of suspension in air or fluid, of death by fire, water, or bolts of electricity, and of other trials and fates. The fact that the prose of the best-loved American humorist is densely permeated with insistent themes of sudden suffering and painful death suggests that Twain's really was the tortured intellect and complexly divided personality that Justin Kaplan and Hamlin Hill depicted. Quite evidently his literary imagination was obsessed with thoughts of entombment and dying and also with fantasies of transcendence (that is, with previewing, and if possible evading, the former conditions). Many of his works depend upon a reader's understanding of the inescapable cruelty of earthly life, innate dread of imminent, premature death, and tortured guilt from unforeseen responsibility for murder or mortal anguish. To ease these persecuting terrors and revulsions, the narrating voice turns repeatedly to the comfort of dream figures or supernatural agents, to deliverance by wealth, or to possible life beyond the grave. A passive, complying, yielding acceptance of death is seldom portrayed, even though the prospect of death is ostensibly welcomed by narrators in Twain's later productions.

All the same, the constantly present comedy in his narratives calls an audience back to reassuring symbols: verdant Cardiff Hill, whitewashed houses in a drowsing village, the gingerbread grandeur of river steamboats. Filled with perils and ironies,

like those murky depths of the "face of the water" penetrated by the contemplative gaze of a pilot in *Life on the Mississippi*, Twain's writings record what their author perceived for humankind: a diabolically conjoined existence of antithetical beauty and ugliness, mirth and tears, elation and remorse, security and terror. That Mark Twain was conscious of maintaining a balance between the two views cannot be doubted. As he explained to an inquisitive newspaper interviewer in 1895: "Look at Thackeray and Dickens, and all the bright host who have gained niches in the gallery of the immortals. They have one thing always in their mind, no matter what parts they make their puppets play. Behind the broadest grins, the most exquisitely ludicrous situations, they know there is the grinning skull, and that all roads lead along the dusty road to death."[40] Subsequent generations would not value Twain's fiction so much without the turmoil of clouds and fire and agony, and the contrasting sunlight, breaking through benignly, would never seem so bright and cheering. The world of his fictions impresses most readers as the more truthfully contrived for those disturbing intervals of the repulsive and the horrific.

NOTES

1   DeLancey Ferguson, "The Case for Mark Twain's Wife," in *A Casebook on Mark Twain's Wound*, ed. Lewis Leary (New York: Thomas Y. Crowell Co., 1962), p. 165.

2   Tom H. Towers, "'I Never Thought We Might Want to Come Back': Strategies of Transcendence in *Tom Sawyer*," *Modern Fiction Studies* 21.4 (Winter 1976): 510.

3   R. G. Collins, "Nineteenth Century Literary Humor: The Wit and Warmth of Wiser Men?," *Mosaic* 9.4 (Summer, 1976): 11, 12.

4   The tastes of this subscription-book market were

analyzed in Hamlin Hill's "Mark Twain: Audience and Artistry," *American Quarterly* 15.1 (Spring 1963): 25–40.

5　The irrepressible cultural critic Leslie Fiedler touched upon the appetite of Mark Twain and many others for human oddities in *Freaks: Myths and Images of the Secret Self* (New York: Simon and Schuster, 1978).

6　*Mark Twain's Letters,* ed. Albert Bigelow Paine, 2 vols. (New York: Harper & Brothers, 1917), p. 607.

7　*Mark Twain's Rubáiyát*, intro. by Alan Gribben, textual note by Kevin Mac Donnell (Austin: Jenkins Publishing Co., 1982), pp. 46, 50. Twain probably composed this imitative homage in 1898.

8　Clemens to William Dean Howells, Vienna, January 22, 1898, *Mark Twain-Howells Letters*, ed. Henry Nash Smith and William M. Gibson, 2 vols. (Cambridge: Belknap Press of Harvard University Press, 1960), p. 670.

9　Clemens to Jane Lampton Clemens and Pamela A. Moffett, July 30, 1866, *Mark Twain's Letters, Volume 1*, ed. Edgar Marquess Branch, Michael B. Frank, and Kenneth M. Sanderson (Berkeley: University of California Press, 1988), pp. 351, 350, 351, and 352.

10　*Roughing It*, ed. Harriet Elinor Smith and Edgar Marquess Branch (Berkeley: University of California Press, 1993), pp. 532–533. In a letter of December 19, 1868 to Olivia Langdon, Clemens recalled that "we were at sea five Sundays. . . . To me comes no vision but a lonely ship in a great solitude of sky & water," as Daryl Jones pointed out ("Mark Twain's Symbols of Despair: A Relevant Letter," *American Literary Realism* 15.2 [Autumn 1982]: 268).

11　Susan K. Harris, *Mark Twain's Escape from Time: A Study of Patterns and Images* (Columbia: University of Missouri Press, 1982), pp. 78–79. Gladys C. Bellamy pioneered the analysis of Mark Twain's water, fire, and light imagery in *Mark Twain as a Literary Artist* (Norman: University of Oklahoma Press, 1950), pp. 249–265.

12　DV331, Mark Twain Papers, Bancroft Library, University of California at Berkeley.

13　*Mark Twain's Which Was the Dream? and Other Symbolic Writings of the Later Years*, ed. John S. Tuckey (Berkeley: University of California Press, 1966), pp. 77–86.

14　For other links with Poe, see "'That Pair of Spiritual Derelicts': The Poe-Twain Relationship," included as a chapter in this present volume.

15　*The Adventures of Tom Sawyer, Tom Sawyer Abroad, Tom Sawyer, Detective*, ed. John C. Gerber, Paul Baender, and Terry Firkins (Berkeley: University of California Press, 1980), p. 277.

16　Speech of April 8, 1889, at Delmonico's in New York City, collected in *Mark Twain Speaking*, ed. Paul Fatout (Iowa City: University of Iowa Press, 1976), p. 244.

17　Notebook 36, TS pp. 7–8, Mark Twain Papers at Berkeley.

18　Samossoud Collection, TS in Mark Twain Papers at Berkeley.

19　*Adventures of Huckleberry Finn*, ed. Victor Fischer and Lin Salamo (Berkeley: University of California Press, 2003), pp. 276–277. Forrest G. Robinson assembled some of the references to Sunday in his insightful article, "The Silences in *Huckleberry Finn*," *Nineteenth-Century Fiction* 37.1 (June 1982): 50–74, though he did not take note of the Sabbath connections, being intent on explaining why Mark Twain associated "solitude" with "melancholy" (p. 51).

20　Henry Nash Smith, *Mark Twain: The Development of a Writer* (Cambridge: Harvard University Press, 1962), pp. 130–131.

21　George C. Carrington Jr., *The Dramatic Unity of "Huckleberry Finn"* (Columbus: Ohio State University Press, 1976), pp. 11, 166, 168.

22　Robinson, pp. 55, 56, 65, 68.

23　Autobiographical Dictation, 30 October 1906; *Autobiography of Mark Twain*, ed. Benjamin Griffin and Harriet Elinor Smith (Berkeley: University of California Press, 2013), 2: 262—hereafter cited as *AutoMT*.

24　*Mark Twain's Correspondence with Henry Huttleston Rogers, 1893–1909,* ed. Lewis Leary (Berkeley: University of California Press, 1969), p. 742.

25　Leland Krauth, "Mark Twain Fights Sam Clemens' Duel," *Mississippi Quarterly* 33.2 (Spring 1980): 141–153.

26　*Adventures of Huckleberry Finn*, pp. 59, 80, 258, 338.

27　*The Adventures of Tom Sawyer, Tom Sawyer Abroad, Tom Sawyer, Detective*, pp. 277–278.

28　Clemens to William Dean Howells, Hartford, December 12, 1886, *Mark Twain-Howells Letters*, p. 575.

29　*AutoMT* 1: 324.

30 Clemens to Henry H. Rogers, Florence, June 6, 1904, *Mark Twain's Correspondence with Henry Huttleston Rogers*, p. 569.

31 I developed these parallels in more detail in "'I Did Wish Tom Sawyer Was There': Boy-Book Elements in *Tom Sawyer* and *Huckleberry Finn*," *One Hundred Years of* Huckleberry Finn*: The Boy, His Book, and American Culture*, ed. Robert Sattelmeyer and J. Donald Crowley (Columbia: University of Missouri Press, 1985), pp. 149–170.

32 *A Connecticut Yankee in King Arthur's Court*, ed. Bernard L. Stein (Berkeley: University of California Press, 1979), p. 92.

33 Louis D. Rubin Jr., *William Elliott Shoots a Bear: Essays on the Southern Literary Imagination* (Baton Rouge: Louisiana State University Press, 1975), p. 50.

34 Forrest G. Robinson recognized this connection in "Why I Killed My Brother: An Essay on Mark Twain," *Literature and Psychology* 30.3–4 (1980): 168–181.

35 See, for example, Tony Tanner's "The Pond of Youth," in *The Reign of Wonder: Naivety and Reality in American Literature* (Cambridge: Cambridge University Press, 1965), pp. 147–149.

36 *Adventures of Huckleberry Finn*, pp. 535–536.

37 Twain related this folk tale in "How to Tell a Story" (1895).

38 The Imagination of Escape," in *Mark Twain's Escape from Time: A Study of Patterns and Images* (1982), pp. 137–160. John S. Tuckey, William M. Gibson, and other commentators also pursued this theme.

39 I elaborated on this idea in "Mark Twain, Business Man: The Margins of Profit," *Studies in American Humor* 1.1 (June 1982): 24–43.

40 "Visit of Mark Twain: Wit and Humour," Sydney *Morning Herald*, 17 September 1895; *Mark Twain: The Complete Interviews*, ed. Gary Scharnhorst (Tuscaloosa: University of Alabama Press, 2006), p. 205.

An earlier version of this chapter appeared in Studies in American Fiction *13.2 (Autumn 1985): 185–200.*

21

'The Master Hand of Old Malory'

Mark Twain's Acquaintance with *Le Morte D'Arthur*

When did Mark Twain first encounter Sir Thomas Malory's prose romance? Most commentators have stated that author George Washington Cable originally introduced Clemens to Malory's *Morte D'Arthur* in a Rochester, New York bookstore in December 1884.[1] After all, this incident is more authoritatively documented than practically any comparable occurrence in American literary history: Clemens himself set down the story in 1889, and Cable repeated essentially the same anecdote in his memorial tribute to Clemens in 1910.[2] Clemens's designated biographer, Albert Bigelow Paine, supplied a dramatized account: "'Cable,' he said, 'do you know anything about this book, the Arthurian legends of Sir Thomas Malory, *Morte Arthure?*' Cable answered: 'Mark, that is one of the most beautiful books in the world. Let me buy it for you. You will love it more than any book you ever read.'"[3]

Unquestionably Clemens and Cable did entertain themselves with the archaic speech of Malory's characters during the joint reading tour they undertook in 1884–85; the railroad journeys were tedious, and this mutual literary interest presumably helped mollify Clemens's emerging dissatisfaction with his companion's personal habits, temperament, and platform artistry. Even Ozias Pond, brother of their lecture agent James B. Pond, joined in the fun. On 3 February 1885 Cable mailed to his wife "a copy of a telegram sent last night after midnight to Ozias by Mark & [me]." The message, addressed to "Sir Sagramore" and signed "Sir Mark Twain" and "Sir Geo. W. Cable," assured Pond that his friends "will well that thou prosper at the hands of the leech, and come lightly forth of thy hurts, and be as thou were tofore."[4] Cable and Clemens were performing in Chicago; Ozias Pond was in Milwaukee. Clemens's letter to Olivia Clemens on 4 February 1885 shows the effects of boredom as much as literary worship: "Some time ago, I gave [Ozias Pond] a full edition of the Morte d'Arthur, & addressed it to him as 'Sir Sagramore le Desirous'—a name which we have ever since called him by. We have all used the quaint language of the book in cars & hotels."[5] Sir Sagramore le Desirous was the knight who insulted Sir Tristram's kingdom of Cornwall ("'For hit is seldom seyne,' seyde sir Sagramoure, 'that ye Cornysshe knyghtes bene valyaunte men in armys'"), causing Tristram to challenge him to combat. Tristram unhorsed Sir Sagramore with a "stronge buffette," breaking his thigh. "Hit is to you shame to sey us knyghtes of Cornwayle dishonour," admonished Sir Tristram, "for hit may happyn a Cornysh knyght may macche you."[6]

Clemens had ordered this "full edition of the Morte d'Arthur" from his business factotum Charles L. Webster on 14 December 1884, more than a month after Clemens and Cable had commenced their extensive tour. "Get a copy of the 'Morte Darthur' (Globe edition)—Macmillan & Co., N.Y.—& leave it with [James B.] Pond for Ozias Pond," Clemens instructed Webster.[7] His directive referred to an edition first published in 1868 and often reprinted.[8]

In 1948 a professor at the University of Texas at Austin, Robert H. Wilson, established the fact that Mark Twain had quoted from Sir Edward Strachey's Globe Edition in composing A Connecticut Yankee in King Arthur's Court (1889), but Wilson could not determine the exact printing of the work that Twain used.[9] Although Albert Bigelow Paine had helpfully referred to Clemens's copy of Malory as a "little green, cloth-bound book,"[10] for many decades no copy that belonged to Clemens was believed to survive. Incredibly, Clemens's signed copy of the Macmillan Globe Edition eventually would make its reappearance in 1997.[11] Mark Twain's manuscript for A Connecticut Yankee had instructed his typist to use passages from the text of Le

Morte Darthur in Chapters 3, 9, and 42, as well as in the "Word of Explanation." The page numbers Twain cited corresponded with those of this Globe Edition.[12]

However much the novelty of Malory's phrasing enlivened the dull routine of travel and rehearsed readings in December 1884 and January 1885, the commonly held assumption that this was Clemens's first introduction to Le Morte D'Arthur cannot withstand scrutiny. Clemens's earliest acquaintance with Malory's Arthurian heroes had evidently taken place through a bowdlerized version edited for children, The Boy's King Arthur; Being Sir Thomas Malory's History of King Arthur and His Knights of the Round Table, edited and with an introduction by the poet Sidney Lanier and illustrated by Alfred Kappes (New York: Charles Scribner's Sons, 1880). On 18 November 1880 someone in the Clemens household purchased "1 Boys King Arthur" for $2.40, according to a bill sent on 1 January 1881 by Brown & Gross, Hartford booksellers. The same statement also recorded another purchase on 13 December 1880 of "1 Boys King Arthur," also for $2.40.[13] Probably the latter copy was destined to be a Christmas gift. Clemens paid up his account with the bookstore on 17 January 1881.[14] His habits of reading aloud to his family[15] and of perusing his daughters' book collections out of a curiosity about prevailing trends in children's literature lend significance to these acquisitions.

Malory's romance was one of four classics that Sidney Lanier (1842–1881), the American poet and (after 1879) lecturer at Johns Hopkins University, adapted for children. His introduction to The Boy's King Arthur, dated October 1880, discussed what was then known of the Arthurian legend, Malory's biography, and Caxton's edition. Lanier assured his readers that "every word in the book . . . is Malory's, unchanged except that the spelling is modernized" (p. xxii). Instead of Caxton's twenty-one books (an arrangement that Lanier termed "wholly unreasonable"), this version is divided into six books. Lanier shortened the narrative considerably, in the process eliminating all suggestions of eroticism such as the chapter that Caxton had dubbed, "How syr Trystram laye wyth the lady, and how her husbond [Sir Segwarydes] faught wyth syr Trystram."[16] Evidently *The Boy's King Arthur* whetted Clemens's interest in Arthurian stories, for at the time Clemens died his personal library included a copy of *The Boy's Mabinogion; Being the Earliest Welsh Tales of King Arthur in the Famous Red Book of Hergest*, edited and with an introduction by Sidney Lanier, illustrated by Alfred Fredericks (New York: Charles Scribner's Sons, 1881). Clemens's daughter Clara donated this volume to the Mark Twain Library at Redding, Connecticut in 1910.

Another piece of evidence corroborates the hypothesis that Clemens was already familiar with *Le Morte D'Arthur* before he toured with Cable in 1884—a letter Clemens wrote to Mrs. Cincinnatus A. Taft on 14 August 1883 when her physician-husband was ill. From Elmira, Clemens urged that no one else be allowed to take up Dr. Taft's practice in Hartford: "For what is Sir Kay in Sir Launcelot's armor, but only Sir Kay, after all, & not Sir Launcelot?"[17] Clemens and Cable would not begin their reading tour until more than a year after Clemens wrote,

dated, and signed this letter. Later, in 1884, Mark Twain would begin his famous entry in Notebook 23, "Dream of being a knight errant in armor in the middle ages."[18]

The resonating tale about Sir Kay and Sir Launcelot to which he alluded in his letter to Mrs. Taft takes place in Chapters 8–12 of Book 2 in Sidney Lanier's abridged version. Its plot would naturally have intrigued the author of *The Prince and the Pauper* (1882), a writer who (under a permanent pseudonym) would soon publish Chapter 32 of *Huckleberry Finn* (1885), in which Sally Phelps mistakes Huck for Tom Sawyer, and whose other stories and personal actions often involved double identities, twins, and impersonations.[19] Malory relates how Launcelot saw three knights attacking a single man, Sir Kay. Angered by such unfair odds even before he recognizes King Arthur's foster brother Sir Kay as the victim, Launcelot enters the fray and vanquishes all three knights single-handedly; he then pledges the defeated knights to journey to Arthur's court, surrender to Queen Guinevere, and place themselves at her mercy as the prisoners of Sir Kay. On the morning following this skirmish, Launcelot arises before Sir Kay, dons Sir Kay's armor and shield, and departs; when Sir Kay awakes he is obliged to wear Launcelot's armor and ride his horse. In Lanier's adaptation Sir Kay recognizes his new security: "On him knights will be bold, and deem that it is I, and that will beguile them; and because of his armor and shield, I am sure that I shall ride in peace."[20]

Protected by these symbolic trappings, Sir Kay proceeds safely to the castle, since the prowess of Launcelot is widely respected. Subsequently Launcelot himself returns to the palace, having overcome several knights who mistook him for the often-defeated Sir Kay. At the royal tale-telling, Sir Kay recounts how, "because Sir Launcelot took my harness, and left me his, I rode in good peace, and no man would have to do with me."[21] The original text is more effective: "'And by Jesu,' seyde sir Kay, 'sir Launcelot toke my harneyse and leffte me his, and I rode in Goddys pece and no man wolde have ado with me.'"[22]

The "Mark Twain" narrator who opens *A Connecticut Yankee* with a prefatory "Word of Explanation" recalls the night he "dipped into old Sir Thomas Malory's enchanting book, and fed at its rich feast of prodigies and adventures, breathed in the fragrance of its obsolete names, and dreamed again." This initial narrator had encountered a fellow named Hank Morgan in Warwick Castle; now in the seclusion of his own quarters at the Warwick Arms he shares with readers a passage from *Le Morte D'Arthur*—the tale of how Launcelot and Kay exchanged armor and shields. The extract he quotes for the reader concludes with these lines: "Because of his armour and shield I am sure I shall ride in peace. And then soon after departed Sir Kay, and thanked his host." Mark Twain next relates: "As I laid the book down there was a knock at the door, and my stranger [the Connecticut Yankee] came in." The transition between the Warwick Arms, where Twain takes up his copy of Malory as "a night-cap," and Hartford, Connecticut, this mysterious stranger's original home; between the ancient "prodigies and adventures" described by Malory on a printed page and the curious manuscript handed to the narrator by his weary acquaintance; between the narrator figure who resembles Samuel L. Clemens

the erudite tourist in England and a literary creation who generally talks in the brash slang of Yankeedom—these juxtapositions all hinge on a medieval tale of switched identities, a story in Malory that obviously held talismanic value for Clemens. (One thinks of his disparaging comparisons of himself to the war hero, General Ulysses S. Grant.) Quite fittingly, the knight who "captures" Hank Morgan upon his arrival in sixth-century England is the usually vulnerable Sir Kay, and in Chapter 3 Hank witnesses the sequel to the Kay/Launcelot change of identities—Sir Kay's revelation to the assembled court of Launcelot's selfless deed. In the *Connecticut Yankee* version, however, Sir Kay has drunk so much wine that he exaggerates Launcelot's feats.

The Launcelot/Kay switch of identities also figures in Chapter 4 of *Pudd'nhead Wilson* (1894), where Chambers "fought himself into such a formidable reputation, by and by, that Tom [Driscoll] could have changed clothes with him, and 'ridden in peace,' like Sir Kay in Launcelot's armor." In a letter written on 22 August 1897 to the Reverend Joseph H. Twichell, Clemens compared the Jubilee Singers (the touring African American vocalists whose performances of spirituals he praised repeatedly) to "Launcelot riding in Sir Kay's armor & astonishing complacent knights who thought they had struck a soft thing."[23]

Clemens admired another passage in Malory's work almost as much: Sir Ector de Maris's grieving eulogy for his dead brother, Sir Launcelot.[24] After a seven-year search for Launcelot, Ector arrives at the Joyous Gard only to see his brother's body on a bier. "Then Sir Ector threw his shield, sword, and helm from him. . . . And it were hard any tongue to tell the doleful complaints that he made for his brother."

Ah, Launcelot, he said, thou were head of all christian knights; and now I dare say, said Sir Ector, thou Sir Launcelot, there thou liest, that thou were never matched of earthly knight's hand; and thou were the courtliest knight that ever bare shield; and thou were the truest friend to thy lover that ever bestrode horse; and thou were the truest lover of a sinful man that ever loved woman; and thou were the kindest man that ever strake with sword; and thou were the goodliest person ever came among press of knights; and thou was the meekest man and the gentlest that ever ate in hall among ladies; and thou were the sternest knight to thy mortal foe that ever put spear in the rest.[25]

The death of Clemens's younger brother Henry in Memphis in 1858 may partially explain why he singled out Sir Ector's apostrophe. Henry Clemens was employed as a clerk aboard the steamboat *Pennsylvania* when it exploded and burned near Helena, Arkansas, on 13 June 1858. Chapter 20 of Twain's *Life on the Mississippi* (1883) describes Henry's suffering and death from burns; he lay lingering for a week in a makeshift hospital for the injured in Memphis, where Sam Clemens hurried upon receiving news of the disaster. Clemens's emotions when he arrived in Memphis and saw Henry's grave condition can be imagined from a letter their older brother Orion wrote from Keokuk, Iowa, on 3 October 1858 to a resident of Memphis named Miss Wood: "His death was horrible! How I could have sat by him, hung

over him, watched day and night every change of expression, and ministered to every want in my power that I could discover. This was denied to me, but Sam, whose organization is such as to feel the utmost extreme of every feeling[,] was there."[26]

Whether or not the deathwatch Samuel Clemens kept in Memphis imbued Sir Ector's address with special poignancy for him, nearly thirty years later, in June 1885, he pronounced "Sir Ector de Maris's eulogy of Launcelot du Lak" to be "Perfect."[27] He employed elements of its language ("the mightiest man of his hands that ever bare shield or strake with sword in the ranks of Christian battle") as part of Sir Kay's encomium to Sir Launcelot in Chapter 3 of *A Connecticut Yankee*. His reverence for Ector's speech is evident in a letter he wrote Mrs. Frank W. Cheney on 21 July 1904, shortly after he returned to the United States following Olivia Clemens's death: "She was beautiful & benignant in death," he reported, "& I knew how Sir Ector felt & thought when he uttered his moving lament over his dead brother." Clemens then went on, rather incongruously, to paraphrase the elegy as a tribute to his lost Olivia:

Ah, Launcelot, there thou liest, . . thou wert the courtliest knight that ever bore shield; and thou wert the truest friend to thy lover that ever bestrode horse; and thou wert the truest lover for a sinful man that ever loved woman; and thou wert the kindest man that ever strake with sword; and thou wert the goodliest person that ever came among press of knights; and thou wert the meekest man and the gentlest that ever sat in hall with ladies.[28]

Hamlin Hill commented in *Mark Twain: God's Fool* (1973) that "silence would have been more convincing" as testimony of Clemens's grief, but if one surveys Clemens's almost quarter-century absorption with Malory's book, especially his fondness for this particular passage, then his ridiculous images of Olivia Clemens's having "bestrode horse" and "strake with sword" become pathetically innocuous. The theme of Sir Ector's words is that of irremediable loss; when he finished his eulogy, "there was weeping and dolour out of measure"[29] The few surviving knights honored Launcelot's remains for fifteen days, buried him with sorrowful ceremony, oversaw the election of a new king, and then scattered to their respective countries, resolved to live thereafter as holy men. The Arthurian order was ended forever. Clemens sought an analogy to convey the realization that his life too was now irreparably altered.

Clemens's esteem for the entire *Morte D'Arthur* never lapsed after he first alluded to the Launcelot/Kay episode in 1883. On 16 November 1886 Clemens wrote the well-known letter to assure Mrs. Fairbanks that "of course in my [*Connecticut Yankee*] story I shall leave unsmirched & unbelittled the great & beautiful *characters* drawn by the master hand of old Malory"—including Sir Galahad, King Arthur, and Sir Launcelot, he specified. Launcelot, he pledged, would "abide & continue 'the kindest man that ever strake the sword,' yet 'the sternest knight to his mortal foe that ever put spear in the rest'"—again quoting Sir Ector's eulogy.[30] These assertions really should be taken at face value, yet they seldom are; critics surmise that Clemens either didn't yet comprehend the satiric thrust of *A Connecticut Yankee*, or else that he was being disingenuous by assuaging Mrs. Fairbanks's misgivings. For a writer of Mark Twain's comic genius, however, the urge to burlesque a literary work was frequently the surest sign of his regard for its merits. Certain popular books—Arthur Conan Doyle's stories about Sherlock Holmes, William Clark Russell's *Wreck of the "Grosvenor,"* even Shakespeare's *Hamlet*—made Twain itch to try out his own humorous versions. *A Connecticut Yankee* is as much homage as travesty.

In "The Secret History of Eddypus," written in 1901 and 1902, the fictional narrator says: "It was in a book called *Morte d'Arthur* that he [Mark Twain] found an English still readable by Tom, Dick and Harry after a lapse of 450 years of verbal wear and waste and change"; the Father of History ordered that this book be preserved.[31] Other favorable allusions occur in "No. 44, The Mysterious Stranger" (Chapter 33), written between 1902 and 1908,[32] "Three Thousand Years Among the Microbes" (written in 1905),[33] and "The Refuge of the Derelicts," written 1905–1906 (*FM*, p. 165). In 1906 Clemens told Albert Bigelow Paine that Malory's book "is one of the most beautiful things ever written in English, and written when we had no vocabulary" (*MTB*, p. 1320). Only the Bible, *The Arabian Nights*, *Don Quixote*, *Robinson Crusoe*, *Gulliver's Travels*, FitzGerald's *Rubáiyát*, and a few other literary works affected Clemens so profoundly and reverberated so persistently through his writings.

NOTES

1 The list of those who accept this sequence of events has encompassed virtually every written account of Mark Twain's composition of *A Connecticut Yankee*

in *King Arthur's Court*; it includes, as a sampling, Justin Kaplan's *Mr. Clemens and Mark Twain* (New York: Simon & Schuster, 1966), pp. 265, 293; Fred W. Lorch's *The Trouble Begins at Eight: Mark Twain's Lecture Tours* (Ames: Iowa State University Press, 1968), p. 178; and Howard J. Baetzhold's study of English literary sources, *Mark Twain and John Bull* (Bloomington: Indiana University Press, 1970), p. 100. In *The Art of Mark Twain* (New York: Oxford University Press, 1976), p. 7, William M. Gibson speculated that Mark Twain based a sketch for the July 1870 issue of *Galaxy*, "The 'Tournament' in A.D. 1870," on Malory's work, but Gibson overlooked the fact that Twain's essay alludes to Ivanhoe's winning the tournament at Ashby-de-la-Zouche and similar details from Sir Walter Scott's *Ivanhoe* (1819) and other books about the Crusades; Twain does not there employ characters or events associated with the Arthurian Round Table.

2   Notebook 23, *Mark Twain Notebooks & Journals, Volume III*, ed. Robert Pack Browning, Michael B. Frank, and Lin Salamo (Berkeley: University of California Press, 1979), 3: 79—hereafter cited as *N&J*. Cable's speech, delivered on 30 November 1910, was published in Arlin Turner's *Mark Twain and George W. Cable: The Record of a Literary Friendship* (East Lansing: Michigan State University Press, 1960), pp. 135–136.

3   *Mark Twain: A Biography* (New York: Harper & Brothers, 1912), p. 790. (Cited hereafter as *MTB*.)

4   Turner, *Mark Twain and George W. Cable*, p. 96.

5   *The Love Letters of Mark Twain*, ed. Dixon Wecter (New York: Harper, 1949), pp. 229–230.

6   *The Works of Sir Thomas Malory*, ed. Eugène Vinaver, 2nd edition, 3 vols. (Oxford: Clarendon Press, 1967), pp. 398–399. The episode occurs in Book 8, "The Book of Sir Tristram de Lyones," Caxton's Chapter 16. In Mark Twain's prefatory "Word of Explanation" to *A Connecticut Yankee*, the guide at Warwick Castle points out an "ancient hauberk, . . . said to have belonged to the knight Sir Sagramore le Desirous," which contains an unaccountable bullet hole in its chain mail. An alleged insult by Hank Morgan in Chapter 9 leads the Boss into a tournament with Sir Sagramore in Chapter 39 "to either destroy knight-errantry or be its victim." The Yankee's lasso conquers Sagramore, and his revolver finishes off the stubborn knight.

7   *Mark Twain, Business Man*, ed. Samuel C. Webster (Boston: Little, Brown, and Co., 1946), p. 283.

8   Malory, *Le Morte Darthur*, edited and with an introduction by Sir Edward Strachey. The third edition (hereafter cited as "Globe Edition") was reprinted in 1870, 1876, 1879, 1883, and 1884.

9   "Malory in the *Connecticut Yankee*," *University of Texas Studies in English* 27 (June 1948): 185–206.

10   Paine, *MTB*, p. 790.

11   It turned out to be a copy of the 509-page *Le Morte Darthur: Sir Thomas Malory's Book of King Arthur and His Noble Knights of the Round Table*. The Globe Edition Series. Edited by Sir Edward Strachey (London and New York: Macmillan and Co., 1879). See the Thomas Malory entry in the Annotated Catalog for additional details about this book.

12   *A Connecticut Yankee in King Arthur's Court*, ed. Bernard L. Stein (Berkeley: University of California Press, 1979), p. 612 n. 90. While the manuscript Mark Twain sent to his typist is extant, the typescript copies are missing.

13   Mark Twain Papers, Bancroft Library, University of California at Berkeley—hereafter cited as MTP.

14   Receipt in MTP.

15   See my essay "'It Is Unsatisfactory to Read to One's Self': Mark Twain's Informal Readings," *Quarterly Journal of Speech* 62.1 (February 1976: 49–56. (A revised version of this essay appears as a chapter in the present volume.)

16   Malory, Caxton's Book 8, Chapter 14.

17   ALS in the Mark Twain House and Museum, Hartford, Connecticut; quoted in Edith Colgate Salsbury's *Susy and Mark Twain* (New York: Harper & Row, 1965), p. 170. Salsbury misdated the letter as 17 August.

18   *N&J* 3: 78.

19   For example, Clemens employed the ruse of using a fictitious name ("because it is mysterious & stylish") when he revisited the Mississippi River in 1882; he registered at hotels in St. Louis and New Orleans as "Mr. C. L. Samuels" (*N&J* 2: 458 n. 84, 466 n. 120).

20   Lanier, ed., *The Boy's King Arthur*, p. 70 (Chapter 11 of Book 6 in Caxton's version).

21   Lanier, ed., *The Boy's King Arthur*, p. 78).

22   *Works of Sir Thomas Malory*, ed. Eugene Vinaver, p. 287.

23   *The Letters of Mark Twain and Joseph Hopkins Twichell*, ed. Harold K. Bush, Steve Courtney, and Peter Messent (Athens: University of Georgia Press, 2017), p. 198.

24   Book 21, Chapter 13 in the Globe Edition of

Malory's *Le Morte Darthur*, Book 6, Chapter 37 in Sidney Lanier's abridged edition, pp. 401–402.

25 Malory, *Le Morte Darthur*, Globe Edition, p. 486.

26 TS in MTP.

27 Notebook 24, *N&J* 3: 159.

28 ALS in the Mark Twain House and Museum, Hartford, Connecticut; quoted by Hamlin Hill, *Mark Twain: God's Fool* (New York, 1973), p. 86.

29 Malory, *Le Morte Darthur*, Globe Edition, p. 486.

30 *Mark Twain to Mrs. Fairbanks*, ed. Dixon Wecter (San Marino, California: Huntington Library, 1949), p. 258.

31 *Mark Twain's Fables of Man*, ed. John S. Tuckey

(Berkeley: University of California Press, 1972), pp. 343–344—hereafter cited as *FM*.

32 *Mark Twain's Mysterious Stranger Manuscripts*, ed. William M. Gibson (Berkeley: University of California Press, 1969), p. 402.

33 *Mark Twain's Which Was the Dream? and Other Symbolic Writings of the Later Years*, ed. John S. Tuckey (Berkeley: University of California Press, 1969), p. 534.

An earlier version of this chapter appeared in English Language Notes *16.1 (September 1978): 32–40.*

22

Anatole France and Mark Twain's Satan

Mark Twain may have absorbed an idea for ending his "No. 44, The Mysterious Stranger," written between 1902 and 1908, from an episode in Anatole France's *Le Crime de Sylvestre Bonnard* (1881). If so, the genesis of the controversial final passage in Twain's story required at least fifteen years. Twain evidently heard someone speak of France's novel in December 1890, for he entered a phonetic approximation of its title in his private notebook: "The Crime of Sylvester Bonar."[1] On January 13, 1891, Clemens wrote to his wife Olivia from the Arlington Hotel in Washington, D.C.: "I've got a charming book for you to read—'The Crime of Sylvester Bonnard,'" and in writing her on the succeeding day he mentioned that he was avoiding people "by clinging as a rule to my room & reading."[2] He returned to France's novel in 1906, when he obtained a copy of the edition published that year by Harper & Brothers.[3] In an inscription written in black ink on the front pastedown endpaper, Clemens described the book as equal or superior to the American type of humor, proof that the French are capable of "humor" as well as "wit" (a significant concession in view of

Clemens's anti-Gallic prejudices); he signed this statement and dated it 1906. Throughout the volume Clemens made numerous markings, corrections, and notes—all in pencil. His marginalia are generally charitable; most annotations in the text simply correct minor grammatical lapses by its translator, the bohemian author, journalist, and Japanophile Lafcadio Hearn (1850–1904).

In Chapter 2 of Part II of *Le Crime de Sylvestre Bonnard* a fairy appears to the bibliophile-pedant Bonnard in the library of the long-deserted Château de Lusance, and he converses with her about the modern disregard for fairies. She lectures Bonnard on the true nature of reality: "Nothing exists except that which is imagined. I am imaginary. That is to exist, I should certainly think! I am dreamed of, and I appear. Everything is only dream; and as nobody ever dreams about you, Sylvestre Bonnard, it is *you* who do not exist. I charm the world; I am everywhere— on a moonbeam, . . . in the thickets of pink brier—everywhere!"[4] In Mark Twain's "No. 44, The Mysterious Stranger," Satan (called "Forty-four" in this version of Twain's work known as *The Mysterious Stranger*) discloses that "*Life itself is only a vision, a dream*," and that "*nothing* exists; all is a dream. God—man—the world,—the sun, the moon, the wilderness of stars: a dream, all a dream, they have no existence." Still more pertinent, Forty-four reveals: "I myself have no existence, I am but a dream—your dream, creature of your imagination."[5]

When the fairy ceases speaking and mischievously throws Bonnard's pen at his nose, Bonnard rubs his face and finds that "she had disappeared."[6] Later Bonnard refers to the episode as "my vision."[7] Mark Twain's Forty-four explains that when August Feldner realizes the truth, "in a moment . . . you will banish me from your visions and I shall dissolve into the nothingness out of which you made me." Forty-four adds that earthly existence "is all a Dream, a grotesque and foolish dream."[8]

The sleepy Bonnard's innocent fantasy about a fairy who interrupts his scholarly labors entirely avoids the dark ironies that Mark Twain injects into his version, but the situations are similar—supernatural beings deliver knowledge to earthlings who seek wisdom, whimsy blends with mocking cruelty (the fairy pelts Bonnard with nutshells, tickles his nose with a feather, and vanishes after hurling his own ink pen at him), both creatures disappear after imparting their startling revelations, and both are figments of dreams by the narrators.

NOTES

1 Notebook 30, *Mark Twain's Notebooks & Journals, Volume III*, ed. Robert Pack Browning, Michael B. Frank, and Lin Salamo (Berkeley: University of California Press, 1979) 3: 595.

2 Both ALS are in the Mark Twain Papers, Bancroft Library, University of California at Berkeley.

3 The Henry W. and Albert A. Berg Collection in the New York Public Library possesses Clemens's copy of *The Crime of Sylvestre Bonnard (Member of the Institute)*. Translation and introduction by Lafcadio Hearn (New York: Harper & Brothers, 1906). This volume was listed as item #229 in the catalog of books sold from Clemens's library in 1911, "The Library and Manuscripts of Samuel L. Clemens," Anderson Auction Company, Catalogue No. 892. To be sold February 7–8, 1911.

4 Quoted from page 100 of the edition of *Le Crime* owned by Clemens.

5 *Mark Twain's Mysterious Stranger Manuscripts*, ed. William M. Gibson (Berkeley: University of California Press, 1969), p. 404.

6 France, *Le Crime*, p. 101.

7 France, *Le Crime*, p. 102.

8 Twain, *Mark Twain's Mysterious Stranger Manuscripts*, pp. 404–405.

_____

An earlier version of this chapter appeared in American Literature *47.4 (January 1976): 634–635.*

23

'I Detest Novels, Poetry & Theology'

Origin of a Fiction Concerning Mark Twain's Reading

The inception of the belief that Mark Twain lacked literary sophistication can be traced partly to Clemens's designated biographer Albert Bigelow Paine, for Paine created an impression much at variance with the one urged by Olin H. Moore and his successors who have studied the scope and quality of Clemens's reading.[1] In spite of the research performed within the past century and the fact that the findings are invariably the same—that Clemens read more widely and with greater emphasis on *belles-lettres* than seems to be realized—the revisionists have still encountered resistance. To understand why this is so requires an appreciation of the importance of the lasting portrait sketched by Paine in *Mark Twain: A Biography* (1912) and *Mark Twain's Letters* (1917). In *Mark Twain's Letters* Paine summarized a concept of Clemens's reading preferences that he had developed in the prior biography: "Mark Twain had a few books that he read regularly every year or two. Among these were *Pepys's Diary*, Suetonius's *Lives of the Twelve Caesars*, and Thomas Carlyle's *French Revolution*. He had

a passion for history, biography, and personal memoirs of any sort. In his early life he had cared very little for poetry, but along in the middle eighties he somehow acquired a taste for Browning."[2]

Paine's *Mark Twain: A Biography* had treated these predilections at greater length: there he summarized Clemens's reading at Quarry Farm in 1874 and quoted Clemens's declaration during that same period that he disliked novels, poetry, and theology.[3] One chapter of the biography Paine titled "Mark Twain's Reading," and there Paine named and quoted marginalia from Mark Twain's favorite books ("not more than a dozen"), all of which happened to be volumes of letters, memoirs, or history.[4] He gave emphasis to Clemens's choice of reading—Suetonius's *Lives of the Twelve Caesars* and Carlyle's *French Revolution*—in his moments of lucidity during his fatal illness.[5] The impression conveyed is that Clemens read narrowly and in subjects extraneous to his writings—and that he read books mainly out of curiosity about celebrated people. While most of this testimony is not exactly incorrect, it distorts the totality of Clemens's reading patterns. Of course Paine became Clemens's companion only during the final four years of his subject's life, so naturally he wrote with greater authority about this phase. When he noticed Clemens's absorption in Suetonius's *Twelve Caesars* and a few other volumes he understandably drew the conclusion that they had exerted an equal influence in preceding periods of Clemens's life.

As it becomes apparent how slanted and incomplete was Paine's estimate of Clemens's familiarity with books, however, the extenuating historical context of the *Biography* should be borne in mind. Paine wrote his narrative in the well-established tradition of the "men of letters" biographies that had carried over from the previous century. He was producing a work that he had been specially selected to execute by its subject himself. This biographical tradition did not encourage the biographer to question seriously the image his subject wished projected to an admiring public.[6] In fairness, too, it must be said that today we can employ the combined scholarship of several generations of scholars in scrutinizing a minute fraction of Paine's labor. Given the scope of his biography, Paine could not hope to concern himself in detail with any single element of Clemens's intellectual development.

On the other hand, Paine possessed several advantages that are no longer available to researchers. Much of Clemens's personal library was still intact until 1911, when Paine and Clemens's daughter Clara presided over the dispersal by auction of a sizable portion of its contents. Paine therefore had access to books and marginalia that have disappeared as a result of the first auction and the final sale

in 1951.[7] With this material at his disposal Paine certainly may be charged with extreme selectivity in characterizing Clemens's library and his reading.

One piece of evidence in particular gives a clue to Paine's methods and motives in outlining Clemens's literary tastes. This is one of the most trusted documents in Mark Twain scholarship—the well-known declaration of his reading preferences that Paine reported Clemens had scribbled on an unused envelope around 1874. Paine quoted this manuscript while analyzing the reading program Clemens and Theodore Crane undertook jointly during the summer of 1874. "On the back of an old envelope," explained Paine, "Mark Twain set down his literary declaration of this period. 'I like history, biography, travels, curious facts and strange happenings, and science. And I detest novels, poetry and theology.'"[8] Its firm tone and sweeping dismissal of the latter three categories coincided with the curmudgeonly pronouncements expected of Twain by many people.

Lest the reader doubt such an absolute statement, Paine reproduced a facsimile of the envelope directly beneath his quotation on page 512 of *Mark Twain: A Biography*. This reproduction has given scholars a sense of security about its authenticity, but its message has puzzled and bothered several who have compared these statements with what is known about Clemens's reading habits. While accepting its authority and its dating by Paine, DeLancey Ferguson fretted in 1943 that though its "affirmation was accurate," he found "the negation too sweeping."[9] Ferguson noted astutely: "He might be said to have loved theology, as an unfailing target

MARK TWAIN

"Correct!" comments Clemens. "He has proceeded from unreasoned selfishness to reasoned selfishness. All our acts, reasoned and unreasoned, are selfish." It was a conclusion he logically never departed from; not the happiest one, it would seem, at first glance, but one easier to deny than to disprove.

On the back of an old envelope Mark Twain set down his literary declaration of this period.

"I like history, biography, travels, curious facts and strange happenings, and science. And I detest novels, poetry, and theology."

But of course the novels of Howells would be excepted; Lecky was not theology, but the history of it; his taste for poetry would develop later, though it would never become a fixed quantity, as was his devotion to history and science. His interest in these amounted to a passion.

Albert Bigelow Paine's facsimile of the envelope as it appeared in Mark Twain: A Biography *(New York: Harper, 1912), p. 512*

Clemens's notes as they actually appear on the envelope (Mark Twain Papers, Bancroft Library, University of California, Berkeley; copyright © 2019)

for his derision, and his avowed dislike of novels and poetry was far from absolute. His use of them for purposes of parody and burlesque shows that he had read most of the standard popular poets of his day." Arthur L. Scott addressed the question of whether this celebrated assertion actually represented a lifelong commitment. "About 1874 Mark Twain jotted several notes on the back of a tiny envelope," Scott conceded. But then Scott brought up Mark Twain's contradictory enthusiasm for theological debates, and pointed out that he also "loved poetry." Consequently Scott called for a re-evaluation of the importance attached to this document: "It is time that we stop judging the literary taste of a volatile man like Mark Twain by a thought hurriedly scrawled near the start of his professional career."[10]

Fortunately the envelope on which Clemens wrote his declaration of reading preferences survives in a file of miscellaneous fragments in the Mark Twain Papers;[11] examination of it proves that Scott and other critics were justified in being baffled by the paradox of its sentiments and the known record of Clemens's reading—but not for the reason Scott supposed. Scott and other scholars such as Walter Blair[12] had too easily accepted the date Paine assigned to the envelope. By including the envelope facsimile in the chapter that described Clemens's summer activities in 1874 and referring to it as "his literary declaration of this period," Paine effectually discouraged anyone from questioning its date. The envelope itself bears no postmark or any other indication of the year in which it was used—except for Paine's note to himself in one corner (" '74"), a method of annotation he applied to many materials in the course of editing the biography and the collected letters. The steadily diminishing size of Clemens's script is a helpful clue in establishing the date of manuscripts, but the handwriting reproduced in the *Biography* facsimile of the envelope, while incongruously cramped and compressed for 1874, might have been reduced in size for the purposes of the illustration. When the envelope itself is inspected, however, there can be no doubt that it is grossly misdated in the *Biography*; Clemens's neat, diminutive, compact style of handwriting clearly belongs to a date after 1900.

In fact Clemens made the comments on that envelope in or after November 1909. Proof of this is contained in the contiguous notes that Paine refrained from mentioning and which he omitted—probably with some difficulty—from the facsimile illustration. Directly above his declaration Clemens had begun his note by listing the titles or authors of five specific books: "The Agony Column./2 books by Rev. C. W. Bardsley/Wanderings in Patagonia./The Martyrs of Science (Brewster)". He then drew a line across the width of the envelope and proceeded to write in the same purple ink: "I like history, biography, travels, curious facts & strange happenings, & science./And I detest novels, poetry &

theology." His pronouncement takes on a different significance when it can be interpreted as a topical reference to specific books: an ephemeral novel, Catharine Dawson Scott's *The Agony Column*, is contrasted with two volumes by the Reverend Charles W. E. Bardsley on the history of English surnames, a travel book that recounts Julius Beerbohm's adventures in a remote region (its full title is *Wanderings in Patagonia: Life Among the Ostrich-Hunters*), and Sir David Brewster's biographies of Galileo, Tycho Brahe, and Kepler. Scott's novel provides the key to dating these notes; the last-published book in the list, it was issued in November 1909.

Obviously Paine wished to give the impression that this dictum represented the early manifestation of a view to which Clemens adhered throughout his life. Yet in actuality Clemens made these notes after his literary career had effectually ended. Because of the prominence that Paine gave this envelope in the *Biography* Mark Twain scholars have struggled to reconcile it with his catholic reading interests. Now it can be relegated to a properly minor status by assigning it to the biographical period to which it really belongs.

With assistance such as Paine was willing to render, the image of Mark Twain that lingers among teachers of English is that of the unbookish folk humorist. Twain, who sought to be accounted a self-taught literary artist, would be gratified. Paine thoroughly implanted and fostered the idea that Twain seldom read and then only haphazardly in unconventional works, and that his responses were invariably opinionative to extremes.

Scholarship has slowly stripped away part of this fallacy. Clemens will eventually be known as a man who was committed to reading as a daily activity, a regular subscriber to urban newspapers and national magazines, an inquisitive, constant, omnivorous (if impulsive and arbitrary) peruser of reading materials. Admittedly his reading was far less programmatic than that of a regular literary reviewer such as William Dean Howells. But the diversity and magnitude of Clemens's acquaintance with books spanned cultures and centuries to an extent seldom appreciated, included large quantities of the fiction, drama, poetry, and theology he supposedly abhorred, and surely represented an astonishing knowledge of literature even for a Nook Farm resident.

Notes

1   Olin H. Moore of Ohio State University launched the study of Mark Twain's literary sources with "Mark Twain and Don Quixote," *PMLA* 37.2 (June 1922): 324–346. Henry A. Pochmann's master's thesis, "The Mind of Mark Twain" (University of Texas at Austin, 1924), concluded correctly that "though unacademic, he was not unread" and urged abandonment of the view that Twain's literary accomplishments were the products of "self-originating genius" (p. 1). A steady procession of scholars has since examined the question of Twain's familiarity with other authors' works. Walter Blair's acknowledgment that Twain "ranged avidly and widely through literature of many sorts" (*Mark Twain & Huck Finn* [Berkeley: University of California Press, 1960], p. 13) is a typical appraisal.

2   *Mark Twain's Letters*, ed. Albert Bigelow Paine (New York: Harper, 1917), pp. 489–490.

3   *Mark Twain: A Biography* (New York: Harper, 1912), pp. 510–512—hereafter cited as *MTB*.

4   Paine, *MTB*, 1536–40.

5   Paine, *MTB*, p. 1576.

6   By the late 1880s Clemens had begun portraying himself as a limited, eccentric reader. "Personally I never cared for a fiction or storybook," he told Rudyard Kipling in 1889. "What I like to read about are facts and statistics of any kind" ("An Interview with Mark Twain," collected in *From Sea to Sea: Letters of Travel*. 2 vols. [New York: Doubleday and McClure, [1899], 2: 180). "With modern writers of fiction I confess I have no very extensive acquaintance," Clemens assured another newspaper interviewer in 1895. "I read little but the 'heaviest' sort of literature—history, biography, travels" ("Visit of Mark Twain: Wit and Humour," Sydney [Australia] *Morning Herald*, 17 September 1895, pp. 5–6, reprinted by Louis J. Budd in "Mark Twain Talks Mostly about Humor and Humorists," *Studies in American Humor* 1.1 [April 1974]: 8 and by Gary Scharnhorst in *Mark Twain: The Complete Interviews* [Tuscaloosa: University of Alabama Press, 2006], p. 205.) Clemens repeatedly made similar professions of literary ignorance.

7   "The Library and Manuscripts of Samuel L. Clemens," Anderson Auction Company, Catalogue No. 892. To be sold 7–8 February 1911. (Items 1–500 are mostly books from Clemens's library.) An additional 310 books are listed in a catalog titled "Mark Twain Library Auction," 10 April 1951, Hollywood, California. See my article, "The Dispersal of Samuel L. Clemens' Library Books," *Resources for American Literary Study* 5.2 (Autumn 1975): 147–165. (A revised version of this essay appears as a chapter in the present volume.)

8   Paine, *MTB*, p. 512.

9   Ferguson, *Mark Twain: Man and Legend* (Indianapolis: Bobbs-Merrill, 1943), p. 206.

10   Scott, *On the Poetry of Mark Twain* (Urbana: University of Illinois Press, 1966), p. 1.

11   Bancroft Library, University of California, Berkeley.

12   Blair, "The French Revolution and *Huckleberry Finn*," *Modern Philology* 55.1 (August 1957): 21.

An earlier version of this chapter appeared in Tennessee Studies in Literature *22 (1977): 154–161.*

24

'Stolen from Books, Tho' Credit Given'

Mark Twain's Use of Literary Sources

When the S.S. *Smyrniote* lay becalmed on its voyage from the Sandwich Islands to San Francisco in 1866, Mark Twain used his unanticipated leisure to ransack the ship's library for material suitable to incorporate in travel sketches and lectures. For twenty-five monotonous days the clipper slowly pursued its return journey from Honolulu, while Twain doggedly plowed through or else skimmed ("few of these books readable," he noted to himself) the numerous volumes that dealt with Hawaii. To his great disappointment most of them proved useless for his purposes. Notebook 5 records his incredulous reaction; there he damned the writer who first invented the phrase "can be better imagined than described" and bemoaned his frustrating situation. "With 100 island books before me, I have thought, now this piece of scenery is described in these, & I can steal and re-hash—turn & find them shirking, with that hackneyed expression, or 'What hath God wrought!'"[1]

Evidently he seldom encountered this frustration thereafter, for most of his travel writings reveal an unabashed dependence on the narratives of preceding tourists. Partly, no doubt, this habit derived from his journalistic training in the Far West, where editors filched from the columns of Eastern newspapers, magazines, and reference books as the exigencies of deadlines demanded. In Chapter 55 of *Roughing It* (1872) Mark Twain claimed that while acting as chief editor of the *Territorial Enterprise* he repeatedly "copied an elaborate editorial out of the 'American Cyclopedia,' that steadfast friend of the editor, all over this land."[2] Perhaps he also remembered the casual manner in which his brother Orion had filled spaces in his Hannibal *Journal* with quotations from Boswell's *Johnson* and other respected literary sources.[3]

Hamlin Hill demonstrated how the requirements for successful subscription book publishing—bulky books chock-full of historical facts and geographical information, interspersed with humor and sensationalism—encouraged Twain to borrow widely from others' writings.[4] That tendency in his works led Sydney J. Krause to remark that "if anything, Twain's were the [reading] tastes of a man of letters in search of literary materials," someone who "read mainly for *use*."[5] This was true at least in regard to his travel volumes. In *Innocents Abroad* (1869) he utilized to good advantage the poorly appointed ship library the *Quaker City* pilgrims collected. A few other volumes, such as William C. Prime's *Tent Life in the Holy Land*, became objects of his satire; from books like the Reverend David Randall's *Handwriting of God* he extracted descriptive details and usable facts. Even his highflown paean to the Sphinx owed much to Alexander William Kinglake's popular *Eōthen*.[6] In *A Tramp Abroad* (1880) the narrator relies on guidebooks wherever he goes, often quoting or paraphrasing their descriptions. If this is unoriginal, he implies, at least he never displays the ignorance of the conceited young American he met in Switzerland, a lad who confided, "I don't read when I'm knocking round like this, having a good time" and then asserted that he had just seen "the chapel where William Tell used to preach" (Chapter 27).

These predilections Mark Twain also displayed in *Roughing It*, of which Robert Regan observed, "The author is . . . a scholarly student of the West who attaches documentary appendices to his humorous book, refers familiarly to austere tomes of anthropology, and approaches phenomena experimentally, in the manner of a natural historian."[7] Yet his studious approach to that volume was outdone a decade later by his procedures for writing *Life on the Mississippi* (1883). On 22 July 1882 his publishers assured him that they were shipping "a lot of books relating to travels in the U.S. by English people in the first half of this century; twentyfive volumes in all. They include Mrs. Trollope, Basil Hall and [Frederick] Marryatt, &c., &c. Their average price is about a dollar per *volume*. Please return any you do not wish for."[8] Twain supplemented these travel guides and descriptions with additional volumes borrowed from George Washington Cable, whom he visited in New Orleans in May 1882. Cable wrote on 7 November 1882, following a visit to Hartford: "I sent the books to you a day or two ago (on the 4th). Mrs. Cable had failed to find them all and even now they do not conform exactly to the list you kept."[9] Clemens notified Cable on 15 January 1883: "I have just finished my book at last & was about to return the volumes you so kindly lent me. I'll get'm started this afternoon or tomorrow."[10]

An idea of his composing methods for sections of *Life on the Mississippi* can be gained from his letter to William Dean Howells of 30 October 1882: "I went to work at nine o'clock yesterday morning, and went to bed an hour after midnight. Result of the day, (mainly stolen from books, tho' credit given,) 9500 words. . . . I have nothing more to borrow or steal; the rest must all be writing."[11] Not only did he openly admit this copying to Howells, but he considered it a praiseworthy feat to have read and incorporated so much within fifteen hours. Remember, advised Hamlin Hill, "the subscription-book readers wanted knowledge and information."[12] Twain contrasted the crude American institutions and ill-mannered people of the Mississippi River Valley sketched half a century earlier by Frances Trollope, Charles Dickens, Harriet

Irene Langdon, widow of Jervis Langdon Jr., donates William C. Prime's Tent Life in the Holy Land *(1857) to Elmira College, 2008. This valuable book—belonging to Charlie Langdon and heavily annotated by Clemens—had remained in the Langdon family collection.*

Martineau, Charles Murray, Basil Hall, Henry Fearon, Frederick Marryat, George Combe, and others with the orderly, prosperous society apparent to the contemporary traveler in the 1880s. Generally he cited his source, but not with scholarly precision; book titles were seldom supplied. In analyzing Twain's use of travel accounts in *Life on the Mississippi*, Dewey Ganzel wrote: "His use of quotation marks is sometimes casual—they do not always mean verbatim reference. Neither does he treat his sources consistently. Although he does not quote Fearon with perfect accuracy,

he does so with little elaboration. . . . Combe, on the other hand, he elaborates with some freedom, embroidering detail for a more dramatic effect."[13]

Twain followed the same procedure in writing *Following the Equator* (1897): "Quote all sorts of authors to back up any doubtful statement about India," he urged himself while touring Jeypore in March 1896.[14] In that book Twain was relatively meticulous (for his historical period) in citing the sources of quotations. Obviously he had found it expedient for a professional humorist to signal to his reader with footnotes and quotation marks that he was not manufacturing or distorting the fiery custom of *Suttee* or the grisly murders committed by the *Thugs*. He was not writing for a scholarly audience, and he merely wanted to indicate the breadth of his research and the unimpeachability of his sources; the perfunctory mention of an author or title therefore sufficed.

Still, he was not finicky about slightly modifying someone else's words to suit his context more appropriately. In Chapter 48 of *Following the Equator* he describes the practice of *Suttee* or self-sacrifice by widows in India, and mentions that "Major Sleeman has a convincing case in one of his books." He narrates the gist of Sleeman's experience (never supplying more than this casual hint of its source), and then quotes the outcome of Sleeman's unsuccessful efforts to prevent a woman from self-immolation in honor of her deceased husband. The original version in Chapter 4 of W. H. Sleeman's *Rambles and Recollections of an Indian Official* (1844) contains two sentences and a word Twain omitted without indicating ellipsis:

I had sentries placed all [a]round, and no other person was allowed to approach within five paces. *As she rose up fire was set to the pile, and it was instantly in a blaze. The distance was about 150 yards.* She came on with a calm and cheerful countenance, stopped once, and, casting her eyes upward, said, 'Why have they kept me five days from thee, my husband?' On coming to the sentries her supporters stopped [and remained standing; she moved on, and]; *she* walked once [a] round the pit, paused a moment, and, while muttering a prayer, threw some flowers into the fire. She then walked up deliberately and steadily to the brink, stepped into the centre of the flame, sat down, and leaning back in the midst as if reposing upon a couch, was consumed without uttering a shriek or betraying one sign of agony.[15]

Mark Twain's minimal additions (the words and letters in square brackets) are intended to aid the reader in visualizing the scene; his deletions (the italicized words) eliminate superfluous details. These purposes are also apparent in another quotation from Sleeman's *Rambles and Recollections of an Indian Official* that Mark Twain used in Chapter 49 of *Following the Equator*: "Sleeman says: 'It is perhaps not known to many of my countrymen, even in India, that in every town and city in the country the right of sweeping the houses and streets is a monopoly, and is supported entirely by the pride of castes among the scavengers, who are all of the lowest class." Actually Sleeman had written in Chapter 8: "It is not, perhaps, known to many of my countrymen in India that in every city and town in the country

the right of sweeping the houses and streets is one of the most intolerable of monopolies, supported entirely by the pride of caste among the scavengers, who are all of the lowest class." Alterations in syntax and a few omissions produce an altogether different tone, less editorial and more circumstantial. Aside from such stylistic liberties, however, Twain's versions of quoted material show fidelity to main points and narrative order. He drops irrelevant or distracting details where possible, amending the passages so that the subject matter comes into clearer focus. It might be said that in his travel books he grew more and more explicit in acknowledging his borrowings and citing his sources, although he never attempted to provide the bibliographic data now normally expected for quotation. The sources in *Following the Equator* are less submerged and easier to detect and identify than those used in *Innocents Abroad* or *Roughing It*. As his literary reputation increased Mark Twain apparently grew more secure about openly quoting other authors.

In his travel writings Twain delved into history whenever he turned up relevant material, but in such works as *The Prince and the Pauper* (1881), *A Connecticut Yankee* (1889), and *Joan of Arc* (1896) he undertook specialized historical research with definite purposes in mind. His self-conscious references to his reading in these works functioned like those in his travel writings that distinguish the factual sightseer from the comic persona. Leon T. Dickinson explained[16] that Twain paraded his sources in order to infuse the novel with a serious tone and to lend credibility to a work written by a well-known humorist. But in *A Connecticut Yankee* he brought forward history books as ammunition. Howard G. Baetzhold noted that

> most of the borrowings illustrate man's subjection to the combined religious and secular "superstitions" underlying the concepts of monarchy, aristocracy, and the Established Church. . . . The author's use of his sources, therefore, suggests that he intended the novel to serve as an implicit examination of man's "slavery" to "superstition," not only as it existed in medieval times but as it had persisted down through the centuries into his own age.[17]

Twain's predilection for supplying documentation implies that he considered books based on actual "facts" to be superior to entirely imaginative writing. During the final decade of his life this inclination led him to prepare autobiographical dictations based entirely on his own experiences that were nevertheless buttressed by extracts from letters, newspaper articles, and other authenticating texts.

His penchant for historical research culminated in a lengthy and exacting study for *Joan of Arc*. To achieve the sense of authority he desired, Twain devoured at least a dozen biographies—a number of them in French. Albert E. Stone Jr. remarked that "few men in his generation were as widely read in the lore of Joan of Arc as Twain himself."[18] As early as September 1891 Mark Twain reminded himself to request Chatto & Windus of London to send him "Joan of Arc books."[19] They complied over a period of years. On 6 March 1893 he wrote to the publishing firm

while he was in Florence: "I thank you ever so much for the Joan of Arc; I knew of this sketch but had not met with it before."[20] He wrote again on 12 June 1893: "I wish to thank you most heartily for the sumptuous Joan of Arc you sent me while I was gone to America."[21] From Paris he informed Henry H. Rogers on 29 January 1895 that "the first two-thirds of the book were easy; for I only needed to keep my historical road straight; therefore I used for reference only one French history and one English one. . . . But on this last third I have constantly used five French sources and five English ones, and I think no telling historical nugget in any of them has escaped me."[22] So fulfilling were these exertions that he was sorry when he completed the book. He described the shock he received upon sending the manuscript to the printer and then reentering his study: "All the litter and the confusion are gone. The piles of dusty reference books are gone from the chairs, the maps from the floor; the chaos of letters, manuscripts, notebooks, paper knives, pipes, matches, photographs, tobacco jars, and cigar boxes is gone from the writing table."[23] Years later he averred that he liked *Joan of Arc* best of all his books because "it furnished me seven times the pleasure afforded me by any of the others: 12 years of preparation & 2 years of writing. The others needed no preparation, & got none."[24]

His other books may not have required the intensive research of his *Joan of Arc* project, but they certainly drew upon extensive reading. Today, however, critics and readers alike agree that the finest passages in his writings are those that give the fewest clues to this reading. We do not employ the same criteria as his subscription-book audience; what we think of as the "real" Mark Twain portions of *Innocents Abroad*, *Roughing It*, or *Following the Equator* are those anecdotal monologues scattered about between his introductions of quoted matter. The modern audience is surfeited with information about foreign lands and historical periods; it cares little or nothing as to whether Twain produces authorities to verify his accounts. The least interesting passages in his travel narratives are those where his reading was inadequately melded with his genius for describing or fictionalizing.

However, an impressive capacity to integrate literary materials seamlessly is on display in *Adventures of Huckleberry Finn* (1885), which received no formal preparatory research. Many researchers, beginning with Olin H. Moore[25] and Henry Pochmann,[26] have traced the ingenious ways in which Twain included in this novel various elements from his lifelong reading. The book-addled character named Tom Sawyer became one means of introducing many of these allusions. In both *The Adventures of Tom Sawyer* (1876) and *Adventures of Huckleberry Finn* Tom Sawyer places unswerving faith in "authorities" such as pirate and robber dime-novels. "I've seen it in books; and so of course that's what we've got to do," emphasizes Tom in Chapter 2 of the latter work. "Do you want to go to doing different from what's in the books, and get things all muddled up?" Subsequently he would flaunt his erudition about the Far West and Indians ("Huck and Tom among the Indians"), Walter Scott's works and the Arabian Nights (*Tom Sawyer Abroad*), and detective stories by Allan

Pinkerton and Arthur Conan Doyle ("Tom Sawyer's Conspiracy"). But the majority of today's readers feel that in the last segment of *Huckleberry Finn*—where Tom Sawyer draws on Baron Trenck, Casanova, Dumas, Cellini, and others for the rope ladder, bloody journal, trained mouse, and smuggled tools foisted upon the helpless Jim—Twain unduly protracted Tom's tendencies. Walter Blair, who decided from a careful sifting of evidence that Mark Twain poured into his masterpiece many years of diverse reading in addition to river lore and childhood memories, conceded that this drawn-out burlesque of dungeon literature was an instance where Twain's literary borrowings led him into excesses. Blair concurred with most critics in perceiving a decline in creative powers from the engrossing river-raft episodes to the boys' horseplay on the Phelps plantation. "A study of Twain's use of sources here shows little about his versatile skill in adaptation," Blair admitted.[27]

Mark Twain's reading of course contributed directly to many other novels, stories, and essays. He played with Malory's *Morte D'Arthur* in *A Connecticut Yankee in King Arthur's Court* in his best-known literary burlesque. He wrote critical reviews of Edward Dowden's *Shelley*, Cooper's *Leather-Stocking Tales*, and Bourget's *Outre-Mer*, and began numerous others. He explicitly parodied Sherlock Holmes's adventures in "A Double-Barrelled Detective Story" (1902). His essay on William Dean Howells (1906) employed a close analysis of Howells's writings.

The modern reader may regret that Twain's reading led him into an investigation of Christian Science; his diatribes against

Mary Baker Eddy and her defenders are dull for any but the most vehement partisan. This type of muckraking preoccupied him during the final decade of his life, and he read avidly as each new reformist crusade occurred to him. If his overt campaign against Eddy now seems a misapplication of his talents and energy, and if his championship of the Francis Bacon cause in the controversy over the Shakespeare canon strikes us as quaintly mistaken, we can at least respect his investing so much time in reading up on American imperialism in the Philippines, mob lynchings in the American South, abuses of animal vivisection, missionary interventions in China, the Russian Czar's edicts, the Russo-Japanese War, copyright laws, the cruelty of bullfights, and colonial atrocities in the Belgian Congo. He read everything he could find that related to these subjects, one by one, as he readied onslaughts at his targets. Reading was always for him the first stage of polemical writing. In the long interval between his taunts at visitors to the Holy Land and his jabs at William McKinley, Theodore Roosevelt, and King Leopold there was scarcely a single year when he did not borrow from books in constructing his own works. For the most part he excelled at his craft in those passages that, if influenced by books, give the least outward sign of it. A knowledge of his reading permits us to judge when and how he incorporated literary resources most successfully.

NOTES

1   *Notebooks & Journals*, ed. Frederick Anderson, Michael B. Frank, and Kenneth M. Sanderson (Berkeley: University of California Press, 1975) 1: 159.

2   *Roughing It*, ed. Harriet Elinor Smith and Robert Pack Browning (Berkeley: University of California Press, 1993), p. 377.

3   Summarized by Minnie M. Brashear, *Mark Twain: Son of Missouri* (Chapel Hill: University of North Carolina Press, 1934), pp. 142–143.

4   Hill, "Mark Twain: Audience and Artistry," *American Quarterly* 15.1 (Spring 1963): 25–40.

5   Krause, *Mark Twain as Critic* (Baltimore: Johns Hopkins Press, 1967), pp. 15, 16.

6   Henry Nash Smith—*Mark Twain: The Development of a Writer* (Cambridge, Massachusetts: Harvard University Press, 1962), p. 29—shows how Twain modeled his description on Kinglake's version.

7   Regan, *Unpromising Heroes: Mark Twain and His Characters* (Berkeley: University of California Press, 1966), pp. 61–62.

8   W. Rowlands of James R. Osgood & Company, Boston, to Clemens, ALS in the Mark Twain Papers, Bancroft Library, University of California, Berkeley—hereafter cited as MTP; partially quoted in *Mark Twain's Letters to His Publishers*, ed. Hamlin Hill (Berkeley: University of California Press, 1967), p. 158 n. 2.

9   Guy A. Cardwell, *Twins of Genius* (East Lansing: Michigan State College Press, 1953), p. 87.

10 Cardwell, *Twins of Genius*, p. 89.

11 *Mark Twain-Howells Letters*, ed. Henry Nash Smith and William M. Gibson (Cambridge, Massachusetts: Harvard University Press, 1960), p. 417.

12 Hill, "Audience and Artistry," p. 31.

13 Ganzel, "Twain, Travel Books, and *Life on the Mississippi*," *American Literature* 34.1 (March 1962): 45.

14 Notebook 36, TS p. 56, MTP.

15 Italics added. Sleeman, *Rambles and Recollections of an Indian Official*, ed. Vincent Arthur Smith, 2 vols. (London: Archibald Constable and Co., 1893), 1, 26–27.

16 Dickinson, "The Sources of *The Prince and the Pauper*," *Modern Language Notes* 64.2 (February 1949): 103–106.

17 Baetzhold, *Mark Twain and John Bull: The British Connection* (Bloomington: Indiana University Press, 1970), p. 132.

18 Stone, *The Innocent Eye: Childhood in Mark Twain's Imagination* (New Haven: Yale University Press, 1961), p. 207.

19 Notebook 31, TS p. 6, MTP.

20 ALS owned in 1979 by Barry Bingham Sr., Louisville, Kentucky.

21 TS in MTP.

22 *Mark Twain's Correspondence with Henry Huttleston Rogers*, ed. Lewis Leary (Berkeley: University of California Press, 1969), p. 125.

23 Mark Twain, "The Finished Book," Paris 1895, collected in *Europe and Elsewhere, The Writings of Mark Twain*, Definitive Edition (New York: Gabriel Wells, 1922), 29: 299.

24 Clemens to an unidentified correspondent, 30 November 1908, MTP.

25 Moore, "Mark Twain and Don Quixote," *PMLA* 37.2 (June 1922), 324–346.

26 Pochmann, "The Mind of Mark Twain," master's thesis, University of Texas at Austin, 1924, especially pp. 15–16, 151–159.

27 Blair, "The French Revolution and *Huckleberry Finn*," *Modern Philology* 55.1 (August 1957): 25.

An earlier version of this chapter appeared in Mosaic: A Journal for the Comparative Study of Literature and Idea*s 12:4 (Summer 1979): 149–155.*

25

The Unfortunate Fate of the Clemenses' Library Collection

The two auctions of the Clemens family's library arranged by Clemens's only surviving daughter Clara would themselves merit an investigative monograph, if only more facts could be obtained about their circumstances and results. As things stand, however, the records of these calamitous disposals are lamentably sketchy. Both Henry Nash Smith and Frederick Anderson, two consecutive editors of the Mark Twain Papers at Berkeley, told me that they had been informed by people who knew Clara Clemens Gabrilowitsch personally that in her father's final days he had advised her and his designated biographer Albert Bigelow Paine not to wait very long to dispose of his literary effects. Having seen the transience of the reputations of most humorists of his generation, he became anxious toward the end of his days about how long his fame was apt to last. In accordance with Clemens's admonitions, Clara and Paine, the latter of whom functioned as Clemens's literary executor, listed nearly five hundred of Clemens's association copies, many of them embellished with fragments of his literary manuscripts, for sale at the Anderson Auction Company in New York City early in 1911. The lucky bidders obtained their prizes at what today seem like bargain prices: Clemens's annotated copy of Richard Irving Dodge's *The Plains of the Great West and Their Inhabitants* (1877) went for only $14 ($336 today); James Parton's two-volume *Life of Voltaire* brought $9 ($216 now); four of Francis Parkman's histories, marked and with notes by Clemens, fetched a total of $22.50 ($540 today). Within months of this original 1911 auction numerous buyers began putting their acquisitions up for resale, and in the years to come many hundreds of the books would change hands over and over again. These association items have almost never failed to gain interest from dedicated and affluent collectors as well as amateur Mark Twain fans.

THE 1951 AUCTION

A second major auction held forty years later in the Hollywood Hills was a much more chaotic and (at least for literary scholars) disastrous affair, scheduled abruptly, conducted by a firm that usually auctioned furniture and interior decorations, and characterized by a general "carnival-like" atmosphere, according to buyers and witnesses. Now married to a man who had persuaded her to part with her five-acre estate and its furnishings, Clara Clemens Gabrilowitsch Samossoud sold both her two-story Mediterranean-style home and the majority of the books from her father's library that she still possessed at a rapidly advertised auction on April 10, 1951. A huge but unknown total of books went under the gavel at Clara's residence. The auctioneer firm only had time to compile for bidders a rudimentary sale sheet of abbreviated authors and titles. In the majority of cases this cryptic two-page list raised more questions about the identities of the books than it answered. The prices for the often-annotated volumes were better than those fetched in the 1911 sale, but not nearly so much as might be expected, largely because of the haste with which the auction was mounted and the lack of national publicity. A bidder walked off with *The Arabian Nights* for $10; someone purchased John Fiske's *A Century of Science* for $12.50; another person bought Howells's autobiographical *Boy Life* for $15; Whittier's nostalgic *Snowbound* sold for $22.50; a copy of Kipling's *Just So Stories for Little Children*, inscribed by Clemens to Olivia Clemens, was hammered down for $27.50; P. T. Barnum's boastful autobiography, *Struggles and Triumphs*, brought only $37. A heavily marked copy of Robert Browning's verse went for $70 (equivalent to $640 today), and a seven-volume,

annotated set of Thomas Macaulay's essays brought $160 ($1,464 now).

The Hollywood event was a literary scholar's nightmare and a forger's windfall; its bad results—including the loss of many books that were acquired by curious passersby or casual buyers attracted by the newspaper

MARK TWAIN LIBRARY

AUCTION

Tuesday, April 10th—1 and 7:30 P. M.

2005 North La Brea Avenue

Inspection: Sunday—12 Noon to 6 P.M. Only

E. F. Whitman, Mgr.   F. B. O'Connor, Auctioneer
    7940 Sunset Blvd.   HO 9-1639

This catalogue is intended only as a guide for the buyers. Care has been taken in listing the following items, but no guarantee is made either by the owner of or the auctioneer as to the description, genuineness, authenticity or condition of any item. Every item is sold "as is" and without recourse.

Personal Notations and Marginal Notes by Mark Twain

1a Personal Memoirs of U. S. Grant, 2 vols., presented to Mr. Clemens by Mrs. U. S. Grant, 1885; signed by S.L.C.
2a The Underground Railroad, by Wm. Still; a story by S. L. C. on flyleaf.
3a Salem Witchcraft, collection by Robert Calef, Cotton Mather and Samuel Fowler.
4a The Life and Letters of Lord Macaulay, by Otto Trevelyan.
5a The Greville Memoirs, reigns of King George IV and King William IV.
6a Views of Religion, by Rufus K. Noyes, M.D.; presented to S. L. C. by the author.
7a William Allingham, a diary by H. Allingham and D. Radford.
8a Memoirs of Wilhelmine, Margravine of Baireuth, translated and edited by Her Royal Highness Princess Christian.
9a Roman Society, by Samuel Dill.
10a Three Generations of English Women, by Janet Ross; presented by author to S. L. C.
11a The Life of Pasteur, by Rene Vallery-Radot.
12a Cuchulain of Muirthemne, by Lady Gregory; presented to S.L.C. by author; letter from author also enclosed.
13a Memoirs of the Duke of Saint-Simon, 3 vols.
14a Letters of James Russell Lowell, 2 vols.
15a A History of the Warfare of Science with Theology in Christendom, by Andrew D. White, 2 vols.; personal notations and newspaper clipping.
16a The Heavens, by Guillemin.
17a The Shakespeare Problem Restate, by Geo. Greenwood.
18a Sidelights on Astronomy, by Simon Newcomb.
19a Society As I Have Found It, by Ward McAllister.
20a The Viper of Milan, by Marjorie Bowen.
21a Salthaven, by W. W. Jacobs, plus a letter from S. L. C. dated 1908.
22a The French Revolution, by Thomas Carlyle.
23a Sir George Grey, the Romance of a Pro-Counsul.
24a Kenelm Chillingly, his Adventures and Opinions.
25a The Life of the Bee, by Maurice Maeterlinck.
26a The Love Letters of Dorothy Osborne to Sir Wm. Temple
27a The Pen and the Book, by Walter Besant.
28a Sketches of Creation, by Alexander Winchell.
29a The Jesuits in North America, by Francis Parkman.
30a Grose's Dictionary of the Vulgar Tongue
31a Origin of Religions, Aryan Sun-Myths.
32a The Pith of Astronomy, by Samuel G. Bayne; clipping of Professor Lowell's Lecture on How the World Dies.
33a The Luck of Roaring Camp and other sketches by Francis Bret Harte.
34a The Celebrated Jumping Frog, by Mark Twain.

Auction, Hollywood, California, 1951

35a Autobiography of Moncure Daniel Conway, 2 vols.
36a History of European Morals, by William Edward Hartpole Lecky, M.A.; Vol. II.
37a Studies in Venetian History, by Horatio Brown, 2 vols.
38a The Sacred Anthology, collected and edited by Moncure Daniel Conway.
39a Life, Letters and Journals of George Ticknor.
40a More Tramps Abroad, by Mark Twain.
41a The First Christmas, by Lew Wallace.
42a The Letters of Madame de Servigne, edited by Mrs. Hale
43a History of European Morals, by William Edward Hartpole Lecky, M.A.
44a Extracts from Adam's Diary, by Mark Twain.
45a Letters of Dr. John Brown, edited by his son and D. W. Forrest.
46a Boer War Lyrics, by Louis Selmer; a personal letter to S. L. C. by the author.
47a The Story of France, by Thomas E. Watson, Vol. I.
48a Robert Browning, 8 vols. Parleyings, Men and Women, Dramas, Aristophane and Other Poems, The Ring and the Book, Dramatic Ilys, Dramatis Personae, etc., Inn Album.
49a The Poetical Works of Levi Bishop.
50a The Country of the Dwarfs, by Paul Du Chaillu.
51a Mark Twain—Adams Tagebuch.
52a The Old Regime in Canada, by Francis Parkman.
53a Mark Twain—A Dog's Tale.
54a Hawthorn and Lavender, by Wm. Ernest Henley.
55a Mary Twain—A Tramp Abroad.
56a Robert Browning—Parleying With Cetrain People.
57a A Frenchman in America, by Max O'Rell.
58a Heart Echoes, by George Edward Lewis.
59a The Myths of the Rhine, by Prof. M. Schele de Vere.
60a Macaulay's Miscellaneous Essays, Vol. I through Vol. VII, incl.
61a The Cycle of Life, by C. W. Saleeby.
62a The Church of St. Bunco, by Gordon Clark.
63a Asia and Europe, by Meredith Townsend.

Autographed by S. L. Clemens

1c History of France, by Francois Pierre Guillavums Guizot, 6 vols.
2c Our Living World (6 books all about animal life with illustrations).
3c Jeanne d'Arc, by Raconte's Par L'Image, with illus.
4c Don Quixote, by Cervantes, with illustrations.
5c Manners: Customs, the Arts and Dress During the Middle Ages, by Paul Lacroix.
6c The Furniture of Our Forefathers, by Esther Singleton. 2 vols. (illustrated).
7c Autobiography of Andrew Dickson White, 2 vols.
8c The Life of Pasteur, by Rene Vallery-Radot.
9c Memoirs of General W. T. Sherman, written by himself, 2 vols.
10c The Indians Book—made and illustratel by Indians.
11c The Thousand and One Nights, by Edward William Lane, 3 vols.
12c Russia's Message, by William English Walling.
13c Old Times in The Colonies, by Charles Carleton Coffin. (illustrated).
14c The Life and Letters of Lord Macaulay, by G. Otto Trevelyan.
15c A Connecticut Yankee in King Arthur's Court, by Mark Twain.
16c Recollections of Baron de Frenilly, by Arthur Chuquet.
17c The History of Signboards, by Jacob Larwood and John Camden Hotten.
18c Memoirs of Barras, Member of the Directorate, 2 vols.
19c Life and Times of Sidney Smith, by Stuart J. Reid.
20c A History of the American People, by Woodrow Wilson. 5 vols.
21c Poems by Oliver Wendell Holmes.
22c Treasures of English Words and Phrases, by Peter Mark Roget, M.D., F.R.S.
23c The Prince and the Pauper, by Mark Twain.
24c The Land Beyond the Forest, by E. Gerard.
25c Silas Strong, Emperor of the Woods, by Irving Bacheller. Given to Mark Twain by the author.
26c Essays on Modern Novelists, by William Lyon Phelps. Given to Mark Twain by the author.
27c A Square Deal, by Theodore Roosevelt.
28c Choyce Drollery; Songs and Sonnets; Several Eminent authors.
29c Reminiscences of the Great Mutiny, by Williams Forbes Mitchell. Given to Mark Twain by the author.
30c In Our Town, by William Allen White. Given to Mark Twain by the author.
31c Two Years in the French West Indie, by Lafcadio Hearn
32c India—What Can It Teach Us? by F. Max Muller.
33c A Child-World, by James Whitcomb Riley. Given to Mark Twain by the author.
34c Rubaiyat of Doc Sifers, by James Whitcomb Riley. With author's signature and verse to Mark Twain.
35c A Pasteboard Crown, by Clara Morris. Given to Mark Twain by the author.
36c History of the War in the Peninsula and In the South South of France, by Maj.-Gen. Sir W.F.P. Napier, K.C.B.
37c English As She Is Taught, by Caroline B. Le Row.
38c Prudence Palfrey, by Thomas Bailey Aldrich. Given to Mark Twain by the author.
39c The New Testament
40c Shelley, by Francis Thompson.
41c The Historical Novel and Other Essays, by Brander Matthews. A book dedicated to Mark Twain and given to him by the author, who gives M. T. credit for the opinions.
42c The Pilgrim's Progress, by John Bunyan.
43c Legends of Florence, Retold by Charles Godfrey Leland.
44c The Canterbury Tales, by Geoffrey Chaucer.
45c Marjorie Daw and Other People, by Thomas Bailey Aldrich. Given to Mark Twain by the author.

Autographed by Mark Twain

46c From Ponapog to Pesth, by Thomas Bailey Aldrich. Given to Mark Twain by the author.
47c Pink Marsh, by George Ade. (illusstrated).
48c A Pair of Patient Lovers, by W. D. Howells. Given to Mark Twain by the author.
49c Ironquill—Moods in rhymes.
50c The Tale of the Great Mutiny, by W. H. Fritchett.
51c A Week in a French Country House, by Adelaide Sartoris.
52c Letters of Mrs. James G. Blaine. 2 vols.
53c Underground Russia, by Stepniak. With a personal note to Mark Twain by the author.
54c Judith of Bethulia, by Thomas Bailey Aldrich. Given to Mark Twain by the author.
55c By Reef and Palm, by Louis Becks. to M.T. from author.
56c Journal of a Voyage Round the World, by Chas. Darwin
57c Secret Memoirs of the Court of Berlin under William II, by H. W. Fischer.
58c London Films, by W. D. Howells.
59c The Five Nations, by Rudyard Kipling.
60c Men and Memoirs, by John Russell Young. Given to Mark Twain by the author.
61c Poets and Dreamers, by Lady Gregory. Given to Mark Twain by the author.
62c Notes on England, by T. Taine.
63c Short Studies on Great Subjects, by James Anthony Froude.
64c Die Letzte Rectenburgerin, by Von Louife Von Francois.
65c The Flight of Pony Baker, by W. D. Howells. Given to Mark Twain by the author.
66c The Jumping Frog, by Mark Twain.
67c The Queen of Sheba, by Thomas Bailey Aldrich. Given to Mark Twain by the author.
68c The Martyrdom of An Empress.
69c A Century of Science and Other Essays, by John Fiske.
70c The Stillwater Tragedy, by T. B. Aldrich. Given to Mark Twain by the author.
71c Snow-Bound, by John Greenleaf Whittier.
72c Wyndham Towers, by Thomas Bailey Aldrich. Given to Mark Twain by the author.
73c The Decameron or Ten Days' Entertainment of Baccaccio. Revised translation by W. K. Kelly.
74c New Conceptions in Science, by Carl Snyder.
75c Marie Bashkirtseff, Translated by Mary J. Serrano.
76c Life and Works of Charlotte Bronte.
77c Cloth of Gold and Other Poems, by Thomas Bailey Aldrich. Given to Mark Twain by the author.
78c Pigs Is Pigs, by Ellis Parker Butler. Given to Mark Twain by the author. Matthews.
79c Parts of Speech—Essays on English, by Brandner
80c Wanderers, by Wm. Winter. Given to M.T. by the author
81c A Chance Acquaintance, by W. D. Howells. Given to Mark Twain by the author.
82c The History of the Hebrew Nation, by Samuel Sharpe. Given to Mark Twain by the author.
83c Mark Twain (in German), The Prince and der Bettljunge.
84c The Chronicle of the Cid, edited by Richard Markham. (illustrated).
85c Holland House, by Princess Marie Liechtenstein.
86c Pottery and Porcelain, by William C. Pine.
87c The Life of Thomas Bailey Aldrich, by Ferris Greenslet. Given to Mark Twain by the author.
88c Inventors at Work, by George Iles. Given to Mark Twain by the author.
89c The Galaxy, an illustrated magazine of entertaining reading.
90c The Maid of France, by Andrew Lang. Story of life and death of Joan d'Arc.
91c Aspects of the Earth, by N. S. Shaler.
92c The Adventures of Baron Munchausen, by Gustave Dore. (illustrated).
93c Laurence and Eleanor Hutton—Their Books of Association.
94c Hana, a Daughter of Japan, by Gensai Murai.
95c The Hanging of the Crane, by Henry Wadsworth Longfellow.

96c Laurel Leaves for Little Folk, by Mary E. Phillips. Given to Mark Twain by the author.
97c Beacon Lights of History, by John Lord, LL.D.
98c The Grandissimes, by George W. Cable (a story of Creole Life).
99c Memoirs of M. De Blowitz.
100c Th. Nast, His Period and His Pictures, by Albert Bigelow Paine.

D1 Tauchnitz Edition—33 beautiful red leather bound volumes: By Mark Twain—Innocents Abroad, Vol. I & II; Roughing It; Stolen White Elephant; The Innocents Abroad; A Tramp Abroad, Vol. I & II; Adventures of Tom Sawyer; The Prince and the Pauper, Vol. I & II; Early Stanhope—The Reign of Queen Anne, Vol. I & II; Cameron—Across Africa, Vol. I & II; Lady Morgan's Memoirs, Vols. I, II & II; Hemans—The Select—Poetical Works; Autobiography of Luftullah; Burton—Mecca and Medina, Vol. I & II; Jefferson—A Book About Doctors, Vol. I & II; Shelley Poems; Mrs. Elliott—Diary of an Idle Woman in Italy, Vol. I & II; Lady Brassey—A Voyage in the Sunbeam, Vol. I & II; Lady Barker—Station Amusements in New Zealand; Lady Barker—Station Life in New Zealand; Grenville Murray — Strange Tales; Miss Burney — Evalina.
D2 The Works of Rudyard Kipling, 18 volumes: Plain Tales from the Hills; Soldiers Three and Miltary Tales, Part I & II; In Black and White; The Phantom Rickshaw; Under the Deodars and Other Stories; The Jungle Book; The Second Jungle Book; The Light That Failed; The Nauklahka; Verses; Captains Courageous; The Day's Work, Part I & II; From Sea to Sea, Part I and II; Early Verse; Stalky & Co.
D3 John William Draper—Human Physiology.
D4 Lorna Doone, a Romance of Exmoor, by R. D. Blackmore.
D5 Memoirs de J. Casanova, by De Seingalt, 10 vols.
D6 Dialogues of Plato, by B. Jowett, 4 vols.
D7 History of the English People, by John Richard Green. 4 vols.
D8 Sir Edward Bulwer Lytton—Last of the Barons; The Last of the Saxon Kings; Last of the Roman Tribunes; Last Days of Pompeii.
D9 Samuel Papys Diary, Vols. I to X, incl.
D10 The Works of Shakespeare, 10 volumes as follows: Vol. I—Love's Labour Lost; Comedy of Errors, Midsummer Nights Dream, etc.; Vol. 2—Taming of the Shrew; Merchant of Venice; As You Like It, and others; Vol. 3—Much Ado About Nothing; All's Wellt That Ends Well, and others; Vol. 4—Pericles Cymbeline; The Winter's Tale; The Tempest; Vol. 5—Henry VI, parts 1, 2 and ; Richard III; Vol. 6—King John; Richard II; Henry IV, Parts I & II; Vol. 7—Henry V; Henry VIII; Titus; Romeo and Juliet; Aneronicus; Vol. 8—Julius Caesar; Hamlet; Othello; Vol. 9—King Lear; Macbeth; Antony and Cleopatra; Vol. 10—Coriolanus Timon of Athens; Poems.
D11 Void.
D12 Thomas Carlyle—History of His Life in London.
D13 Rudyard Kipling—9 vols. leather bound: Abaft the Funnel; Puck of Pooks Hill; The Light That Failed; Many Inventions; Actions and Reactions; Traffics and Discoveries; The Day's Work; Life's Handicap; Kim.
D14 Mark Twain — 27 vols. leather bound: Huckleberry Finn, 2 vols.; Joan of Arc, 2 vols.; More Tramps Abroad, 2 vols.; The Prince and the Pauper, 2 vols.; A Yankee at King Arthur's Court, 2 vols.; Tom Sawyer, Tom Sawyer Abroad; Tow Sawyer Detective; Hadleyburg, 2 vols.; Life on the Missippi, 2 vols.; Sketches; 1,000,000 Bank-Note; American Claimant; Roughing It; Pudd'nhead Wilson; Innocents at Home; American Humour; Stolen White Eelephant.
D15 Little Masterpieces, 8 vols., by famous authors.
D16 The Life of the Universe, by Svante Arrhenius, 2 vols. Crete, the forerunner of Greece, by Charles H. Hawes.
D17 London, Its Celebrated Characters and Places, by J. Heneage Jess, 3 vols.
D18 Mottoes and Aphorisms from Shakespeare.
D19 Life of Oliver Wendell Holmes, by E. E. Brown.
D20 The Last Act, being the funeral rites of Nations and Individuals.
D21 Uncle Remus—Folk Lores of the Old Plantation, by Joel Harris.
D22 Tacitus, the Oxford translation. Vol. I.
D23 Mark Twain, a Tramp Abroad.
D24 Wolfville Nights, by Alfred Henry Lewis.
D25 The Story of My Life, Helen Keller.
D26 History of the United States, by Thomas Higginson and Wm. MacDonald.
D27 The New International Encyclopedia, 17 vols.
D28 The Genesis of the United States, by Alex. Brown,
D29 History of the Inquisition, by W. H. Rule, M.D. 2 vols.
D30 History of the German Struggle, by Poultney Bigelow. 4 vols.

D31 Curiosities of Literature, by Disraeli. 4 vols.
D32 Thomas Carlyle, by Froude. 4 vols.
D33 Old Yorkshire, by W. Smith, Vols. I & III. to Mark Twain by the author.
D34 The Merry Adventures of Robin Hood, by Howard Pyle.
D35 The Letters of Queen Victoria. Vol. III.
D36 A Family Flight, by Rev. E. E. Hale and Susan Hale.
D37 The Age of Reason, by Thomas Paine, M.A.
D38 Rudyard Kipling, Just So Stories.
D39 The Life, Times and Scientific Labours of the Marquis of Worcester.
D40 The Story of France, by Watson. Vol. II.
D41 Eccentricities of Genius, by Major J. B. Pond and given by the author.
D42 Autobiograph, by Joh nStuart Mill.

Autographed by S. L. Clemens

D43 Curiosities of the Sky, by Garrett Serviss.
D44 Roman Holidays and others, by W. D. Howells.
D45 The Day's Work, by Rudyard Kipling.
D46 Napoleon III, from the Poular Caricatures of the last 30 years.
D47 Evolution, the Master-Key, by C. W. Saleeby.
D48 Captain Bill McDonald, Texas Ranger, by Albert Bigelow Paine. Autographed by the author.
D49 The Leopard's Spots, by Thomas Dixon, Jr.
D50 Joan of Arc, by John Presland.
D51 Dissertations, by Mr. Dooley.
D52 Memoirs of Madame Desbordes-Valmore.
D53 Void
D54 Void
D55 The Betrothed, by Manzoni.
D56 The Undiscovered Country, by W. D. Howells, autographed by the author.
D57 Fond Adventures, by Maurice Kewlett.
D58 Westminster Drolleries, No. 124.
D59 The Friendly Stars, Martha Evans Martin.
D60 The Mutineers of the Bounty, by Lady Belcher.
D61 The Strength of the Hills, by Florence Wilkinson.
D62 The Thousand One Nights or Arabian Nights.
D63 Astronomy with the Naked Eye, by Garrett P. Serviss.
D64 The Conquest of Rome, by Matilde Serao.
D65 The Stickit Minister, by S. R. Crockett.
D66 Lady Byron Vindicated, by Harriett Beecher Stowe.
D67 Clarissa Harlowe, by Samuel Richardson.
D68 The Ruinous Face, by Maurice Hewlett.
D69 A Woman's Part in a Revolution, by Mrs. John Hays Hammond and signed by the author to Mark Twain.
D70 Home Folks, by James Whitcomb Riley, and signed by the author to M.T.
D71 Boy Life, by W. D. Howells.
D72 Things Not Generally Known, by John Timbs.
D73 London, by Guastave Dore and Blanchard Jerrold (Ill.)
D74 The Ancient Mariner, by Gustave Dore (Illustrations).
D75 Birds of North America, with illustrations.
D76 Froude's History of England. 10 vols. incomplete.
D77 Struggles and Triumphs or Forty Years Recollections, by P. T. Barnum, and signed by author to S.L.C.

D78 Flower and Thorn, by Thomas Bailey Aldrich, and signed by author to S.L.C.
D79 The Age of Fable or Beauties of Mythology, by Thos. Bullfinch, Vols. I & II.

Jean Clemens. Clara Clemens—Children

J1 Shakespeare—20 volumes, beautifully bound.
1. Titus, Andronicus; Henry VI, Part 1.
2. Henry VI, Part 2; Henry VI, Part 3.
3. Richard II; Love's Labour Lost.
4. Comedy of Errors; Two Gentlemen of Verona.
5. Midsummer Nigths' Dream; Romeo and Juliet.
6. King John; Richard II.
7. Merchant of Venice; Taming of the Shrew.
8. Henry IV, Part 1; Henry IV, Part 2.
9. Henry V; Merry Wives of Windsor.
10. Twelfth Night; Much Ado About Nothing.
11. As You Like It; All's Well That Ends Well.
12. Measure for Measure; Troilus and Cressida.
13. Hamlet; Julius Caesar.
14. Macbeth; Othello.
15. King Lear; Antony and Cleopatra.
16. Coriolanus; Timon of Athens.
17. Pericles; Tempest.
18. Cymbeline; Winter's Tale.
19. Henry VIII; Two Nobel Kinsmen.
20. Poems; Sonnets.
J2 Undine, by De La Motte Fouque.
J3 The Poetical Works of Percy Bysshe Shelley.
J4 The Children of the Nations, by Poultney Bigelow.
J5 An Inland Voyage, by Robert Louis Stevenson.
J6 The Religious Mysticism of the Unanishada, by Robert Milburn.
J7 The Light of Asia, by Sir Edwin Arnold.
J8 Are You a Bromide, by Gelett Burgess and presented

J9 The Land of the Fathers, Sergey Gussiev Orenburgsky.
J10 The Portrait of Zelide, by Geoffrey Scott.
J11 Mark Twain's Reise VM Die Welt.
J12 Bimbi, story for children by Ouida.
J13 Schnurrdiburr oder Die Bienen, by Von Wilhelm Busch.
J15 Daddy Darwin's Dovecote, by Julian Horatio Ewing. (Children Tales) 2 vols.
J16 Goldsmith's She Stoops to Conquer.
J17 Brenstone Poems, by Witter Bynner.
J18 Novellen, by Paul Feyfe; 3 vols.
J19 Deutfche Gefchichte - Beitalter der Reformation; 3 vols.
J20 Poganuc People, by H. B. Stowe.
J21 History of the United Netherlands, by John Lothrop Motley; 2 vols.
J22 Golden Cat, by Albert Bigelow Paine.
J23 Schopenhauer's Essays, by Saunders.
J24 Quo Vadis, by Sienkiewicz.
J25 Life and Lillian Gish, by Albert Bigelow Paine; autographed by the author and Lillian Gish.
J26 Herod, by Stephen Phillips.
J27 Susy's Six Teachers, by Mrs. Prentiss.
J28 Young Folks' History of England, by Charlotte M. Yonge
J29 Literary and Social Silhouettes, Hjalmar Hjorth Boyeson
J30 Latin Lessons—Elementary Latin Reading, by R. F. Leighton.
J31 Susy's Six Birthdays, by Mrs. Prentiss.
J32 Leather Stocking Tales, by James Fenimore Cooper.
J33 The Laws of Scientific Hand Reading, by William G. Benham.
J34 The Good Natured Man, by Oliver Goldsmith.
J35 Fruit Gathering, by Tagore.
J36 Little Ann, by Kate Greenaway.
J37 The Rollo Books, by Jacob Abbot; 24 vols. 1. Water; 2. Vaporation; 3. Air; 4. Sky; 5. Work; 6. Experiments; 7. Correspondence; 8. Play; 9. Read; 10. Travels; 11. Fire; 12. School; 13. Museum; 14. Talk; 15. Europe; 16. On the Atlantic; 17. Scotland; 18. Paris; 19. Rome; 20. Switzerland; 21. Geneva; 22. On the Rhine; 23. Naples; 24. Holland.
J38 Paolo and Francesca, by Stephen Phillips.
J39 The Makers of Venice, by Mrs. Oliphant.

Signature of Olivia L. Clemens.

O1 Heroines of Fiction, by W. D. Howells.
O2 Russia Under the Tzars, by Stepniak.
O3 The Ascent of Man, by Henry Drummond.
O4 The Heir of Redclyffe, by Mrs Yonge; 2 vols.
O5 Youma, Story of a West Indian Slave, by Lafcadio Hearn.
O6 Painters, Sculptors, Architects and Engravers, by Mrs. Clement.
O7 A Japanese Nightingale, by Onoto Watanna. H. Lewes.
O8 Female Characters of Goethe, from the original drawings of William Kaulbach with text by G. H. Lewis.
O9 Homer's Odyssey.
O10 Poems by Jean Ingelow.
O11 Poenamo, Sketches of the Early Days of New Zealand, by Eugene Campbell, with note from author to O.L.C.
O12 Handbook of Marks and Monograms on Pottery and Porcelain, by Wm. Chaffers.
O13 Heroines of Fiction, by W. D. Howells.
O14 Poems, by Matthew Arnold.
O15 Hints on Household Taste.
O16 Poems, by Mrs. Browning.
O17 Literature of the South of Europe, by J.C.L. Simonde De Sismondi, Vol. II.
O18 In the Garden of Dreams, by Louise Chandler Moulton.
O19 Breakfast, Luncheon and Tea, by Marion Harland.
O20 Taine's History of English Literature, H. Van Laun; 2 vol
O21 History of England, by Macaulay; 2 vols.
O22 McCarthy—The Four Georges, Vol. I & II; and the Four Georges and William IV, Vol. III & IV.
O23 Cooper's Leather Stocking Tales: 1. The Pathfinder; 2. Deerslayer; 3. Mohicans.
O24 Concise History of France, by Guizot; Gustave Massoon
O25 Honore De Balzac, 6 vols.: 1. Louis Lambert; 2. The Magic Skin; 3. Seraphita; 4. Cousin Pons; 5. Bureaucracy; 6. Ursula.
O26 The Deserted Village, by Oliver Goldsmith, (illus.)
O27 The Household Book of Poetry, collected and edited by Charles Dana.
O28 Robert Browning, by William Sharp.
O29 Literary Friends and Acquaintances, by W. D. Wowells and autographed by the author.

Memos, Letters, Clippings and Other Papers of Interest

Adam,s Expulsion—Unpublished manuscript on Adam.
Heidelberg Notes—Mark Twain Travels (Crowded out of Tramp Abroad to make room for more vital statistics).
A Rubinstein Photograph inscribed with an allegretto and note.
Letters to Mark Twain from Johannes Brahms, Johann Srtouss, Karl Goldmark, Novitz Moszkowsky, Rudyard Kipling, Andrew Carnegie, Mr. Forhan, his publisher.
Pablo Sarasate—Picture and inscription.
Charles Sunnod—Picture and inscription.
Mark Twain, letter to his friend regarding his love.
Letter from J. Langdon to his son.
Mark Twain Letter, unmailed.
Newspaper Clipping in re Mark Twain.
Notes by Mark Twain on a play.
Mark Twain—An Incident—an unpublished Manuscript.
Manuscript—Only Known Poem by Mark Twain.
Music Collection and Mementos of Ossip Gabrilowitsch (former husband of Mark Twain's daughter.
Balance of Unlisted Books to Follow

notices and then were not recognized and valued by subsequent generations of their families—will be felt for many decades to come. Public and private research libraries had little opportunity to assemble adequate funds and dispatch representatives to the sale, owing to the haste with which it was arranged.[1] That 1951 auction has to rank as one of the memorable debacles of American literary history. It should be noted that this regrettable sale was both preceded and followed by the habit of Clara Clemens Samossoud and her husband Jacques of giving away to their friends as "souvenirs" assorted books that once belonged to Clemens's library. These gifts naturally went unrecorded and thus resulted in additional holes in any inventory of his library. Miraculously, more than a hundred association copies that somehow escaped the Hollywood auction were included with the notebooks, letters and literary manuscripts that formed the nucleus of the Mark Twain Papers, the invaluable collection now housed in the Bancroft Library at the University of California at Berkeley.

LOCATING SURVIVING REMNANTS OF THE CLEMENS FAMILY LIBRARY

In 1970 I decided to set about tracking down the approximately 700 books once owned by the Clemenses that were then known to exist (many more have since surfaced), making several trips along the California coast, repeated visits to Connecticut and New York, and research stops in Wisconsin, Illinois, Virginia, North Carolina, Indiana, Missouri, Texas, and Nevada to verify the authenticity of these volumes and transcribe marginal notations that Clemens left behind. In the course of this scholarly sleuthing I discovered a number of spurious association copies that forgers had attributed to Clemens's library and had sold to private and public archives across the nation.

A Discovery in Redding, Connecticut

My detective work paid off monumentally in May 1977 when, revisiting the public library in Redding, Connecticut, I learned from library volunteers Dorothy Munro and Marge Webb that a long-lost record of a major portion of Clemens's book donations had finally turned up there. In the 152 ruled pages of this bound notebook an early librarian had neatly inscribed the authors, titles, publishers, pages, numbers of illustrations, bindings, prices, dates of publication, and—most important of all— the donors of 2,315 books given to the Mark Twain Library shortly after its founding in 1908. Some of the books were the gifts of Dan Beard and other Redding residents, but the librarian had labeled 1,751 of them as the donations of "S. L. Clemens" and (beginning on page 118, accession number 1827) "Mrs. Gabrilowitsch." (Clara Clemens had married Ossip Gabrilowitsch on 6 October 1909.) Evidently Clemens donated books to the library in 1908 and 1909, to judge

from certain dates of publication. Since Clara's donations included a few volumes published in 1909, she presumably went through her father's library at the time of his death and added books to his previous gifts to the community library. The librarian apparently catalogued the books in the order of donation.

An article in the New York *Times* titled "Twain Books for Library" reported from Redding on 10 July 1910 that "Mrs. Clara Clemens Gabrilowitsch . . . has formally notified the Director of the Mark Twain Free Library here that she will present to that institution practically the entire library of her father, now in the Redding residence, Stormfield. The gift includes nearly 2,500 volumes." As we know, Clara Clemens kept back enough books to furnish two lively auctions in 1911 and 1951, but she nonetheless must have donated at least the 2,500 volumes she promised. The numbered book donations in the extant accession book of the Mark Twain Library end at the bottom of the last facing pages (150–151), indicating that the record was continued in another, still-missing accession book. The final title in the last column was assigned the number 2315. Various books survive from the Clemenses' donations to the Mark Twain Library that were not included in this list. Some display accession numbers quite subsequent to those recorded there—William Smith's *Morley: Ancient and Modern* (1886), for example, was assigned 3460, Isaac Hull Platt's *Bacon Cryptograms* (1905) is labeled 3549, and others, too, are numbered in the 3,000 range—suggesting that Clara Clemens Gabrilowitsch made many additional contributions. But in the existing accession record we learn the titles and dates of novels by Walter Scott, Charles Dickens, Jane Austen, and many other books notably absent from Clemens's library when he died in 1910. This list of 1,751 volumes constituted a massive addition to Twain's known library, even though he may have donated a percentage of them without marking or even reading their pages. (Donations published by Harper & Brothers between 1906 and 1909 could have been books he persuaded his publisher to contribute.)

During the first half-century after the library's founding many hundreds of volumes were either lost or damaged and therefore discarded as the result of being circulated to patrons. These extensive depletions were compounded in 1952 when a librarian—wishing to make space on the shelves for newer acquisitions and unaware at the time of the monetary and scholarly value of Mark Twain association copies—culled the collection of seldom-loaned volumes and sold them to a used book dealer. After the first accession record of the Mark Twain Library surfaced in 1977, documenting perhaps half of the volumes contributed by Clemens and his daughter Clara, and upon my study of the list of donated books, I came to realize that the librarians in Redding had faithfully followed Clemens's wishes and in fact had used his library volumes exactly as he intended. He did not bequeath the collection as a monument to his thought and writings, but rather as a core of books for the founding of a public library—a community institution he always supported wherever he lived.

In general Clemens was very respectful of a book as a physical artifact; in 1872 he had deplored the "Vandals" who desecrated the Library of the British Museum when they "tear leaves out of valuable books."[2] Still, very possibly it was Clemens himself, his secretary Isabel Lyon, or his daughter Clara who defaced some of the volumes donated to the Redding library by ripping out endpapers and flyleaves that (presumably) contained intimate family inscriptions. (On the other hand, the signatures or inscriptions by Clemens might have presented tempting prizes for souvenir-hunters in the 1940s, 1950s, and 1960s.) If Clemens considered the presence of his marginalia in the donated books, he likely believed that his annotations could be instructive in showing library users how to interpret any texts he had bothered to mark. Future generations of Mark Twain students would thereby lose the opportunity to see most of these comments, but it should be recalled that only in the middle of the twentieth century did the cataloguing and describing of an author's library become recognized as important components of literary research.

THE ANTENNE COLLECTION

Another group of books from Clemens's library, approximately ninety volumes given to his housekeeper Katy Leary (1856–1934) after her employer died in 1910, eventually ended up in Rice Lake, Wisconsin. These books belonged to the descendants of Katy Leary. In 1993 this collection began to be donated in installments to the Mark Twain Archive at Elmira College, until virtually all of those books joined the volumes already deposited there that Clemens had read and annotated while sojourning at Quarry Farm.

When I stumbled upon such exciting finds as Katy Leary's collection my investigation took on aspects of a literary detective's case. There were clues, informants, false leads, dull surveillance, dazzling breakthroughs. What required solving were the contents of this lost collection, now changing locations ceaselessly and attracting forgeries that no doubt would have fascinated him.

NOTES

1   Much later, in 1987, I was asked by the family who then owned Clara Clemens Samossoud's former residence in Hollywood to search its bookshelves for any Clemens library books that might have escaped the 1951 auction. (Clara had known the couple who purchased her house, and since a bundle of Clemens letters had been found in the home it seemed likely that she might have left behind some books as well.) I located several volumes that seemed to have belonged to Clemens's personal library, and Nick Karanovich of Fort Wayne, Indiana purchased them from that family.

2   Clemens's English journals of 1872 (*MTLet* 5: 596).

26

Critical Bibliography

Books, Articles, Doctoral Dissertations, and Master's Theses Related to Samuel L. Clemens's Reading

(NUMEROUS WORKS OMITTED HERE ARE LISTED IN THE RELEVANT CATALOG ENTRIES IN VOLS. 2-3.)

ALDEN, HENRY M. "Mark Twain—An Appreciation," *The Bookman* (New York) 31 (June 1910): 366–369.

Alden reflects on Clemens's choices in reading matter, particularly in the author's last hours. A mixture of pathos and curiously reserved praise.

ANDREWS, KENNETH R. *Nook Farm: Mark Twain's Hartford Circle.* Cambridge: Harvard University Press, 1950.

In Chapter 5, "Literature in Hartford 1871–1891" (pp. 144–215), Andrews presents a vivid analysis of the literary milieu that Samuel L. Clemens first visited on 21 January 1868 and into which he moved on 1 October 1871. "The writing of books was a profession in Hartford," a city containing many printing and bookbinding firms (p. 149). Andrews's discussions of Harriet Beecher Stowe and Charles Dudley Warner are especially worthwhile.

ASPIZ, HAROLD. "Mark Twain's Reading—A Critical Study." Doctoral dissertation. University of California, Los Angeles, 1949.

The only systematic, full-scale survey of Samuel L. Clemens's reading that preceded Alan Gribben's *Mark Twain's Library: A Reconstruction* (1980). Unfortunately in 1949 it was impossible for a graduate student to consult the unpublished collection eventually known as the Mark Twain Papers; Aspiz could only study those of Twain's writings that were in print. He did not examine the *A1911* sale catalogue, nor does he refer to the large library then in Clara Clemens Samossoud's possession and soon (1951) to be sold at auction. But he included information from the memoirs of many of Clemens's contemporaries, and he usefully sorted out the studies of Clemens's reading that were beginning to accumulate. Aspiz grouped his discussions by genre and period ("Later American Humor," "The Novel," etc.). His dissertation contains appendixes on (a) Daniel Defoe, W. E. H. Lecky, and Thomas Malory as sources for *A Connecticut Yankee*, and (b) Clemens's knowledge of foreign languages.

AUGUR, MARGARET ELIZABETH. "Mark Twain's Reading and Its Effect Upon His Writing." Master's thesis. University of Illinois, Urbana, 1939.

"He was unacademic, but was he unliterary?" (p. 3). Augur proposes to answer this question, or at least begin to answer it. She takes us at a dog-trot through Samuel L. Clemens's reading of a lifetime, limited by the resources on which she could draw in 1939. She gives no indication of having read the master's thesis on this topic that preceded hers by fifteen years—Henry A. Pochmann's "The Mind of Mark Twain."

BAENDER, PAUL. "Alias Macfarlane: A Revision of Mark Twain's Biography," *American Literature* 38.2 (May 1966): 187–197.

Baender here disputed biographer Albert Bigelow Paine's description of a Cincinnati boardinghouse-philosopher named "Macfarlane," arguing that this "Macfarlane" was merely another fictitious persona for Twain's cynicism about historical progress. However, William Baker—"Mark Twain in Cincinnati: A Mystery Most Compelling," *American Literary Realism* 12.2 (Autumn 1979): 299–315—subsequently turned up evidence that a similarly named printer was employed in the same shop as Clemens.

BAETZHOLD, HOWARD G. "The Course of Composition of *A Connecticut Yankee*: A Reinterpretation," *American Literature* 33.2 (May 1961): 195–214.

Reworked and expanded, this exacting study of Mark Twain's sources was incorporated throughout *Mark Twain and John Bull*. In this article Baetzhold is intent on correcting John B. Hoben regarding the phases in Twain's composition of *A Connecticut Yankee* (1889).

_____. *Mark Twain and John Bull: The British Connection*. Bloomington: Indiana University Press, 1970.

This is Baetzhold's most comprehensive study of Twain's indebtedness to major and minor British writers. It remains an often-cited secondary source about Twain's works.

_____. "Samuel L. Clemens" entry, *American Literary Critics and Scholars, 1850–1880*, eds. John W. Rathbun and Monica M. Grecu. Dictionary of Literary Biography Series. Detroit: Bruccoli Clark Layman, 1988, pp. 34–47.

Baetzhold sketches Mark Twain's opinions of numerous writers, including Bret Harte, W. E. H. Lecky, and Walter Scott, stressing Twain's "antipathy toward affected diction . . . and romantic excesses in general" (p. 38).

_____. "'Well, My Book is Written—Let it Go . . .': The Making of *A Connecticut Yankee in King Arthur's Court*," in *Biographies of Books*, eds. James Barbour and Tom Quirk. Columbia: University of Missouri Press, 1996, 64: 41–77.

An updated, revised account of Twain's writing of one of his best novels, all the more important as a work of scholarship because Baetzhold's name became synonymous with the study of Twain's process of composition in *A Connecticut Yankee*. This article provides Baetzhold's most concise and articulate summation of his findings about Twain's sources, allusions, and authorial decisions. (See also Joe B. Fulton's *Mark Twain in the Margins* [2000]).

BARBARESE, J. T. "The Last Word Goes to Scribblers in the Margins," *Wall Street Journal*, 13 January 2014, A-13.

Discusses the impact of marginalia left behind in a book by a previous reader, especially if that reader is a prominent author. Clemens is not mentioned, but the points are applicable to his frequent marginal comments.

BELLAMY, GLADYS CARMEN. *Mark Twain as a Literary Artist*. Norman: University of Oklahoma Press, 1950.

Bellamy's "starting point was . . . [a] conviction that Mark Twain was much more the conscious craftsman than is generally believed" (Foreword, p. vii). She produced a sprightly, perceptive, reasoned study. This book formally integrated and built upon the assertions of Minnie M. Brashear, and Walter Blair's *Mark Twain & Huck Finn* (1960) would then cement the foundations of this view. Bellamy did not concern herself for the most part with tracing sources; in establishing Mark Twain's familiarity with other writers she relied on Henry A. Pochmann, Minnie M. Brashear, and Edward Wagenknecht.

BERRET, ANTHONY J. "Huck Finn's Library: Reading, Writing, and Intertextuality," *Making Mark Twain Work in the Classroom*, ed. James S. Leonard. Durham, North Carolina: Duke University Press, 1999, pp. 200–215.

Berret skillfully followed up Walter Blair's *Mark Twain & Huck Finn* (1960) in investigating the literary allusions in Twain's famous novel. See also the related studies of Dale Billingsley (1979) and Alan Gribben (2002).

BILLINGSLEY, DALE. "'Standard Authors' in *Huckleberry Finn*," *Journal of Narrative Technique* 9.2 (Spring 1979): 126–131.

Billingsley illustrated how literary motifs link various episodes in Twain's novel. See also the related studies of Anthony J. Berret (1999) and Alan Gribben (2002).

BLAIR, WALTER. "The French Revolution and *Huckleberry Finn*," *Modern Philology* 55.1 (August 1957): 21–35.

Blair argued against assuming—as Mark Twain and Brander Matthews *(Tocsin of Revolt,* pp. 268–269) urged us to do—that Twain's only excellences derive from actual episodes that he or his friends experienced. Twain's own comments "justify a study of some possible sources of his masterpiece" (p. 21). Blair here explored Twain's reading in the history of the French Revolution.

_____. *Mark Twain & Huck Finn.* Berkeley: University of California Press, 1960.

Blair's book constitutes a meticulous companion to Mark Twain's masterpiece. It traces numerous literary works that show up in *Huckleberry Finn.*

_____. *Native American Humor, 1800–1900.* New York: American Book Company, 1937; San Francisco: Chandler Publishing Company, 1960.

This volume is both an anthology and a critical survey of its field. An absolutely indispensable handbook for delving into the pseudonyms and publications of nineteenth-century humorists who anticipated, surrounded, and imitated Mark Twain, *Native American Humor* is also a superlative collection of representative tales. Blair compiled his volume at a time when American humor was practically a virgin field, and his work survives its successors because of his astounding labor, comprehensiveness, and wit. A section on Mark Twain (pp. 147–162) begins to trace some of his literary predecessors, research that Blair would develop more fully in *Mark Twain & Huck Finn* (1960).

_____. "On the Structure of *Tom Sawyer*," *Modern Philology* 37.1 (August 1939): 75–88.

Blair compared the structure of *The Adventures of Tom Sawyer* with patterns prevalent in juvenile fiction at the time. He demonstrated the prevalence of "a common conception of the humor of childhood and the nature of children" of which Mark Twain took advantage. The article discussed connections between *Tom Sawyer* and Sunday-school books.

BLANCK, JACOB. "Farewell Tour," *Antiquarian Bookman* 7 (5 May 1951): 1543–44; "Mark Twain Sale Postscript," *Antiquarian Bookman* 7 (26 May 1951): 1775.

Both articles described the extraordinary Hollywood *C1951* auction. Its sale catalog was "the briefest sort of checklist which succeeded in being exasperating rather than informative" (p. 1543). Blanck extracted amusing examples from the catalog. He quoted Clara Clemens Samossoud's declaration that she and her husband "are going to become gypsies" (p. 1544). In his second column Blanck compiled several book dealers' accounts of the auction proceedings. Maxwell Hunley reported that "the sale was conducted in a carnival atmosphere complete with flood-lights, hot-dog stands and pop" (p. 1775). John Valentine of Glendale, California wrote (in the Los Angeles *Daily News*) that the sale was "held out of doors before the huge mansion in the Hollywood Hills, complete with loud-speakers, flashing bulbs, and hot-dog stand. . . . An attending collector swore that he heard Injun Joe whooping from the darkened woods" (p. 1775). Satirical in tone, sketchy, secondhand, but fascinating.

BLODGETT, HAROLD. "A Note on *Mark Twain's Library of Humor*," *American Literature* 10.1 (March 1938): 78–80.

Blodgett called attention to Mark Twain's generally ignored anthology of American humorists that appeared in 1888.

BOEWE, MARY. "Smouching Towards Bedlam; or, Mark Twain's Creative Use of Some Acknowledged Literary Sources," *Mark Twain Journal* 29.1 (Spring 1991): 8–12.

Boewe investigated Twain's attitudes toward borrowing literary material, focusing on "A Horse's Tale" but covering other works as well.

BRADLEY, SCULLEY, RICHMOND CROOM BEATTY, AND E. HUDSON LONG, eds. *Adventures of Huckleberry Finn: An Annotated Text, Backgrounds and Sources, Essays in Criticism.* Norton Critical Edition. New York: W. W. Norton & Company, 1962.

The editors reprinted and explained five literary sources on pp. 237–254, including the writings of Julia A. Moore, Johnson J. Hooper, and Artemus Ward.

BRANCH, EDGAR M., ed. *Clemens of the "Call": Mark Twain in San Francisco.* Berkeley: University of California Press, 1969.

Clemens's newspaper pieces from 1864 are reprinted and annotated, with glosses that interpret his allusions.

_____. *The Literary Apprenticeship of Mark Twain, with Selections from His Apprentice Writing.* Urbana: University of Illinois Press, 1950.

In tracing the development of Mark Twain's forms and style of writing between 1852 and 1867, Branch commented upon probable influences from his reading.

_____. "Mark Twain: Newspaper Reading and the Writer's Creativity," *Nineteenth-Century Fiction* 37.4 (March 1983): 576–603.

Branch reviewed Twain's "use of newspaper items as sources for his fiction."

BRASHEAR, MINNIE M. "Mark Twain Juvenilia," *American Literature* 2.1 (March 1930): 25–53.

Brashear reprinted Clemens's contributions to Orion's Hannibal *Daily Journal* in 1852 and 1853, with some attention to his literary sources.

_____. *Mark Twain: Son of Missouri.* Chapel Hill: University of North Carolina Press, 1934.

Chapter 6 takes up "Sam Clemens' Reading" during his Missouri residence, speculating about its impact on his writing (pp. 196–224). Brashear also assesses the intellectual climate of the Hannibal village, disputing Vernon Parrington's belittlement of its library resources in *Main Currents in American Thought* (1928), and explores Clemens's debt to eighteenth-century authors in a separate chapter, "The Shadow of Europe" (pp. 225–253). She has inevitably been overtaken in various areas where subsequent research among newly accessible materials has supplanted her speculations of many years ago. Yet she is shrewdly perspicacious in spotting and analyzing Mark Twain's "unliterary" pose, and her conclusions regarding Clemens's reading in general are not likely to be overturned.

BROOKS, VAN WYCK. *The Ordeal of Mark Twain.* New York: E. P. Dutton and Co., 1920. Revised edition, 1933.

Brooks' discussion of Clemens's reading tastes is disparaging (see especially pages 146–183). "An animal repugnance to Jane Austen,

an irritated schoolboy's dislike of Scott and Cooper—is not that the measure of the literary criticism he has left us?" (p. 160).

BROWN, GEORGE ROTHWELL. *Washington: A Not Too Serious History.* Baltimore: Norman Publishing Co., 1930.

In this affectionate guide to historical locations and personages Brown mentions Samuel L. Clemens's patronage of a Washington bookstore. Although he does not cite his source for this information he does provides a general bibliography.

BUDD, LOUIS J. *Mark Twain: Social Philosopher.* Bloomington: Indiana University Press, 1962.

This remains the standard work on Mark Twain's shifting political views. Budd incidentally commented on a few works by W. E. H. Lecky, Robert G. Ingersoll, and George Standring that affected Mark Twain's philosophies, but treats none in depth.

BURHANS, CLINTON S., JR. "Mark Twain's View of History," *Papers of the Michigan Academy of Science, Arts, and Letters* 46, Part 3 (1961): 617–627.

From Mark Twain's "confused pattern of historical attitudes" (p. 627) Burhans concluded that he "has no theory of history because his view of history is an uneasy mixture of conflicting and inconsistent elements which he never reconciles" (p. 617). Burhans blamed this partly on weaknesses in the American historical imagination. The problem of Twain's concept of history is indeed complex, but Roger B. Salomon produced a more charitable treatment of the topic in *Twain and the Image of History* (1961). To Burhans it was a jumble of contradictions; he found only Mark Twain's "split-vision, seeing it as both change and repetition, evolution and decadence, progress and the lack of progress" (p. 626).

CARTER, PAUL J., JR. "The Social and Political Ideas of Mark Twain." Doctoral dissertation. University of Cincinnati, 1939.

Carter included a chapter on Mark Twain as "The Reader" (pp. 125–152) that was restricted to a consideration of reading related to "his social and political criticism." Carter concluded that Twain was "impervious to the deeper and broader aspects of his reading. What he sought was largely material of human interest" (p. 152). The dissertation discussed Thomas Carlyle, W. E. H. Lecky, and Thomas Paine. Today most of these suppositions have been superseded, particularly since we now have access to Clemens's Lecky marginalia, the absence of which Carter lamented on page 135. Carter's was a commendable effort to treat a difficult topic, but it was largely dependent on Minnie M. Brashear's work.

CLARK, CHARLES H. "Mark Twain at 'Nook Farm' (Hartford) and Elmira," *The Critic* 6 (17 January 1885): 25–26.

Clark's article contains revealing comments about Clemens's reading inclinations.

CLARK, HARRY HAYDEN. See James Woodress, ed., *Eight American Authors* (1972).

CLEMENS, CLARA. *My Father, Mark Twain.* New York: Harper & Brothers, 1931.

First-hand information about Clemens's reading habits from his daughter is unquestionably valuable, even when the recollections are jumbled together without many dates of association. Clara quoted certain letters from Clemens to her mother that do not appear in *Love Letters of Mark Twain*, and some of these allude to his reading.

CLEMENS, CYRIL. "Mark Twain's Reading," *Commonweal* 24 (7 August 1936): 363–364.

Essentially this essay summarized the work of Albert Bigelow Paine, Henry A. Pochmann, and Minnie M. Brashear. But by enumerating Clemens's likes and dislikes, Cyril Clemens may have contributed to a growing awareness of Mark Twain's literary knowledge.

CLEMENS, JAMES ROSS, M.D. "Reminiscences of Mark Twain," *Overland Monthly* 87 (April 1929): 105 and 125.

These recollections by Samuel L. Clemens's distant cousin, whom he met in London in 1897 (not 1898, as Dr. Clemens reports), contain several references to Clemens's reading habits and play-going. Dr. Clemens (1866–1918) later returned to St. Louis, Missouri to practice medicine; he was Cyril Clemens's father.

COGELL, ELIZABETH A. "The Influence of Mark Twain's Reading in Science on the Ideas in *What Is Man?*" Master's thesis. University of South Dakota, 1962.

Not consulted.

COLEMAN, PHILIP YATES. "Mark Twain's Desperate Naturalism." Doctoral dissertation. University of Illinois, Urbana, 1964.

Coleman took account of Clemens's reading in examining his philosophical attitudes. There are limited discussions of W. E. H. Lecky, Jonathan Edwards, Robert G. Ingersoll, and a few other writers.

COTTON, MICHELLE L. "Olivia Susan Clemens." Senior thesis. Elmira College. December 1982.

Directed by Herbert A. Wisbey Jr., this thesis transcribes the letters that Susy Clemens wrote to her former Bryn Mawr roommate, Louise Brownell, between 1891 and 1894. Cotton provided identifications for the literary allusions mentioned in the letters along with other explanatory notes. The Hamilton College Archives have since made these letters digitally accessible online.

COVICI, PASCAL, JR. *Mark Twain's Humor: The Image of a World.* Dallas: Southern Methodist University Press, 1962.

Concerned with isolating and tracing the "strategy" and evolution of Mark Twain's forms of humor, Covici pays attention to the Southwest humorists, Edgar Allan Poe, and a few additional authors.

COWAN, ALLISON LEIGH. "Scrawled in the Margins, Signs of Twain as a Critic," New York *Times*, 19 April 2010, A-17.

Using Alan Gribben's *Mark Twain: A Reconstruction* (1980) as a guide, the reporter quotes from Clemens's association copies belonging to the Mark Twain Library in Redding, Connecticut. The *Times* simultaneously made available on the Internet a digital list of the books Clemens's donated to the community library, which can be found online at "Twain's Bookshelf," 19 April 2010.

CUMMINGS, SHERWOOD. "Mark Twain and Science." Doctoral dissertation. University of Wisconsin, 1950.

Chapter 2, "Mark Twain's Reading in

Science" (pp. 17–45), added to Hyatt H. Waggoner's previous (1937) article. Cummings concluded that Mark Twain's "approach to science was that of an amateur," but his reading was "extensive and catholic enough" so that he "had a good layman's knowledge of science" (p. 45). Cummings conveniently listed by author and title the thirty scientific books and articles Clemens was known to have read (pp. 374–376).

_____. *Mark Twain and Science: Adventures of a Mind.* Baton Rouge: Louisiana State University Press, 1988.

This signal study brought together Cummings's lifetime investigations of Clemens's knowledge of scientific fields. There are several chapters on individual novels and careful examinations of many aspects of Clemens's curiosity about the scientific inquiries that had made an intellectual impact on his generation.

_____. "Mark Twain's Acceptance of Science," *The Centennial Review* 6.2 (Spring 1962): 245–261.

Cummings's article examined Mark Twain's attitudes toward science itself, noting inconsistencies and vacillations. Pages 252–255 summarized Clemens's "extensive reading in science"—totaling more than sixty books and articles. Cummings provided "a sampling of the marginalia" from three books housed in the Mark Twain Papers in the Bancroft Library at the University of California at Berkeley—Charles Darwin's *Descent of Man*, Andrew D. White's *Warfare of Science with Theology*, and Alexander Winchell's *Sketches of Creation*. This was Cummings's most concise summary of his research on Clemens and science, a helpful look at the manifestations of the author's sometimes contradictory views.

_____. "Mark Twain's Social Darwinism," *Huntington Library Quarterly* 20.2 (February 1957): 163–175.

The "social pronouncements" of Mark Twain's last decade "show the stamp of his knowledge of evolutionary science" (p. 165). Cummings traced references to Darwin's ideas in *Roughing It, Following the Equator, What Is Man?*, and other works. He maintained that Twain's pessimism "was expressed in terms of a nineteenth-century ideology" and he disputed

Minnie M. Brashear's contention that Twain was "intellectually a child of the eighteenth century" (p. 169). "From accepting Darwin's theory that the fitness of individual organisms to survive was tested in an eternal struggle for existence to applying that theory to the human organism, who was part of the natural world, was a simple step" (p. 169). Cummings concentrated on *The American Claimant* (pp. 169–173) in demonstrating the social Darwinism implicit in Twain's writings. Cummings placed greater credibility in Twain's account of his Cincinnati friend Macfarlane's philosophizing than Paul Baender would allow—though Macfarlane's identity remains a matter of contention owing to a finding by William Baker reported in "Mark Twain in Cincinnati: A Mystery Most Compelling," *American Literary Realism* 12.2 (Autumn 1979): 299–315.

_____. "Science and Mark Twain's Theory of Fiction," *Philological Quarterly* 37.1 (January 1958): 26–33.

From "Darwin, who demonstrated the inexorable influence of environment on organic life, and H. A. Taine, who applied the Darwinian theory of environment to human society, Twain undoubtedly received instruction in the formulation of his own explicitly stated theory that fictional characters achieve reality only when depicted with reference to their formative environment" (p. 27). Cummings drew attention to Clemens's fascination with the twin influences of training and environment.

_____. "*What is Man?*: The Scientific Sources," in *Essays on Determinism in American Literature,* ed. Sydney J. Krause, *Kent Studies in English* 1 (1964): 108–116.

This study of Twain's scientific sources for *What Is Man?* revealed that he joined Stephen Crane, Theodore Dreiser, Ambrose Bierce, and other "conscious participants in a broad literary movement based on the scientific ideas of their time." Therefore Twain's treatise did not simply reflect—as Edward Wagenknecht, Carl Van Doren, and Alexander E. Jones had claimed—his Calvinistic upbringing, his guilt complex, or his distaste for bourgeois Protestant society. Cummings contended that Oliver Wendell

Holmes's *Autocrat of the Breakfast-Table* and Charles Darwin's *The Descent of Man* "express or imply every single idea that is contained in Mark Twain's 'gospel.'" Four other books—Thomas Paine's *Age of Reason*, W. E. H. Lecky's *European Morals*, John Lubbock's *Ants, Bees, and Wasps*, and Thomas Henry Huxley's *Evolution and Ethics*—were among the "hundred-plus" that Twain read for the ideas in *What Is Man?* Cummings considered Twain "a second-rate thinker, but at his best a great creative artist. Although *What Is Man?* is simplistic and doctrinaire as an intellectual statement, his considerable novels (unlike those of some naturalists) transcend doctrine" (p. 115).

DAVID, BEVERLY R. *Mark Twain and His Illustrators, Volume I (1869–1875); Volume II (1875–1883).* 2 vols. Troy, New York: Whitston Publishing Co., 1986 (Volume I); Albany, New York: Whitston Publishing Co., 2001 (Volume II).

In the course of describing the decisions made by Mark Twain and his publishers about who should illustrate his books and what the drawings should look like, David makes references to many preceding and contemporary authors, works, artists, and public figures.

DAVIS, CHESTER. See *The Twainian*.

[DAWSON, GLEN.] "Mark Twain Library Auction," *American Book-Prices Current, 1950–1951* (New York: R. R. Bowker, 1951), pp. 105–106.

Glen Dawson of Dawson's Bookshop in Los Angeles contributed the information reported in this brief description of the *C1951* sale. E. F. Whitman and F. B. O'Connor, 7940 Sunset Boulevard, Hollywood, the realtor auctioneers retained to dispose of the books, distributed brief printed list of the lots that would be up for bid. Bookseller-buyers who attended the auction included Dawson, Maxwell Hunley, and John Valentine of Glendale. A "carnival atmosphere" prevailed. Dawson mentioned a few specific manuscripts and books.

DERRICK, L. E. "A Study of Mark Twain's Sources." Master's thesis. University of Texas at Austin, 1930.

Not consulted.

DEVOTO, BERNARD. *Forays and Rebuttals.* Boston: Little, Brown, and Co., 1936.

DeVoto's literary columns, essays, and addresses in this collection expound his critical views. The final piece, "Mark Twain and the Limits of Criticism" (his 1936 address to the Modern Language Association) knocked the prevailing academic systems of criticism and particularly castigated "the study of influences." Behind DeVoto's indignant contempt is a sound philosophy about the ideal purposes of criticism; his comments furnished a beneficial astringent for those undertaking the now-outmoded "source-study."

_____. *Mark Twain's America.* Boston: Little, Brown, and Company, 1932.

Stimulated by angry dissent but unmarred by it, DeVoto's feisty, contentious book set out to disprove the notion that Mark Twain was handicapped by his origins or environment. In so doing it provided a non-stop listing of background legends, tales, songs, superstitions, novels, and anecdotes that Clemens might have absorbed. DeVoto wove a gripping narrative from the materials he sifted concerning the American Mississippi and Far West. For DeVoto these folkways were fully as rich—and less inhibited and constrained—than the elegant environs of the Eastern literati into which Clemens moved. On pages 150–154 DeVoto showed that two episodes in *Huckleberry Finn* originated from sketches written by pre-Civil War humorists.

DICKINSON, LEON T. "Mark Twain's *Innocents Abroad*: Its Origins, Composition, and Popularity." Doctoral dissertation. University of Chicago, 1945.

Discussed the guidebooks Mark Twain employed in his tour of the Holy Land.

_____. "The Sources of *The Prince and the Pauper*," *Modern Language Notes* 64.2 (February 1949): 103–106.

Dickinson puzzled over the dissimilarity of Charlotte M. Yonge's *The Prince and the Page* (1865) and Mark Twain's *The Prince and the Pauper*, then briefly summarized Twain's employment of J. Hammond Trumbull's *The True-Blue Laws* (1876), Richard Head and Francis Kirkman's *The English Rogue* (1665–1671), and other probable literary resources. He suggested that Twain's meticulousness about citing his sources in *Prince and the Pauper* stemmed from his desire to see the novel taken seriously, despite its author's reputation as a humorist.

DONNER, STANLEY T. "Mark Twain as a Reader," *Quarterly Journal of Speech* 33.3 (October 1947): 308–311.

Donner briefly reviewed Mark Twain's artistry as a platform reader and lecturer. Twain preferred to speak from memory so that his performances would be free from stiffness and formality. Donner did not discuss the selections from others' writings that Twain often read in public.

DOYNO, VICTOR A. "Beginning to Write *Huck Finn*," in *Huck Finn: The Complete Buffalo & Erie County Public Library Manuscript—Teaching and Research Digital Edition*, eds. Vic A. Doyno *et al.* CD Version. Buffalo, New York: State University of New York at Buffalo, Buffalo and Erie County Public Library, and the Mark Twain Foundation, 2003.

The first half of the iconic manuscript having returned to Buffalo after some legal skirmishing, Doyno now studied it as closely as he had previously analyzed the second half. He paid special attention to Twain's emphasis on the importance of literacy.

_____. *Writing* Huck Finn: *Mark Twain's Creative Process*. Philadelphia: University of Pennsylvania Press, 1991.

This book followed up on Walter Blair's groundbreaking studies. Although Doyno was restricted to the second half of Twain's manuscript (the first half of it had turned up in 1990 in Hollywood, California, only to become embroiled in lengthy legal tussles), he traced new patterns in the novel. Subsequently Doyno would edit the first integrated version of the two halves of the manuscript, *Adventures of Huckleberry Finn* (New York: Random House, 1996), and there Doyno would explain the different paths taken by the two parts of Twain's manuscript.

DRISCOLL, KERRY. *Mark Twain among the Indians and Other Indigenous Peoples*. Oakland, California: University of California Press, 2018.

Driscoll frequently takes Mark Twain's reading into account in following the permutations of his attitudes toward Native Americans and the indigenous people of other colonized countries. Her treatment of Richard Irving Dodge's influence, for example, is careful and perceptive.

ELLSWORTH, WILLIAM W. *A Golden Age of Authors: A Publisher's Recollection*. Boston: Houghton Mifflin Company, 1919.

Chapter 15 contains Ellsworth's impressions of Mark Twain, including an account of his oral readings to the Saturday Morning Club in Hartford and a description of his appearance while reading in bed (pp. 224–226).

EMERSON, EVERETT. "Mark Twain: The Writer as Reader," *Thoughts: A Collection of Essays on English Language and Literature*. Bangkok, Thailand: Chullongkorn University 3 (3 January 1983): 1–7.

This essay briefly reviewed some of Clemens's favorite books. Emerson also analyzed a menu decorated with clever literary references that Clemens prepared for a Civil War veterans dinner in June 1881. It was preserved by the Reverend Joseph H. Twichell and is now part of the Beinecke Rare Book and Manuscript Library at Yale University.

ENSOR, ALLISON R. "Mark Twain and the Bible." Doctoral dissertation. Indiana University, 1965.

In this general survey Ensor finds at least 1,000 allusions to the Bible in Mark Twain's writings.

_____. *Mark Twain and the Bible*. Lexington: University of Kentucky Press, 1969.

Ensor here rehearsed the successive stages of Mark Twain's attitudes toward, and literary use of, the Bible. This is the most accessible treatment of the subject, though it does not claim comprehensiveness. Certain books of the Bible received separate treatment in Ensor's index—Genesis, Exodus, and Matthew, for instance. The most valuable section of the book summarized the "three major biblical images: the Prodigal Son; Adam, Eve, and the Fall; Noah and the flood" (pp. 29–72). Ensor concluded that Twain's "use of the first eleven chapters of Genesis is far out of proportion to the importance of that section to the Bible as a whole" (p. 99), that most of Twain's biblical knowledge "had come by aural rather than visual acquaintance with the Scriptures" (p. 100), and that, "lacking the guidance which biblical scholarship might have provided, Twain overstressed certain of the Bible's shortcomings" (p. 101).

_____. "Music" entry, *The Mark Twain Encyclopedia*, eds. J. R. LeMaster and James D. Wilson (New York: Garland Publishing, 1993), pp. 527–528.

A brief but helpful glance at Clemens's musical predilections, with references for further reading on the subject.

FANNING, PHILIP ASHLEY. *Mark Twain and Orion Clemens: Brothers, Partners, Strangers.* Tuscaloosa: University of Alabama Press, 2003.

Fanning tells the uncomfortable story of how Orion Clemens in later life came to submit to his younger brother's dictates. This joint biography mentions a number of books that the two men shared.

FATOUT, PAUL, ed. *Mark Twain Speaking.* Iowa City: University of Iowa Press, 1976.

Collecting 195 of Mark Twain's public addresses, *Mark Twain Speaking* superseded the unreliable editions of *Mark Twain's Speeches* published in 1910 and 1923. Fatout's succinct notes often glossed literary allusions.

FEARS, DAVID H. *Mark Twain Day by Day: An Annotated Chronology of the Life of Samuel L. Clemens.* 4 vols. Banks, Oregon: Horizon Micro Publishing, 2008–2013. [A second edition of Volume 1, revised and enlarged, was issued in 2014 as Volume 1.2.]

Aided by research begun by Thomas A. Tenney, David H. Fears completed a herculean task that no other scholar besides Tenney had dared to undertake, a documented record of Clemens's whereabouts and activities for every day of his life. In the process Fears resolved many existing conundrums, such as the exact day and year that Rudyard Kipling went to Quarry Farm in Elmira, New York to interview Clemens (see the Kipling entry below). Inevitably this vast compendium also incorporated references to Clemens's reading, and Fears' detailed index is a helpful guide to these facts as well as to Clemens's personal encounters with notable authors.

FEINSTEIN, GEORGE W. "Mark Twain's Literary Opinions." Doctoral dissertation. University of Iowa, 1945.

Feinstein compiled Mark Twain's literary opinions "in an easily referable form" with "a maximum of direct quotation" (p. ii). Part I is an alphabetical catalogue of "Elements of Literature" with Twain's comments on "Adjectives," "Autobiography," "Classic," "Critics," "Drama," etc. Part II lists "Authors and Works" by name. A forty-page preface discussing Twain's critical standards precedes these lists. The first catalogue is engaging, a kind of Mark Twain dictionary of critical terms, adroitly arranged and edited. Part II makes no attempt to specify sources or publication dates or titles or editions, but reading Twain's comments in this format can be illuminating. Twain's references to authors are grouped under the heading "Reading; Miscellaneous" (pp. 148–154). Feinstein also lists a long series of comments by Mark Twain on his *own* writings (pp. 171–190). Feinstein refrained from commenting on or interpreting any of Twain's remarks.

_____. "Twain as Forerunner to Tooth-and-Claw Criticism," *Modern Language Notes* 63.1 (January 1948): 49–50.

Feinstein argued that Mark Twain's literary criticism, springing from "eruptive antipathies and enthusiasms," should be partially credited for "the American drift toward a trenchant style in criticism," including that of H. L. Mencken.

FERGUSON, DELANCEY. *Mark Twain: Man and Legend.* Indianapolis: Bobbs-Merrill Company, 1943.

Ferguson's biography listed a few of the books Clemens is known to have read, recapitulating Albert Bigelow Paine's information on this subject. *Mark Twain: Man and Legend* gave indications of Ferguson's sense of mission to establish Clemens as a man of letters.

FIELDS, MRS. JAMES T. See M. A. DeWolfe Howe, ed.

FISHER, HENRY W. *Abroad with Mark Twain and Eugene Field: Tales They Told to a Fellow Correspondent.* New York: Nicholas L. Brown, 1922.

Fisher (who sometimes spelled his name Fischer) met Mark Twain in the United States and came to know him in Berlin, Vienna, London, and Paris while Fisher was a foreign correspondent. His editor, Merle Johnson, believed that Fisher "retained the substance and the manner, if not always the exact language" of Twain's anecdotes (p. x). Fisher kept a few notes about their conversations, but much of his book was dictated from memory after a lapse of twenty years or more. Still, his reports of Twain's preferences in reading generally accord with those obtained from other sources. Pages 1–219 of Fisher's book described Twain; only the final section (pp. 223–246) recounted anecdotes about Eugene Field. Presumably most of Fisher's stories about Twain took place in the 1890s, but he almost never supplies dates.

FLACK, FRANK M. "Mark Twain and Music." Master's thesis. University of Iowa, 1942.

Not consulted.

FRANTZ, RAY W., JR. "The Role of Folklore in *Huckleberry Finn*," *American Literature* 28.3 (November 1956): 314–327.

An authoritative study of a topic not treated in the present study of Clemens's library and reading.

FRENCH, BRYANT MOREY. *Mark Twain and* The Gilded Age: *The Book That Named the Era*. Dallas: Southern Methodist Press, 1965.

French insisted that the novel cannot be appreciated without an understanding (which some contemporary reviewers lacked) of Mark Twain's intention of burlesquing romantic and sensation novels of the time. In support of this contention he suggested certain novelists who might have been Twain's targets. This is a rewarding handbook for readers of *The Gilded Age* (1873).

FRIED, MARTIN B. "The Sources, Composition, and Popularity of Mark Twain's *Roughing It*." Doctoral dissertation. University of Chicago, 1951.

Not consulted.

FULTON, JOE B. *Mark Twain in the Margins: The Quarry Farm Marginalia and* A Connecticut Yankee in King Arthur's Court. Tuscaloosa: University of Alabama Press, 2000.

Fulton opens the covers of books already known to have influenced Twain's novel—and it so happened that these particular copies were available to Twain primarily at Quarry Farm, his summer retreat in Elmira, New York. This is a detailed and illuminating examination of four historical works that establishes how much they were at the heart of Twain's ruminations about European history and human behavior: Thomas Carlyle's *The French Revolution*, W. E. H. Lecky's *History of England in the Eighteenth Century* and *History of the Rise and Influence of the Spirit of Rationalism in Europe*, and Thomas Macaulay's *History of England*. Fortunately the actual volumes annotated by Twain survived so that Fulton could transcribe Twain's markings and comments.

GANZEL, DEWEY. *Mark Twain Abroad: The Cruise of the "Quaker City."* Chicago: University of Chicago Press, 1968.

Mark Twain Abroad pays considerable attention to the guidebooks employed by Mark Twain to write his *Quaker City* letters in 1867 and incorporates information that Ganzel had compiled for his "Guidebooks" article in 1965. His study of four guidebooks as primary literary sources is sound and useful. Ganzel's book treats each stage of the *Quaker City* voyage, drawing on documents, diaries, and newspaper sketches to supplement Twain's own account.

_____. "Samuel Clemens, Guidebooks and *The Innocents Abroad*," *Anglia* 83 (1965): 78–88.

An informative article that specified the guidebooks Mark Twain used as resources in writing *The Innocents Abroad*. (A reworked version appeared in Ganzel's *Mark Twain Abroad*.) Ganzel extended and occasionally disputed Leon T. Dickinson's earlier (1945) work on this topic.

_____. "Twain, Travel Books, and *Life on the Mississippi*," *American Literature* 34.1 (March 1962): 40–55.

Ganzel argued that some of the so-called "Group A" *Huckleberry Finn* notes are actually related to Clemens's perusal of nearly twenty travel books preparatory to writing *Life on the Mississippi* (1883). Thus these working notes would have been made in 1882 rather than in 1880, as Walter Blair had estimated in "When Was *Huckleberry Finn* Written?," *American Literature* 30.1 (March 1958): 1–25. Ganzel's theory is not conclusive, but he usefully listed the books Twain mentioned in a section of manuscript ultimately deleted from *Life on the Mississippi* (p. 41).

GILDER, RODMAN. "Mark Twain Hated the Theatre," *Theatre Arts Monthly* 24.2 (February 1940): 109–116

This was in 1949 "the best available treatment of Mark Twain's relation to the stage," according to Harold Aspiz (p. 251 n. 2). Gilder reviewed Twain's published reactions to stage productions, and questioned William Dean Howells's assertion that Twain detested drama. Gilder engaged in no detailed analysis or theorizing, but merely laid out a tentative definition of this seeming contradiction.

GOOLD, EDGAR H, JR. "Mark Twain's Literary Theories and Opinions." Doctoral dissertation. University of North Carolina, 1949.

Thorough and documented, this was generally superior to the average doctoral dissertation. Six essays evaluated Mark Twain's standards for literary criticism. Chapter 3, "Mark Twain's Tastes and Temperament," considered a list of 411 books he was known to have read and then analyzed them by the percentages devoted to various subjects in two categories, "before 1870" and "after 1870." The relatively small size of this sample (Goold did not provide the book titles) and the possibility that they distorted Clemens's reading (only three history books are considered in the "pre-1870 group) partly detract from his conclusions. Goold examined Clemens's famous "I like history, biography, travels" statement very closely, comparing it with the 411 books Clemens definitely read. His conclusion: Clemens didn't dislike all poetry, but merely sentimental poetry, and he read considerably more fiction than he implied. Chapter 4 analyzed Clemens's critical criteria as explicitly revealed in his comments about various authors' works. A lengthy and detailed Chapter 5 (pp. 251–323) reviewed Clemens's critical standards as applied to individual writers, classified by genre. In the final (sixth) chapter Goold asserted that Clemens held well-defined critical tenets (p. 334), but that his judgments were on the whole "superficial" (p. 331).

GRIBBEN, ALAN. "Boy Books, Bad Boy Books, and *The Adventures of Tom Sawyer*," in *The Adventures of Tom Sawyer*, ed. Beverly Lyon Clark. Norton Critical Edition Series. New York: W. W. Norton, 2007), pp. 290–306.

Sets Mark Twain's novel within the context of other Boy Book fiction, looks closely at an antecedent, Thomas Bailey Aldrich's *The Story of a Bad Boy* (1869), and defends Twain's often-attacked character, Tom Sawyer, as an essential foil for Huckleberry Finn.

_____. "The Dispersal of Samuel L. Clemens' Library Books," *Resources for American Literary Study* 5.2 (Autumn 1975): 147–165. (A revised version of this essay appears as a chapter in the present volume.)

Chronicles the sale, loss, and donation of the contents of Clemens's personal library. Discusses a cache of nearly ninety books that had ended up in Rice Lake, Wisconsin. Lists the then-known locations of extant volumes from Clemens's personal library.

_____. "The Formation of Samuel L. Clemens' Library," *Studies in American Humor* 2.3 (January 1976): 171–182. (A revised version of this essay appears as a chapter in the present volume.)

Clemens partly accumulated his large personal library through purchases from retail bookstores, especially in initially filling the shelves of the Hartford house, but he increasingly relied on his publishers for acquisitions. Admirers donated hundreds of complimentary copies. Gribben describes Clemens's manner of signing and inscribing books. Clemens's library shared the vicissitudes of his fortunes and travels, and eventually he discarded a large portion of its contents.

_____. "'Good Books & a Sleepy Conscience': Mark Twain's Reading Habits," *American Literary Realism* 9.4 (Autumn 1976): 294–306. (A revised version of this essay appears as a chapter in the present volume.)

Despite the fact that Clemens took seriously his occupation as a writer and lecturer, he felt strangely guilty about spending much time with books written by others. There were a few exceptions: periods when he was too ill or tired to work, and stints of literary research in preparation for his own historical or travel narratives. Gribben details Clemens's methods of annotating the volumes in his library, emphasizing that he enjoyed reading leisurely and pausing to savor certain passages.

_____. "'I Detest Novels, Poetry & Theology': Origin of a Fiction Concerning Mark Twain's Reading," *Tennessee Studies in Literature* 22 (1977): 154–161. (A revised version of this essay appears as a chapter in the present volume.)

The notion that Samuel Clemens lacked literary sophistication can be partly traced to his designated biographer, Albert Bigelow Paine, who created an impression that Clemens scorned *belles-lettres*. A document in the Mark Twain Papers in the Bancroft Library at the University of California at Berkeley—Clemens's undated note asserting "I detest novels, poetry & theology"—reveals that in at least one instance Paine distorted information to strengthen this thesis. Gribben reproduces the note in facsimile and assigns it a much later date than Paine implied.

_____. "'I Did Wish Tom Sawyer Was There': Boy-Book Elements in *Tom Sawyer* and *Huckleberry Finn*," in *One Hundred Years of* Huckleberry Finn: *The Boy, His Book, and American Culture*, eds. Robert Sattelmeyer and J. Donald Crowley (Columbia: University of Missouri Press, 1985), pp. 149–170.

Examines the insufficiently recognized impact on Mark Twain's boy books of Thomas Bailey Aldrich's *The Story of a Bad Boy* (1869) and traces the allusions to romances about imprisonment in dungeons that led Tom Sawyer astray in the concluding section of *Huckleberry Finn*. (Corrective note: in 1985, when this essay appeared, Twain's "A Boy's Manuscript" had long been dated as belonging to 1870; subsequently its composition date was moved forward to 1868 or early in 1869. However, it still seems significant that Aldrich's *The Story of a Bad Boy* began appearing serially in *Our Young Folks* in January 1869.)

_____. "'If I'd Knowed What a Trouble It Was to Quote a Book': Literary Knowledge in Mark Twain's *Huckleberry Finn*," CD Project, *Huck Finn: The Complete Buffalo & Erie County Public Library Manuscript—Teaching and Research Digital Edition*, eds. Victor A. Doyno *et al.* (Buffalo, New York: State University of New York at Buffalo, Buffalo and Erie County Library, and the Mark Twain Foundation, 2002), pp. 1–9. (A revised version of this essay appears as a chapter in the present volume.)

Surveys the multitudinous and sometimes hidden literary allusions in Mark Twain's masterpiece. On the same CD, Alan Gribben provides "Works Related to Mark Twain's *Adventures of Huckleberry Finn*," pp. 10–68. See also the related studies of Dale Billingsley (1979) and Anthony J. Berret (1999).

_____. "'I Kind of Love Small Game': Mark Twain's Library of Literary Hogwash," *American Literary Realism* 9.1 (Winter 1976): 64–76. Reprinted in *Mark Twain's Humor: Critical Essays*, ed. David E. E. Sloane. New York: Garland Publishing Co., 1993, pp. 295–315. (A substantially expanded version of this essay appears as a chapter in the present volume.)

For truly atrocious writing Clemens developed an insatiable appetite, and he avidly collected examples. Around 1870 he began referring to these as "hogwash"; later, in 1876, he labeled several volumes in his personal library as belonging to "S. L. Clemens's Library of Literary 'Hogwash.'" Though he never actually compiled a list of his "Hogwash" books, it is possible to construct this hypothetical library. Gribben catalogues numerous volumes that Clemens might have included and reproduces in facsimile some of his marginalia from the pages of Edward P. Hammond's *Sketches of Palestine*.

_____. "The Importance of Mark Twain," *American Quarterly* 31.1 (Spring 1985): 30–49. Revised version collected in *American Humor*, ed. Arthur P. Dudden (New York: Oxford University Press, 1987), pp. 24–49.

Situates Mark Twain among the authors who were his contemporaries and summarizes his lasting value to the writers who followed him.

_____. "'It Is Unsatisfactory to Read to One's Self': Mark Twain's Informal Readings," *Quarterly Journal of Speech* 62.1 (February 1976): 49–56. (A revised version of this essay appears as a chapter in the present volume.)

Clemens viewed the reading of books and

magazines as ideally a social pastime—an opportunity for sharing selected passages orally. His fireside readings grew to include neighbors and friends. In 1886 and 1887 he performed oral interpretations of Robert Browning's poetry for a study group in Hartford. Besides Browning, he often read from William Dean Howells, Joel Chandler Harris's Uncle Remus tales, Rudyard Kipling, and Shakespeare. Gradually Clemens came to rely on oral readings in judging the caliber of any author's writing—including his own.

_____. "The Library and Reading of Samuel L. Clemens." Doctoral dissertation. University of California at Berkeley, 1974.

Five chapters analyzed Clemens's use of literary materials; various sections of these would appear in revised form as articles in scholarly journals. An annotated catalog documented Clemens's familiarity with many hundreds of books, essays, poems, stories, plays, operas, songs, newspapers, and magazines. At 2,370 total pages, including its Finding List, the study at that time constituted the largest dissertation ever filed for a doctoral degree at the University of California, Berkeley; however, since it was an inductive study, the credit for this distinction properly belonged to Clemens and his literary appetites.

_____. "Manipulating a Genre: *Huckleberry Finn* as Boy Book," *South Central Review* 5.4 (Winter 1988): 15–21. (A revised version of this essay appears as a chapter in the present volume.)

Situates Mark Twain's masterpiece among various other British and American entries in the literary Boy Book subgenre.

_____. "Mark Twain, Phrenology and the 'Temperaments': A Study of Pseudoscientific Influence," *American Quarterly* 24.1 (March 1972): 45–68. (A revised version of this essay appears as a chapter in the present volume.)

Discussed Clemens's lifelong curiosity about phrenology and the indications that he read George Sumner Weaver's *Mental Science*, George Combe's *Notes on the United States*, and Orson S. and Lorenzo N. Fowler's *New Illustrated Self-instructor in Phrenology*, as well as books by American humorists who satirized phrenology.

_____. *Mark Twain's Library: A Reconstruction* 2

vols. Boston: G. K. Hall & Co., 1980.

A revised and enlarged version of the 1974 dissertation listed above that added 1,751 additional titles discovered in the accession records of the Mark Twain Library at Redding, plus numerous new catalog entries and corrections as well as a list of 350 books, magazines, and newspapers that Albert Bigelow Paine had borrowed after Clemens's death in 1910. In 958 pages containing nearly 5,000 entries Gribben attempted to create the first catalog of the library and reading of Clemens and his family. He invented a new format to accommodate the disparate types of information he was making available. The publication of *Mark Twain's Library* would elicit hundreds upon hundreds of new leads that have resulted in this present, much-expanded study and its revised catalog.

_____. "Mark Twain's Library Books in the Humanities Research Center," *The Library Chronicle* (University of Texas at Austin), N.s., no. 11 (1979): 11–26.

Catalogs more than thirty books from Clemens's personal library, most of them assembled by Frank C. Willson (1889–1960) and sold by his widow Margarete Willson in 1962. The collection includes editions of Homer, Chaucer, Byron, Carlyle, and a copy of the Bible that accompanied Clemens on his travels in the Holy Land. The former Humanities Research Center is now known as the Harry Ransom Center. That library's ability to obtain this and thousands of other major acquisitions is recounted in Alan Gribben's *Harry Huntt Ransom: Intellect in Motion* (Austin: University of Texas Press, 2008).

_____. "Mark Twain's Lifelong Reading," in *Mark Twain and Youth: Studies in His Life and Writings*, eds. Kevin Mac Donnell and R. Kent Rasmussen (London: Bloomsbury Academic, 2016), pp. 30–43.

Surveys discernible patterns in the entirety of Clemens's acquaintance with books and journals. Despite the brevity of his formal schooling, Clemens became a voracious and intrepid reader.

_____ AND GRETCHEN SHARLOW. "Mark Twain's Travel Trunk: An Impromptu Notebook," *Mark Twain Journal* 42.2 (Fall 2004): 15–18.

Clemens sometimes utilized any available

surface for making notes, and the inner lid of a trunk from the Langdon home in Elmira, New York was found to contain jottings that included a few literary references.

_____. Private Libraries of American Authors: Dispersal, Custody, and Description," *Journal of Library History* 21.2 (Spring 1986): 300–314. Reprinted in *Libraries, Books, and Culture*, ed. Donald G. Davis Jr. (Austin, Texas: Graduate School of Library and Information Science, University of Texas at Austin, 1986), pp. 300–314.

Compares the cavalier treatment and limited documentation of the contents of Samuel L. Clemens's personal library to the fates of book collections owned by other prominent American writers.

_____. "Reconstructing Mark Twain's Library," *A B Bookman's Weekly* 66 (11 August 1980): 755–773. Reprinted in *A B Bookman's Yearbook I* (1980), ed. Jacob Chernofsky (Clifton, New Jersey: A B Bookman's Weekly, 1982), pp. 3–11.

Describes Gribben's decade-long search for the Clemens family's scattered library books.

_____. "'Stolen from Books, Tho' Credit Given': Mark Twain's Use of Literary Sources," *Mosaic: A Journal for the Comparative Study of Literature and Ideas* 12.4 (Summer 1979): 149–155. (A revised version of this essay appears as a chapter in the present volume.)

Mark Twain's travel writings display an unabashed dependence on the narratives of tourists and historians. Partly this resulted from the demands of the subscription-book industry; readers wanted historical facts and geographical information as well as comedy. Acknowledged quotations also imparted credibility to descriptions penned by a well-known humorist. Twain frequently made slight modifications in quoted material. Toward the latter part of his career he grew more straightforward about crediting his literary sources. Some of his novels are based very substantially upon historical research. His most engrossing passages, however, reveal the fewest traces of Twain's literary indebtedness.

_____. "Those Other Thematic Patterns in Mark Twain's Writings," *Studies in American Fiction* 13.2 (Autumn 1985): 185–200. (A revised version of this essay appears as a chapter in the present volume.)

Identifies three large configurations in Twain's literature that involve the grotesque, distasteful, and disastrous. Nearly all of the examples had literary predecessors.

_____. "Tom Sawyer, Tom Canty, and Huckleberry Finn: The Boy Book and Mark Twain," *Mark Twain Journal: The Author and His Era* 55.1–2 (Spring/Fall 2017): 127–144. (A slightly revised version of this essay appears as a chapter in the present volume.)

Speculates about why Twain and other male writers were drawn to the Boy Book subgenre, and examines *The Prince and the Pauper* (1881) as the middle work in Twain's composition of a trio of novels about boys confronting decisions that involved secrets.

_____. "'When Other Amusements Fail': Mark Twain and the Occult," *The Haunted Dusk: American Supernatural Fiction, 1820–1920*, eds. Howard Kerr, John W. Crowley, and Charles L. Crow (Athens: University of Georgia Press, 1983), pp. 169–189.

Examines Clemens's fascination with supernatural explanations and pseudoscientific practices, taking note of his reading on these subjects.

HARNSBERGER, CAROLINE. *Mark Twain: Family Man*. New York: The Citadel Press, 1960.

Reports on some marginalia in books from Clemens's library.

_____. *Mark Twain's Views of Religion*. Evanston, Illinois: Schori Press, 1961.

An unsystematic, brief survey of Clemens's opinions concerning religion. In the course of her narrative Harnsberger quoted previously unpublished marginalia from Clemens's copies of Rufus K. Noyes' *Views of Religion* (1906) and Alexander Winchell's *Sketches of Creation* (1903). She made few distinctions between these extremely "late" opinions and those Clemens had set down previously. Even so, the quoted comments are valuable. Harnsberger's opening thesis is that Mark Twain's "preoccupation with God as a Supreme Being proved him to be far from an atheist" (p. 1).

HARRINGTON, PAULA AND RONALD JENN. *Mark Twain & France: The Making of a New American Identity.* Columbia: University of Missouri Press, 2017.

A wide-ranging survey of Clemens's shifting attitudes toward France and its eminent writers, political figures, and historical events. Twain's *Personal Recollections of Joan of Arc* of course forms a centerpiece of *Mark Twain & France,* but numerous other revealing topics are explored, such as Clemens's rhapsodic memories of a trip he made down the Rhône River in 1891. The study concludes that in the final decades of his life, "having worked through—as the representative American of his day—the rivalry between France and America, Twain left France behind as a foil. . . . He would turn increasingly to narratives that investigated the darker side of all humankind, not only the French." Related to this research is an article documenting Clemens's selection of, and notations in, the works that helped him write his historical romance—Ronald Jenn and Linda A. Morris, "The Sources of Mark Twain's *Personal Recollections of Joan of Arc,*" *Mark Twain Journal: The Author and His Era* 55.1–2 (2017): 55–74.

HARRIS, SUSAN K. *The Courtship of Olivia Langdon and Mark Twain.* Cambridge: Cambridge University Press, 1996.

Harris's first chapter provides a rich discussion of Olivia Langdon's reading before her marriage as recorded in her commonplace book and other sources. (See also Resa A. Willis, "'Quietly and Steadily': Olivia Langdon Clemens' Commonplace Book" [1986]). Chapter 4 of Harris's *Courtship,* "Conning Books: Olivia Langdon and Samuel Clemens's Joint Reading," probes their wide-ranging interests and occasional differences in interpretations.

HELLWIG, HAROLD H. *Mark Twain's Travel Literature: The Odyssey of a Mind.* Jefferson, South Carolina: McFarland and Co., 2008.

Hellwig's study of Twain's travel narratives concludes with a useful list of other authors' travel writings that evidently caught Twain's attention.

HEMMINGHAUS, EDGAR H. *Mark Twain in Germany.* New York: Columbia University Press, 1939.

Chiefly relevant because it summarized (and thus made available in English) Friedrich Schönemann's *Mark Twain als literarische Persönlichkeit* (1925) as Chapter 6 (pp. 97–122).

_____. "Mark Twain's German Provenience," *Modern Language Quarterly* 6.4 (December 1945): 459–478.

Hemminghaus's purpose was "to examine more closely the record and extent of Clemens's German reading and acquaintanceship with German writers, and to ascertain . . . his own impressions and opinions of them" (p. 459). Hemminghaus began with a lengthy survey of Mark Twain's contact with the German language and German-speaking peoples, from his days in Hannibal and Virginia City to his many visits to Europe. It is impressive to see Clemens's encounters with the German language and people mount in this chronicle. Hemminghaus appears correct in observing that Clemens commonly "deprecate[d] the level of competence which he had attained in the German language" (p. 465). On pages 467–477 Hemminghaus attempted to "determine what German books Clemens may have read." He concluded that "Mark Twain's approach to the Germans, their language, and their literature was unquestionably one of great amicability and affectionate admiration" (p. 477). His reading in German had a range that "was unusually wide and varied, covering a multitude of fields—political, literary, technical, and journalistic. Much he read in the original" (p. 477). Having visited the Mark Twain Library in Redding, Connecticut, Hemminghaus listed the books Clemens and his daughter Clara donated to this community library that related to German language or literature.

HERRICK, GEORGE H. "Mark Twain, Reader and Critic of Travel Literature," *Mark Twain Journal* 10.1 (Summer 1955): 9–10, 22.

A note intending to demonstrate that Mark Twain "read and read widely in the realm of travel literature" (p. 9). Primarily Herrick repeated Twain's comments published in his better-known works—*The Innocents Abroad,*

Life on the Mississippi, Following the Equator, and others.

HILL, HAMLIN. *Mark Twain and Elisha Bliss.* Columbia: University of Missouri Press, 1964.

Hill's study analyzed the formula for subscription book authorship that Mark Twain mastered so profitably. It listed and discussed most of the subscription volumes published by Elisha Bliss with which Mark Twain might have been familiar and that probably influenced his own narrative structures.

_____. "Mark Twain: Audience and Artistry," *American Quarterly* 15.1 (Spring 1963): 25–40.

An excellent essay outlining the effects that the standard format and contents of subscription books had on Mark Twain's writing. Hill demonstrated how, in order to meet the requirements for a 600- to 700-page book, "Twain snatched up material from other authors, from his own earlier published works, from notes and suggestions in his notebooks" (p. 30).

_____. *Mark Twain: God's Fool.* New York: Harper & Row, 1973.

Hill's biography of Clemens's final decade discussed a few books that affected his writings and speeches significantly, including Dana's *Two Years Before the Mast.*

_____ AND WALTER BLAIR, eds. *The Art of Huckleberry Finn: Text, Sources, Criticisms.* San Francisco: Chandler Publishing Co., 1962.

A facsimile reproduction of the first edition of Mark Twain's novel was accompanied by (also in facsimile) selections from his literary sources, including W. E. H. Lecky's *History of European Morals,* J. J. Hooper's *Simon Suggs' Adventures,* Julia A. Moore's *The Sentimental Song Book,* and others (pp. 399–491).

HIRST, ROBERT H. "The Making of *The Innocents Abroad*: 1867–1872." Doctoral dissertation. University of California, Berkeley, 1975.

A major study, broad in scope yet meticulous about details. Hirst—who later became editor of the Mark Twain Papers and general editor of the Mark Twain Project in the Bancroft Library at the University of California at Berkeley—developed an interest in the composition of *The Innocents Abroad* while employed there as a research editor, and his dissertation drew on many primary materials. His dissertation investigated some of Twain's literary sources, including William C. Prime, William M. Thomson, and Charles W. Elliott.

HOBEN, JOHN B. "Mark Twain's *A Connecticut Yankee*: A Genetic Study," *American Literature* 18.3 (November 1946): 197–218.

Succeeded but not entirely supplanted by later studies, this readable essay treats Malory among the other literary influences on *A Connecticut Yankee* (1889). See Howard G. Baetzhold's 1961 correction of certain points in Hoben's article.

HOLMES, RALPH. "Mark Twain and Music," *Century Magazine* 104 (October 1922): 844–850.

Samuel Clemens developed a "passion for music" (p. 845), but he preferred "the simplest of familiar songs"—spirituals, ballads, and popular ditties. "Mark Twain passed middle life without music meaning more to him than a pretty tune or a prodigious performance" (p. 847). His extraordinary sense of hearing made the ticking of clocks or the barking of dogs intolerable to him. After Olivia Clemens died, the beleaguered Clemens took Clara's advice "to seek some solace in music—in music that offered a tortured heart a balm more efficacious than the simple and soon exhausted virtues of mere melody" (p. 849). Clara says that she suggested the orchestrelle and selected its records. "Beethoven, Wagner, Schubert, Chopin, even Brahms, soon became his daily companions" (p. 850). Yet except for one or two of Clara's recitals, she could not recall that "he ever sat through an entire concert of any kind" (p. 850). Clara remembered singing the Scotch air "Flow Gently, Sweet Afton" and various Scottish ballads to Clemens during his final illness. Holmes says that Clara set down her recollections for his article, which gives the essay its primary value. Sketchy as it is, this is one of the most comprehensive surveys of Clemens's tastes in music appreciation.

HOWE, M. A. DEWOLFE, ed. *Memories of a Hostess: A Chronicle of Eminent Friendships Drawn Chiefly from the Diaries of Mrs. James T. Fields.* Boston: Atlantic Monthly Press, 1922.

Pages 244–250 contain several allusions to Clemens's preferences in reading.

HOWELLS, WILLIAM DEAN. *My Mark Twain: Reminiscences and Criticisms*, ed. Marilyn Austin Baldwin. Baton Rouge: Louisiana State University Press, 1967. (The first edition of this biographical sketch appeared in 1910.)

An early memoir and critical evaluation, its comments on Clemens's literary predilections became nearly as influential as those set down by Albert Bigelow Paine. Balanced, lucid, and thoughtful overall, but surprisingly inaccurate regarding various aspects of Clemens's reading.

HUNLEY, MAXWELL AND JOHN VALENTINE. "Mark Twain Autograph Sale, Hollywood," *Autograph Collectors' Journal* 4 (Fall 1951): 54–55.

Listed and described a few items sold at the auction of Mark Twain's library books and manuscripts in April 1951. Hunley and Valentine mentioned the "loud-speakers, flashing bulbs, and hot-dog stands" that characterized the sale. They supplied several low prices that resulted because the auctioneers failed to distribute advance catalogs to antiquarian book dealers.

HUNT, PAUL. "Mark Twain's Library: A Postscript," *A B Bookman's Weekly* 66 (13 October 1980): 2376–86.

Hunt reprinted the amateurish catalog provided for the auction of Mark Twain's library books held in Hollywood, California in 1951.

HUNTER, JIM. "Mark Twain and the Boy-Book in 19th-Century America," *College English* 24.6 (March 1963): 430–438.

Hunter's essay discussed books *about* children composed for the amusement of adults, rather than tales written *for* the amusement of children (p. 431). He examined books about American boys such as *Huckleberry Finn* that reacted against the idealized view of the child as full of heavenly grace, pure and innocent and spiritual in an adult way, beginning with Thomas Bailey Aldrich's *The Story of a Bad Boy* (1869). Hunter also reviewed *The Adventures of Tom Sawyer* (1876), G. W. Peck's *Peck's Bad Boy and His Pa* (1883), Edward Eggleston's *The Hoosier Schoolboy* (1883), William Dean Howells's *A Boy's Town* (1890), William Allen White's *The Court of Boyville* (1899), and Stephen Crane's *Whilomville Stories* (1900), and related these to Twain's *Huckleberry Finn* (1885). Hunter was not interested in ascertaining whether Twain read any or all of these books—or when—but rather looked for similarities in attitudes toward boyhood and a boy's world.

JACOBSON, MARCIA. *Being a Boy Again: Autobiography and the American Boy Book*. Tuscaloosa: University of Alabama Press, 1994.

Thomas Bailey Aldrich, Charles Dudley Warner, and Mark Twain are among the founding authors of the American boy book tradition investigated in this sweeping study.

JENN, RONALD AND LINDA A. MORRIS. "The Sources of Mark Twain's *Personal Recollections of Joan of Arc*," *Mark Twain Journal: The Author and His Era* 55.1–2 (2017): 55–74.

This is almost certainly the most detailed investigation of the works Twain consulted and how he employed them in composing the book of which he was so fond. His marginalia in several of the sources, including Antoine Ricard's *Jeanne d'Arc la vénérable*, are transcribed and analyzed.

JENSEN, FRANKLIN L. "Mark Twain's Comments on Books and Authors," *Emporia State Research Studies* 12.4 (June 1964): 5–53.

Jensen's study, originally written as a master's thesis at Kansas State College of Emporia, attempted the difficult task of surveying Clemens's reading in an article of fifty pages. As an outline of Clemens's responses to major writers it is a useful introduction; he managed to supply brief reports on Clemens's responses to many authors. Jensen prefaced his two checklists (pre-1869 and post-1869) with a sketch of Clemens's critical approaches and his attacks on James Fenimore Cooper, Sir Walter Scott, and Jane Austen. He concluded the study with an analysis of Clemens's critical criteria. His bibliography listed fifty-three books and articles and picked up several nearly forgotten studies.

JONES, ALEXANDER E. "Mark Twain and Freemasonry," *American Literature* 26.3 (November 1954): 363–373.

Peripherally related to Clemens's reading, it examines his uses of the Masonic lodge rituals in his writings.

_____. "Mark Twain and Religion." Doctoral dissertation. University of Minnesota, 1950.

Jones paid attention to Mark Twain's use of the Bible as a literary source.

KARANOVICH, NICK. "Sixty Books from Mark Twain's Library," *Mark Twain Journal* 25.2 (Fall 1987): 9–20.

This article reviewed the seven Christie's auctions (held between October 1987 and May 1989) that dispersed the Mark Twain association copies formerly in the Doheny Collection of St. John's Seminary in Camarillo, California. Karanovich included prices, inscriptions, and reproductions of marginalia.

KEMBLE, EDWARD WINDSOR. "Illustrating *Huckleberry Finn*," *The Colophon: A Book Collectors' Quarterly* (New York City), Part One (1930), 4 leaves, no page numbers.

Mark Twain's former illustrator, reminiscing in 1929, recalled hearing Twain praise the drawings of Edwin Austin Abbey (1852–1911)— especially those Abbey made for an 1882 edition of Robert Herrick's poems, an edition of Oliver Goldsmith's *She Stoops to Conquer*, and Henry Austin Dobson's compilation of poetry, *The Quiet Life* (1899). Twain also had good words for the "humor" of Arthur Burdett Frost (1851–1928), and for the artistic work of "a little group of shining lights undimmed by time"—illustrators and painters William Thomas Smedley (1858–1920), Charles Stanley Reinhart (1844–1896), and Frederic Remington (1861–1909).

KERR, HOWARD. *Mediums, and Spirit-Rappers, and Roaring Radicals: Spiritualism in American Literature.* Urbana: University of Illinois Press, 1972.

Kerr documented Clemens's curiosity about spiritualism. He "left San Francisco evidently still on good terms with spirits, mediums, and believers" (p. 161), but in the 1870s he probably read about exposures of their equipment, and in the 1880s his attitude became increasingly skeptical. Kerr's chronological survey convincingly demonstrated Clemens's lifelong interest in psychical phenomena.

KING, GRACE. *Memories of a Southern Woman of Letters.* New York: Macmillan Co., 1932.

King offered her impressions of Clemens garnered from her visits to his home in the 1880s, with a few references to books she saw him read and plays he attended.

KIPLING, RUDYARD. "An Interview with Mark Twain," collected in *From Sea to Sea: Letters of Travel.* 2 vols. New York: Doubleday and Mc-Clure, 1899.

This highly entertaining account of Kipling's first (1889) meeting with Clemens humorously stresses Kipling's difficulty in locating his summer residence at Quarry Farm. It is one of the earliest first-hand accounts we possess of Clemens's replies to questions about his preferences in reading. He assured Kipling that he ignores novels, but then showed a knowledge of the specific title about which Kipling questioned him. Kipling reported that Clemens remarked, "Personally I never care for fiction or story-books. What I like to read about are facts and statistics of any kind" (2:180). The article was first published in the United States as "Rudyard Kipling on Mark Twain," New York *Herald*, 17 August 1890. It was reprinted in *Mark Twain: Life As I Find It*, ed. Charles Neider (Garden City, New York: Hanover House, 1961), pp. 310–321, and in *Mark Twain: The Complete Interviews*, ed. Gary Scharnhorst (Tuscaloosa: University of Alabama Press, 2006), pp. 117–126. David H. Fears—*Mark Twain Day by Day: An Annotated Chronology of the Life of Samuel L. Clemens* (Banks, Oregon: Horizon Micro Publishing, 2009), 2: 402–405—authoritatively dated Kipling's visit with Clemens as having occurred on 15 August 1889.

KOLB, HAROLD H., JR. "Mark Twain, Huckleberry Finn, and Jacob Blivens: Gilt-Edged, Tree-Calf Morality in *The Adventures of Huckleberry Finn*," *Virginia Quarterly Review* 55.4 (Autumn 1979): 653–669.

A look at literary child characters, particularly Huckleberry Finn, and their moral values.

KRAUSE, SYDNEY J. *Mark Twain as Critic.* Baltimore: Johns Hopkins Press, 1967.

Krause's is an especially useful book in connection with any study of Clemens's literary interests. It summarized Clemens's reading tastes on pages 13–16 and referred frequently to his reading throughout. Krause provided excellent interpretations of Twain's comments on James

Fenimore Cooper, Walter Scott, Bret Harte, Thomas Macaulay, William Dean Howells, Edgar Watson Howe, Émile Zola, and Adolf von Wilbrandt.

KRUSE, HORST. *Mark Twain and "Life on the Mississippi."* Amherst: University of Massachusetts Press, 1981.

Thus far Kruse's remains the only book-length study of the narrative that Twain intended to become the "standard work" about the greatest American river. This is the best starting-point for a grasp of Twain's motives, sources, and structure for a travel book that clearly realized his ambitious intention.

LANGDON, JERVIS. *Samuel Langhorne Clemens: Some Reminiscences and Some Excerpts from Letters and Unpublished Manuscripts.* Privately printed, 1938.

Langdon here shared his recollections of a few of Clemens's private reading habits. More important is Langdon's lengthy quotation from a previously unpublished manuscript of the 1870s, "Comments on English Diction," pages 20–22, in which Clemens expressed himself on William Shakespeare, Walter Scott, Charles Dickens, and Abraham Lincoln. This has been reprinted as Appendix B (pp. 197–220) in *Mark Twain in Elmira*, ed. Robert D. Jerome, Herbert A. Wisbey Jr., and Barbara E. Snedecor. Second edition. Elmira, New York: Elmira College Center for Mark Twain Studies, 2013.

LAWTON, MARY. *A Lifetime with Mark Twain. The Memories of Katy Leary, for Thirty Years His Faithful and Devoted Servant.* New York: Harcourt, Brace and Company, 1925.

An account of the Clemenses' family life by their housekeeper, valuable for its firsthand perspective but possibly somewhat distorted in Lawton's retelling. It contains disappointingly few clues to Clemens's preferences and habits in reading. The literary references it does include are sometimes suspect; as she recalls Clemens's literary classes, for example, their subject was Charles Dickens rather than Robert Browning (pp. 39–40). Katy Leary (1856–1934) worked for Clemens between 1880 and 1910.

LEARY, KATY. See Mary Lawton, *A Lifetime with Mark Twain.*

LEHMANN-HAUPT, HELLMUT. *The Book in America: A History of the Making and Selling of Books in the United States.* Second edition. New York: R. R. Bowker Co., 1952.

Clemens was a regular customer of Israel Witkower's bookshop in Hartford, according to pages 243–244 of this book. (Actually Lehmann-Haupt must have meant Brown & Gross, the bookseller's shop at 77 Asylum Street; Israel Witkower would not become proprietor of the successor to this firm until the second quarter of the twentieth century.)

The Letters of Mark Twain and Joseph Hopkins Twichell, eds. Harold K. Bush, Steve Courtney, and Peter Messent. Athens: University of Georgia Press, 2017.

The correspondence between Clemens and Twichell is rife with literary allusions, but the surprising thing is that Twichell's prolific references to authors and books outweigh those by Clemens. Presumably Twichell felt that with such a well-read friend as Clemens he could quote frequently from literature without intimidating or embarrassing the recipient of his letters.

LILJEGREN, S[TEN]. B[ODVAR]. "The Revolt Against Romanticism in American Literature as Evidenced in the Works of S. L. Clemens," in *Essays and Studies on American Language and Literature* (The American Institute in the University of Upsala, Sweden) 1 (1945): 9–60.

The Swedish scholar Liljegren (1885–1984) persuasively develops the thesis that in Mark Twain's writings he was reacting against the conventions of the terror (i.e., "Gothic") novel, the terror ballad, the churchyard elegy, the historical novel, medieval pageantry, and other holdovers from the previous literary era. This study predates Sidney J. Krause's admirable *Mark Twain as Critic*, but should be read in conjunction with it. Liljegren urges scholars to view American writers as part of larger Continental movements, especially regarding English and European Romanticism and Realism (p. 11). Liljegren also condemns the notion, prevalent in Europe, that Twain's work "is absolutely original," the product of "a practically unlettered visionary of busy young America"; in fact, Mark Twain "is well read in English and American literature"

(p. 14). Liljegren concludes: "He was neither unlettered nor uncouth, as [Vernon] Parrington, in his endeavor to fit in Mark Twain into his system, seems to imply. . . . If we are content to interpret him in this comfortable way, we cannot account for his literary work at all, nor for his life in general." Twain was "a cultured and 'literary' man" (p. 51). Unfortunately Liljegren wrote in 1945 without access to materials that might have enabled him to prove, rather than merely state, his case.

LONG, E. HUDSON. *Mark Twain Handbook*. New York: Hendricks House, 1957.

Long's six-page section (pp. 294–299) on Mark Twain's literary sources listed the main books mentioned by Albert Bigelow Paine's biography, Edward Wagenknecht's *Mark Twain: The Man and His Work*, Dixon Wecter's *Love Letters of Mark Twain*, and miscellaneous studies. Although not contributing any original research, this listing is a useful gathering of book titles within the compass of a few pages. Long also summarized the conclusions of previous critics, made a few generalizations, and supplied examples of Clemens's opinions on certain writers.

LORCH, FRED W. *The Trouble Begins at Eight: Mark Twain's Lecture Tours*. Ames: Iowa State University Press, 1968.

A helpful chapter titled "Art of Reading" (pp. 152–160) distinguished between Mark Twain's "lectures" and his "readings" (see page 155 especially). Too often commentators refer to these two types of public performances interchangeably, and Lorch made a significant contribution in explaining the differences. He also included a useful account of Mark Twain's reading tour with George Washington Cable (pp. 161–182).

LOVING, JEROME. *Mark Twain: The Adventures of Samuel L. Clemens*. Berkeley: University of California Press, 2010.

Loving's index bristles with the names of authors whom Clemens either knew personally or became familiar with through their names and their writings.

LYNN, KENNETH S. *Mark Twain and Southwestern Humor*. Boston: Little, Brown and Company, 1959.

The first half of Lynn's book outlined the background of Southwestern humor (now often termed Southern frontier humor), setting up the context for Mark Twain's appearance on the scene. Lynn usefully reviewed the life and literary career of numerous humorists, supplementing Walter Blair's *Native American Humor* (1937) with attention to themes and types of characters. Then on pages 140–288 he treated Twain's own literary works in a fairly standard thematic appreciation, seldom relating them to the Southwestern humorists.

LYON, ISABEL V. Journals and Appointment Calendars, 1903–1909. Mark Twain Papers, Bancroft Library, University of California at Berkeley.

Isabel Lyon kept two sets of daybooks during her tenure as a secretary in the Clemens household—a private series of journals meant for her eyes alone, and an "official" group of calendars filled with reminders of and records about Clemens's appointments. Though they are suffused with a worshipful view of her "King," they afford an invaluable glimpse into his daily activities, particularly his reading. Unfortunately there are many gaps during periods when Lyon was not in Clemens's company, or when her emotional state did not permit her to attend to this daily chore. Most of these journals reside in the Mark Twain Papers in the Bancroft Library at the University of California at Berkeley. In 1970 I discovered that the Antenne-Dorrance Collection then in Rice Lake, Wisconsin included a journal which Lyon had kept in 1905. (A photocopy of it is now on deposit in the Mark Twain Archive at Elmira College.) In addition, the Harry Ransom Center at the University of Texas at Austin also possesses one of her journals, this one chronicling events in 1906; much of it was published by Laurie Lentz in "Mark Twain in 1906: An Edition of Selected Extracts from Isabel V. Lyon's Journal," *Resources for American Literary Study* 11.1 (Spring 1981): 1–36.

McKEITHAN, D[ANIEL]. M[ORLEY]. *Court Trials in Mark Twain and Other Essays*. The Hague, Netherlands: Martinus Nijhoff, 1958.

The last fifty pages of this book are devoted to six essays that concern Mark Twain's literary sources; the remainder of the book treats court trials in his fiction. McKeithan's essays are valuable for the summaries and extracts of the sources behind Twain's stories.

McNUTT, JAMES C. "Mark Twain and the American Indian: Earthly Realism and Heavenly Idealism," *American Indian Quarterly* 4.3 (August 1978): 223–242.

McNutt illustrated how Clemens's reading of anthropological and military writings affected his attitudes toward the American Indian. He also explored in some detail the works of John George Wood, D. Randolph Keim, Richard I. Dodge, and Henry Rowe Schoolcraft. McNutt's insightful article opened up new perspectives in our understanding of Twain's contradictory references to the Native American.

MADIGAN, FRANCIS V., JR. "Mark Twain's Passage to India: A Genetic Study of *Following the Equator.*" Doctoral dissertation. New York University, 1974.

Directed by William M. Gibson, this substantial study explores Mark Twain's celebrated world lecture tour and the book that resulted from this travel. Appendixes A and B supplied the passages that Twain decided to delete from the text of *Following the Equator*, mainly several long extracts from Marcus Clarke's writings. In Appendix C, "Mark Twain's Sourcebooks" (pp. 353–368), Madigan helpfully listed and described forty-six books to which Twain was indebted for material in *Following the Equator*.

Mark Twain and Philosophy, ed. Alan H. Goldman. Great Authors and Philosophy Series. Lanham, Maryland. Rowman & Littlefield, 2017.

Without claiming (or investigating) whether Twain owed or read specific philosophical works, fifteen scholars point out parallels between concepts displayed in Twain's writings and ideas propounded by philosophers from Socrates to Nietzsche. The results are intriguing.

Mark Twain Encyclopedia, eds. J. R. LeMaster and James D. Wilson. New York: Garland Publishing, 1993. Reprinted as *The Routledge Encyclopedia of Mark Twain.* New York: Routledge, 2011.

Many of the entries by multiple scholars discuss the literary antecedents for Twain's writings or the published works to which he alludes.

"MARK TWAIN HOUSE BRINGS CLEMENS BOOKS HOME TO STAY," *Mark Twain News* 41.3 (Fall 1997): 6–7.

A newsletter column recounting the details of the purchase at an auction in San Francisco of 271 books formerly belonging to the Clemenses' library. The Mark Twain House and Museum paid $200,500 for the volumes, which had been sold in Clara Clemens Samossoud's 1951 auction in Hollywood. "The July 16 [1997] purchase tripled the number of books from Twain's library that The Mark Twain House owns."

Mark Twain-Howells Letters, eds. Henry Nash Smith and William M. Gibson. Cambridge: Harvard University Press, Belknap Press, 1960.

Smith and Gibson's annotation of the two authors' correspondence, scrupulously edited, includes a wealth of material related to literary sources.

Mark Twain Journal: The Author and His Era (1936-). Its title from 1936 until 1953 was the *Mark Twain Quarterly*; in 1954 it became the *Mark Twain Journal.* A subtitle was added with the Fall 2016 issue.

Founded by Cyril Clemens in 1936, this journal soon became a repository for biographical notes and articles, including those related to Clemens's reading. Thomas A. Tenney continued to be receptive to such studies when he became the editor in 1983. Alan Gribben assumed the editorship upon Dr. Tenney's death in 2012 and he affiliated the journal with the Center for Mark Twain Studies at Elmira College as well as the Mark Twain Circle of America. It has remained interested in scholarship involving Clemens's social and intellectual background as well as articles about people either connected with him or prominent during his historical period, but also publishes critical essays of general interest.

Mark Twain: Life As I Find It. Essays, Sketches, Tales, and Other Material, ed. Charles Neider. Garden City, N.Y.: Hanover House, 1961.

Neider's collection reprinted numerous manuscripts, documents, and interviews relevant to Clemens's reading interests.

Mark Twain's Letters, ed. Albert Bigelow Paine. 2 vols. New York: Harper & Brothers, 1917.

Paine bowdlerized or abbreviated without

editorial indications, but this collection nevertheless remains useful.

Mark Twain: The Complete Interviews, ed. Gary Scharnhorst. Tuscaloosa: University of Alabama Press, 2006.

Mark Twain was interviewed so many times that he developed these opportunities into another type of oral performance at which he excelled. In the nearly 300 newspaper and magazine interviews assembled here, beginning in 1871 and ending in 1910, Twain often discussed his literary likes and dislikes. Scharnhorst's meticulous notes tracked down nearly all of these allusions, and his index is a scholar's dream.

MATTHEWS, BRANDER. *Essays on English*. New York: Charles Scribner's Sons, 1921.

See the essay titled "Mark Twain and the Art of Writing" (pp. 243–268) for Twain's comments on Walter Scott, Edward Dowden, Jane Austen, and others. Matthews notes that Twain sometimes failed to take a historical view of styles he considered mannered or ornate, always preferring directness and naturalness.

_____. *The Tocsin of Revolt and Other Essays*. New York: Charles Scribner's Sons, 1922.

Matthews alluded to his impressions of Clemens's reading tastes on pages 266–270, an essay titled "Memories of Mark Twain."

MEINE, FRANKLIN J., ed, *Tall Tales of the Southwest: An Anthology of Southern and Southwestern Humor 1830–1860*. New York: Alfred A. Knopf, 1930.

Meine preceded even Walter Blair in opening up certain areas of investigation regarding Mark Twain's Southern frontier sources. For instance, he pointed out parallels between *Huckleberry Finn* and J. J. Hooper's "Simon Suggs Attends a Camp Meeting."

MELTON, JEFFREY A. *Mark Twain, Travel Books, and Tourism: The Tide of a Great Popular Movement*. Tuscaloosa: University of Alabama Press, 2002.

Melton demonstrated how thoroughly Mark Twain's travel narratives were embedded among, and often reacted against, the writings of travelers who had preceded him.

MOORE, OLIN HARRIS. "Mark Twain and Don Quixote," *PMLA* 37.2 (June 1922): 324–346.

As the earliest essay to examine in depth Mark Twain's indebtedness to specific sources its points met initial resistance among those who conceived of Twain as an unlettered original. Moore devoted much space to a refutation of the readings of Twain's novels as essentially autobiography. He noted a number of works by European authors utilized by Twain in *Huckleberry Finn*—including Trenck, Dumas, Casanova, and Cellini. "Today, Moore is seen as a perspicacious pioneer of a view that has grown more and more important, and the notion that Mark Twain was a kind of unconscious artist has been demolished by many scholars," Edward Wagenknecht would explain in his preface to the third (1967) edition of his *Mark Twain: The Man and His Work* (viii-ix), noting his own change of title for Chapter 3 from "The Divine Amateur" to "The Man of Letters."

MUTALIK, KESHAV. *Mark Twain in India*. Bombay, India: Noble Publishing House, 1978.

Narrates Mark Twain's itinerary during his tour of 1896. Appendix D (pp. 112–114) briefly describes Twain's use of literary sources in *Following the Equator*, especially Edward Buck's *Indo-Anglican Literature* and W. H. Sleeman's *Report*.

OTNESS, HAROLD M. "A Room Full of Books: The Life and Slow Death of the American Residential Library," *Libraries & Culture* 23.2 (Spring 1988): 111–134.

Discusses the history and trends of "separate rooms in the home dedicated to the keeping and using of books" (p. 111). Several of Otness's examples fit the Clemenses' decisions about building and maintaining their sumptuous library room in the Hartford house.

PAINE, ALBERT BIGELOW. *Mark Twain: A Biography*. 2 vols. New York: Harper & Brothers, 1912.

Contains considerable information about Clemens's reading not to be found elsewhere, but projects his reading interests during his final four years (1906–1910) onto other periods of his life as well. A chapter titled "Mark Twain's Reading" discusses Clemens's favorite books and publishes selected marginalia (pp. 1536–1540). A faulty index and Paine's casual approach to dating sometimes hinder the usefulness of his still-essential biography.

PARSONS, COLEMAN O. "The Background of *The Mysterious Stranger*," *American Literature* 32.1 (March 1960): 55–74.

Parsons identified a number of Mark Twain's "background materials" for the novel. "Twain's sources were formative, corroborative, and illustrative. They shaped his outlook, supported and clarified attitudes already formed, and afforded graphic instances of life as he understood it" (p. 73).

PATTEE, FRED LEWIS. *Mark Twain.* New York: American Book Company, 1935.

Pattee discounts the impact of Clemens's reading and stresses his originality.

POCHMANN, HENRY AUGUST. "The Mind of Mark Twain." Master's thesis. University of Texas, 1924.

The earliest guide to Clemens's reading, and a fascinating collection of curious and disparate items that fell within his notice. It was an overly ambitious endeavor ("I soon saw . . . that it would be necessary to restrict my inquiry," Pochmann acknowledged in his preface), but he proceeded to gather references to Clemens's reading and his knowledge of folklore, nature, and various other topics with such system and erudition that this master's thesis continued to set an example for Mark Twain scholarship.

QUICK, DOROTHY. *Enchantment: A Little Girl's Friendship with Mark Twain.* Norman: University of Oklahoma Press, 1961.

Unabashedly sentimental, Quick's recollections of her relationship with Clemens during the last three years of his life placed some new letters in print and produced her version of Clemens's reading advice for children. She became one of his "Angel Fish," was invited to his home, and was addressed as a young adult.

QUIRK, TOM. "Backgrounds and Sources," *Mark Twain's* Adventures of Huckleberry Finn*: A Documentary Volume*, ed. Tom Quirk. Dictionary of Literary Biography Series. Volume 343. Detroit, Michigan: Gale/Cengage Learning, 2009.

Pages 9–110 reprint numerous primary sources and scholarly articles related to the literary resources behind Mark Twain's masterpiece.

Quirk's volume is one of the most valuable reference tools available to Twain scholars.

RASMUSSEN, R. KENT. *Critical Companion to Mark Twain: A Literary Reference to His Life and Work.* 2 vols. New York: Facts On File, 2007.

Many entries include detailed information about the literary sources involved in Twain's writings. In this respect *Critical Companion* is even more valuable than Rasmussen's earlier, very impressive *Mark Twain A-Z: The Essential Reference to His Life and Writings* (1995).

REGAN, ROBERT. *Unpromising Heroes: Mark Twain and His Characters.* Berkeley: University of California Press, 1966.

This astute study of a recurrent folklore motif in Mark Twain's works incidentally noticed a few literary influences as well.

REIGSTAD, THOMAS J. *Scribblin' for a Livin': Mark Twain's Pivotal Period in Buffalo.* Amherst, New York: Prometheus Books, 2013. Revised, enlarged edition, Buffalo: NFB Publishing, 2018.

Reigstad describes Clemens's reading, the Buffalo cultural milieu, and his literary associates during this important phase of his life.

RICE, CLARENCE C., M.D. "Mark Twain as His Physician Knew Him," *Mentor* 12 (May 1924): 48–49.

A brief sketch of Clemens's personality by a close friend. Rice emphasized his constant reading, but gave no book titles.

_____. "What Mark Twain's Doctor Remembers"; "The Missouri Writer's Humor and Philosophy as Related in the Anecdotes of a Friend"; "Incidents in a Long Friendship with the Missouri Author and Humorist," *Kansas City Star Magazine*, 1 November 1925, continued in the 8 November 1925 issue.

Rice mentioned that on Henry H. Rogers's yacht and at Rogers's home, usually with Rice and Thomas Reed, "Mr. Clemens was always reading during the card games [which Clemens didn't join]. He read anything that came to hand. He wasn't particular about the author. He seemed as much interested in a second reader schoolbook or any child's story as in a great literary effort—and often he would repeat to the party some of the childish sentences he had been reading, in the manner of a small boy doing his recitation."

ROGERS, FRANKLIN R. *Mark Twain's Burlesque Patterns as Seen in the Novels and Narratives 1855–1885*. Dallas: Southern Methodist University Press, 1960.

An instructive, judicious survey of Mark Twain's fixation on literary burlesque as a satiric mode. Rewards the reader with numerous clues to Twain's models and resources for various burlesques. Rogers was especially interested in identifying Twain's concept of narrative structure, or what Twain once called his "narrative-plank."

RUSSELL, JAMES R. "The Origin, Composition, and Reputation of Mark Twain's *A Connecticut Yankee*." Doctoral dissertation. University of Chicago, 1966.

Discussed some of Mark Twain's literary sources that were apparent in the novel.

RYAN, PAT M., JR. "Mark Twain: Frontier Theatre Critic," *Arizona Quarterly* 16.1 (Autumn 1960): 197–209.

Ryan's article quoted from Mark Twain's journalistic reviews of the 1860s and juxtaposed against them some passages from his later books.

SALOMON, ROGER B. *Twain and the Image of History*. New Haven: Yale University Press, 1961.

In the process of bringing together Mark Twain's reactions to the nineteenth-century doctrine of historical progress, Salomon traced his reading in history and quoted from his marginalia. Salomon's book has proved to be a lasting contribution to Twain studies.

SCHIRER, THOMAS. *Mark Twain and the Theatre*. Nuremberg, Germany: Hans Carl, 1984.

Schirer provided a comprehensive overview of Clemens's affection for the stage, from his praise of Edwin Forrest in 1853 to his admiration for the young actress Billie Burke toward the end of his life. Further profitable studies seem possible on this topic. Those should especially consult Rodman Gilder's "Mark Twain Hated the Theatre" (1940) and Robert A Wiggins's "Mark Twain and the Drama" (1953), along with articles on the subject by Pat M. Ryan Jr. (1960) and James W. Tuttleton (1964).

SCHMIDT, BARBARA. "The Life and Art of True Williams," *Mark Twain Journal* 39.2 (Fall 2001): 1–60.

Schmidt's is the fullest account of Williams's life and career before, during, and after his stint as a Hartford illustrator for Mark Twain's subscription books. In outlining the complex course of Williams's artistic work she introduced many titles with which Clemens was acquainted.

SCHÖNEMANN, FRIEDRICH. *Mark Twain als literarische Persönlichkeit*. Jenaer Germanistische Forschungen 8. Jena: Verlag der Frommannschen Buchhandlung, 1925.

This German critic's monograph had a considerable impact on Mark Twain studies in America as well as abroad, particularly after Edgar H. Hemminghaus summarized Schönemann's ideas as Chapter 6 of *Mark Twain in Germany* ("Schönemann's Appraisal of Mark Twain's Literary Personality," pp. 97–122) in 1939. To a large extent Schönemann was reacting against Van Wyck Brooks' hostile interpretations of Twain's literary career. Schönemann appraised Twain's reading on the basis of letters and literary works in print by 1925; his was one of the earliest studies of the literary influences reflected in Twain's works. Schönemann's subsequent affiliation with Nazism and his admiration of Hitler would greatly diminish his reputation, according to Joe B. Fulton's *Mark Twain Under Fire, Reception and Reputation, Criticism and Controversy, 1851–2015* (Rochester, New York: Camden House, 2018).

SCOTT, ARTHUR L. *Mark Twain at Large*. Chicago: Henry Regnery Co., 1969.

In a cogent book about Mark Twain's opinions concerning foreign countries and international affairs Scott necessarily paid some attention to Twain's reading of books by foreign authors. He quoted marginalia from relevant books in the Mark Twain Papers in the Bancroft Library at the University of California at Berkeley.

———. *On the Poetry of Mark Twain, with Selections from His Verse*. Urbana: University of Illinois Press, 1966.

Scott's ingeniously conceived book reviewed the poems that Mark Twain composed and reprinted many of his generally infelicitous efforts. Scott only followed up clues to Twain's poetic models in a few cases, but this is a handy compilation of Twain's experiments with verse.

SEARLE, WILLIAM. *The Saint & the Skeptics: Joan of Arc in the Work of Mark Twain, Anatole France, and Bernard Shaw.* Detroit: Michigan State University Press, 1976.

Searle offered a salutary perspective on Mark Twain's seemingly contradictory determinism and his adoration of the Maid. He made use of several of Twain's source-books that were available in the Mark Twain Papers in the Bancroft Library at the University of California at Berkeley.

SHELDEN, MICHAEL. *Mark Twain, Man in White: The Grand Adventures of His Final Years.* New York: Random House, 2010.

In the course of producing one of the most gracefully written (and highly readable) biographical studies of Mark Twain, Shelden pauses in numerous places to explore Twain's relationships with various authors and their books. Shelden's book is more upbeat in recounting the events occurring in Twain's last years than the biographies of most other writers. *Mark Twain, Man in White* is also notable for providing the cultural and historical context within which Twain lived, wrote, and spoke.

SHERMAN, STUART P. "Mark Twain," in *The Cambridge History of American Literature.* New York: G. P. Putnam's Sons, 1917–1921. 3:1–20.

In appraising Mark Twain's career in this biographical sketch, Sherman discounted the effect of literary influences. "Mark Twain's literary independence is generally conceded," he noted.

SKANDERA TROMBLEY, LAURA. *Mark Twain in the Company of Women.* Philadelphia: University of Pennsylvania Press, 1994.

Dozens of women authors (along with a few male writers) figure in Skandera Trombley's narrative about the crucial role that female influences played in Mark Twain's life and literature.

_____. *Mark Twain's Other Woman: The Hidden Story of His Final Years.* New York: Alfred A. Knopf, 2010.

A fearless exposé of the close but ill-fated friendship between a famous author and his secretarial companion. Prominent authors often make appearances, and Skandera Trombley's evocation of Twain's seventieth birthday celebration at Delmonico's in 1905 brings that epochal gathering to life.

SLATER, JOSEPH. "Music at Colonel Grangerford's: A Footnote to *Huckleberry Finn*," *American Literature* 21.1 (March 1949): 108–111.

Slater's article described the music that Huckleberry Finn praises in Chapter 17 of *Adventures of Huckleberry Finn* (1885).

SLOANE, DAVID E. E., ed. *The Literary Humor of the Urban Northeast, 1830–1890.* Baton Rouge: Louisiana State University Press, 1983.

Sloane reprinted examples of the Literary Comedians who were centered in the northeastern United States in order to demonstrate the techniques and approaches to humor that they had in common. This work implicitly drew attention to the fact that Twain had other models of humor in front of him than those of the Southern frontier (the Old Southwest) region.

_____. *Mark Twain as a Literary Comedian.* Baton Rouge: Louisiana State University Press, 1979.

Although Sloane conceded an indebtedness on Mark Twain's part to the Southern frontier humorists, he argued that the group known as the Literary Comedians who were regionally identified with the Northeast (especially Artemus Ward but also including Josh Billings, B. P. Shillaber, and others) exerted a far greater influence in shaping Twain's humor.

SMITH, HENRY NASH, ed. *Mark Twain of the "Enterprise."* Berkeley: University of California Press, 1957.

Reprinted and annotated much of Clemens's early journalism in the Far West, with attention to his literary allusions.

_____. *Mark Twain's Fable of Progress: Political and Economic Ideas in "A Connecticut Yankee."* New Brunswick, New Jersey: Rutgers University Press, 1964.

Too brief (108 pages) to take up Mark Twain's sources, but Smith's book sketched the outlines of a few books with similar themes that were issued in the same period as *A Connecticut Yankee in King Arthur's Court* (1889).

_____. *Mark Twain: The Development of a Writer.* Cambridge: Harvard University Press, Belknap Press, 1962.

Smith's landmark critical study contained numerous references to Mark Twain's literary resources, though it was not his intention to defend these parallels in detail.

_____. "'That Hideous Mistake of Poor Clemens's,'" *Harvard Library Bulletin* 9.2 (Spring 1955): 145–180.

In an article that became the definitive study of this fascinating moment in America's cultural history, Smith incidentally identified the poems that Mark Twain quoted or misquoted in his burlesque speech at the Whittier Birthday Dinner in 1877.

SMITH, J. H. "The Expressed Opinions of Mark Twain on Heredity and Environment." Doctoral dissertation. University of Wisconsin, 1955.

Not consulted.

SMITH, THOMAS RUYS. "'The Mississippi Was a Virgin Field': Reconstructing the River Before Mark Twain, 1865–1875," *Mark Twain Journal* 53.2 (Fall 2015): 24–66.

Surveys the surprisingly rich and diverse descriptions of the river and its travelers that preceded Twain's claim to be the most authentic voice and authoritative expert on these subjects. Smith takes nothing away from Twain, but makes it clear that the author had excellent previous material on which to build his masterful accounts.

SMYTHE, CARLYLE. "The Real 'Mark Twain,'" *The Pall Mall Magazine* (London) 16 (September 1898): 29–36.

On pages 30–31 Smythe, a member of Mark Twain's travel group for part of his 1895–96 lecture tour, holds forth with convincing assurance about Twain's literary preferences and dislikes.

SPOTTS, CARLE BROOKS. "The Development of Fiction on the Missouri Frontier (1830–1860)," *Missouri Historical Review* 28–29 (April 1934-July 1935): 195–205, 275–286, 17–26, 100–108, 186–194, 279–294.

A broad study of literary genres popular in the American West, centering on the writers in St. Louis. Such a study is relevant to the literature that might have influenced young Samuel Clemens.

STONE, ALBERT E., JR. *The Innocent Eye: Childhood in Mark Twain's Imagination*. New Haven: Yale University Press, 1961.

Stone's perceptive book paid attention to those writers of juvenile fiction who seem to have influenced Mark Twain's technique and subject matter—particularly in relation to Twain's less well-known stories and novels.

_____. "Mark Twain's *Joan of Arc*: The Child as Goddess," *American Literature* 31.1 (March 1959): 1–20.

Stone discussed thirteen works used by Mark Twain as source material. "*Joan of Arc* is the most historical of all Twain's novels and shows on every page its debt to the history books he read so carefully" (p. 7). Edward Wagenknecht called Stone's article "the fullest study of the sources . . . and the most important paper on that work" (*MTMW*, p. 64 n. 20). Slightly revised, Stone's essay appeared as Chapter 7 of his *The Innocent Eye*.

TANNER, TONY. *The Reign of Wonder: Naivety and Reality in American Literature*. Cambridge: Cambridge University Press, 1965.

In his eighty-six-page section on Mark Twain (pp. 97–183) Tanner extended Kenneth S. Lynn's ideas in discussing a few of Twain's predecessors in Old Southwestern humor. His observations on Twain's attitudes toward literary idols and neglected writers were accurate and to the point.

TARNOFF, BEN. *The Bohemians: Mark Twain and the San Francisco Writers Who Reinvented American Literature*. New York: Penguin Press, 2014.

The Bohemians concentrates on the careers of Twain, Ina Coolbrith, Bret Harte, and Charles Warren Stoddard, but it makes many references to Charles H. Webb and other California literary figures whom Clemens knew.

TAYLOR, COLEY B. "Personal Recollections of Mark Twain," *Perspectivas* (Universidad de las Americas, Santa Catarina Martir, Puebla, 1982), pp. 34–43.

Taylor gave us a first-hand account of Clemens's days in Redding, Connecticut, including his donations to the community library he helped found there.

TENNEY, THOMAS ASA. *Mark Twain: A Reference Guide.* Boston: G. K. Hall & Co., 1977.

Tenney's reference work listed and described thousands of books, articles, and reviews about Twain. It brought order to a field of study where duplication of efforts and ignorance of previous work were common. In 1977 he began adding supplements in *American Literary Realism* and later published installments in the *Mark Twain Journal.*

———. "Seclusion in Tedworth Square," *Mark Twain Journal* 36.2 (Fall 1998): 30–31.

This note reproduced in facsimile one of Clemens's reader's cards for the Chelsea Public Libraries in 1898. Clemens was then living in London at 23 Tedworth Square.

TUCKEY, JOHN S. *Mark Twain and Little Satan: The Writing of "The Mysterious Stranger."* West Lafayette, Indiana: Purdue University Studies, 1963.

Tuckey astutely reconstructed Mark Twain's composition and Albert Bigelow Paine and Frederick A. Duneka's editing of the *Mysterious Stranger* manuscripts. *Mark Twain and Little Satan* additionally speculated about Twain's familiarity with several books on psychology.

TUTTLETON, JAMES W. "Twain's Use of Theatrical Traditions in the Old Southwest," *College Language Association Journal* 8.2 (December 1964): 190–197.

Tuttleton connected elements of Southern frontier drama with Mark Twain's *Adventures of Huckleberry Finn* (1885).

The Twainian (issued 1939–2005).

Chester L. Davis (1903–1987), Executive Secretary of the Mark Twain Research Foundation of Perry, Missouri, published slightly bowdlerized transcriptions of Clemens's annotation in the dozen-plus books that his group had purchased at the 1951 Hollywood auction. These notes are scattered through the columns of *The Twainian* in bi-monthly issues of the 1950s, 1960s, and 1970s. The most significant marginalia were those reproduced from Clemens's copy of *History of European Morals* by W. E. H. Lecky. Davis published these notes in consecutive issues from May 1955 until December 1955, and then added a few more

notes in the November-December 1962 issue. In transcribing the Lecky marginalia Davis omitted "those things which . . . are too rough for the eyes of some of our young people"; he also left out "many short corrections of language . . . or short exclamations."

TWICHELL, JOSEPH H. "Mark Twain," *Harper's Magazine* 92.552 (May 1896): 817–827.

On page 818 Twichell observed that in 1872 Clemens had a limited acquaintance with books, but on page 822 he described how Clemens had subsequently rectified this deficiency.

WAGENKNECHT, EDWARD. *Mark Twain: The Man and His Work.* Third edition. Norman: University of Oklahoma Press, 1967. First edition 1935; revised edition 1961.

Pages 29–41 and 61–66 summarized the major findings about Mark Twain's reliance on literary materials in his writings. A useful if opinionated and occasionally cantankerous critical bibliography on pages 247–294 included many works related to Clemens's reading. Wagenknecht declared: "It may be doubted that any modern writer has used 'sources' more freely than Mark Twain" (p. 61). Wagenknecht's breezy, informal prose style is refreshing, but his omission of substantiating citations—while it removes cumbersome footnotes from his volume—leaves the reader a laborious task to determine the sources he employed.

WAGGONER, HYATT HOWE. "Science in the Thought of Mark Twain," *American Literature* 8.4 (January 1937): 357–370.

Waggoner's was the earliest study that addressed exclusively "just what Mark Twain knew of science, what books he read," so numerous books and articles subsequently depended upon Waggoner's research. He listed eighteen scientists with whose books Twain was seemingly acquainted. The first part of the article is now largely superseded because of Waggoner's admission that (in 1937) "we do not know when Mark Twain read these books" (p. 363). But Waggoner's speculations about the impact of each book on Twain's thought still deserve to be taken into account. Waggoner primarily focused on *What Is Man?* as the later work most explicitly stating Twain's scientific philosophy.

He accepted Twain's story about the philosophical "Macfarlane" as his early teacher, which is a matter still in dispute. The essay closed by countering Minnie M. Brashear's hypothesis that Mark Twain's philosophy sprang from the eighteenth century and was essentially unaffected by the intellectual developments of his own period. Waggoner was especially opposed to her assertions that Twain's deterministic "Gospel" derived from Thomas Paine's *The Age of Reason*.

WALLACE, ELIZABETH. *Mark Twain and the Happy Island*. Chicago: A. C. McClury & Co., 1913.

Wallace recollected her days with Mark Twain in Bermuda in 1908. A well-written if saccharine book, limited to her perceptions as recalled five years afterwards. She devoted considerable attention to Twain's interest in Rudyard Kipling's works. Wallace also visited Twain at Stormfield, and their letters of 1909–1910 in this volume alluded to books they were mutually reading.

WECTER, DIXON. *Sam Clemens of Hannibal*. Boston: Houghton Mifflin Co, 1952.

This engaging, unsentimental, balanced examination of Clemens's family and his boyhood made use of everything known about the literary culture of Hannibal. Wecter's appraisal of Clemens's early reading (pp. 208–209) is frank in conceding the paucity of evidence and presents the best information about his youth that we have. He corrected Van Wyck Brooks and Minnie M. Brashear on certain points.

WELLAND, DENNIS. *Mark Twain in England*. London: Chatto & Windus; Atlantic Highlands, New Jersey: Humanities Press, 1978.

Welland chronicled Mark Twain's sometimes rocky relationship with his English audience and publishers. *Mark Twain in England* often mentioned Clemens's reading and the books that he requested from his London publisher. An appendix listed Twain's books published by Chatto & Windus.

_____. "Mark Twain's Last Travel Book," *Bulletin of the New York Public Library* 69.1 (January 1965): 31–48.

In assessing the variations between the American edition of *Following the Equator* (1897) and the British version, *More Tramps*

Abroad, Welland made use of the book's manuscript in the Henry W. and Albert A. Berg Collection of the New York Public Library. He incidentally noted pages inserted from various published sources, some containing Twain's marginalia. Welland inferred that Twain's reliance on lengthy quotations "betokens no flagging inspiration or loss of inventive power on Twain's part: it is rather as though he were seeking almost desperately for some independent verification of his own view of man" (p. 45). Nine years later Francis V. Madigan Jr. disputed this conclusion; rather, Madigan insisted, Twain passed over material more pessimistic than the extracts he chose, "looking for opportunities in his book to allow other voices to be heard" (see Madigan, [1974], p. 354).

WIGGINS, ROBERT A. "Mark Twain and the Drama," *American Literature* 25.3 (November 1953): 279–286.

Wiggins's article laid the basis for more properly appreciating the influence of dramatic works on Mark Twain's writings. See also Rodman Gilder, "Mark Twain Hated the Theatre" (1940) and Thomas Schirer, *Mark Twain and the Theatre* (1984).

WILLIAMS, JAMES D. "The Genesis, Composition, Publication and Reception of Mark Twain's *A Connecticut Yankee*." Doctoral dissertation. New York University, 1961.

Williams devoted an entire chapter to connections between Clemens's known reading and *A Connecticut Yankee in King Arthur's Court* (pp. 74–105). Portions of this dissertation appeared later, revised, as an article in *PMLA* (1965).

_____. "The Use of History in Mark Twain's *A Connecticut Yankee*," *PMLA* 80.1 (March 1965): 102–110.

"The historical reading behind the novel was wide but eclectic, and there is no evidence that Mark Twain attempted any thorough or scholarly historical preparation," Williams explained. Indeed, Twain lacked the temperament or desire to "present accurately 'the life of the day'" (p. 110). "Mark Twain's attempts at historical accuracy in *A Connecticut Yankee* were sporadic and strictly limited by the demands of farce, outrage, or the theme of progress. He drew his material largely from modern historians and largely from post-Renaissance history" (p. 102). Williams seemed to blame Twain for not using medieval resources and for preferring histories with a nineteenth-century melioristic bias. All the same, this study is a usefully compact survey of Twain's known sources in writing *A Connecticut Yankee*. Williams here introduced a previously unnoticed source used by Twain: an *Atlantic Monthly* article on economy (1869) written by Edward Jarvis.

WILLIS, RESA A. "'Quietly and Steadily': Olivia Langdon Clemens' Commonplace Book," *Mark Twain Journal* 24.1 (Spring 1986): 17–20.

Willis quoted and discussed Olivia Langdon's early reading as revealed in her commonplace book. "All the entries attest to Livy's sheltered background, her intelligence, her feeling of her role in the world and her religious faith." Willis summarized Olivia's record of her reading in *Mark and Livy: The Love Story of Mark Twain and the Woman Who Almost Tamed Him* (New York: Atheneum Publishers, 1992), pp. 29–30, 62. See also Susan K. Harris's *The Courtship of Olivia Langdon and Mark Twain* (1996).

WILSON, JAMES D. "'The Monumental Sarcasm of the Ages': Science and Pseudoscience in the Thought of Mark Twain," *South Atlantic Bulletin* 40.2 (May 1975): 72–82.

Twain's relationship with phrenology and faith-healing duplicated his response toward legitimate science and technology—infatuation led to eventual disillusionment. This article overlooked some previous studies of its topics but otherwise makes valid points.

_____. *A Reader's Guide to the Short Stories of Mark Twain*. Boston: G. K. Hall & Co., 1987.

A valuable summary of sources for, and critical studies of, Twain's short fiction.

WISBEY, HERBERT A., JR. AND MARK WOODHOUSE. "Elmira College's Mark Twain Collection," *Mark Twain Society Bulletin* 20.2 (July 1997): 1–3.

Described the collections of books, manuscripts, and periodicals that would form the core of the Mark Twain Archive at Elmira College, including the donation of the Antenne Collection of Rice Lake, Wisconsin—at one time "the largest number of books from Mark Twain's personal library in private hands." These books had been given to Katy Leary, the Clemenses' housekeeper, after Clemens's death in 1910.

WOODRESS, JAMES, ed. *Eight American Authors: A Review of Research and Criticism*. Revised edition. New York: W. W. Norton, 1972.

In rapid-fire notes Harry Hayden Clark surveyed most scholarly books and articles that had treated Clemens's reading (pp. 283–287, 290–295, and 304–305). His summaries were occasionally biased.

WYATT, EDITH. "An Inspired Critic," *North American Review* 205.737 (April 1917): 603–615.

Complaining that "the United States is filled with what may be called an excessive moderation concerning the telling of truth" (p. 607), Wyatt praised Mark Twain's "penetrating and imaginative" literary and social criticism for its "conscientiousness, truth and independence" (p. 614).

Index

R

Rabelais, François 34

Rambles and Recollections of an Indian Official (Sleeman) 232, 233

Randall, David 231

Ranke, Leopold von 43

Rasmussen, R. Kent ix, x, 268

"The Raven" (Poe) 193

Reade, Charles xvi, 38

Reader's Handbook (Brewer) 45

Redding, Connecticut xxii, xxiv, xxvi, 9, 13, 49, 59, 63, 67–71, 76, 97, 121, 129, 131, 217, 243, 250, 258, 260, 271

Redpath, James 100

Regan, Robert xx, 69, 231

Reid, Whitelaw 42, 143, 149

Reinhart, Charles Stanley 263

Remington, Frederic 263

Renan, Ernest 43

Report (Sleeman) 267

Representative Actors (Russell) 69

A Reverie and Other Poems (Chesebrough) 96

Rhône River 50, 81, 260

Ricard, Antoine 262

Rice, Clarence C. 80

Rice Lake *Chronotype* xxiii, 76

Rice Lake, Wisconsin xv, xxii, xxiii, 75, 76, 244, 256, 265, 274

Richard II (Shakespeare) 111, 112

Richard III (Shakespeare) 110, 111, 184

Riley, James Whitcomb xvi, 34, 183

The Rime of the Ancient Mariner (Coleridge) 37, 60, 83, 202, 205

The Ring and the Book (Browning) 127, 128

Riverdale Library Association 13

Riverdale, New York City 13, 40, 49, 62, 63, 67

Robert Elsmere (Ward) 37, 118

Roberts, William Culver, Jr. 103

Robin Hood 25, 135–138

Robin Hood and His Merry

Foresters (Cundall) xxi, 135, 137, 138

Robin Hood and His Merry Foresters (Percy) 26

Robinson Crusoe (Defoe) xxii, 30, 32, 67, 125, 179, 183, 184, 194, 220

Robinson, Forrest G. 204, 213

Rochester, New York 215

Rockingham, Vermont 145

Rogers, Henry H. 12, 96, 120, 208, 211, 234, 268

Rohrbach, Augusta 18

Rollo Books (Abbott) 36

The Romance of Gilbert Holmes: An Historical Novel (Kirkman) 61

Romance of a Pro-consul (Milne) 92

Roman Society in the Last Century of the Western Empire (Dill) xxxiii

Rome, Italy 38, 42

Rome (Zola) xxiii

Romeo and Juliet (Shakespeare) 111

Roosevelt, Theodore xxxiii, 236

Rose, George 103

Ros, Emanda 92, 103

Rossini, Gioachino 41

Ross, Janet xiv, 40

Ross, Malcolm 58

Ross, Margaret Anne 97, 103

Roughing It (Twain) 14, 147, 202, 203, 206, 207, 210, 230, 231, 233, 235, 251

Rousseau, Jean-Jacques 39

Royston, Samuel Watson 94, 103

Rubáiyát of Omar Khayyám (FitzGerald) xv, xxiii, 33, 129, 183, 202, 220

Rubin, Louis D., Jr. 209

Rule, W. H. 43

Ruskin, John 36, 125

Russell, William Clark 34, 69, 202, 220

Russia 44, 132, 236

Ryan, Pat M., Jr. 269

S

Sage, Dean 81

Saintine, Joseph Xavier Boniface 184

The Saints' Everlasting Rest (Baxter) 11

Saint-Simon, Henri de 31, 39, 42, 52, 74, 87

Saleeby, C. W. 44

Salem Athenaeum 12

Salem Witchcraft (Fowler) 52

Salomon, Roger B. 42, 249

Salt Lake City, Utah xxxi

Samossoud, Jacques 109, 242

Sandwich Islands 34, 202, 203, 230

Sanford, Peggy xxv

San Francisco, California xxviii, 29, 40, 80, 202, 203, 230, 263, 266

San Francisco *Call* 40

San Marino, California 76

Santa Barbara, California 73, 110

Sartor Resartus (Carlyle) 4, 132

Saturday Morning Club 253

The Satyricon (Petronius) 43

Savage Club 12

The Scarlet Letter (Hawthorne) xxiii, 37

Schiller, Friedrich 35

Schirely, Edwin F. 96

Schönemann, Friedrich 15, 260, 269

Schoolcraft, Henry Rowe 266

Schopenhauer, Arthur 43

Scotland xvi, 84, 140, 158, 261

Scott, Albert J. 100

Scott, Arthur L. 47, 128, 227, 269

Scott, Catharine Dawson 228

Scott, James H. 89

Scott, Walter 8, 11, 28, 35, 51, 53, 59, 80, 94, 125, 184, 185, 194, 195, 207, 221, 235, 244, 247, 249, 262, 264, 267

Scrambles Amongst the Alps (Whymper) 51

Select Orations (Cicero) 42

FORTHCOMING IN 2020 —

Volumes Two and Three of *Mark Twain's Literary Resources: A Reconstruction of His Library and Reading*

The forthcoming volumes consist of the Annotated Catalog, arranged alphabetically under authors' names. Their birth and death dates are provided, along with the birth and death dates of illustrators, editors, and translators. Catalog entries for books give the basic bibliographic data—places of publication, publishers' names, and dates of publication—for editions Clemens owned, borrowed, knew of, or, shall we say, brushed against. These facts were often obtained from auction catalogs when the books themselves could not be studied. The reader is informed of signatures or inscriptions on endpapers or flyleaves; marginalia in the text by Clemens or his family; descriptions of the volumes in bookdealers' catalogs; provenance of the books, if determined; current locations of the volumes, if known; and whether the original association copies, photocopies, or other sources were consulted for this study.

New to the Annotated Catalog: A title-author-subject Index for Volumes Two and Three assists the researcher or browser. Entries list Mark Twain's reading about travel, slavery, American humorists, ancient Greece, the Roman Empire, and scores of other subjects.

Here is a sample Annotated Catalog entry:

Maeterlinck, Maurice (1862–1949). *The Life of the Bee.* Translated by Alfred Sutro (1863-1933). Original green cloth, front hinge cracked, light rubbing to extremities, water damage to rear half of the book, dampstaining. New York: Dodd, Mead and Co., 1902. 427 pp.

Inscription: front pastedown endpaper signed in black ink, "S L. Clemens".

Marginalia: profuse annotations by Clemens in pencil amount to approximately 120 words, with notes or marked passages on approximately fifty pages. The notes begin on page 36 of "The Swarm" (where Clemens wrote in pencil, "Drawing room bee") and end on page 146, where he wrote "in bottle" in pencil. On page 40, Clemens wrote vertically: "Order to the queen: 300 a day wanted now. Later: Reduce the output 25%". On page 51 Clemens noted, "bad morals". Clemens jotted a sentence that he felt Maeterlinck should have inserted before the last sentence of a footnote on page 106: "First they *remove* the reigning queen. Then". On page 107 he added, "This is the place." Page 114 contains another comment: "very good". Vertically on page 115 Clemens objected, "[John] Lubbock says no." (This referred to Maeterlinck's statement about the queen bee that "her people . . . venerate her.") Again on page 127 Clemens noted, "L says no."

Catalogs: C1951, #25a, listed among volumes containing Clemens's marginal notes, $30; "Property from the Library of Mark Twain," Butterfield & Butterfield, San Francisco, Sale 6613 (16 July 1997), lot 2683.

Location: Mark Twain House and Museum, Hartford, Connecticut.

Copy examined: Clemens's copy. Viewed in 1997 and 2019 in Hartford. "It was Maeterlinck who introduced me to the bee. I mean, in the psychical & scientific way, & in the poetical way" ("The Bee," written around 1902, MS in Box #1, no. 1, MTP; *DE,* 26: 280). Farther on in this essay, which discusses the bee's habits in a comical but informed manner, Mark Twain alludes to François Huber, Sir John Lubbock, and Maeterlinck as "the great authorities." Paine, *MTB,* p. 1162.

For ordering information, consult www.newsouthbooks.com/twain